200

A GUIDE to CONSENT and CAPACITY LAW in ONTARIO

D'Arcy Hiltz
Anita Szigeti

A Guide to Consent and Capacity Law in Ontario, 2006 Edition
© LexisNexis Canada Inc. 2005
July 2005

All rights reserved. No part of this publication may be reproduced, stored in any material form (including photocopying or storing it in any medium by electronic means and whether or not transiently or incidentally to some other use of this publication) without the written permission of the copyright holder except in accordance with the provisions of the Copyright Act. Applications for the copyright holder's written permission to reproduce any part of this publication should be addressed to the publisher.

Warning: The doing of an unauthorized act in relation to a copyrighted work may result in both a civil claim for damages and criminal prosecution.

Members of the LexisNexis Group worldwide

Canada	LexisNexis Canada Inc, 123 Commerce Valley Drive, East, Suite 700, MARKHAM, Ontario
Argentina	Abeledo Perrot, Jurisprudencia Argentina and Depalma, BUENOS AIRES
Australia	Butterworths, a Division of Reed International Books Australia Pty Ltd, CHATSWOOD, New South Wales
Austria	ARD Betriebsdienst and Verlag Orac, VIENNA
Chile	Publitecsa and Conosur Ltda, SANTIAGO DE CHILE
Czech Republic	Orac sro, PRAGUE
France	Éditions du Juris-Classeur SA, PARIS
Hong Kong	Butterworths Asia (Hong Kong), HONG KONG
Hungary	Hvg Orac, BUDAPEST
India	Butterworths India, NEW DELHI
Ireland	Butterworths (Ireland) Ltd, DUBLIN
Italy	Giuffré, MILAN
Malaysia	Malayan Law Journal Sdn Bhd, KUALA LUMPUR
New Zealand	Butterworths of New Zealand, WELLINGTON
Poland	Wydawnictwa Prawnicze PWN, WARSAW
Singapore	Butterworths Asia, SINGAPORE
South Africa	Butterworth Publishers (Pty) Ltd, DURBAN
Switzerland	Stämpfli Verlag AG, BERNE
United Kingdom	Butterworths Tolley, a Division of Reed Elsevier (UK), LONDON, WC2A
USA	LexisNexis, DAYTON, Ohio

Library and Archives Canada Cataloguing in Publication

Hiltz, D'Arcy
A guide to consent and capacity law in Ontario / D'Arcy Hiltz, Anita Szigeti — 2006 edition.

Includes index.

ISBN 0-433-45002-9

1. Informed consent (Medical law) — Ontario. 2. Capacity and disability — Ontario. 3. Power of attorney — Ontario. I. Szigeti, Anita.
II. Title.

KEO382.5.H54 2005 344.71304'12 C2005-903540-4
KF1347.H54 2005

Printed and Bound in Canada

DEDICATION

For families and individuals who live courageously with mental illness, the good doctors who try to give them what they need and the dedicated lawyers who try to get them what they want.

To Jay
My cherished
colleague
And favorite (OK, so only)
Hospital counsel
Anita

ABOUT THE AUTHORS

D'ARCY HILTZ and ANITA SZIGETI are partners in the Toronto law firm of HILTZ SZIGETI LLP. The firm's practice focuses on mental health law litigation, including consent and capacity issues, guardianship and estate matters. The firm recently received a national award for outstanding legal advocacy in the area of mental health.

D'Arcy Hiltz graduated from the University of Windsor Law School (1981), and was admitted to the Ontario Bar (1983). Mr. Hiltz has been an advocate in the field of consent and capacity matters for over twenty years, acting as counsel to individuals with mental health issues, their families and physicians. For a ten-year period (1991-2001), he was Chair of the Ontario Psychiatric Review Board (Toronto East Region), the Senior Vice Chair of the Consent and Capacity Board for Ontario and the Regional Vice Chair of the Board for Toronto. He presided over thousands of hearings involving consent and capacity matters. Mr. Hiltz has taught at the University of Toronto Faculty of Law. He has published widely and is a frequent lecturer on consent and capacity, guardianship and estate matters.

Anita Szigeti graduated from the University of Toronto's Faculty of Law (1990), and was admitted to the Ontario Bar (1992). Ms. Szigeti was Amicus Curiae in the Starson case in the Supreme Court of Canada. She appears frequently in the Court of Appeal as Amicus Curiae to mentally disordered accused. She is also the Chair of the Mental Health Legal Committee, an organization of lawyers who represent persons with mental health issues and a former Chair of the Mental Health Law and Policy Advisory Committee to Legal Aid Ontario. In anticipation of significant changes to the *Mental Health Act* in December 2000, she co-chaired a certification program for lawyers seeking admission to Legal Aid's Consent and Capacity Panel. In addition to providing education to physicians and their counsel, she has for many years taught mental health law to families of persons with mental health issues.

TABLE OF CONTENTS

PREFACE

The Legislation

Ontario's law governing involuntary committal and consent and capacity matters is contained in four complex and interrelated statutes: the *Mental Health Act*, the *Health Care Consent Act, 1996*, the *Substitute Decisions Act, 1992*, and the *Personal Health Information Protection Act, 2004*. All four statutes affect individual liberty and autonomy. They address psychiatric admissions and the rights of individuals to make their own decisions in relation to medical or psychiatric treatment, admission to long-term care facilities, personal care, finances and records of personal health information It is essential to have an understanding of all four statutes, failing which, effective use of the law will be an elusive and frustrating journey.

Purpose of the Commentary to the Consolidation

We have selected these four Acts as the focus of this consolidation because Ontario's Consent and Capacity Board adjudicates exclusively under them. This volume is meant primarily to assist the reader in navigating the legislation and applications to the Board. To this end, we have included the Board's Rules of Practice. Whether you are applying to the Board or responding to an application, it is sometimes difficult to ascertain where to begin. Although a sophisticated analysis of the interrelationship of the four Acts falls outside the scope of this introduction, we hope to provide basic direction for what you need to address a particular issue. We have also provided a more detailed guide to each statute, together with cross-references to the others where applicable. In the 2006 edition, we have also included the *Statutory Powers Procedure Act* and an introduction to its application to proceedings of the Consent and Capacity Board. We have also updated the jurisprudence before the Board and in the appellate courts.

Policy Considerations

Legislation governing involuntary committal and capacity seeks to balance individual rights against the interest of the State. On the one hand citizens have certain constitutionally protected rights to liberty, autonomy and self-determination. On the other hand, the State has the right and obligation to protect the safety of the community and to protect incapable individuals from self-harm, exploitation by others or needless suffering.

All four Acts in this consolidation represent Ontario's attempt to strike an appropriate balance between these competing rights and interests. The intent of the legislation is to enhance autonomy and self-determination as much as possible while employing the principle of minimal restriction on liberties which is a constant theme throughout this area of law. At the same time the State must accomplish its goal and duty of beneficence in relation to those individuals who are truly incapacitated. Some restriction on liberty is necessary where the restriction operates to the ultimate benefit or protection of the individual or the community. The principles of fundamental justice must be adhered to in providing due process to the individual, whenever the individual's liberty is at stake. As a result, all four pieces of legislation are replete with procedural safeguards, checks and balances.

Acknowledgements

We extend a special thanks to Danann Hawes of LexisNexis Canada Inc. for his personal involvement with the first edition of this project, his good humour and extraordinary effort throughout, and for the valuable assistance of John Cambridge as editor. We were also assisted in the preparation of the 2006 edition by the patience of Teresa Chan of LexisNexis. We also wish to thank our administrative assistant Joanna Olek for her help in preparation of this manuscript.

D'Arcy Hiltz
Anita Szigeti

PENDING LEGISLATIVE CHANGES

Note: The legislation reproduced in this consolidation is current to The Ontario Gazette Vol. 138, No. 26 (June 25, 2005). Amendments not yet in force are shown as shaded text; no other legislative changes were pending at the time this consolidation went to print.

DETAILED TABLE OF CONTENTS

SUBSTITUTE DECISIONS ACT

Part I — Property

General

Continuing Powers of Attorney for Property

Statutory Guardians of Property

Court-Appointed Guardians of Property

Property Management

Part II — The Person

General

Powers of Attorney for Personal Care

Court-Appointed Guardians of the Person

Duties of Guardians of the Person and Attorneys for Personal Care

Part III — Procedure in Guardianship Applications

Part IV — Miscellaneous

Regulations

Forms

POWERS OF ATTORNEY ACT

HEALTH CARE CONSENT ACT

Part I — General

Part II — Treatment

General

Consent to Treatment

Capacity

Consent on Incapable Person's Behalf

Emergency Treatment

Protection from Liability

Applications to Board

Part III — Admission to Care Facilities

General

Consent on Incapable Person's Behalf

Crisis Admission

Protection from Liability

Applications to Board

Part IV — Personal Assistance Services

General

Decision on Incapable Recipient's Behalf

Protection from Liability

Applications to Board

Part V — Consent and Capacity Board

Part VI — Miscellaneous

Regulation

Evaluators — O. Reg. 104/96

Forms

ADVOCATING FOR CLIENTS

CONSENT TO MEDICAL TREATMENT

STANDARD OF PRACTICE FOR SOCIAL WORKERS COMMUNICATING POST EVALUATION, A FINDING OF INCAPACITY WITH RESPECT TO ADMISSION TO CARE FACILITIES OR PERSONAL ASSISTANCE SERVICES

MENTAL HEALTH ACT

Part I — Standards

Part II — Hospitalization

Part III — Estates

Part IV — Veterans, Etc.

Part V — Miscellaneous

Regulations

Part I — Operating Grant Assistance

Part II — Capital Grant Assistance

Forms

PERSONAL HEALTH INFORMATION PROTECTION ACT

Part I
Interpretation and Application

Purposes, Definitions and Interpretation

Part III
Consent Concerning Personal Health Information

General

Part IV
Collection, Use and disclosure of Personal Health Information

Disclosure

Part V
Access to Records of Personal Health Information and Correction

Access

Correction

Part VIII
Complementary Amendments

Regulation

Forms

STATUTORY POWERS PROCEDURE ACT

Contents

THE CONSENT AND CAPACITY BOARD

Commentary

Rules of Practice

COMMENTARY

CONSENT AND CAPACITY LAW IN ONTARIO

INTRODUCTION

THE BROAD CONCEPTS: "PROPERTY", "TREATMENT/PLACEMENT", "DETENTION" AND "PERSONAL HEALTH INFORMATION"

In this introduction, we set out the circumstances in which others take over making important decisions on behalf of incapable persons. These circumstances most often arise in the context of feared serious adverse consequences. The general principle is that capable people have the right to take risks where incapable people have the right to informed decision-making based on their prior capable wishes or best interests.

Conceptually, issues of consent, capacity and involuntary committal addressed by the legislation may be grouped into the four[1] broad areas of "property," "treatment/placement", "detention" and "personal health information." These categories correspond to areas of decision-making autonomy that capable individuals enjoy regardless of the wisdom of the choices. We are all presumed to have the capacity to manage our own property, to make our own decisions regarding treatment and disclosure of personal health information, and to live freely where we choose.

Once we become sufficiently incapacitated that we or others are at serious risk of harm, the State owes us a duty to protect our interests and that of the community. The legislation in this consolidation governs how these protections are afforded to incapable persons.

There is no substitute for reading the legislation; however, a more detailed review of each Act introduces the particular Act in the body of this consolidation. In the pages which follow, we provide only a brief overview to assist the reader in identifying the applicable statutory provisions for consideration of a particular issue.

---

[1] Community treatment orders (established under the *Mental Health Act* (MHA) s. 33.1 to 33.9) do not fit neatly into any one of these four categories, as they constitute a hybrid between treatment issues (treatment is provided to the subject of the CTO while the individual resides in the community) and involuntary detention of the individual (which may result from treatment non-compliance.) As a result, they are introduced under a special heading between the discussion on Treatment/Placement and Detention.

Property

Findings of Incapacity under the Mental Health Act and the Substitute Decisions Act, 1992

A finding of incapacity to manage property may arise under the *Mental Health Act* (MHA) or the *Substitute Decisions Act, 1992* (SDA). Both Acts provide mechanisms for the assessment and determination of capacity to manage property. A finding under the *Mental Health Act*, may be made only in relation to bona fide patients in psychiatric facilities. In all other cases, the finding must be made under the SDA. A finding made under either Act results (with very few exceptions)[2] in the Public Guardian and Trustee becoming the statutory guardian of the person's property. However, neither Act can be considered in isolation.

Definitions of Incapacity

Although the application of the *Mental Health Act* is restricted to patients in a psychiatric facility, the MHA does not provide a complete code in relation to issues of capacity to manage property. For example, incapacity to manage property is not defined in the MHA. The definition set out in the SDA is accepted as applying to both Acts. The *Substitute Decisions Act, 1992* defines incapacity to manage property as follows:

> A person is incapable of managing property if the person is not able to understand information that is relevant to making a decision in the management of his or her property, or is not able to appreciate the reasonably foreseeable consequences of a decision or lack of decision.[3]

While the *Substitute Decisions Act, 1992* must be employed to assess the capacity of anyone who is not a patient in a psychiatric facility, a certificate of incapacity to manage property issued under that Act arguably may be cancelled by a physician who otherwise has the authority to make the corresponding finding under the *Mental Health Act*, provided that at the relevant time the individual is a patient in a psychiatric facility.[4]

---

[2] The exception under the *Substitute Decisions Act, 1992* is if the assessment of incapacity is in support of an application to the court for the appointment of a guardian of property pursuant to s. 22. The exception under the *Mental Health Act* is if the assessment of incapacity is in relation to a patient who has a court-appointed guardian of property or a continuing power of attorney for property. Provisions regarding court-appointed guardianship of property and continuing powers of attorney for property are contained within the SDA.

[3] s. 6, SDA.

[4] s. 56, MHA.

Rights Advice/Information Subsequent to the Finding of Incapacity

A patient whose physician finds him or her incapable of managing property under the *Mental Health Act* is entitled to receive rights advice promptly after the finding is made.[5] A person who is found incapable of managing his or her property by a capacity assessor under the *Substitute Decisions Act, 1992* for the purpose of determining whether the Public Guardian and Trustee should become the person's statutory guardian of property, does not receive rights advice, but is entitled to receive a copy of the certificate of incapacity. It is left to the Public Guardian and Trustee to inform the individual of the right to apply to the Consent and Capacity Board.[6] A person assessed not capable of managing property for the purpose of an application to the court for the appointment of a guardian of property, must receive written notice of the assessor's finding.[7] There is no right to apply to the Consent and Capacity Board in relation to such a finding.

Applications to Review the Finding of Incapacity

Individuals assessed not capable of managing property under the *Mental Health Act* or under the *Substitute Decisions Act, 1992* for the purposes of determining whether the Public Guardian and Trustee should become statutory guardian of property, have the same right to apply to the Board for a review of the finding[8] and may only make an application in this regard once every six months[9]. However, if a patient found incapable under the MHA fails to apply to the Board while a patient of the psychiatric facility, he or she must apply under the SDA and incur the cost of a capacity assessment.[10] The application the person makes to the Board is a Form 18 application in each case. However, there are significantly different forms approved by the Minister of Health under each Act. A Form 18 under the MHA provides the Board with far less information in relation to the matter than the approved Form 18 under the SDA.

---

[5] s. 59, MHA.

[6] s. 16(4) and (6), SDA.

[7] s. 78(5), SDA.

[8] The language identifying the applicant and the scope of the review is different: Under the MHA (s. 60), a patient in a psychiatric facility in respect of whom a finding of incapacity to manage his or her property has been made or continued can apply for a review of the issue of his or her capacity to manage property; Under the SDA (s. 20.2) a person who has a statutory guardian of property may apply for a review of the finding of incapacity.

[9] An individual assessed not capable of managing property under the SDA for the purposes of a summary application to the court for the appointment of a guardian of property, has no right to apply to the Consent and Capacity Board.

[10] s. 20.2(1) SDA.

Authority to make Findings of Incapacity

Under the *Substitute Decisions Act, 1992* only a qualified capacity assessor[11] may conduct[12] assessments of capacity for the purposes of creating a statutory guardianship.[13] Under the *Mental Health Act,* only physicians may conduct assessments of incapacity to manage property. Capacity assessors under the SDA may perform an assessment of either the person requesting the assessment or any other person's capacity for the purpose of determining whether the Public Guardian and Trustee should become the person's statutory guardian of property.[14]

Procedural Safeguards Prior to the Finding of Incapacity

There are significant procedural safeguards in the SDA which do not apply to MHA assessments of financial capacity. Under the SDA, for the purposes of statutory guardianship, no assessment of another person's capacity shall be performed by an assessor unless the request is in the prescribed form and the person requesting the assessment states that certain requirements are met.[15] This is in sharp contrast to the operation of the MHA, which compels a physician to assess a patient's capacity to manage property forthwith upon admission to the psychiatric facility[16] (again, with very few exceptions.)[17]

Under the SDA, a person can refuse the assessment.[18] This is not the case under the *Mental Health* Act. There is also a requirement under the SDA that before performing an assessment of capacity, the assessor explain to the person to be assessed the purpose of the assessment, the significance and effect of the finding of capacity or incapacity, and the person's right to refuse to be assessed.[19] Absent

---

[11] "assessor" is a defined term under the Act and means "a member of a class of persons who are designated by the regulations as being qualified to do assessments of capacity"; O. Reg. 293/96, s.1 sets out the qualifications of an assessor, including the requirement to complete a training course and approval by the Attorney General. A list of assessors may be obtained from the Capacity Assessment Office of the Attorney General.

[12] Pursuant to O. Reg. 293/96 s. 2, an assessor shall perform assessments of capacity in accordance with the "Guidelines for Conducting Assessments of Capacity" established by the Attorney General and dated June 7, 1996. To request a copy of the guidelines, contact the Capacity Assessment Office of the Attorney General.

[13] For the purpose of a summary application to the court for the appointment of a guardian of property, two statements are required: one from an assessor and the other from "a person who knows the person alleged to be incapable".

[14] s. 16(1) SDA.

[15] s. 16(2) SDA.

[16] s. 54 (1) MHA.

[17] s. 54 (6) MHA. The exceptions are if the patient has a guardian of property or the physician believes on reasonable grounds that the patient has a continuing power of attorney that provides for the management of the patient's property.

[18] s. 78(1).

[19] s. 78(2).

such an explanation, any assessment of a person's capacity is unlawful. Again, these safeguards are not in the *Mental Health* Act. The case of *Re Koch* illustrates the significance of procedural safeguards under the SDA.[20] However, it does not apply to assessments of financial capacity conducted under the MHA.

Treatment/Admission To or Placement In Long-Term Care Facilities/Personal Assistance Services/Personal Care:

Findings of Incapacity under the HCCA and the SDA

A finding of incapacity regarding medical or psychiatric "treatment,[21] "admission to a long-term care facility" or "personal assistance services" may be made under the *Health Care Consent Act, 1996* (HCCA). A finding of incapacity regarding "personal care" may be made under the SDA

"Personal assistance service" is defined in the *Health Care Consent Act, 1996* as assistance with or supervision of hygiene, washing, dressing, grooming, eating, drinking, elimination, ambulation, positioning or any other routine activity of living provided to residents of long-term care facilities (defined as Care facilities under the HCCA including nursing homes but not retirement homes.)[22] Findings of incapacity regarding personal assistance services may be made only in relation to residents of care facilities as defined under the Act.

Personal care is defined in the SDA as "health care, nutrition, shelter, clothing, hygiene or safety."[23] Findings of incapacity regarding personal care may be made in relation to anyone. Although personal care decisions include decisions regarding treatment and admission to care facilities, they are broader than the decisions to which the HCCA applies.

A finding of incapacity regarding "treatment", "admission to a care facility" or "personal assistance services" made under the HCCA results in a substitute decision maker (SDM) being called upon to make decisions for the incapable person.

A finding of incapacity regarding "personal care" made under the SDA does not result in a substitute decision maker being called upon to make the decision.

A finding of incapacity in relation to personal care has relevance only for the purpose of activating a power of attorney for personal care or in support of an

---

[20] A 1997 decision of the (then) Ontario Court, General Division (1997), 33 O.R. (3d) 485, the judgment of Quinn J. is still the leading case on this issue.

[21] The HCCA, s. 2, defines "treatment" as anything done for a therapeutic purpose including, among other things, a course of treatment, plan of treatment or community treatment plan. Community treatment plan has a defined meaning in the *Mental Health Act* as described by s. 33.7 of the MHA and as a required part of a community treatment order under the MHA (the CTO is based on the CTP under s. 33.1(4)(b) of the MHA.).

[22] s. 2(1) HCCA.

[23] s. 45 SDA.

application to the court for the appointment of a guardian of the person.[24] The procedure for such an application is set out in Part III of the SDA. A court-appointed guardian for a person found not capable of personal care is the highest-ranking substitute decision maker. The next highest-ranking substitute decision maker is an attorney under a power of attorney for personal care. The requirements for a power of attorney for personal care are also contained in the SDA and not in the *Powers of Attorney Act*.[25] Although one would expect the identification of substitute decision makers and their rights, duties and obligations as substitute decision makers to be found in the SDA, these provisions are all actually contained within the HCCA.[26]

Definition of Capacity

The test for capacity is the same under each Act. In fact, it is the same test as the test for capacity to manage property. A person is capable with respect to treatment, admission to a care facility, personal assistance services or personal care if the person is able to understand the information that is relevant to making the decision and able to appreciate the reasonably foreseeable consequences of a decision or lack of decision.[27]

Rights Advice/Information Subsequent to the Finding of Incapacity

A patient in a psychiatric facility, 14 years old or older, who is found not capable with respect to psychiatric treatment, is entitled to receive written notice of the finding together with rights advice. A rights adviser must meet with the person and explain the significance of the finding and the right to apply to the Board for a review of the finding.[28]

A person who is not a patient in a psychiatric facility and found not capable with respect to either medical or psychiatric treatment, is not entitled to receive written notice of the finding or rights advice. In such a case, the health practitioner or evaluator must comply with the guidelines established by their respective professional governing body in terms of notifying the person of the finding and the individual's right to apply to the Board to have the finding reviewed. This is also the case with respect to a finding made under the HCCA in relation to personal assistance services and admission to a care facility.[29]

Individuals who are assessed in relation to personal care under the SDA must be given written notice of the finding; however, they do not receive rights advice.[30]

---

[24] s. 55(1) SDA.

[25] ss. 46-50.

[26] s. 20, 21, 41, 42, 58 and 59.

[27] s. 4(1) HCCA and s. 45, SDA.

[28] s. 15 Reg. 741 to MHA.

[29] s. 17.

[30] s. 78(5).

Application to Review the Finding of Incapacity

Individuals assessed not capable with respect to treatment, personal assistance services or admission to a care facility under the HCCA have a right to apply to the Consent and Capacity Board for a review of the finding and may make an application in this regard only once every six months, unless leave is obtained.[31]

Individuals assessed not capable of personal care under the provisions of the *Substitute Decisions Act, 1992* do not have a right to apply to the Board for a review of the finding.

Authority to make Findings of Incapacity

A finding of treatment incapacity may be made only by a health practitioner, a term defined under the HCCA as including a broad class of professionals. Some health practitioners are also defined as "evaluators" under the Act. In addition to determining treatment capacity, evaluators may also make findings of incapacity with respect to admission and personal assistance services.[32] In the event a summary application[33] is made to the court under the SDA for the appointment of a guardian of the person, a finding of incapacity to make personal care decisions may be made only by a capacity assessor.[34,35]

Procedural Safeguards

There are significant procedural safeguards in the *Substitute Decisions Act, 1992* relating to a finding of incapacity for personal care which do not apply to assessments under the HCCA. Under the SDA, there is a requirement that before performing an assessment of capacity, the assessor explain to the person to be assessed the purpose of the assessment, the significance and the effect of the finding of capacity or incapacity, and the person's right to refuse to be assessed.[36] Absent such an explanation, the assessment of a person's capacity is unlawful. These safeguards are not in the HCCA. The case of *Re Koch* illustrates the significance of procedural safeguards under the SDA.[37] Although *Re Koch*

---

[31] ss. 32(1), 50(1) and 65(1), HCCA and sections 32(5), 50(4) and 65(4).

[32] s. 2 HCCA.

[33] s. 74(1), SDA.

[34] "assessor" is a defined term under the Act and means "a member of a class of persons who are designated by the regulations as being qualified to do assessments of capacity"; O. Reg. 293/96, s.1 sets out the qualifications of an assessor, including the requirement to complete a training course and approval by the Attorney General. A list of assessors may be obtained from the Capacity Assessment Office of the Attorney General.

[35] There is no requirement that a finding of incapacity in relation to personal care be made by an assessor if the application for the appointment is not by way of summary disposition.

[36] s. 78.

[37] *Re Koch* (1997), 33 O.R., (3d) 485 (Gen.Div.).

imported these procedural safeguards to the HCCA, decisions of the Consent and Capacity Board have treated these statements as *obiter*. As a result, the procedural safeguards of the SDA have not been applied by the Board to the HCCA.

Community Treatment Orders: A Special Case

Community treatment orders (CTOs) were established by amendments to the *Mental Health Act* in December, 2000.[38] In essence, they require the subject's compliance[39] with a community treatment plan (CTP),[40] failing which the individual may be forcibly returned to the issuing physician for an examination.[41] In addition, the criteria for issuing a CTO, in respect of an individual who is not a patient in a psychiatric facility, include the requirement that the individual meet the criteria for an application for psychiatric assessment (Form 1) under the *Mental Health Act*.[42] All subjects of proposed CTOs must, without ongoing treatment, meet one of the harm, impairment or deterioration criteria for involuntary committal.[43] However, the criteria for issuing or renewing a CTO do not include the incapacity of the subject. Capable individuals may consent to their own CTOs. Incapable persons' SDMs may consent to CTOs on their behalf. For all of these reasons and depending on one's philosophical perspective[44] regarding the complex issues raised by CTOs, the CTO is a hybrid of the concepts of treatment and detention.

The CTP is meant to provide a "comprehensive community-based plan of treatment or care and supervision"[45] which generally includes at least the requirement to take prescribed medication as well as regular attendance with a psychiatrist or other physician who issued the order.[46] Some CTPs may oblige the subject to do any number of other things, which, but for their inclusion as part of the CTP, would not otherwise constitute "treatment," such as participation in daily meetings with members of an assertive community treatment team (ACT) or living in housing as specified in the CTP. The validity of some CTPs has been

---

[38] MHA, ss. 33.1 to 33.9 inclusive.

[39] MHA, s. 33.1(9).

[40] MHA, s. 33.7.

[41] The order for examination (Form 47) the MHA under s. 33.3(1) is referenced below in this introduction, under "Detention".

[42] MHA, s. 33.1(4)(c)(ii).

[43] MHA, s. 33.1(4)(c)(i) and (iii).

[44] In the United States, "CTOs" are known as Involuntary Outpatient Commitment (IOC); For example, on February 17, 2004, New York's highest court upheld the constitutionality of "Kendra's Law", which required compliance with medication in the community. Nearly 40 other states have similar statutes. The challenge was brought on the ground that it violated the constitutional guarantee of due process because it did not require that a court declare a psychiatric patient mentally incapacitated (which is not an issue in Ontario) before forcing the patient into treatment.

[45] MHA, s. 33.1(3), the purpose clause to CTO provisions.

[46] MHA, s. 33.1(9)(a).

questioned before the Board,[47] but these issues have not yet received judicial consideration. This is the case as well with the question of the constitutionality of the CTO regime.[48]

The CTO regime,[49] and even the subsection which sets out the criteria for issuing CTOs,[50] are simply too cumbersome to set out in detail here. A somewhat more comprehensive discussion is included, in this consolidation, in the introduction to the *Mental Health Act*. There are some aspects of a CTO which require recourse to the provisions of the *Health Care Consent Act, 1996* regarding treatment, and others which rest on an understanding of the involuntary psychiatric examination, assessment and detention of individuals pursuant to the *Mental Health Act*. A CTO may be issued by a physician for a particular purpose[51] provided all the criteria for issuing or renewing[52] a CTO are met.

CTOs may be issued in respect of an individual who is a patient in a psychiatric facility or someone who is living in the community. A CTO requires consent to the CTP either from the capable individual, or if incapable, from the person's SDM. The SDM is entitled to all the information the subject would receive if capable in relation to the CTP. In these, and some other ways, the CTO relates to the treatment provisions of the HCCA just as any other "treatment" issues do, given that the CTP is specifically included in the definition of "treatment."

Finding of Incapacity Relating to CTP, Right to Apply to the Board

One would expect, then, that in the event a physician finds an individual incapable with respect to a CTP which relates to the treatment of mental disorder, the individual would be entitled to written notice of the finding in the approved form, together with prompt rights advice on that specific issue, as discussed above. However, the Board does not necessarily interpret the statute as requiring independent[53] notice of a finding of incapacity regarding a CTP. On the other

---

47 A more detailed discussion on these issues is contained in the MHA chapter under the heading of "Community Treatment Orders." The Board has interpreted broadly the types of things that may comprise a CTP; for instance, a condition prescribing where and with whom a subject of a CTO may reside has been affirmed as a valid clause requiring the subject's compliance, see In *re M.B.G.* TO-030685 July 7, 2003.

48 See the Introduction to the MHA in this consolidation.

49 MHA s. 33.1 to s. 33.9.

50 MHA s. 33.1(4).

51 The purpose is set out in s. 33.1(3) of the MHA.

52 The criteria for issuing and renewing a CTO are the same, as set out in s. 33.1(4) of the MHA.

53 Apart from a notice of a finding of incapacity regarding treatment of a mental disorder which has already been provided during the same admission as the one which culminates in the issuance of a CTO, pursuant to Reg. 741, s. 15 (1) and (2), [see In *re DB* TO 021079, October 17, 2002 and In *re P.B.* (aka *O.(P.) B.*) TO-01/1330, March 16, 2002]; or apart from the notice of intent to issue or renew a CTO (Form 49 under the MHA) which includes a statement indicating that the subject of the proposed CTO

hand, the Board consistently has held that a review of the individual's capacity in relation to the CTP is a necessary part of every review of a community treatment order which is in effect pursuant to an SDM's consent. This is the case even where the subject of the order has made no independent application to review the finding of incapacity to consent to the CTP; indeed the Board considers these applications superfluous.[54]

Application to the Board to Review a CTO

A person who is the subject of a CTO, or anyone on the person's behalf, may apply to the Board to inquire into whether or not the criteria for issuing or renewing the CTO are met on the date of hearing[55] each time a CTO is issued or renewed.[56] A mandatory hearing on the issue is held when the CTO is renewed for the second time and on the occasion of every second renewal thereafter.[57]

Procedural Safeguards

A physician who is considering issuing or renewing a CTO must give the individual (and his or her SDM if applicable) and a rights adviser written notice of the intention to do so.[58] The rights adviser who receives such notice must promptly meet with the individual and the SDM[59] to explain the requirements for issuing or renewing a CTO, the significance of the order, and any obligations each person may be required to meet under the order. This is the only time a rights adviser is required to meet with any party to a CTO. At this meeting, the rights adviser cannot take an application from the subject of a CTO for a review of the CTO[60] as no CTO exists. Although the issuing physician must give the subject (and the SDM if applicable)[61] a copy of the CTO,[62] including the CTP,[63] together with notice of the right to a hearing before the Board[64], there is no requirement to

---

has been found incapable with respect to the CTO. See In *re K.M.* TO 021453 April 2, 2003.

54 See for example, In re C.I. TO 030704 July 31, 2002.

55 MHA, s. 39.1(1).

56 MHA, s. 39.1(2).

57 MHA, s. 39.1(3) and (5).

58 Reg. 741, s. 14.3(1); the approved form is Form 49 under the MHA.

59 Reg. 741, s. 14.3(2), (3). If the rights adviser believes it is in the subject's best interest to receive rights advice from another rights adviser, he or she will ensure that the rights adviser providing rights advice to the individual is not the same rights adviser as the individual who provided the service to the SDM. See, Reg. 741, s. 14.3(4).

60 Form 48 application under the MHA.

61 MHA, s. 33.1(10)(b).

62 Form 45 under the MHA.

63 MHA, s. 33.1(10).

64 Form 46 pursuant to MHA s. 33.1(10) (a).

provide rights advice to the subject or the SDM following the issuance of the CTO.

Detention

The *Mental Health Act, Substitute Decisions Act, 1992* and *Health Care Consent Act, 1996* all have provisions allowing for the detention of individuals. With the exception of certain provisions in the MHA, detention of an individual is grounded in a finding of incapacity in relation to either treatment (HCCA and MHA), personal care (SDA) or personal assistance services (HCCA).

Detention Not Based on Incapacity

The Mental Health Act

The *Mental Health Act* allows for the detention of individuals in psychiatric facilities without a finding of incapacity, primarily in five areas:

1. Action by police officers;
2. Order of the justice of the peace;
3. Application for psychiatric assessment;
4. Involuntary committal;
5. Order for examination by physician.

1. Action by Police Officers

Where a police officer has reasonable and probable grounds to believe a person is acting or has acted in a disorderly manner and has reasonable cause to believe that the person has: (a) threatened or attempted or is threatening or attempting to cause harm to himself or herself; (b) has behaved or is behaving violently toward another person or has caused or is causing another person to fear bodily harm from him or her; or (c) has shown or is showing a lack of competence to care for himself or herself,[65] and in addition the police officer is of the opinion that the person is apparently suffering from mental disorder of a nature or quality that likely will result in (d) serious bodily harm to the person; (e) serious bodily harm to another person; or (f) serious physical impairment of the person[66] and that it would be dangerous to proceed to obtain an order of the justice of the peace, the police officer may take the person in custody to an appropriate place for examination by a physician.[67] The examination of the individual should take place at a psychiatric facility at which point the individual may be further detained in the event the physician completes an application for psychiatric assessment. There

---

[65] The "past harm or threat of harm" criteria.

[66] The "future harm" criteria.

[67] MHA s. 17.

is no requirement that the individual be assessed incapable of consenting to treatment of a mental disorder.

2. Order of the Justice of the Peace

A justice of the peace may issue an order for the examination of a person by a physician, provided the justice of the peace is satisfied by sworn testimony that the person meets the "past harm or threat of harm" criteria and the justice of the peace has reasonable cause to believe that the person also meets the "future harm" criteria as set out above in relation to the authority of the police.[68] The order of the justice of the peace is sufficient authority for any police officer to take the person in custody forthwith to an appropriate place where he or she may be detained for examination by an physician.[69] There is no right to apply to the Consent and Capacity Board to have the order reviewed. Once examined by a physician, the person can be further detained in the event the physician completes an application for psychiatric assessment. There is no requirement that the individual be assessed incapable of consenting to treatment of a mental disorder.

3. Application for Psychiatric Assessment

Any physician in the province of Ontario may complete an application for psychiatric assessment (Form 1 under the MHA), provided the physician has examined the subject of the application within the past seven days and has reasonable cause to believe that the person meets the "past harm or threat of harm" criteria and if, in addition, the physician is of the opinion that the person meets the "future harm" criteria as set out above in relation to the authority of police and that of J.P.s.[70] The application for psychiatric assessment is sufficient authority for seven days from and including the day on which it is signed

(a) for any person to take the person who is the subject of the application in custody to a psychiatric facility forthwith; and

(b) to detain the person who is the subject of the application in a psychiatric facility and to restrain, observe and examine him or her in the facility for not more than seventy-two hours.

There is no right to apply to the Consent and Capacity Board to have the application reviewed.

Prior to the expiration of the seventy-two hour period, a physician other than the physician who completed the Form 1 application[71] must examine the person in a psychiatric facility and either (a) release the person from the psychiatric facility if the physician is of the opinion that the person is not in need of the treatment provided in the psychiatric facility;[72] (b) admit the person as an informal or voluntary patient if the attending physician is of the opinion that the person is

---

[68] MHA s. 16.

[69] MHA s. 16(3).

[70] MHA s. 15(1).

[71] MHA s. 20(2).

[72] MHA s. 20(1)(a).

suffering from mental disorder of such a nature or quality that the person is in need of the treatment provided in the psychiatric facility and is suitable for admission as an informal or voluntary patient;[73] or (c) admit the person as an involuntary patient by completing and filing with the officer in charge a certificate of involuntary admission, if the attending physician is of the opinion that the conditions for involuntary admission are met. [74] There is no requirement that the individual be assessed incapable of consenting to treatment of a mental disorder.

4. Involuntary Committal

A person may be detained indeterminably in a psychiatric facility notwithstanding that he or she may be capable of making decisions regarding treatment, provided the following criteria are met: (a) he or she is suffering from mental disorder of a nature or quality that likely will result in either serious bodily harm to themselves, serious bodily harm to another person, or serious physical impairment of themselves, unless he or she remains in the custody of a psychiatric facility; and (b) he or she is not suitable for admission or continuation as an informal or voluntary patient.[75] There is no requirement that the individual be assessed incapable of consenting to treatment of a mental disorder.

The initial period of involuntary detention is for two weeks. Subsequent periods of detention are for one month under a first certificate of renewal, two additional months under a second certificate of renewal and three additional months under a third or subsequent certificate of renewal. Given that there is no limit to the number of certificates of renewal, an individual may be detained indeterminably provided the certificates are completed and filed with the officer in charge by the attending physician at the required intervals.[76] Whenever a certificate of involuntary admission or renewal is completed,[77] the subject of the detention has the right to apply to the Consent and Capacity Board for a hearing to determine whether or not the criteria for detention continue to be met.[78] There is a mandatory review of an individual's detention before the Consent and Capacity Board on the completion of a fourth certificate of renewal and on the completion of every fourth certificate of renewal thereafter.[79]

5. Order for Examination by Physician

The *Mental Health Act* allows a physician to issue a community treatment order for a person, notwithstanding that the individual may be capable of providing their own consent or refusal to the treatment. If capable, the subject of the order

---

[73] MHA s. 20(1)(b).

[74] MHA s. 20(1)(c).

[75] MHA s. 20(5).

[76] MHA s. 20(4).

[77] But not an application for psychiatric assessment or order for examination by a justice of the peace or a physician.

[78] MHA s. 39(2).

[79] MHA s. 39(4).

must consent to the community treatment plan which forms the basis of the order. In the event the person withdraws his or her consent to the plan, or fails to comply with the terms of the plan, the physician who issued or renewed the community treatment order may order an examination of the person upon having reasonable and probable grounds to believe that the criteria set out in s. 33.1(4)(c)(i)(ii) and (iii) of the *Mental Health Act* (which include the criterion that the subject meet the pre-requisites for issuing a Form 1 application for psychiatric assessment[80]) continue to be met. However, these criteria are not dependent on the individual being incapable of consenting to their own treatment.

The order for examination[81] is sufficient authority, for thirty days after it is issued, for a police officer to take the person named into custody and then promptly to the physician who issued the order. There is no right to apply to the Consent and Capacity Board to have the order reviewed. However, issuance of the order for examination terminates the CTO.[82]

Upon receiving the individual desired pursuant to an order for examination under this section, the physician must promptly examine the person to determine whether, (a) the physician should make an application for a psychiatric assessment; (b) the physician should issue another community treatment order, where the person, or his or her SDM, consents to the community treatment plan; or (c) the person should be released without being subject to a community treatment order.[83]

Detention Based on Incapacity

The Mental Health Act

The *Mental Health Act* allows for the detention of individuals based on findings of incapacity (provided certain additional criteria exist) in four areas:

1. Order of the justice of the peace;
2. Application for psychiatric assessment;
3. Involuntary committal;
4. Order for examination by physician.

Detention in these four areas is based on the "expanded" criteria for examination, assessment or committal of incapable persons pursuant to amendments to the *Mental Health Act* in December, 2000. These expanded criteria are not available to police officers acting independently.

---

[80] MHA s. 33.1(4)(c)(ii).

[81] MHA Form 47.

[82] For a fuller discussion of the operation of the CTO provisions, including termination of the order for failure to comply, or because of a withdrawal of consent, see the introduction to the MHA and s. 33.3(1) and 33.4(1) and (3).

[83] MHA s. 33.3(4) and s. 33.4(5).

1. Order of the Justice of the Peace

A justice of the peace may make an order for the examination of an individual without the necessity of being satisfied as to any of the criteria of dangerousness (the "future harm" criteria) previously discussed,[84] based solely on the likelihood of the individual suffering either "substantial mental deterioration" or "substantial physical deterioration", provided the justice of the peace is satisfied that the individual: (a) is apparently incapable, within the meaning of the HCCA, of consenting to his or her treatment in a psychiatric facility and the consent of his or her substitute decision maker has been obtained, (b) has previously received treatment for mental disorder of an ongoing or recurring nature that, when not treated, is of a nature or quality that likely will result in either substantial mental or physical deterioration of the person; (c) has shown clinical improvement as a result of the treatment; (d) is apparently suffering from the same mental disorder as the one for which the individual previously received treatment or from a mental disorder that is similar to the previous one; and (e) given the individual's history of mental disorder and current mental or physical condition, is likely to suffer substantial mental or physical deterioration.[85] The order of the justice of the peace is sufficient authority for a period not to exceed seven days from, and including, the day that it is made for any police officer to take the person in custody forthwith to an appropriate place where the individual may be detained for examination by a physician.[86] There is no right to apply to the Consent and Capacity Board to review the order.

The physician conducting the examination may then determine whether or not to complete an application for psychiatric assessment.

2. Applications for Psychiatric Assessment

Any physician in the province of Ontario who has examined an individual within the past seven days may complete an application for psychiatric assessment of the individual based solely on the ground of substantial mental or physical deterioration, (*i.e.* the dangerousness criteria previously discussed need not be present) provided the physician forms the opinion based on reasonable cause to believe that the "expanded" criteria in relation to incapable persons described above, with respect to the authority of the J.P., are met.[87] The physician, as opposed to the J.P., must be of the opinion that the individual is incapable, rather than "apparently incapable."

The authority to detain, restrain and observe the subject of the Form 1 application under this section is the same as previously set out above, in relation to the

---

[84] (the "future harm" criteria of serious bodily harm to self or others/serious physical impairment)

[85] MHA s. 16(1.1), the "expanded" criteria for examination, assessment or committal, as referenced above and below.

[86] MHA s. 16(3).

[87] MHA s. 15(1.1).

Form 1 application for assessment not based on incapacity.[88] There is no right to apply to the Consent and Capacity Board to review the application. Prior to the expiration of the seventy-two hour period of detention, the individual must be: (1) released, (2) admitted as a voluntary or informal patient; or (3) admitted as an involuntary patient.[89]

3. Involuntary Committal

A person who has been found incapable of consenting to his or her treatment in a psychiatric facility within the meaning of the HCCA may be detained indeterminably in a psychiatric facility based solely on the ground of substantial mental or physical deterioration, provided all of the "expanded" criteria as described above in relation to the Form 1 application for psychiatric assessment of incapable persons exist.[90]

The renewals of the periods of detention and the right of the individual to apply to the Consent and Capacity Board to have the detention reviewed, are the same as previously set out.[91]

4. Order for Examination by Physician

The *Mental Health Act* allows a physician to issue a community treatment order for a person incapable of consenting to his or her treatment in the community, provided the individual's SDM has consented to the community treatment plan. In the event the SDM withdraws his or her consent to the plan, or the person subject to the plan fails to comply with the terms of the plan, the physician who issued or renewed the community treatment order may order an examination of the individual upon having reasonable and probable grounds to believe that the criteria set out in s. 33.1(4)(c)(i)(ii) and (iii) continue to be met. As set out above, these criteria include the requirement that the individual continue to meet the pre-requisites for issuing a Form 1 application for psychiatric assessment. The order for examination may be issued in relation to incapable individuals even where the only ground on which a Form 1 could be issued in relation to the individual is the likelihood of either substantial "mental" or "physical" deterioration. The balance of the comments in relation to the order for examination set out above[92] apply here.

---

[88] MHA s. 15(5).

[89] MHA s. 20(1).

[90] MHA s. 20(1.1).

[91] In relation to involuntary committal not based on incapacity.

[92] See the commentary relating to Orders For Examination as Detention not Based on Incapacity.

The Substitute Decisions Act, 1992

1. Court-Appointed Guardian of the Person

The SDA authorizes a court to appoint a guardian for a person who is not capable of personal care and, as a result, needs decisions to be made on his or her behalf by a person who is authorized to do so.[93]

An order of the court appointing a guardian of the person must include a finding that the person is incapable of personal care.[94]

Provided the court is satisfied that the individual is not capable in all areas of personal care, the court may make an order for full guardianship.[95] Under an order for full guardianship, the guardian may exercise custodial power over the person under guardianship, determine his or her living arrangements and provide for his or her shelter and safety. In addition, the court may, in its order, authorize the guardian to apprehend the person if required, in which case the guardian may, with the assistance of a police officer, enter any premises specified in the order during the hours specified and search for and remove the person, using such force as may be necessary.

2. Power of Attorney for Personal Care

The SDA authorizes an individual to make a power of attorney for personal care granting the named attorney extraordinary powers of custody over the grantor provided certain conditions exist.[96] The provisions that may be included in such a power of attorney are as follows:

1. A provision that authorizes the attorney and other persons under the direction of the Attorney to use force that is necessary and reasonable in the circumstances, i) to determine whether the grantor is incapable of making a decision to which the *Health Care Consent Act, 1996,* applies, ii) to confirm in accordance with s. 49(2) whether the grantor is incapable of personal care, if the power of attorney contains a condition described in clause 49(1)(b), or iii) to obtain an assessment of the grantor's capacity by an assessor in any other circumstances described in the power of attorney.
2. A provision that authorizes the attorney and other persons under the direction of the attorney to use force that is necessary and reasonable in the circumstances to take the grantor to any place for care or treatment, to

[93] SDA s. 55(1).

[94] SDA s. 58(1).

[95] SDA s. 59(1).

[96] This special form of a power of attorney is colloquially referred to as a "Ulysses Contract"; the idea being that an individual executes such a document to allow the attorney to keep the grantor safe from him or herself at a time of anticipated or at least potential incapacity in relation to the grantor's personal care.

admit the grantor to that place and to detain and restrain the grantor in that place during the care or treatment.

3. A provision that waives the grantor's right to apply to the Consent and Capacity Board under sections 32, 50, and 65 of the *Health Care Consent Act, 1996,* for a review of a finding of incapacity that applies to a decision to which that Act applies.[97]

These extraordinary provisions are not effective unless both of the following circumstances exist: (1) at the time the power of attorney was executed or within thirty days afterward, the grantor made a statement in the prescribed form indicating that he or she understood the effect of the provision and that they could only revoke the power of attorney if within thirty days before the revocation, an assessor performed an assessment of the grantor's capacity and provided a statement that the grantor was capable of personal care and (2) within thirty days after the power of attorney was executed, an assessor made a statement in the prescribed form indicating that after the power of attorney was executed, the assessor performed an assessment of the grantor's capacity and was satisfied that the grantor was capable of personal care and was capable of understanding the effect of the provisions contained in the power of attorney and the provisions for revocation.[98]

3. Court-Appointed Guardians and Attorneys for Personal Care

In the event an individual has either a court-appointed guardian with full custodial and apprehension power, or a power of attorney for personal care containing the special provisions effective in section 50 of the SDA, the guardian or attorney has authority to consent to the individual's admission and treatment in a psychiatric facility, notwithstanding any objection of the individual to the admission. The authority to admit, treat and detain the individual in the psychiatric facility for the purposes of receiving the treatment is not based on the criteria for detention or involuntary committal under the *Mental Health Act*. Rather, the authority derives from the powers granted to the guardian or to the attorney by virtue of the provisions of the SDA. This authority is specifically recognized by section 24(2) of the HCCA, which states:

> (2) If the incapable person is 16 years old or older and objects to being admitted to a psychiatric facility for treatment of a mental disorder, consent to his or her admission may be given only by,
>
> (a) his or her guardian of the person, if the guardian has authority to consent to the admission; or
>
> (b) his or her attorney for personal care, if the power of attorney contains a provision authorizing the attorney to use force that is necessary and reasonable in the circumstances to admit the incapable person to the

---

[97] SDA s. 50(2).

[98] SDA s. 50(1).

psychiatric facility and the provision is effective under subsection 50 (1) of the *Substitute Decisions Act, 1992.*[99]

An application may be made by a person to the Consent and Capacity Board for a review of a decision to consent on the person's behalf to the person's admission to a hospital, psychiatric facility, or other health facility referred to in section 24 for the purpose of treatment.[100] There are no exceptions (which apply to individuals in these circumstances),[101] barring the application.[102]

In reviewing the decision to admit the person to a hospital, psychiatric facility, or other health facility for the purpose of the treatment, the Board may either direct that the person be discharged from the hospital, psychiatric facility, or health facility or confirm the decision to admit the person to a hospital, psychiatric facility, or health facility.

4. Orders for Assessment and Apprehension

The SDA allows the court to order the Public Guardian and Trustee, together with police, to apprehend a person whose capacity (either in relation to property or personal care) is in issue in a proceeding under the SDA. Provided an order has been previously made for the assessment of the individual's capacity, the court's subsequent order may permit the individual to be taken into custody and brought to a specified place to be assessed. In making such an order, the court must be satisfied that, (1) the assessor named in the assessment order has made all efforts that are reasonable in the circumstances to assess the person; (2) the assessor was prevented from assessing the person by the actions of the person or others; (3) a restraining order[103] is not appropriate under the circumstances, or has already been used without success; and (4) there is no less intrusive means of permitting the assessment to be performed than an order for enforcement. The Public Guardian and Trustee and police may use such force as necessary to bring the person to a health facility for the assessment. The order is sufficient authority to detain the individual at the health facility for not longer than seventy-two hours.[104]

The SDA also authorizes the court to permit the Public Guardian and Trustee to enter premises and remove a person using such force as may be necessary

---

[99] HCCA, s. 24(2).

[100] HCCA s. 34.

[101] The only exception is s. 34.(2) of the HCCA, which prohibits the application of informal minors (12-16 years of age) admitted to psychiatric facilities pursuant to substitute consent.

[102] HCCA, s. 34(1) would appear to permit an application to review the decision of the guardian or attorney to consent to the admission in these circumstances, as applications by individuals detained pursuant to the consent of the guardian or attorney in such situations are not barred by statute. It is unclear what, if any, legal effect the Board's decision may have in these applications, however, since the authority of the guardian, in any event, may be varied or terminated only by the court.

[103] Against another individual who may be hindering or obstructing the assessment, s. 80.

[104] SDA s. 79-81.

provided the Public Guardian and Trustee has been appointed guardian of the person by the Court.[105]

The Health Care Consent Act, 1996

The HCCA authorizes a substitute decision maker for a person assessed not capable of personal assistance services, to give consent to the use of confinement, monitoring devices, or restraint provided the practice is essential to prevent serious bodily harm to the person or to others, or allows the person greater freedom or enjoyment.[106]

This is the only authority (subject to a court-appointed guardian of the person with custodial power or an attorney for personal care with the extraordinary powers effective under s. 50 of the SDA), which permits individuals to be detained in long-term care facilities.[107] Personal Health Information Protection Act, 2004

PERSONAL HEALTH INFORMATION

The Personal Health Information Protection Act, 2004

As of November 1, 2004, the *Personal Health Information Protection Act, 2004* sets out the rules for the collection, use and disclosure of personal health information. These rules apply to all health information custodians operating within the Province of Ontario and to individuals and organizations that receive personal health information from health information custodians. Subject to certain exceptions, the legislation requires health information custodians to obtain consent before they collect, use, or disclose personal health information. There is also the right, subject to certain exceptions, to access and request correction of personal health information.

If an individual is mentally capable, they have the right, subject to certain exceptions[108] to access and consent to the use, disclosure, and collection of their personal health information. In the event the collection, use, or disclosure is refused based on a finding of incapacity, the individual may apply to the Consent and Capacity Board, subject to certain exceptions.[109]

---

[105] SDA s. 62.

[106] HCCA s. 59(3).

[107] An argument may be made that an attorney for personal care with the necessary authority may have the ability to detain the individual pursuant to s. 67 of the SDA which affords attorneys for personal care the same rights and duties as guardians have under s. 66.(10)(1) among others. Section 66(10)(1)(a) of the SDA allows the guardian to consent to confinement, monitoring or restraint if the practice allows the individual greater freedom or enjoyment.

[108] PHIPA, s. 52 .

[109] PHIPA, s. 22(3), see also s.20 of the HCCA for the list of substitute decision makers

In the event collection, use, or disclosure is refusad based on grounds other than incapacity, the individual may complain to the Information and Privacy Commissioner of Ontario.[110]

Refusal Based on Incapacity

In the event a health information custodian is of the opinion that an individual is either: (a) unable to understand the information that is relevant to deciding whether to consent to the collection, use, or disclosure as the case may be, or (b) unable to appreciate the reasonably foreseeable consequences of giving, not giving, withholding, or withdrawing consent, the custodian may refuse the request of the individual. In such a case, the individual has the right to apply to the Consent and Capacity Board of Ontario to review the finding of incapacity. It is to be noted that the individual does not have the right to apply to the Consent and Capacity Board for a review of the determination if there is a person who is entitled to act as their substitute decision-maker in relation to treatment, admission to a care facility, or personal assistance services under the provisions of the *Health Care Consent Act.*[111] It is also to be noted that the requirement of the health information custodian to provide notice of the assessment of incapacity to the individual is vague. The Act states that if it is reasonable in the circumstances, a health information custodian shall provide, to an individual determined incapable, information about the consequences of the determination of incapacity, including the information, if any, that is prescribed.[112] The Act, to date, does not contain any regulation prescribing information to be provided.

Refusal Based on Grounds Other Than Incapacity

Although an individual may have the requisite capacity to access and disclose their personal health information, a health information custodian may refuse access and disclosure in a number of circumstances, including where: disclosure could reasonably be expected to result in a risk of serious bodily harm; the information in question is subject to a legal privilege; the information was collected as part of an investigation; or another law prohibits the disclosure of the information.[113] In the event a health information custodian denies an individual access to their personal health information based on any grounds other than incapacity, the individual has the right to file a complaint with the Information Privacy Commissioner.[114]

Appointment of Representatives and Compliance of Substitute Decision Makers

In addition to the application to the Board to review a finding of incapacity, the Act also allows applications to the Board for the appointment of representatives

---

[110] PHIPA, s.54(8)

[111] PHIPA, s.22(3)

[112] PHIPA, s.22(2)

[113] PHIPA, s.52

[114] PHIPA, s.54(8)

for individuals determined not capable. It is to be noted that such applications give rise to a deemed application to review a finding of incapacity.[115] One question yet to be determined is whether or not there may be a deemed application if the application would otherwise be prohibited by virtue of the incapable person having a SDM for the purposes set out in the HCCA.

This would also appear to be the case in relation to an application by a health information custodian to determine whether or not a SDM is complying with the rules for making decisions regarding the collection, use, or disclosure of the information.[116]

Correction of Personal Health Information

Section 55 of the Act sets out the procedure for correcting information in the record of personal health information maintained by a custodian.

[115] s. Ontario Regulation 329/04, s.9

[116] Ontario Regulation 329/04, s. 24(2) and s. 9

SUBSTITUTE DECISIONS ACT, 1992

COMMENTARY

The *Substitute Decisions Act, 1992*,[1] (SDA) proclaimed in force on April 3, 1995, significantly affected the law of capacity in a number of areas by creating:

1. A definition for capacity to manage property;
2. A definition for capacity to make personal care decisions;
3. Powers of attorney for personal care;
4. Definitions for capacity to make powers of attorney for personal care and property;
5. Statutory guardians of property;
6. Court-appointed guardians of property;
7. Court-appointed guardians of the person;
8. Duties of the Public Guardian and Trustee to investigate and act when incapacity may result in serious adverse effects for an incapable person or his or her property.

The Act, in addition to an Introduction, is divided into four sections:

I. Property
II. The Person
III. Procedure in Guardianship Applications
IV. Miscellaneous

This commentary will discuss each of the above areas.

Introduction

Presumptions of Capacity

In addition to the usual definition section, the Introduction to the Act contains three significant presumptions of capacity.

The first presumption is that a person eighteen years of age or more is capable of entering into a contract.[2]

The second presumption is that a person sixteen years of age or more is capable of giving or refusing consent[3] in connection to his or her own personal care.[4]

The third presumption is that a person is deemed capable to retain and instruct counsel in circumstances where their capacity is in issue in a proceeding under the

[1] S.O. 1992, c. 30.
[2] s. 2(1).
[3] s. 2(2).
[4] This is to be contrasted with section 4(2) of the *Health Care Consent Act, 1996* where there is a presumption of capacity with respect to treatment without a minimum age.

Act[5] and the Public Guardian and Trustee is ordered by the court to arrange legal representation for the individual.[6]

In relation to the first two presumptions, the Act entitles a person to rely upon these presumptions unless there are reasonable grounds to believe the person is not capable of entering into the contract or giving or refusing consent as the case may be.[7] What constitutes reasonable grounds will of course depend on the particular facts of any case. A useful guide in determining when reasonable grounds may exist in the context of a treatment decision was contained in a regulation to the former *Consent to Treatment Act, 1992* (proclaimed in 1995) of Ontario as follows:

> A health practitioner may have reason to believe that a person may be incapable with respect to a proposed treatment based on the following observations:
>
> a. The person shows evidence of confused or delusional thinking;
>
> b. The person appears to be unable to make a settled choice about treatment;
>
> c. The person is experiencing severe pain or acute fear or anxiety;
>
> d. The person appears to be severely depressed;
>
> e. The person seems to be impaired by alcohol or drugs;
>
> f. Any other observations that give rise to a concern about the person's capacity, including observations about the person's behaviour or communication.

The third presumption regarding capacity to retain and instruct counsel can be extremely problematic. In the case of *Banton v. Banton*,[8] Mr. Justice Cullity stated:

> The position of lawyers retained to represent a client whose capacity is in issue in proceedings under the *Substitute Decisions Act, 1992* is potentially one of considerable difficulty. Even in cases where the client is deemed to have capacity to retain and instruct counsel pursuant to section 3(1) of the Act, I do not believe that counsel is in the position of a litigation guardian with authority to make decisions in the client's interests. Counsel must take instructions from the client and must not, in my view, act if satisfied that capacity to give instructions is lacking. A very high degree of professionalism may be required in borderline cases where it is possible that the client's wishes may be in conflict with his or her best interests and counsel's duty to the court.

The difficulty of counsel acting for clients in this area of law is increased by the obvious fact that in the majority of cases and by most standards: (a) capacity of the client to give instructions is significantly diminished or lacking and (b) given that it is not appropriate for counsel to make decisions in the client's interest as

---

5 s. 3(1)(b). Also see section 81 of the *Health Care Consent Act, 1996* for a similar presumption for persons who are or may be incapable of treatment, admission or personal assistance decisions.

6 s. 3 (1)(a).

7 s. 2(3) SDA.

8 (1998), 164 D.L.R. (4th) 176 at 218. (Ont. Gen. Div.)

would a litigation guardian, is it also not appropriate for counsel to determine what he or she believes to be in the best interest of the client? What then is the role of counsel?

At the minimum, counsel who acts pursuant to a section 3 appointment must: (1) identify the requirements of the law in relation to the particular issue;[9] (2) ensure that the law has been complied with; and (3) to the extent possible, present evidence to the court that reflects the wishes of the client and the circumstances in which those wishes were expressed. Appointed counsel should not make decisions or express their personal view to the court as to what he or she feels to be in the best interest of the client.

I. PROPERTY

The Act divides property into the following five areas:

1. General
2. Continuing Powers of Attorney for Property
3. Statutory Guardians of Property
4. Court-Appointed Guardians of Property
5. Property Management

1. General

Definition

Incapacity to manage property is defined as follows:[10]

> A person is incapable of managing property if the person is not able to understand information that is relevant to making a decision in the management of his or her property, or is not able to appreciate the reasonably foreseeable consequences of a decision or lack of decision.

This definition of incapacity to manage property is also accepted for the purposes of the *Mental Health Act*. It is significant to recognize that capacity to manage property is grounded in an individual's ability to understand and to appreciate. It is not measured subjectively by right or wrong decisions. The fact that a decision may be unwise does not mean the individual making the decision lacks capacity. There is a distinction between an individual failing to understand or appreciate risks and consequences and being unable to understand or appreciate risks or consequences. Only inability may lead to a finding of incapacity.

A number of capacity studies are frequently referred to in decisions of the Consent and Capacity Board. Two of these are the Weisstub Report in 1990 of the Ontario Government entitled, Enquiry on Mental Competency: Final Report, and the other is a submission of Dr. F.M. Mai of the University of Ottawa for the

---

[9] ss. 55, 57, 22 and 24 sets out the criteria to be considered by the court to appoint guardians of the person and property.

[10] s. 6.

Ontario Government Report. The Weisstub Report set out the test to be applied in assessing financial competency as follows:

In order to be considered mentally capable to make a financial decision, an individual must have the ability to:

1. Understand the nature of the financial decision and the choices available to him or her;
2. Understand his or her relationship to the parties to and/or potential beneficiaries of the transaction or transactions which give rise to the decision;
3. Appreciate the consequences of making the decision.

The submission of Dr. Mai set out the following questions:

1. Does the patient suffer from delusions or hallucinations which will likely materially affect the patient's understanding and management of finances?
2. Is the patient oriented to time, place and person?
3. Is the patient's memory sufficiently intact so as to allow the patient to keep track of financial matters and decisions?
4. Is the patient's calculating ability sufficient in the circumstances?
5. Does the patient suffer specific thought process deficits which give rise to the conclusion that deficits in financial judgment exist?
6. Does the patient possess or have the capacity to learn skills necessary to make the sort of decision required in an estate of the size, nature and complexity that he or she possesses?

Dr. Mai's last point should always be kept in mind when applying the test for capacity. The size and nature of an individual's estate can significantly alter the requisite level of capacity required to manage it.

2. Continuing Powers of Attorney for Property

Definition

A continuing power of attorney for property is a document signed by the maker (grantor) naming another person (the attorney) to do on the grantor's behalf anything in respect of property the grantor can do if capable, except make a will.[11] Two or more persons may be named as attorneys in which case the attorneys shall act jointly unless the power of attorney provides otherwise.[12] The grantor may also appoint one or more substitute attorneys in the event that an attorney is or becomes unable or unwilling to act.

A power of attorney is a continuing power of attorney if it expresses the intention that the authority given may be exercised during the grantor's incapacity to manage property.[13] The significance of such a document for individuals who do

---

[11] s. 7(2).

[12] s. 7(4).

[13] s. 7(1)(b).

not want the Public Guardian and Trustee to take control of their property in the event of a finding of incapacity, cannot be overstated. In essence, without a continuing power of attorney for property, the Public Guardian and Trustee takes control of an individual's property in the event the individual is found not capable of managing property. This is referred to as statutory guardianship.[14]

Capacity to give a Continuing Power of Attorney for Property

A person is capable of giving a continuing power of attorney[15] if he or she: (a) knows what kind of property he or she has and its approximate value; (b) is aware of obligations owed to his or her dependents; (c) knows that the attorney will be able to do on the person's behalf anything in respect to property that the person could do if capable, except make a will, subject to the conditions and restrictions set out in the power of attorney; (d) knows that the attorney must account for his or her dealings with the person's property; (e) knows that he or she may, if capable, revoke the continuing power of attorney; (f) appreciates that unless the attorney manages the property prudently its value may decline; and (g) appreciates the possibility that the attorney may misuse the authority given to him or her.[16]

The capacity required to make a power of attorney for property is less than that required to manage property. Accordingly, capacity to make a continuing power of attorney for property may exist even though the grantor has been found incapable of managing property.[17] However, a continuing power of attorney for property made after a certificate of incapacity to manage property is issued will not terminate a statutory guardianship of property. A statutory guardianship of property, (a guardianship created following an initial finding of incapacity to manage property) may only be terminated if the person found not capable of managing property made a continuing power of attorney before a certificate of incapacity was issued.[18]

Revocation

A person is capable of revoking a continuing power of attorney if he or she is capable of giving one.[19]

A revocation of a power of attorney must be in writing and must be executed by the grantor in the same way as a continuing power of attorney.[20]

---

[14] s. 15 and 16.

[15] s. 8.

[16] s. 8(1)(a)-(g).

[17] s. 9(1).

[18] s. 16.1.

[19] s. 8(2).

[20] s. 12(2).

Determining when a Continuing Power of Attorney Takes Effect

A continuing power of attorney for property is effective on the date it is signed unless it provides otherwise.[21]

If a continuing power of attorney provides that it comes into effect when the Grantor becomes incapable of managing property but does not provide a method for determining whether that situation has arisen, the continuing power of attorney comes into effect when: (a) the attorney is notified in the prescribed form by an assessor that the assessor has performed an assessment of the grantor's capacity and has found that the grantor is incapable of managing property; or (b) the attorney is notified that a certificate of incapacity has been issued in respect of the grantor under the *Mental Health Act*.[22]

Form

A power of attorney need not be in any particular form. A sample of a power of attorney form can be obtained from the Public Guardian and Trustee's website and is also contained in the forms section.

Execution

Similar to a will, a continuing power of attorney must be signed by the grantor in the presence of two witnesses, each of whom must sign the power of attorney as witnesses.[23] The attorney does not sign the document nor is it necessary to obtain the attorney's written consent. In the event however, the grantor wishes to appoint the Public Guardian and Trustee as attorney, the Public Guardian and Trustee's written consent must be obtained before the power of attorney is signed by the grantor.[24]

Who may not be Witnesses to a Power of Attorney for Property

The following persons shall not be witnesses:[25]

1. The attorney or the attorney's spouse or partner;
2. The grantor's spouse or partner;
3. A child of the grantor or a person whom the grantor has demonstrated a settled intention to treat as his or her child;
4. A person whose property is under guardianship or who has a guardian of the person;
5. A person who is less than eighteen years old.

Although a continuing power of attorney that is not properly executed is not effective, the court may on any person's application, declare it to be effective if

---

[21] s. 7(7).

[22] s. 9(3).

[23] s. 10(1).

[24] s. 7(3).

[25] s. 10(2).

the court is satisfied that it is in the interest of the grantor or his or her dependents to do so.[26]

Resignation of Attorney for Property

An attorney under a continuing power of attorney may resign but, if the attorney has acted under the power of attorney, a resignation is not effective until the attorney delivers a copy of the resignation to: (a) the grantor; (b) any other attorneys under the power of attorney; (c) the person named by the power of attorney as the substitute for the attorney who has resigned, if the power of attorney provides for the substitution of another person; and (d) unless the power of attorney provides otherwise, the grantor's spouse or partner and the relatives of the grantor who are known to the attorney and reside in Ontario, if, (i) the attorney is of the opinion that the grantor is incapable of managing property; (ii) the power of attorney does not provide for the substitution of another person or the substitute is not able or willing to act.[27]

Termination of Power of Attorney for Property

A continuing power of attorney is terminated in the following circumstances:[28]

1. When the attorney dies, becomes incapable of managing property or resigns unless another attorney is authorized to act or the power of attorney provides for the substitution of another person and that person is able and willing to act;
2. If the court appoints a guardian of property for the grantor;
3. When the grantor executes a new continuing power of attorney unless the grantor provides that there should be multiple continuing powers of attorney;
4. When the power of attorney is revoked;
5. When the grantor dies.

Use by Attorney after Revocation

In the event a continuing power of attorney is terminated or becomes invalid, any subsequent exercise of the power by the attorney remains valid as between the grantor or the grantor's estate and any person, including the attorney, who acted in good faith and without knowledge of the termination or invalidity.[29] This is also the case if a continuing power of attorney is ineffective because of an improper execution.[30]

---

[26] s. 10(4).

[27] s. 11(a)-(d).

[28] s. 12(1)(a)-(f).

[29] s. 13(1).

[30] s. 13(2).

Powers of Attorney prior to April 3, 1995

Powers of attorney executed prior to the coming into force of the *Substitute Decisions Act, 1992* or within six months after that date are deemed to be continuing powers of attorney for the purposes of the *Substitutions Act* provided, (a) the power of attorney contains a provision expressly stating that it may be exercised during any subsequent legal incapacity of the grantor;[31] and (b) it is executed in accordance with the *Powers of Attorney Act* (R.S.O. 1990, c. P. 20) and is otherwise valid.[32]

No Assessments of Capacity to Manage Property when Power of Attorney Exists

Under the *Substitute Decisions Act, 1992*, no assessment of another person's capacity to manage property, for the purpose of determining whether the Public Guardian and Trustee should become statutory guardian, may be performed in the event there is knowledge that the person has a continuing power of attorney to manage all of their property.[33] A person requesting an assessment must state in the prescribed form (Form 4)[34] that they have made reasonable inquiries and have no knowledge of the existence of any attorney under a continuing power of attorney that gives the attorney authority over all of the person's property.[35] It is an offence to make an untrue statement in a prescribed form, the penalty for which on conviction is a fine not exceeding $10,000.00.[36]

Under the *Mental Health Act*, a physician is required to assess a patient's capacity to manage property upon the patient's admission to a psychiatric facility. However, such an assessment is not required in the event the physician has reasonable grounds to believe that the patient has a continuing power of attorney that provides for the management of the patient's property.[37]

3. Statutory Guardians for Property

Public Guardian and Trustee as Statutory Guardian of Property

The Public Guardian and Trustee becomes a person's statutory guardian of property upon receipt of: (1) a certificate of incapacity (Form 21) issued by a physician under the *Mental Health Act*[38] or (2) a certificate of incapacity (Form A) issued by an assessor under the *Substitute Decisions Act, 1992.*[39] "Assessor" is

---

[31] s. 14(a)

[32] s. 14(b).

[33] s. 16(2)(b).

[34] s. 16(2).

[35] s. 16(2)(b).

[36] s. 89(5) and 89(6).

[37] s. 54(6) of the *Mental Health Act.*

[38] s. 15.

[39] s. 16(5).

defined as a member of a class of persons designated by the regulations as being qualified to do assessments of capacity.[40]

Under the *Substitute Decisions Act, 1992*, a person may request an assessor perform an assessment of another person's capacity or of the person's own capacity for the purpose of determining whether the Public Guardian and Trustee should become the statutory guardian of property of the subject of the assessment.[41] No assessment shall be performed unless the request is in the prescribed form[42] (Form 4)[43] and, if the request is made in respect of another person, the request states that, (a) the person requesting the assessment has reason to believe that the other person may be incapable of managing property; (b) the person requesting the assessment has made reasonable inquiries and has no knowledge of the existence of any attorney under a continuing power of attorney that gives the attorney authority over all of the other person's property; and (c) the person requesting the assessment has made reasonable inquiries and has no knowledge of any spouse, partner or relative of the person who intends to make an application to the court under section 22 for the appointment of a guardian of property for the other person.[44]

Procedural Safeguards

Subject to very few exceptions, an assessor must explain to the person to be assessed the purpose of the assessment, the significance and effect of a finding of capacity or incapacity, and the person's right to refuse to be assessed.[45] The assessor, subject to few exceptions,[46] shall not perform an assessment of a person's capacity if the person refuses to be assessed.

Information and Documentation to be Provided following a Finding of Incapacity

In the event an assessor issues a certificate of incapacity, the assessor must promptly give a copy to the incapable person and to the Public Guardian and Trustee.[47] It is the obligation of the Public Guardian and Trustee to ensure that the person is informed in a manner that the Public Guardian and Trustee considers appropriate that (a) the Public Guardian and Trustee has become the person's statutory guardian of property; and (b) the person is entitled to apply to the

---

40 A list of assessors may be obtained from the Capacity Assessment Office of the Attorney General.

41 s. 16(1).

42 s. 16(2).

43 *Re A.B.* TO 03 1296, November 3, 2003 underscores the importance of using the prescribed form. In this case, a telephone request for an assessment was found to be of no force or effect and the resulting statutory guardianship failed as invalid.

44 s. 16(2)(a)-(c).

45 s. 78.

46 s. 79.

47 s. 16(4).

Consent and Capacity Board for a review of the assessor's finding that the person is incapable of managing property.[48]

Application to Consent and Capacity Board Contingent upon Existence of Statutory Guardianship

Under the *Substitute Decisions Act, 1992* a person may only apply to the Consent and Capacity Board for a review of a finding that the person is incapable of managing property if the person has a statutory guardian of property.[49] In the event the Public Guardian and Trustee has terminated a statutory guardianship in favour of an attorney acting under a continuing power of attorney for property, there is no authority for the person to apply to the Board for a review of the finding of incapacity to manage property. The only remedy in such a case would be for the individual to either have his or her capacity reassessed by a capacity assessor, or apply to the court, as discussed below.[50] The existence of a statutory guardianship under the *Substitute Decisions Act, 1992* as a precondition to applying to the Consent and Capacity Board for a review of a finding of incapacity, is to be contrasted with the *Mental Health Act*. The *Mental Health Act* does not require the existence of a statutory guardianship in order for an individual to apply to the Board.[51]

Termination of Statutory Guardianship

A statutory guardianship of property is terminated in the event the incapable person gave a continuing power of attorney before the certificate of incapacity was issued, the power of attorney gives authority over all of the incapable person's property and the Public Guardian and Trustee receives a copy of the power of attorney as well as a written undertaking signed by the attorney to act in accordance with the power of attorney.[52] In the event someone other than the Public Guardian and Trustee is statutory guardian of property,[53] the statutory guardianship of property is terminated if this person receives a copy of the power of attorney and a written undertaking signed by the attorney to act in accordance with the power of attorney.

---

48 s. 16(6)(a), (b).

49 s. 20.2.

50 s. 20.3 allows an application to be made to the court (pursuant to s. 69(0.1), (8), (9)) to terminate a statutory guardianship. There is no specific authority granted in the *Substitute Decisions Act, 1992* which permits an application to be made to the court to terminate the authority of an attorney for property. Section 39(1) of the *Substitute Decisions Act, 1992* however, allows an application to be made to the court for directions.

51 Section 60 of the *Mental Health Act*.

52 Section 16.1(a), (b), (c).

53 Section 17 sets out who may apply to replace the Public Guardian and Trustee as statutory guardian.

In addition to providing for the termination of a statutory guardianship of property by the attorney under a continuing power of attorney for property, the Act also allows a statutory guardianship of property to be terminated[54] if any of the following events occurs:

1. A guardian of property is appointed by the court;
2. Notice of the guardian's resignation is given by the guardian to the person and the Public Guardian and Trustee if the Public Guardian and Trustee is not the guardian;
3. In the case of a statutory guardianship created under the *Mental Health Act*, (i) notice is given to the guardian that the certificate of incapacity has been cancelled under section 56 of the *Mental Health Act* (Form 23), (ii) notice is given to the guardian that the person has been discharged, unless the guardian has also received a notice of continuance issued under subsection 57(2) of the *Mental Health Act* (Form 24), (iii) notice is given to the guardian from an assessor or from a physician who has authority to issue certificates if incapacity under the *Mental Health Act* stating that the assessor or physician has performed an assessment of the person's capacity and is of the opinion that the person is capable of managing property, if the person has been discharged and a notice of continuance was issued under subsection 57(2) of the *Mental Health Act*, (iv) the Consent and Capacity Board has determined the person capable of managing property and no appeal is taken or the time for appeal from a decision has expired, or (v) if an appeal is taken from a decision of the Consent and Capacity Board and it is finally determined that the person is capable of managing property.[55]
4. In the case of a statutory guardianship created under the *Substitute Decisions Act, 1992*, (i) notice is given to the guardian from an assessor stating that the assessor has performed an assessment of the person's capacity and is of the opinion that the person is capable of managing property, (ii) the time for appeal from a decision of the Consent and Capacity Board on an application under section 20.2 has expired if the Board determines that the person is capable of managing property and no appeal is taken or (iii) an appeal from a decision of the Consent and Capacity Board on an application under section 20.2 is finally disposed of if an appeal is taken and it is finally determined that the person is capable of managing property.[56]

Although there is no reference in the Act to terminating a statutory guardianship created under the *Substitute Decisions Act, 1992*, by way of a subsequent finding of capacity to manage property under the provisions of the *Mental Health Act*, it would appear that an attending physician of a patient with respect to whom a certificate of incapacity has been issued may, after examining the patient for that purpose, cancel the certificate and thereby terminate the

---

[54] s. 16.1(d).

[55] s. 20(i)-(v).

[56] s. 20(i)-(iii).

statutory guardianship.[57] In addition to the foregoing, a statutory guardianship may also be terminated by application to the court.[58] A court application may prove effective in terminating the guardianship if there is concern that an application to the Consent and Capacity Board may result in a decision of the Board declining jurisdiction.[59]

Replacing the Public Guardian and Trustee as Statutory Guardian

Only certain individuals may replace the Public Guardian and Trustee as statutory guardian of property. These individuals are: (1) the incapable person's spouse or partner (2) a relative of the incapable person (3) the incapable person's attorney under a continuing power of attorney, if the power of attorney was made before the certificate of incapacity was issued and does not give the Attorney authority over all of the incapable person's property (4) a trust corporation within the meaning of the *Loan and Trust Corporations Act*, if the incapable person's spouse or partner consents in writing to the application.[60]

The application to replace the Public Guardian and Trustee must be in the prescribed form (Form 1) and must be accompanied by a management plan for the property in the prescribed form (Form 2).[61] The Public Guardian and Trustee may refuse to appoint the applicant unless the applicant provides security in a manner approved by the Public Guardian and Trustee for an amount fixed by the Public Guardian and Trustee.[62] In the event the Public Guardian and Trustee appoints the applicant, it shall give the applicant a certificate certifying the appointment as statutory guardian. The certificate is proof of the guardian's authority.[63]

In the event the Public Guardian and Trustee refuses to issue a certificate for a statutory guardian of property, the applicant must be provided with written reasons for the refusal.[64] In the event the applicant disputes the refusal by giving the Public Guardian and Trustee notice in writing, the Public Guardian and Trustee has an obligation to apply to the court to decide the matter.[65]

Death/Incapacity/Resignation of Statutory Guardian

In the event a statutory guardian of property dies, becomes incapable of managing property or gives notice to the Public Guardian and Trustee of his or her

---

[57] s. 56 of the *Mental Health Act*.

[58] s. 20.3.

[59] Unreported case of *Cerget (a.k.a. Swyarchuk) v. The Public Guardian and Trustee*, Ontario Superior Court of Justice. Court File No.: 03-CV-001921CM, January 5, 2004, per GATES S.C.J.

[60] s. 17(1).

[61] s. 17(2) and (3).

[62] s. 17(6).

[63] s. 17(8).

[64] s. 18(1).

[65] s. 18(2).

resignation, the Public Guardian and Trustee may elect to become the incapable person's statutory guardian until another person is appointed as guardian of property under section 17 or 22 of the Act.[66]

Applications to review a Finding of Incapacity

In the event a person's property is under statutory guardianship created under the *Mental Health Act* and the person has been discharged from the psychiatric facility before (or without) making an application to the Board, the person may only apply to the Consent and Capacity Board under the *Substitute Decisions Act, 1992* to review the finding made under the *Mental Health Act*.[67] To do so, however, the person must undergo a reassessment of their capacity. Once the re-assessment has been completed, the person must apply to the Board within six months. The reassessment of capacity must be done by an assessor or by a physician who has authority to issue certificates of incapacity under the *Mental Health Act*. Applications may be made to the Board every six months. If a re-assessment of capacity finds the person capable of managing property, and is provided to the Public Guardian and Trustee, the statutory guardianship is terminated and there is no authority for the person to apply to the Board. Thus, a person who may at one time have been found incapable by the Board is prevented from re-applying to the Board to reverse the finding. This may be disconcerting to those individuals who would prefer a formal decision of a tribunal over the opinion of a capacity assessor. In the event this situation does arise, and the individual wishes to have a decision of the Board confirming that he or she is capable of managing property, it would appear that provided the assessment is not delivered to the Public Guardian and Trustee, jurisdiction exists for the Board to hear the application and to render a decision. At the hearing of the matter, the assessment of capacity may be relied upon by the applicant in support of his or her position.

In the event a person has a statutory guardian resulting from a finding of incapacity made under the *Substitute Decision Act, 1992*, the person may apply to the Consent and Capacity Board to review the finding of incapacity provided the finding of incapacity was made by an assessor within six months preceding the date the application is submitted to the Board.[68]

The parties to an application to the Consent and Capacity Board to review a finding of incapacity to manage property are:[69]

1. The applicant;
2. The assessor or physician who made the finding of incapacity;
3. Any other person whom the Board specifies.

The Board may confirm the finding of incapacity or may determine that the person is capable of managing property, and in so doing may substitute its

---

[66] s. 19.

[67] s. 20.2(1)(a).

[68] s. 20.2(1)(b) and 20.2(3).

[69] s. 20.2(4).

opinion for that of the assessor or physician.[70] Appeals to the Superior Court of Justice may be taken from decisions of the Board. The appeal procedure is set out in section 80 of the *Health Care Consent Act, 1996.*

4. Court-Appointed Guardians of Property

Who may Apply

Any person may apply to the court to have a guardian of property appointed for a person who is incapable of managing property, provided it is necessary for decisions to be made on the incapable person's behalf by a person who is authorized to do so.[71]

Requirements for Appointment of Guardian

The court shall not appoint a guardian if it is satisfied that the need for decisions to be made will be met by an alternative course of action that (a) does not require the court to find a person incapable of managing property; and (b) is less restrictive of the person's decision-making rights than the appointment of a guardian.[72]

Who may not be Appointed Guardian

A person who provides health care or residential, social, training or support services to an incapable person for compensation shall not be appointed a guardian of the person's property unless such a person is the incapable person's spouse, partner, relative, attorney for personal care, or an attorney under a continuing power of attorney for the incapable person.[73]

The court shall not appoint the Public Guardian and Trustee as guardian for property unless the application proposes the appointment of the Public Guardian and Trustee and there is no other suitable person who is available and willing to be appointed.[74]

A person who does not reside in Ontario shall not be appointed a guardian of property unless the person provides security, in a manner approved by the court, for the value of the property. The court may order that this requirement for security does not apply to a person or that the amount required be reduced and may make its order subject to conditions.[75]

---

[70] s. 20.2(5).

[71] s. 22 (1).

[72] In the case of *Deschamps v. Deschamps*, [1997] O.J. No. 4894 (Gen. Div.), the court concluded guardianship was not required given that capacity to make a new power of attorney existed.

[73] s. 22 and s. 24.

[74] s. 24(2.1).

[75] s. 24(3), (4).

The Public Guardian and Trustee and trust corporations within the meaning of the *Loan and Trust Corporations Act* are not required to post security.[76]

Factors in Determining who should be Appointed

In determining who shall be appointed guardian of property in all applications other than those by way of summary disposition (section 77 applications), the court must consider (a) whether the proposed guardian is the attorney under a continuing power of attorney; (b) the incapable person's current wishes, if they can be ascertained; and (c) the closeness of the applicant's relationship to the incapable person.[77] Two or more persons may be appointed as joint guardians of property by the court with their consent or the court may appoint each of them as guardian for a specified part of the property.[78]

Requirements of Court Order

An order appointing a guardian of property must include a finding that the person is incapable of managing property and that as a result it is necessary for decisions to be made on behalf of the incapable person by a person who is authorized to do so. An order of the court appointing a guardian of property may require the guardian to post security in a manner and amount the court considers appropriate; make the appointment for a limited period as the court considers appropriate; or impose such other conditions of the appointment as the court considers appropriate.[79]

Variations of Court Order

Any order made by the court may be varied on a motion in the proceeding in which the guardianship was created.[80]

Duty of Public Guardian and Trustee when Serious Adverse Effects to Property may Occur

In the event a person's property may suffer "serious adverse effects" defined as "loss of a significant part of a person's property, or a person's failure to provide necessities of life for himself or herself or for dependants",[81] any person may notify the Public Guardian and Trustee of the situation. The Public Guardian and Trustee must investigate any allegation that a person is incapable of managing property and that serious adverse effects are occurring or may occur as a result.[82]

---

[76] s. 25(3).

[77] s. 24(5).

[78] s. 24(6).

[79] s. 25.

[80] s. 26.

[81] s. 27(1).

[82] s. 27(2).

If as a result of the investigation, the Public Guardian and Trustee has reasonable grounds to believe that a person is incapable of managing property and that the prompt appointment of a temporary guardian of property is required to prevent serious adverse effects, the Public Guardian and Trustee shall apply to the court for an order appointing her as temporary guardian of property.[83]

Appointment of Public Guardian and Trustee
as Temporary Guardian of Property

The court may by order appoint the Public Guardian and Trustee as temporary guardian of property for a period not exceeding ninety days.[84] The order may suspend the powers of any attorney under a continuing power of attorney during the term of the temporary guardianship.[85] On motion in the proceedings the court may terminate the guardianship, reduce or extend its term or otherwise vary the order.[86]

5. Property Management

Sections 31 to 42 of the Act contain a comprehensive guide setting out rights and obligations of a guardian of property. The duties, including the duty to account, apply to court-appointed as well as statutory guardians of property. They also, with few exceptions, apply to attorneys under continuing powers of attorney for property.

II. THE PERSON

The Act divides personal care into the following four areas:

1. General
2. Powers of Attorney for Personal Care
3. Court-Appointed Guardians of the Person
4. Duties of Guardians of the Person and Attorneys for Personal Care

1. General

Definition

The Act defines incapacity to manage personal care as follows:

> A person is incapable of personal care if the person is not able to understand information that is relevant to making a decision concerning his or her own health care, nutrition, shelter, clothing, hygiene or safety, or is not able to appreciate the reasonably foreseeable consequences of a decision or lack of decision.[87]

[83] s. 27(3.1).

[84] s. 27(6).

[85] s. 27(8).

[86] s. 27(9.1).

[87] Section 45

A person may be incapable in one or more areas of personal care (*e.g.* health care, nutrition and safety) and capable in others (*e.g.* clothing and shelter).

2. Powers of Attorney for Personal Care

Definition

A power of attorney for personal care is a document signed by the maker (grantor) authorizing another person (the attorney) to make on the grantor's behalf, decisions concerning the grantor's personal care. Two or more persons may be named as attorneys in which case the attorneys shall act jointly unless the power of attorney provides otherwise. The grantor may also appoint one or more substitute attorneys in the event that an attorney is or becomes unable or unwilling to act.

A power of attorney for personal care is not referred to as a "continuing power of attorney for personal care" since such a document only takes effect when an individual becomes incapable of making personal care decisions. Unlike decisions respecting management of property, decisions for personal care cannot be made on behalf of others who are capable of personal care.

The importance of a power of attorney for personal care for individuals who do not want the provisions of the *Health Care Consent Act, 1996* to apply in the event they become incapable of making decisions regarding either: (a) psychiatric or medical treatment; (b) admission to a long-term care facility; or (c) personal assistance services, cannot be overstated. In essence, without a power of attorney for personal care, if an individual is found not capable of making a decision to which the *Health Care Consent Act, 1996* applies, decisions in these areas will be made for the incapable person by the highest-ranked person on a hierarchy of substitute decision makers set out in the *Health Care Consent Act, 1996*. In the event an individual does not want this hierarchy to apply, (with the exception of a guardian of the person) it is critical that the individual have a power of attorney for personal care. An attorney for personal care is the highest-ranking substitute decision maker second only to a court-appointed guardian of the person. It is also critical to have such a document if the grantor wishes his or her attorney to make decisions in accordance with directives which may be expressed in the document. The attorney is bound to follow such directives unless it is impossible to do so. In certain circumstances the attorney may also apply to the Consent and Capacity Board in the event the decision the attorney must make is a decision to which the *Health Care Consent Act, 1996* applies and the attorney is uncertain whether he or she must follow the directive.[88]

---

[88] *i.e.* Sections of the *Health Care Consent Act, 1996* which allow the substitute decision maker to apply to the Board for directions etc., ss. 35 and 36 of the *Health Care Consent Act, 1996*.

Capacity to give a Power of Attorney for Personal Care

A person is capable of giving a power of attorney for personal care if the person: (a) has the ability to understand whether the proposed attorney has a genuine concern for the person's welfare; and (b) appreciates that the person may need to have the proposed attorney make decisions for the person.[89]

The capacity required to make a power of attorney for personal care is less than that required to make personal care decisions. Accordingly, capacity to make a power of attorney for personal care may exist even though the grantor has been found incapable of making personal care decisions.[90]

Revocation

A person is capable of revoking a power of attorney for personal care if he or she is capable of giving one.[91] A revocation must be in writing and executed in the same way as a power of attorney for personal care.[92]

When Power of Attorney becomes Effective

A power of attorney for personal care only becomes effective when one of the following events occurs:

1. The *Health Care Consent Act, 1996* applies to the decision and that Act authorizes the Attorney to make the decision;
2. The *Health Care Consent Act, 1996* does not apply to the decision and the attorney has reasonable grounds to believe that the grantor is incapable of making the decision, subject to any condition of the power of attorney that prevents the attorney from making the decision, unless the fact that the grantor is incapable of personal care has been confirmed.[93]

A power of attorney for personal care may prescribe the method for confirming whether the grantor is incapable of personal care; however, if no method is specified, the finding of incapacity may be confirmed by notice to the attorney in the prescribed form (Form B) from an assessor stating that the assessor has performed an assessment of the grantor's capacity and has found that the grantor is incapable of personal care.[94]

Who may not be an Attorney for Personal Care

A person may not act as an attorney under a power of attorney for personal care if the person provides health care to the grantor for compensation or provides residential, social training or support services to the grantor for compensation.

---

[89] s. 47(1)(a), (b).

[90] s. 47(2).

[91] s. 47(3).

[92] s. 53(2).

[93] s. 49(1)(a), (b).

[94] s. 49(2).

This prohibition does not apply if the person is the grantor's spouse, partner or relative.

Form

A power of attorney need not be in any particular form. A sample is obtainable from the Public Guardian and Trustee and is reproduced in the forms section.

Execution

Similar to a will, a power of attorney for personal care must be executed in the presence of two witnesses, each of whom must sign the power of attorney as witnesses.[95] The attorney does not sign the document nor is it necessary to obtain the attorney's written consent. In the event a person wishes to appoint the Public Guardian and Trustee as his or her attorney for personal care, the written consent of the Public Guardian and Trustee must be obtained before the power of attorney is signed by the grantor.

Who may not be Witnesses to a Power of Attorney for Personal Care

The following persons shall not be witnesses:[96]

1. The attorney or the attorney's spouse or partner;
2. The grantor's spouse or partner;
3. A child of the grantor or a person whom the grantor has demonstrated a settled intention to treat as his or her child;
4. A person whose property is under guardianship or who has a guardian of the person;
5. A person who is less than eighteen years old.

Although a power of attorney for personal care that is not properly executed is not effective, the court may on any person's application, declare the power of attorney for personal care to be effective if the court is satisfied that it is in the grantor's interest to do so.[97]

Extraordinary Powers of Attorney for Personal Care

Provided they fulfill certain statutory requirements, powers of attorney for personal care may contain the following extraordinary provisions:

1. A provision that authorizes the attorney and other persons under the direction of the attorney to use force that is necessary and reasonable in the circumstances, (a) to determine whether the grantor is incapable of making a decision to which the *Health Care Consent Act, 1996* applies; (b) to confirm in accordance with subsection 49(2) whether the grantor is incapable of personal care, if the power of attorney contains a condition

---

95 s. 48(1).

96 s. 48(2) and s. 10(2).

97 s. 48(4).

described in clause 49(1)(b); or (c) to obtain an assessment of the grantor's capacity by an assessor in any other circumstances described in the power of attorney;

2. A provision that authorizes the attorney and other persons under the direction of the attorney to use force that is necessary and reasonable in the circumstances to take the grantor to any place for care or treatment, to admit the grantor to that place and to detain or restrain the grantor in that place during the care or treatment;
3. A provision that waives the grantor's right to apply to the Consent and Capacity Board under sections 32, 50 and 65 of the *Health Care Consent Act, 1996* for a review of a finding of incapacity in relation to a decision to which the *Health Care Consent Act, 1996* applies.

In order for any of the above provisions contained in the power of attorney for personal care to be effective, both of the following circumstances must exist:

1. At the time the power of attorney was executed or within thirty days afterwards, the grantor made a statement in the prescribed form (Form 5) indicating that he or she understood the effect of the provision and that the power of attorney may only be revoked by an assessor performing an assessment of the grantor's capacity within thirty days before the revocation in the prescribed form (Form E) indicating that the assessor performed an assessment of the grantor's capacity and that the assessor is of the opinion that the grantor was capable of personal care and setting out the facts upon which the opinion is based;
2. Within thirty days after the power of attorney was executed, an assessor made a statement in the prescribed form (Form D), (a) indicating that after the power of attorney was executed, the assessor performed an assessment of the grantor's capacity; (b) stating the assessor's opinion that at the time of the assessment the grantor was capable of personal care and was capable of understanding the effect of the provision and of the means of revocation; and (c) setting out the facts on which the opinion is based.[98]

Assessments of Capacity

An attorney under a power of attorney for personal care must, on the request of and on behalf of the grantor, assist in arranging an assessment of the grantor's capacity by an assessor, provided an assessment has not been performed in the previous six months.[99]

Resignation

An attorney under a power of attorney for personal care may resign; however, if the attorney has acted under the power of attorney, the resignation is not effective until the attorney delivers a copy of the resignation to, (a) the grantor;

---

[98] s. 50.

[99] s. 51(1).

(b) any other attorneys under the power of attorney; (c) the person named by the power of attorney as a substitute for the attorney who is resigning, if the power of attorney provides for the substitution of another person; and (d) unless the power of attorney provides otherwise, the grantor's spouse or partner and the relatives of the grantor who are known to the attorney and reside in Ontario, if the power of attorney does not provide for the substitution of another person or the substitute is not able and willing to act.[100] A copy of the resignation need not be delivered to the grantor's spouse if the grantor and the spouse are living separate and apart within the meaning of the *Divorce Act* or a relative of the grantor, if the grantor and the relative are related only by marriage and the grantor and his or her spouse are living as separate and apart within the meaning of the *Divorce Act*.[101]

An attorney who resigns must make reasonable efforts to give notice of the resignation to persons with whom the attorney previously dealt on behalf of the grantor and with whom further dealings are likely to be required on behalf of the grantor.[102]

Termination

A power of attorney for personal care is terminated in the following circumstances:[103] (a) when the attorney dies, becomes incapable of personal care or resigns, unless (i) another attorney is authorized to act under subsection 46(5) of the Act, or (ii) the power of attorney provides for the substitution of another person and that person is able and willing to act; (b) when the court appoints a guardian under section 55; (c) when the grantor executes a new power of attorney for personal care, unless the grantor provides that there shall be multiple powers of attorney for personal care; (d) when the power of attorney is revoked.

No Statutory Guardian for Personal Care

Unlike the creation of statutory guardianship of property upon a finding of incapacity to manage property, there is no statutory guardianship of personal care created upon a finding of incapacity to make personal care decisions.

No Review of a Finding of Incapacity for Personal Care

There is no application to the Consent and Capacity Board to review a finding that an individual is incapable of personal care. In essence, a finding by an assessor that a person is incapable of personal care is of no legal consequence except for the purposes of: (1) triggering the effectiveness of a power of attorney for personal care; or (2) evidence in support of a court application for appointment of a guardian for the person.

---

[100] s. 52(1)(a) - (d).

[101] s. 52(1.1).

[102] s. 52(2).

[103] s. 53(1)(a)-(d).

In the event a finding of incapacity triggers a power of attorney for personal care, the consequences for an individual who disagrees with the assessment are significant since there is no statutory review of the assessment. The only remedy for the individual who disagrees with the assessment of incapacity would be to either request an assessment by another assessor or apply to the court.[104] Unfortunately, applications to the court, unlike applications to the Consent and Capacity Board, are costly, paper intensive and prone to delays. In the event the assessment directly impacts on a decision to which the *Health Care Consent Act, 1996* applies, the individual would be provided an opportunity to apply to the Board under that Act for a review of the finding of incapacity insofar as it relates to a decision to be made under that Act. Otherwise, the individual for all practical purposes is without a remedy of review. The individual is also free, absent a court-appointed guardian of the person, to ignore the finding.

Procedural Safeguards

Subject to few exceptions, an assessor shall not perform an assessment of a person's capacity to make personal care decisions if the person refuses to be assessed. The assessor must explain to the person to be assessed the purpose of the assessment, the significance and effect of a finding of capacity or incapacity and the person's right to refuse to be assessed.

Although these procedural safeguards are not contained in the *Health Care Consent Act, 1996,* they would apply to a decision under the *Health Care Consent Act, 1996* if the assessment was conducted by an assessor under the provisions of the *Substitute Decisions Act, 1992*. The case of *Re Koch*[105] illustrates the significance of procedural safeguards in the *Substitute Decisions Act, 1992* and imported them to the *Health Care Consent Act, 1996*. The importation of the *Substitute Decisions Act, 1992* procedural safeguards to the *Health Care Consent Act, 1996* has not been followed by the Consent and Capacity Board. For the most part, the statements of the court in *Re Koch* have been considered *obiter dicta* by the Board.

Information to be Provided

In the event an assessor performs an assessment of capacity, the assessor must give the person written notice of the assessor's findings.

---

[104] Although there is no specific section of the *Substitute Decisions Act, 1992* allowing an application to the court, s. 68 allows an application to be made to the court for directions.

[105] *Re Koch*, (1997), 33 O.R. (3d) 485 (Gen. Div.).

3. Court-Appointed Guardians of the Person

Who may Apply

Any person may apply to have a guardian of the person appointed by the court for a person who is incapable of personal care and, as a result, needs decisions to be made on his or her behalf by a person who is authorized to do so.[106]

Requirements

The court shall not appoint a guardian if it is satisfied that the need for decisions to be made will be met by an alternative course of action that, (a) does not require the court to find the person incapable of personal care; (b) is less restrictive of the person's decision-making rights than the appointment of a guardian.[107]

Who may not be Appointed

A person who provides health care or residential, social, training or support services to an incapable person for compensation shall not be appointed as his or her guardian of the person unless such person is the incapable person's spouse, partner or relative or the attorney for personal care or an attorney under a continuing power of attorney. This prohibition does not apply if the court is satisfied that there is no other suitable person who is available and willing to be appointed.[108]

The court shall not appoint the Public Guardian and Trustee as a guardian unless the Application proposes the Public Guardian and Trustee and there is no other suitable person that is available and willing to be appointed.[109]

Factors to Determine who should be Appointed

In determining who shall be appointed guardian of the person in all applications other than those by way of summary disposition (section 77 Applications) the court must consider, (a) whether the proposed guardian is the attorney under a continuing power of attorney for property; (b) the incapable person's current wishes, if they could be ascertained; and (c) the closeness of the applicant's relationship to the incapable person. Two or more persons may be appointed, with their consent, as joint guardians or the court may appoint each of them as guardian in respect of a specified period.[110]

---

[106] s. 55(1).

[107] s. 55(2)(a), (b).

[108] s. 57(1).

[109] s. 57(2.2).

[110] s. 57(3)(a), (b), (c) and 57(4).

Requirements of Court Order

An order appointing a guardian of the person must include a finding that the person is incapable in respect of the functions referred to (*i.e.* health care, nutrition, shelter, clothing, hygiene or safety) or in respect of some of them, and, as a result, decisions need to be made on his or her behalf by a person who is authorized to do so. An order of the court appointing a guardian of the person may make the appointment for a limited period or impose such other conditions as the court considers appropriate.[111]

Custodial Power

An order for full guardianship is necessary in the event that custodial power over the incapable person is required.

A requirement for an order for full guardianship is a finding by the court that a person is incapable in respect of all functions of personal care.[112]

Powers of a Guardian under Full Guardianship

Under an order for full guardianship, the guardian may exercise the following powers:[113] (a) custodial power over the person under guardianship, determining his or her living arrangements and provide for his or her shelter and safety; (b) be the person's litigation guardian, except in respect of litigation that relates to the person's property or to the guardian's status or powers; (c) settle claims and commence and settle proceedings on the person's behalf, except claims and proceedings that relate to the person's property or to the guardian's status or powers; (d) have access to personal information, including health information and records, to which the person could have access if capable, and consent to the release of that information to another person, except for the purposes of litigation that relates to the person's property or to the guardian's status or powers; (e) on behalf of the person make any decisions to which the *Health Care Consent Act, 1996* applies; (e) make decisions about the person's health care, nutrition and hygiene; (f) make decisions about the person's employment, education, training, clothing and recreation and about any social services provided to the person; and (g) exercise the other powers and perform the other duties that are specified in the order.

If the guardian has custodial power over the person and the court is satisfied that it may be necessary to apprehend him or her, the court may in its order authorize the guardian to do so. In such a case, the guardian may, with the assistance of police, enter the residence specified in the order, between 9:00 a.m.

---

[111] s. 58(2)(a), (b).

[112] s. 59(1).

[113] s. 59(2)(a)-(g).

and 4:00 p.m. or during the hours specified in the order, and search for and remove the person using such force as may be necessary.[114]

Unless the order expressly provides otherwise, the guardian does not have power to change existing arrangements in respect of custody of or access to a child or to give consent on the person's behalf to the adoption of a child.[115]

Powers of Guardian under Partial Guardianship

In the event the court does not make an order for full guardianship, it may make an order for partial guardianship if it finds the person incapable in respect of some but not all of the personal care functions.[116] The order must specify in respect of which functions the person is found to be incapable[117] and under such an order the guardian may exercise those powers specified in the order.[118]

Variation of Order

The court may vary an order appointing a guardian or substitute another person as guardian on a motion in a proceeding in which the guardian was appointed. Such a motion may be made by the guardian, the applicant in the proceeding in which the guardian was appointed or any person who was entitled to be served with notice of that proceeding.[119]

Duty of Public Guardian and Trustee when Serious Adverse Effects may Occur to the Person

In the event a person may be incapable of personal care and may be suffering serious adverse effects as a result, defined as "serious illness or injury, or deprivation of liberty or personal security", any person may notify the Public Guardian and Trustee of such an occurrence. The Public Guardian and Trustee must investigate any allegation that a person is incapable of personal care and that as a result serious adverse effects are occurring or may occur.

If as a result of the investigation, the Public Guardian and Trustee has reasonable grounds to believe that a person is incapable of personal care and that the prompt appointment of a temporary guardian of the person is required to prevent serious adverse effects, the Public Guardian and Trustee shall apply to the court for an order appointing him or her as temporary guardian of the person.

---

[114] s. 59(3).

[115] s. 59(4)(b).

[116] s. 60(1).

[117] s. 60(2).

[118] s. 60(3).

[119] s. 61 and s. 69.

Appointment of Public Guardian and Trustee as Temporary Guardian

The court may by order appoint the Public Guardian as temporary guardian of the person[120] for a period not exceeding ninety days.[121] The order may suspend the powers of any attorney under a power of attorney for personal care during the term of the temporary guardianship.[122] The court may also authorize the Public Guardian and Trustee to apprehend the person if satisfied that it may be necessary to do so.[123]

The court may, by order, vary or terminate the guardianship on a motion in the proceeding in which the guardian was appointed.[124]

4. Duties of Guardians of the Person and Attorneys for Personal Care

Prior Capable Wishes and Best Interests

Sections 66, 67 and 68 contain a comprehensive guide to the duties required of guardians of the person and attorneys for personal care. The Act requires guardians and attorneys to make decisions on the incapable person's behalf to which the *Health Care Consent Act, 1996* applies in accordance with that Act and if that Act does not apply, the guardian or attorney must make the decision in accordance with a prior capable wish. If the guardian or attorney does not know of a wish or instruction applicable to the circumstances that the incapable person expressed while capable or if it is impossible to make the decision in accordance with the wish or instruction, the guardian must make the decision in the incapable person's best interest. The Act sets out a number of criteria which the guardian and attorney must use in determining the best interest of the incapable person.[125]

Records and Consultation

The guardian or attorney as the case may be must keep records of the decisions they make[126] and encourage the incapable person, to the best of his or her ability, to participate in the guardian's decisions.[127] The guardian/attorney must seek to foster regular personal contact between the incapable person and supportive family members and friends.[128] The guardian/attorney must also consult with

[120] s. 62(6).
[121] s. 62(7).
[122] s. 62(9).
[123] s. 62(10).
[124] s. 62(11).
[125] subs. 66(4).
[126] s. 66(4.1).
[127] s. 66(5).
[128] s. 66(6).

these individuals and as far as possible seek to foster the incapable person's independence.[129]

Confinement, Monitoring, Duties and Restraint

A guardian/attorney must choose the least restrictive and intrusive course of action that is available and appropriate in the particular case. Confinement, monitoring devices or restraint should not be consented to by the guardian unless the practice is essential to prevent serious bodily harm to the person or to others or to allow the person greater freedom or enjoyment.[130] A guardian or attorney shall not use electric shock as aversive conditioning and shall not give consent on the person's behalf to the use of electric shock as aversive conditioning unless the consent is given to a treatment in accordance with the *Health Care Consent Act, 1996.*[131]

Application for Directions

In the event a guardian or attorney requires directions from the court, an application may be made seeking direction on any question arising in the guardianship or under the power of attorney. Any person may also request directions provided leave is granted.[132]

III. PROCEDURE IN GUARDIANSHIP APPLICATIONS

Sections 69 to 77 set out the process, including the documentation required for a court to appoint either a guardian of property or a guardian of the person. Conversely, there is also a process set out for termination of such an order. In the event there is no opposition to the application, a summary process is set out which requires additional documentation to be submitted with the application.

IV. MISCELLANEOUS

Sections 78 to 90 contain various provisions including: the right to refuse to be assessed, the information to be provided prior to an assessment, court orders for assessment and the process to enforce such orders; extraordinary powers granted to the Public Guardian and Trustee for the purposes of conducting investigations into serious adverse effects, conflict of laws regarding powers of attorney; foreign orders; mediation of disputes by the Public Guardian and Trustee; offences and penalties for offences; and regulations.

---

[129] s. 66(7).

[130] s. 66(10)(a).

[131] s. 66(12).

[132] s. 68(1).

SUBSTITUTE DECISIONS ACT, 1992

(S.O. 1992, c. 30)

Amendments: 1994, c. 27, ss. 43 (2), 62; 1996, c. 2, ss. 3-60; 1998, c. 26, s. 108; 2001, c. 13, s. 30; 2002, c. 17, Sched. F, Table; 2002, c. 18, Sched. A, s. 20; 2004, c. 3, Sched. A, s. 97; 2005, c. 5, s. 65.

GENERAL

1. (1) **Interpretation** — In this Act,

"assessor" means a member of a class of persons who are designated by the regulations as being qualified to do assessments of capacity;

"capable" means mentally capable, and "capacity" has a corresponding meaning;

"controlled-access residence" means premises, other than a facility, where one or more persons live and that are operated for remuneration by a person who controls access to the premises;

"court" means the Superior Court of Justice;

"dependant" means a person to whom another has an obligation to provide support;

"facility" means,

(a) a facility governed or funded under an Act mentioned in the Schedule,

(b) police detention facilities provided by a municipality under the *Police Services Act*,

(c) a detention facility maintained under section 16.1 of the *Police Services Act*, or

(d) a prescribed facility;

"incapable" means mentally incapable, and "incapacity" has a corresponding meaning;

"partner" means,

(a) [Repealed, 2005, c. 5, s. 65]

(b) either of two persons who have lived together for at least one year and have a close personal relationship that is of primary importance in both persons' lives;

"prescribed" means prescribed by the regulations;

"psychiatric facility" has the same meaning as in the *Mental Health Act*;

"regulations" means the regulations made under this Act;

"spouse" means a person

(a) to whom the person is married, or

(b) with whom the person is living in a conjugal relationship outside marriage, if the two persons,

(i) have cohabited for at least one year,

(ii) are together the parents of a child, or

(iii) have together entered into a cohabitation agreement under section 53 of the *Family Law Act*;

"will" has the same meaning as in the *Succession Law Reform Act*.

(2) [Repealed, 2002, c. 18, Sched. A, s. 20]

(2.1) **Relatives** — Two persons are relatives for the purpose of this Act if they are related by blood, marriage or adoption.

(3) **Meaning of "explain"** — A person whom this Act requires to explain a matter satisfies that requirement by explaining the matter to the best of his or her ability and in a manner that addresses the special needs of the person receiving the explanation, whether that person understands it or not.

[1996, c. 2, s. 3; 2002, c. 17, Sched. F, Table; 2002, c. 18, Sched. A, s. 20; 2005, c. 5, s. 65]

2. (1) **Presumption of capacity** — A person who is eighteen years of age or more is presumed to be capable of entering into a contract.

(2) **Same** — A person who is sixteen years of age or more is presumed to be capable of giving or refusing consent in connection with his or her own personal care.

(3) **Exception** — A person is entitled to rely upon the presumption of capacity with respect to another person unless he or she has reasonable grounds to believe that the other person is incapable of entering into the contract or of giving or refusing consent, as the case may be.

(4) **Onus of proof, contracts and gifts** — In a proceeding in respect of a contract entered into or a gift made by a person while his or her property is under guardianship, or within one year before the creation of the guardianship, the onus of proof that the other person who entered into the contract or received the gift did not have reasonable grounds to believe the person incapable is on that other person.

3. (1) **Counsel for person whose capacity is in issue** — If the capacity of a person who does not have legal representation is in issue in a proceeding under this Act,

(a) the court may direct that the Public Guardian and Trustee arrange for legal representation to be provided for the person; and

(b) the person shall be deemed to have capacity to retain and instruct counsel.

(2) **Responsibility for legal fees** — If legal representation is provided for a person in accordance with clause (1) (a) and no certificate is issued under the *Legal Aid Services Act, 1998* in connection with the proceeding, the person is responsible for the legal fees.

[1998, c. 26, s. 108]

Part I

Property

General

4. Application of Part — This Part applies to decisions on behalf of persons who are at least eighteen years old.

5. Age — To exercise a power of decision under this Part on behalf of another person, a person must be at least eighteen years old.

6. Incapacity to manage property — A person is incapable of managing property if the person is not able to understand information that is relevant to making a decision in the management of his or her property, or is not able to appreciate the reasonably foreseeable consequences of a decision or lack of decision.

Continuing Powers of Attorney for Property

7. (1) **Continuing power of attorney for property** — A power of attorney for property is a continuing power of attorney if,

(a) it states that it is a continuing power of attorney; or

(b) it expresses the intention that the authority given may be exercised during the grantor's incapacity to manage property.

[Note: S.O. 1996, c. 2, s. 4(5) provides that subsection 7 (1), as re-enacted by the S.O. 1996, c. 2, subs. 4 (1), applies to powers of attorney given before or after March 29, 1996.]

(2) **Same** — The continuing power of attorney may authorize the person named as attorney to do on the grantor's behalf anything in respect of property that the grantor could do if capable, except make a will.

(3) **P.G.T. may be attorney** — The continuing power of attorney may name the Public Guardian and Trustee as attorney if his or her consent in writing is obtained before the power of attorney is executed.

(4) **Two or more attorneys** — If the continuing power of attorney names two or more persons as attorneys, the attorneys shall act jointly, unless the power of attorney provides otherwise.

(5) **Death, etc., of joint attorney** — If two or more attorneys act jointly under the continuing power of attorney and one of them dies, becomes incapable of

managing property or resigns, the remaining attorney or attorneys are authorized to act, unless the power of attorney provides otherwise.

(6) **Conditions and restrictions** — The continuing power of attorney is subject to this Part, and to the conditions and restrictions that are contained in the power of attorney and are consistent with this Act.

(7) **Postponed effectiveness** — The continuing power of attorney may provide that it comes into effect on a specified date or when a specified contingency happens.

(7.1) **Form** — The continuing power of attorney need not be in any particular form.

(8) **Same** — The continuing power of attorney may be in the prescribed form.

[1996, c. 2, s. 4]

8. (1) **Capacity to give continuing power of attorney** — A person is capable of giving a continuing power of attorney if he or she,

(a) knows what kind of property he or she has and its approximate value;

(b) is aware of obligations owed to his or her dependants;

(c) knows that the attorney will be able to do on the person's behalf anything in respect of property that the person could do if capable, except make a will, subject to the conditions and restrictions set out in the power of attorney;

(d) knows that the attorney must account for his or her dealings with the person's property;

(e) knows that he or she may, if capable, revoke the continuing power of attorney;

(f) appreciates that unless the attorney manages the property prudently its value may decline; and

(g) appreciates the possibility that the attorney could misuse the authority given to him or her.

(2) **Capacity to revoke** — A person is capable of revoking a continuing power of attorney if he or she is capable of giving one.

9. (1) **Validity despite incapacity** — A continuing power of attorney is valid if the grantor, at the time of executing it, is capable of giving it, even if he or she is incapable of managing property.

(2) **Same** — The continuing power of attorney remains valid even if, after executing it, the grantor becomes incapable of giving a continuing power of attorney.

(3) **Determining incapacity** — If the continuing power of attorney provides that it comes into effect when the grantor becomes incapable of managing property but does not provide a method for determining whether that situation has arisen, the power of attorney comes into effect when,

(a) the attorney is notified in the prescribed form by an assessor that the assessor has performed an assessment of the grantor's capacity and has found that the grantor is incapable of managing property; or

(b) the attorney is notified that a certificate of incapacity has been issued in respect of the grantor under the *Mental Health Act*.

[1996, c. 2, s. 5]

10. (1) **Execution —** A continuing power of attorney shall be executed in the presence of two witnesses, each of whom shall sign the power of attorney as witness.

(2) **Persons who shall not be witnesses —** The following persons shall not be witnesses:

1. The attorney or the attorney's spouse or partner.
2. The grantor's spouse or partner.
3. A child of the grantor or a person whom the grantor has demonstrated a settled intention to treat as his or her child.
4. A person whose property is under guardianship or who has a guardian of the person.
5. A person who is less than eighteen years old.

(3) [Repealed, 1996, c. 2, s. 6]

(4) **Non-compliance —** A continuing power of attorney that does not comply with subsections (1) and (2) is not effective, but the court may, on any person's application, declare the continuing power of attorney to be effective if the court is satisfied that it is in the interests of the grantor or his or her dependants to do so.

[1996, c. 2, s. 6]

11. (1) **Resignation of attorney —** An attorney under a continuing power of attorney may resign but, if the attorney has acted under the power of attorney, the resignation is not effective until the attorney delivers a copy of the resignation to,

(a) the grantor;

(b) any other attorneys under the power of attorney;

(c) the person named by the power of attorney as a substitute for the attorney who is resigning, if the power of attorney provides for the substitution of another person; and

(d) unless the power of attorney provides otherwise, the grantor's spouse or partner and the relatives of the grantor who are known to the attorney and reside in Ontario, if,

(i) the attorney is of the opinion that the grantor is incapable of managing property, and

(ii) the power of attorney does not provide for the substitution of another person or the substitute is not able and willing to act.

(1.1) **Exception —** Clause (1) (d) does not require a copy of the resignation to be delivered to,

(a) the grantor's spouse, if the grantor and the spouse are living separate and apart as a result of a breakdown of their relationship; or

(b) a relative of the grantor, if the grantor and the relative are related only by marriage and the grantor and his or her spouse are living separate and apart as a result of a breakdown of their relationship.

(2) **Notice to other persons** — An attorney who resigns shall make reasonable efforts to give notice of the resignation to persons with whom the attorney previously dealt on behalf of the grantor and with whom further dealings are likely to be required on behalf of the grantor.

[1996, c. 2, s. 7; 2005, c. 5, s. 65]

12. (1) **Termination** — A continuing power of attorney is terminated,

(a) when the attorney dies, becomes incapable of managing property or resigns, unless,

(i) another attorney is authorized to act under subsection 7 (5), or

(ii) the power of attorney provides for the substitution of another person and that person is able and willing to act;

(b) [Repealed, 1996, c. 2, s. 8]

(c) when the court appoints a guardian of property for the grantor under section 22;

(d) when the grantor executes a new continuing power of attorney, unless the grantor provides that there shall be multiple continuing powers of attorney;

(e) when the power of attorney is revoked;

(f) when the grantor dies.

(2) **Execution of revocation** — The revocation shall be in writing and shall be executed in the same way as a continuing power of attorney.

[1996, c. 2, s. 8]

13. (1) **Exercise after termination or invalidity** — If a continuing power of attorney is terminated or becomes invalid, any subsequent exercise of the power by the attorney is nevertheless valid as between the grantor or the grantor's estate and any person, including the attorney, who acted in good faith and without knowledge of the termination or invalidity.

(2) **Same, improper execution** — If a continuing power of attorney is ineffective because a person listed in subsection 10 (2) witnessed its execution, subsection (1) applies, with necessary modifications.

14. **Certain existing powers of attorney preserved** — Despite the repeal of section 5 of the *Powers of Attorney Act*, by subsection 24 (3) of the *Consent and Capacity Statute Law Amendment Act, 1992*, a power of attorney that is executed on or before the day this Act comes into force or within six months after that day shall be deemed to be a continuing power of attorney for the purposes of this Act if,

(a) it contains a provision expressly stating that it may be exercised during any subsequent legal incapacity of the grantor, as described in section 5 of the *Powers of Attorney Act*; and

(b) it is executed in accordance with the *Powers of Attorney Act* and is otherwise valid.

Statutory Guardians of Property

15. P.G.T. as statutory guardian — If a certificate is issued under the *Mental Health Act* certifying that a person who is a patient of a psychiatric facility is incapable of managing property, the Public Guardian and Trustee is the person's statutory guardian of property.

[1996, c. 2, s. 9]

16. (1) **Assessment of capacity for statutory guardianship** — A person may request an assessor to perform an assessment of another person's capacity or of the person's own capacity for the purpose of determining whether the Public Guardian and Trustee should become the statutory guardian of property under this section.

(2) **Form of request** — No assessment shall be performed unless the request is in the prescribed form and, if the request is made in respect of another person, the request states that,

(a) the person requesting the assessment has reason to believe that the other person may be incapable of managing property;

(b) the person requesting the assessment has made reasonable inquiries and has no knowledge of the existence of any attorney under a continuing power of attorney that gives the attorney authority over all of the other person's property; and

(c) the person requesting the assessment has made reasonable inquiries and has no knowledge of any spouse, partner or relative of the other person who intends to make an application under section 22 for the appointment of a guardian of property for the other person.

(3) **Certificate of incapacity** — The assessor may issue a certificate of incapacity in the prescribed form if he or she finds that the person is incapable of managing property.

(4) **Copies** — The assessor shall ensure that copies of the certificate of incapacity are promptly given to the incapable person and to the Public Guardian and Trustee.

(5) **Statutory guardianship** — As soon as he or she receives the copy of the certificate, the Public Guardian and Trustee is the person's statutory guardian of property.

(6) **Information to be given** — After becoming a person's statutory guardian of property under subsection (5), the Public Guardian and Trustee shall ensure

that the person is informed, in a manner that the Public Guardian and Trustee considers appropriate, that,

(a) the Public Guardian and Trustee has become the person's statutory guardian of property; and

(b) the person is entitled to apply to the Consent and Capacity Board for a review of the assessor's finding that the person is incapable of managing property.

[1996, c. 2, s. 10]

16.1 Termination by attorney — A statutory guardianship of property is terminated if,

(a) the incapable person gave a continuing power of attorney before the certificate of incapacity was issued;

(b) the power of attorney gives the attorney authority over all of the incapable person's property;

(c) the Public Guardian and Trustee receives a copy of the power of attorney and a written undertaking signed by the attorney to act in accordance with the power of attorney; and

(d) if someone has replaced the Public Guardian and Trustee as the statutory guardian under section 17, the statutory guardian receives a copy of the power of attorney and a written undertaking signed by the attorney to act in accordance with the power of attorney.

[1996, c. 2, s. 10]

17. (1) **Replacement of P.G.T.** — Any of the following persons may apply to the Public Guardian and Trustee to replace the Public Guardian and Trustee as an incapable person's statutory guardian of property:

1. The incapable person's spouse or partner.
2. A relative of the incapable person.
3. The incapable person's attorney under a continuing power of attorney, if the power of attorney was made before the certificate of incapacity was issued and does not give the attorney authority over all of the incapable person's property.
4. A trust corporation within the meaning of the *Loan and Trust Corporations Act*, if the incapable person's spouse or partner consents in writing to the application.

(2) **Form of application** — The application shall be in the prescribed form.

(3) **Management plan** — The application shall be accompanied by a management plan for the property in the prescribed form.

(4) **Appointment** — Subject to subsection (6), the Public Guardian and Trustee shall appoint the applicant as the incapable person's statutory guardian of property if the Public Guardian and Trustee is satisfied that the applicant is suitable to manage the property and that the management plan is appropriate.

(5) **Considerations** — The Public Guardian and Trustee shall consider the incapable person's current wishes, if they can be ascertained, and the closeness of the applicant's relationship to the person.

(6) **Security** — The Public Guardian and Trustee may refuse to appoint the applicant unless the applicant provides security, in a manner approved by the Public Guardian and Trustee, for an amount fixed by the Public Guardian and Trustee.

(7) **Same** — If security is required under subsection (6), the court may, on application, order that security be dispensed with, that security be provided in a manner not approved by the Public Guardian and Trustee, or that the amount of security be reduced, and may make its order subject to conditions.

(8) **Certificate** — The Public Guardian and Trustee shall give the person appointed as statutory guardian of property a certificate certifying the appointment.

(9) **Effect of certificate** — The certificate is proof of the guardian's authority.

(10) **Conditions** — The Public Guardian and Trustee may make an appointment under this section subject to conditions specified in the certificate.

(11) **Two or more guardians** — The Public Guardian and Trustee may certify that two or more applicants are joint statutory guardians of property, or that each of them is guardian for a specified part of the property.

(12) **Duty of guardian** — A person who replaces the Public Guardian and Trustee as statutory guardian of property shall, subject to any conditions imposed by the Public Guardian and Trustee or the court, manage the property in accordance with the management plan.

[1996, c. 2, s. 11]

18. (1) **Refusal to issue certificate of statutory guardianship** — If the Public Guardian and Trustee refuses to issue a certificate for a statutory guardian of property under section 17, he or she shall give the applicant reasons, in writing, for the refusal.

(2) **Dispute, application to court** — If the applicant disputes the refusal by giving the Public Guardian and Trustee notice in writing, the Public Guardian and Trustee shall apply to the court to decide the matter.

(3) **Review by court** — The court shall decide whether the applicant should, in the circumstances, replace the Public Guardian and Trustee.

(4) **Criteria** — The court shall take into consideration the incapable person's current wishes, if they can be ascertained, and the closeness of the applicant's relationship to the person.

(5) **Order** — The court may, in its order, impose such conditions on the guardian's powers as it considers appropriate.

[1996, c. 2, s. 12]

19. (1) **Death, etc., of statutory guardian** — If a statutory guardian of property dies, becomes incapable of managing property or gives notice to the

Public Guardian and Trustee of his or her resignation, the Public Guardian and Trustee may elect to become the incapable person's statutory guardian until another person is appointed as guardian of property under section 17 or 22.

(2) **Delivery of accounts, etc. —** If a statutory guardian of property gives notice to the Public Guardian and Trustee of his or her resignation, the Public Guardian and Trustee may require the guardian to provide the Public Guardian and Trustee with his or her accounts in respect of the guardianship, any property in his or her possession or control that is subject to the guardianship and any information requested by the Public Guardian and Trustee in respect of the guardianship.

(3) **Same —** Subsection (2) applies with necessary modifications to the personal representative of a statutory guardian of property who dies.
[1996, c. 2, s. 13]

20. Termination of statutory guardianship — A statutory guardianship of property for a person is terminated if any of the following events occurs:

1. A guardian is appointed for the person by the court under section 22.
2. Notice of the guardian's resignation is given by the guardian to,
   i. the person, and
   ii. the Public Guardian and Trustee, if the Public Guardian and Trustee is not the guardian.
3. In the case of a statutory guardianship created under section 15,
   i. notice is given to the guardian that the certificate of incapacity has been cancelled under section 56 of the *Mental Health Act*,
   ii. notice is given to the guardian that the person has been discharged, unless the guardian has also received a notice of continuance issued under subsection 57 (2) of the *Mental Health Act*,
   iii. notice is given to the guardian from an assessor or from a physician who has authority to issue certificates of incapacity under the *Mental Health Act* stating that the assessor or physician has performed an assessment of the person's capacity and is of the opinion that the person is capable of managing property, if the person has been discharged and a notice of continuance was issued under subsection 57 (2) of the *Mental Health Act*,
   iv. the time for appeal from a decision of the Consent and Capacity Board on an application under section 20.2 of this Act or section 60 of the *Mental Health Act* has expired, if the Board determines that the person is capable of managing property and no appeal is taken, or
   v. an appeal from a decision of the Consent and Capacity Board on an application under section 20.2 of this Act or section 60 of the *Mental Health Act* is finally disposed of, if an appeal is taken and it is finally determined that the person is capable of managing property.

4. In the case of a statutory guardianship created under section 16,
   i. notice is given to the guardian from an assessor stating that the assessor has performed an assessment of the person's capacity and is of the opinion that the person is capable of managing property,
   ii. the time for appeal from a decision of the Consent and Capacity Board on an application under section 20.2 has expired, if the Board determines that the person is capable of managing property and no appeal is taken, or
   iii. an appeal from a decision of the Consent and Capacity Board on an application under section 20.2 is finally disposed of, if an appeal is taken and it is finally determined that the person is capable of managing property.

[1996, c. 2, s. 13]

20.1 (1) **Assessment of incapacity —** A statutory guardian of property shall, on behalf of the incapable person, assist in arranging an assessment of the person's capacity by an assessor if the assessment is requested by the incapable person and,

(a) in the case of a statutory guardianship created under section 15, the person has been discharged from the psychiatric facility, a notice of continuance was issued under subsection 57 (2) of the *Mental Health Act*, and six months have elapsed since the notice of continuance was issued; or

(b) in the case of a statutory guardianship created under section 16, six months have elapsed since the guardianship was created.

(2) **Limit —** Subsection (1) does not require a statutory guardian of property to assist in arranging an assessment if an assessment has been performed in the six months before the request.

[1996, c. 2, s. 13]

20.2 (1) **Application for review of finding of incapacity —** A person who has a statutory guardian of property may apply to the Consent and Capacity Board for a review of a finding that the person is incapable of managing property,

(a) in the case of a statutory guardianship created under section 15, if the finding was made by an assessor, or by a physician who has authority to issue certificates of incapacity under the *Mental Health Act*, following an assessment of capacity that was performed after a notice of continuance was issued in respect of the person under subsection 57 (2) of the *Mental Health Act*; or

(b) in the case of a statutory guardianship created under section 16, if the finding,

   (i) resulted in the issuance of the certificate of incapacity under subsection 16 (3), or

   (ii) was made by an assessor following an assessment of capacity that was performed after the creation of the statutory guardianship.

(2) **Limit** — A person may not make an application under this section if he or she made an application under this section in the previous six months.

(3) **Time for application** — An application under this section must be made within six months after the finding of incapacity was made.

(4) **Parties** — The parties to the application are:

1. The applicant.
2. The assessor or physician who made the finding of incapacity.
3. Any other person whom the Board specifies.

(5) **Power of Board** — The Board may confirm the finding of incapacity or may determine that the person is capable of managing property, and in doing so may substitute its opinion for that of the assessor or physician.

(6) **Procedure** — Sections 73 to 80 of the *Health Care Consent Act, 1996* apply with necessary modifications to an application under this section.
[1996, c. 2, s. 13]

20.3 (1) **Termination by court** — The court may, on application by a person who is subject to a statutory guardianship of property, terminate the statutory guardianship.

(2) **Suspension** — In an application under this section, the court may suspend the powers of the statutory guardian.

(3) **Procedure** — Subsections 69 (0.1), (8) and (9) apply to an application under this section and, except for the purpose of subsection 69 (9), subsection 69 (6) does not apply.
[1996, c. 2, s. 13]

21. **P.G.T. to forward notices** — If the Public Guardian and Trustee receives a notice concerning a statutory guardianship although another person is the guardian, he or she shall ensure that it is promptly forwarded to that person.

Court-Appointed Guardians of Property

22. (1) **Court appointment of guardian of property** — The court may, on any person's application, appoint a guardian of property for a person who is incapable of managing property if, as a result, it is necessary for decisions to be made on his or her behalf by a person who is authorized to do so.

(2) **Same** — An application may be made under subsection (1) even though there is a statutory guardian.

(3) **Prohibition** — The court shall not appoint a guardian if it is satisfied that the need for decisions to be made will be met by an alternative course of action that,

(a) does not require the court to find the person to be incapable of managing property; and

(b) is less restrictive of the person's decision-making rights than the appointment of a guardian.

23. Procedure — Part III (Procedure) applies to applications to appoint guardians of property.

24. (1) **Appointment criteria** — A person who provides health care or residential, social, training or support services to an incapable person for compensation shall not be appointed under section 22 as his or her guardian of property.

(2) **Exception** — Subsection (1) does not apply to the incapable person's spouse, partner or relative or to the following persons:

1. [Repealed, 1996, c. 2, s. 14]
2. The attorney for personal care.
3. The attorney under a continuing power of attorney.

(2.1) **P.G.T.** — The court shall not appoint the Public Guardian and Trustee as a guardian under section 22 unless the application proposes the Public Guardian and Trustee as guardian and there is no other suitable person who is available and willing to be appointed.

(3) **Non-residents** — A person who does not reside in Ontario shall not be appointed as a guardian of property unless the person provides security, in a manner approved by the court, for the value of the property.

(4) **Same** — The court may order that the requirement for security under subsection (3) does not apply to a person or that the amount required be reduced, and may make its order subject to conditions.

(5) **Criteria** — Except in the case of an application that is being dealt with under section 77 (summary disposition), the court shall consider,

(a) whether the proposed guardian is the attorney under a continuing power of attorney;

(b) the incapable person's current wishes, if they can be ascertained; and

(c) the closeness of the applicant's relationship to the incapable person.

(6) **Two or more guardians** — The court may, with their consent, appoint two or more persons as joint guardians of property or may appoint each of them as guardian for a specified part of the property.

[1996, c. 2, s. 14]

25. (1) **Finding of incapacity** — An order appointing a guardian of property for a person shall include a finding that the person is incapable of managing property and that, as a result, it is necessary for decisions to be made on his or her behalf by a person who is authorized to do so.

(2) **Contents of order** — An order appointing a guardian of property may,

(a) require that the guardian post security in the manner and amount that the court considers appropriate;

(b) make the appointment for a limited period as the court considers appropriate;

(c) impose such other conditions on the appointment as the court considers appropriate.

(3) **Exception** — Clause (2) (a) does not apply if the guardian is the Public Guardian and Trustee or a trust corporation within the meaning of the *Loan and Trust Corporations Act*.

26. (1) **Variation or substitution of appointment order** — The court may vary an order appointing a guardian of property under section 22 or substitute another person as guardian, on motion in the proceeding in which the guardian was appointed.

(2) **Who may make motion** — A motion under subsection (1) may be made by the guardian, the applicant in the proceeding in which the guardian was appointed, or any person who was entitled under section 69 to be served with notice of that proceeding.

(3) **Motion to vary** — Subsection 69 (2), subsections 69 (5) to (9) and section 77 apply, with necessary modifications, to a motion to vary an order.

(4) **Motion to substitute** — Subsection 69 (1), subsections 69 (5) to (9), subsection 70 (1) and section 77 apply, with necessary modifications, to a motion to substitute another person as guardian.

[1996, c. 2, s. 15]

27. (1) **Serious adverse effects** — Loss of a significant part of a person's property, or a person's failure to provide necessities of life for himself or herself or for dependants, are serious adverse effects for the purposes of this section.

(2) **Duty to investigate** — The Public Guardian and Trustee shall investigate any allegation that a person is incapable of managing property and that serious adverse effects are occurring or may occur as a result.

(3) **Extent of investigation** — In conducting an investigation under subsection (2), the Public Guardian and Trustee is not required to take any steps that, in his or her opinion, are unnecessary for the purpose of determining whether an application to the court is required under subsection (3.1).

(3.1) **Application for temporary guardianship** — If, as a result of the investigation, the Public Guardian and Trustee has reasonable grounds to believe that a person is incapable of managing property and that the prompt appointment of a temporary guardian of property is required to prevent serious adverse effects, the Public Guardian and Trustee shall apply to the court for an order appointing him or her as temporary guardian of property.

(4) **Notice** — Notice of the application shall be served on the person alleged to be incapable, unless the court dispenses with notice in view of the nature and urgency of the matter.

(5) [Repealed, 1996, c. 2, s. 16]

(6) **Order appointing temporary guardian** — The court may by order appoint the Public Guardian and Trustee as temporary guardian of property for a period not exceeding ninety days.

(7) **Same —** The order shall set out the temporary guardian's powers and any conditions imposed on the guardianship.

(8) **Power of attorney —** The order may suspend the powers of any attorney under a continuing power of attorney during the term of the temporary guardianship.

(9) **Service of order —** If the order was made without notice, it shall be served on the person as soon as possible.

(9.1) **Termination, variation —** On motion by the Public Guardian and Trustee or by the person whose property is under guardianship, the court may terminate the guardianship, reduce or extend its term, or otherwise vary the order.

(10) **Duty if no application made —** If the Public Guardian and Trustee conducts an investigation under this section and decides not to make an application under subsection (3.1), the Public Guardian and Trustee shall, within three years,

- (a) destroy all information collected during the investigation and during any previous investigations in respect of the person under this section; and
- (b) notify the person who was alleged to be incapable that,
  - (i) an allegation was made that the person was incapable of managing property and that serious adverse effects were occurring or might occur as a result,
  - (ii) the Public Guardian and Trustee investigated the allegation as required by this Act and decided not to make an application for temporary guardianship, and
  - (iii) the Public Guardian and Trustee has destroyed all information collected during the investigation.

(11) **Exception —** Subsection (10) does not apply if, within three years after the decision is made not to make an application under subsection (3.1),

- (a) another investigation is commenced in respect of the person under this section or section 62; or
- (b) the Public Guardian and Trustee becomes the person's guardian of property or guardian of the person.

[1996, c. 2, s. 16]

28. (1) **Termination —** The court may terminate a guardianship created under section 22, on motion in the proceeding in which the guardian was appointed.

(2) **Who may make motion —** A motion under subsection (1) may be made by the guardian, the applicant in the proceeding in which the guardian was appointed, or any person who was entitled under section 69 to be served with notice of that proceeding.

[1996, c. 2, s. 17]

29. **Suspension —** In a motion to terminate a guardianship or temporary guardianship, the court may suspend the powers of the guardian or temporary guardian.

[1996, c. 2, s. 17]

30. **Procedure, termination** — Part III (Procedure) applies to motions to terminate guardianships of property.
[1996, c. 2, s. 18]

Property Management

31. (1) **Powers of guardian** — A guardian of property has power to do on the incapable person's behalf anything in respect of property that the person could do if capable, except make a will.

(2) [Repealed, 1996, c. 2, s. 19]

(3) **Same** — The guardian's powers are subject to this Act and to any conditions imposed by the court.
[1996, c. 2, s. 19]

32. (1) **Duties of guardian** — A guardian of property is a fiduciary whose powers and duties shall be exercised and performed diligently, with honesty and integrity and in good faith, for the incapable person's benefit.

(1.1) **Personal comfort and well-being** — If the guardian's decision will have an effect on the incapable person's personal comfort or well-being, the guardian shall consider that effect in determining whether the decision is for the incapable person's benefit.

(1.2) **Personal care** — A guardian shall manage a person's property in a manner consistent with decisions concerning the person's personal care that are made by the person who has authority to make those decisions.

(1.3) **Exception** — Subsection (1.2) does not apply in respect of a decision concerning the person's personal care if the decision's adverse consequences in respect of the person's property significantly outweigh the decision's benefits in respect of the person's personal care.

(2) **Explanation** — The guardian shall explain to the incapable person what the guardian's powers and duties are.

(3) **Participation** — A guardian shall encourage the incapable person to participate, to the best of his or her abilities, in the guardian's decisions about the property.

(4) **Family and friends** — The guardian shall seek to foster regular personal contact between the incapable person and supportive family members and friends of the incapable person.

(5) **Consultation** — The guardian shall consult from time to time with,

(a) supportive family members and friends of the incapable person who are in regular personal contact with the incapable person; and

(b) the persons from whom the incapable person receives personal care.

(6) **Accounts** — A guardian shall, in accordance with the regulations, keep accounts of all transactions involving the property.

(7) **Standard of care —** A guardian who does not receive compensation for managing the property shall exercise the degree of care, diligence and skill that a person of ordinary prudence would exercise in the conduct of his or her own affairs.

(8) **Same —** A guardian who receives compensation for managing the property shall exercise the degree of care, diligence and skill that a person in the business of managing the property of others is required to exercise.

(9) **P.G.T. —** Subsection (8) applies to the Public Guardian and Trustee.

(10) **Management plan, policies of P.G.T. —** A guardian shall act in accordance with the management plan established for the property, if the guardian is not the Public Guardian and Trustee, or with the policies of the Public Guardian and Trustee, if he or she is the guardian.

(11) **Amendment of plan —** If there is a management plan, it may be amended from time to time with the Public Guardian and Trustee's approval.

(12) **Application of *Trustee Act* —** The *Trustee Act* does not apply to the exercise of a guardian's powers or the performance of a guardian's duties.

[1996, c. 2, s. 20]

33. (1) **Liability of guardian —** A guardian of property is liable for damages resulting from a breach of the guardian's duty.

(2) **Same —** If the court is satisfied that a guardian of property who has committed a breach of duty has nevertheless acted honestly, reasonably and diligently, it may relieve the guardian from all or part of the liability.

33.1 Will — A guardian of property shall make reasonable efforts to determine,

(a) whether the incapable person has a will; and

(b) if the incapable person has a will, what the provisions of the will are.

[1996, c. 2, s. 21]

33.2 (1) **Property in another person's control —** A person who has custody or control of property belonging to an incapable person shall,

(a) provide the incapable person's guardian of property with any information requested by the guardian that concerns the property and that is known to the person who has custody or control of the property; and

(b) deliver the property to the incapable person's guardian of property when required by the guardian.

(2) **Property includes will —** For the purposes of subsection (1), the property belonging to a person includes the person's will.

(3) **Copies of documents —** A person who has custody or control of any document relating to an incapable person's property that was signed by or given to the incapable person shall, on request, provide the incapable person's guardian of property with a copy of the document.

[1996, c. 2, s. 21]

34. **Completion of transactions** — A guardian of property has power to complete a transaction that the incapable person entered into before becoming incapable.

35. **P.G.T., powers of executor** — When the Public Guardian and Trustee is the guardian of property for an incapable person who dies, he or she may, until notified of another person's appointment as personal representative, exercise the powers of an executor to whom the incapable person's property is given in trust for the payment of debts and the distribution of the residue.

35.1 (1) **Disposition of property given by will** — A guardian of property shall not dispose of property that the guardian knows is subject to a specific testamentary gift in the incapable person's will.

(2) **Application** — Subsection (1) does not apply in respect of a specific testamentary gift of money.

(3) **Permitted dispositions** — Despite subsection (1),

(a) the guardian may dispose of the property if the disposition of that property is necessary to comply with the guardian's duties; or

(b) the guardian may make a gift of the property to the person who would be entitled to it under the will, if the gift is authorized by section 37.

[1996, c. 2, s. 22]

36. (1) **Proceeds of disposition** — The doctrine of ademption does not apply to property that is subject to a specific testamentary gift and that a guardian of property disposes of under this Act, and anyone who would have acquired a right to the property on the death of the incapable person is entitled to receive from the residue of the estate the equivalent of a corresponding right in the proceeds of the disposition of the property, without interest.

(2) **If residue insufficient** — If the residue of the incapable person's estate is not sufficient to pay all entitlements under subsection (1) in full, the persons entitled under subsection (1) shall share the residue in amounts proportional to the amounts to which they would otherwise have been entitled.

(3) **Will prevails** — Subsections (1) and (2) are subject to a contrary intention in the incapable person's will.

[1996, c. 2, s. 23]

36.1 Proof of P.G.T. guardianship — A recital, in a document executed by the Public Guardian and Trustee, that the Public Guardian and Trustee is the incapable person's guardian of property under this Act is proof of the facts recited, in the absence of evidence to the contrary.

[1994, c. 27, s. 62]

37. (1) **Required expenditures** — A guardian of property shall make the following expenditures from the incapable person's property:

1. The expenditures that are reasonably necessary for the person's support, education and care.

2. The expenditures that are reasonably necessary for the support, education and care of the person's dependants.

3. The expenditures that are necessary to satisfy the person's other legal obligations.

(2) **Guiding principles** — The following rules apply to expenditures under subsection (1):

1. The value of the property, the accustomed standard of living of the incapable person and his or her dependants and the nature of other legal obligations shall be taken into account.

2. Expenditures under paragraph 2 may be made only if the property is and will remain sufficient to provide for expenditures under paragraph 1.

3. Expenditures under paragraph 3 may be made only if the property is and will remain sufficient to provide for expenditures under paragraphs 1 and 2.

(3) **Optional expenditures** — The guardian may make the following expenditures from the incapable person's property:

1. Gifts or loans to the person's friends and relatives.

2. Charitable gifts.

(4) **Guiding principles** — The following rules apply to expenditures under subsection (3):

1. They may be made only if the property is and will remain sufficient to satisfy the requirements of subsection (1).

2. Gifts or loans to the incapable person's friends or relatives may be made only if there is reason to believe, based on intentions the person expressed before becoming incapable, that he or she would make them if capable.

3. Charitable gifts may be made only if,

   i. the incapable person authorized the making of charitable gifts in a power of attorney executed before becoming incapable, or

   ii. there is evidence that the person made similar expenditures when capable.

4. If a power of attorney executed by the incapable person before becoming incapable contained instructions with respect to the making of gifts or loans to friends or relatives or the making of charitable gifts, the instructions shall be followed, subject to paragraphs 1, 5 and 6.

5. A gift or loan to a friend or relative or a charitable gift shall not be made if the incapable person expresses a wish to the contrary.

6. The total amount or value of charitable gifts shall not exceed the lesser of,

   i. 20 per cent of the income of the property in the year in which the gifts are made, and

ii. the maximum amount or value of charitable gifts provided for in a power of attorney executed by the incapable person before becoming incapable.

(5) **Increase, charitable gifts** — The court may authorize the guardian to make a charitable gift that does not comply with paragraph 6 of subsection (4),

(a) on motion by the guardian in the proceeding in which the guardian was appointed, if the guardian was appointed under section 22 or 27; or

(b) on application, if the guardian is the statutory guardian of property.

(6) **Expenditures for person's benefit** — Expenditures made under this section shall be deemed to be for the incapable person's benefit.

[1996, c. 2, s. 24]

38. (1) **Attorney under continuing power of attorney** — Section 32, except subsections (10) and (11), and sections 33, 33.1, 33.2, 34, 35.1, 36 and 37 also apply, with necessary modifications, to an attorney acting under a continuing power of attorney if the grantor is incapable of managing property or the attorney has reasonable grounds to believe that the grantor is incapable of managing property.

(2) **Authority under subs. 37 (5)** — An attorney under a continuing power of attorney shall make an application to the court to obtain the authority referred to in subsection 37 (5).

[1996, c. 2, s. 25]

39. (1) **Directions from court** — If an incapable person has a guardian of property or an attorney under a continuing power of attorney, the court may give directions on any question arising in the management of the property.

(2) **Form of request** — A request for directions shall be made,

(a) on application, if no guardian of property has been appointed under section 22 or 27; or

(b) on motion in the proceeding in which the guardian was appointed, if a guardian of property has been appointed under section 22 or 27.

(3) **Applicant; moving party** — An application or motion under this section may be made by the incapable person's guardian of property, attorney under a continuing power of attorney, dependant, guardian of the person or attorney under a power of attorney for personal care, by the Public Guardian and Trustee, or by any other person with leave of the court.

(4) **Order** — The court may by order give such directions as it considers to be for the benefit of the person and his or her dependants and consistent with this Act.

(5) **Variation of order** — The court may, on motion by a person referred to in subsection (3), vary the order.

[1996, c. 2, s. 26]

40. (1) **Compensation** — A guardian of property or attorney under a continuing power of attorney may take annual compensation from the property in accordance with the prescribed fee scale.

(2) **Same** — The compensation may be taken monthly, quarterly or annually.

(3) **Same** — The guardian or attorney may take an amount of compensation greater than the prescribed fee scale allows,

(a) in the case where the Public Guardian and Trustee is not the guardian or attorney, if consent in writing is given by the Public Guardian and Trustee and by the incapable person's guardian of the person or attorney under a power of attorney for personal care, if any; or

(b) in the case where the Public Guardian and Trustee is the guardian or attorney, if the court approves.

(4) **Effect of power of attorney** — Subsections (1) to (3) are subject to provisions respecting compensation contained in a continuing power of attorney executed by the incapable person if,

(a) the compensation is taken by the attorney under the power of attorney; or

(b) the compensation is taken by a guardian of property who was the incapable person's attorney under the power of attorney.

[1996, c. 2, s. 27]

41. [Repealed, 1996, c. 2, s. 28]

42. (1) **Passing of accounts** — The court may, on application, order that all or a specified part of the accounts of an attorney or guardian of property be passed.

(2) **Attorney's accounts** — An attorney, the grantor or any of the persons listed in subsection (4) may apply to pass the attorney's accounts.

(3) **Guardian's accounts** — A guardian of property, the incapable person or any of the persons listed in subsection (4) may apply to pass the accounts of the guardian of property.

(4) **Others entitled to apply** — The following persons may also apply:

1. The grantor's or incapable person's guardian of the person or attorney for personal care.
2. A dependant of the grantor or incapable person.
3. The Public Guardian and Trustee.
4. The Children's Lawyer.
5. A judgment creditor of the grantor or incapable person.
6. Any other person, with leave of the court.

(5) **P.G.T. a party** — If the Public Guardian and Trustee is the applicant or the respondent, the court shall grant the application, unless it is satisfied that the application is frivolous or vexatious.

(6) **Filing of accounts** — The accounts shall be filed in the court office and the procedure in the passing of the accounts is the same and has the same effect as in the passing of executors' and administrators' accounts.

(7) **Powers of court** — In an application for the passing of an attorney's accounts the court may, on motion or on its own initiative,

(a) direct the Public Guardian and Trustee to bring an application for guardianship of property;

(b) suspend the power of attorney pending the determination of the application;

(c) appoint the Public Guardian and Trustee or another person to act as guardian of property pending the determination of the application;

(d) order an assessment of the grantor of the power of attorney under section 79 to determine his or her capacity; or

(e) order that the power of attorney be terminated.

(8) **Same** — In an application for the passing of the accounts of a guardian of property the court may, on motion or on its own initiative,

(a) adjust the guardian's compensation in accordance with the value of the services performed;

(b) suspend the guardianship pending the determination of the application;

(c) appoint the Public Guardian and Trustee or another person to act as guardian of property pending the determination of the application; or

(d) order that the guardianship be terminated.

[1994, c. 27, s. 43]

Part II

The Person

General

43. **Application of Part** — This Part applies to decisions on behalf of persons who are at least sixteen years old.

44. **Age** — To exercise a power of decision under this Part on behalf of another person, a person must be at least sixteen years old.

45. **Incapacity for personal care** — A person is incapable of personal care if the person is not able to understand information that is relevant to making a decision concerning his or her own health care, nutrition, shelter, clothing, hygiene or safety, or is not able to appreciate the reasonably foreseeable consequences of a decision or lack of decision.

[1996, c. 2, s. 29]

Powers of Attorney for Personal Care

46. (1) **Power of attorney for personal care** — A person may give a written power of attorney for personal care, authorizing the person or persons named as attorneys to make, on the grantor's behalf, decisions concerning the grantor's personal care.

(2) **P.G.T. may be attorney** — The power of attorney may name the Public Guardian and Trustee as attorney if his or her consent in writing is obtained before the power of attorney is executed.

(3) **Prohibition** — A person may not act as an attorney under a power of attorney for personal care, unless the person is the grantor's spouse, partner or relative, if the person,

(a) provides health care to the grantor for compensation; or

(b) provides residential, social, training or support services to the grantor for compensation.

(4) **Two or more attorneys** — If the power of attorney names two or more persons as attorneys, the attorneys shall act jointly, unless the power of attorney provides otherwise.

(5) **Death, etc., of joint attorney** — If two or more attorneys act jointly under the power of attorney and one of them dies, becomes incapable of personal care or resigns, the remaining attorney or attorneys are authorized to act, unless the power of attorney provides otherwise.

(6) **Conditions and restrictions** — The power of attorney is subject to this Part, and to the conditions and restrictions that are contained in the power of attorney and are consistent with this Act.

(7) **Instructions** — The power of attorney may contain instructions with respect to the decisions the attorney is authorized to make.

(8) **Form** — The power of attorney need not be in any particular form.

(9) **Same** — The power of attorney may be in the prescribed form.

(10) [Repealed, 1996, c. 2, s. 30]

(11) [Repealed, 1996, c. 2, s. 30]

(12) [Repealed, 1996, c. 2, s. 30]

[1996, c. 2, s. 30]

47. (1) **Capacity to give power of attorney for personal care** — A person is capable of giving a power of attorney for personal care if the person,

(a) has the ability to understand whether the proposed attorney has a genuine concern for the person's welfare; and

(b) appreciates that the person may need to have the proposed attorney make decisions for the person.

(2) **Validity** — A power of attorney for personal care is valid if, at the time it was executed, the grantor was capable of giving it even if the grantor is incapable of personal care.

(3) **Capacity to revoke** — A person is capable of revoking a power of attorney for personal care if he or she is capable of giving one.

(4) **Capacity to give instructions** — Instructions contained in a power of attorney for personal care with respect to a decision the attorney is authorized to make are valid if, at the time the power of attorney was executed, the grantor had the capacity to make the decision.

48. (1) **Execution** — A power of attorney for personal care shall be executed in the presence of two witnesses, each of whom shall sign the power of attorney as witness.

(2) **Persons who shall not be witnesses** — The persons referred to in subsection 10 (2) shall not be witnesses.

(3) [Repealed, 1996, c. 2, s. 31]

(4) **Non-compliance** — A power of attorney for personal care that does not comply with subsections (1) and (2) is not effective, but the court may, on any person's application, declare the power of attorney for personal care to be effective if the court is satisfied that it is in the grantor's interests to do so.

[1996, c. 2, s. 31]

49. (1) **When power of attorney effective** — A provision in a power of attorney for personal care that confers authority to make a decision concerning the grantor's personal care is effective to authorize the attorney to make the decision if,

(a) the *Health Care Consent Act, 1996* applies to the decision and that Act authorizes the attorney to make the decision; or

(b) the *Health Care Consent Act, 1996* does not apply to the decision and the attorney has reasonable grounds to believe that the grantor is incapable of making the decision, subject to any condition in the power of attorney that prevents the attorney from making the decision unless the fact that the grantor is incapable of personal care has been confirmed.

(2) **Method for confirmation** — A power of attorney that contains a condition described in clause (1) (b) may specify the method for confirming whether the grantor is incapable of personal care and, if no method is specified, that fact may be confirmed by notice to the attorney in the prescribed form from an assessor stating that the assessor has performed an assessment of the grantor's capacity and has found that the grantor is incapable of personal care.

(3) **Instructions to assessor** — A power of attorney that contains a condition described in clause (1) (b) may require an assessor who performs an assessment of the grantor's capacity to consider factors described in the power of attorney.

(4) **Application** — This section applies to powers of attorney given before or after the coming into force of section 32 of the *Advocacy, Consent and Substitute Decisions Statute Law Amendment Act, 1996*.

[1996, c. 2, s. 32]

50. (1) **Special provisions, use of force** — A power of attorney for personal care may contain one or more of the provisions described in subsection (2), but a provision is not effective unless both of the following circumstances exist:

1. At the time the power of attorney was executed or within 30 days afterwards, the grantor made a statement in the prescribed form indicating that he or she understood the effect of the provision and of subsection (4).
2. Within 30 days after the power of attorney was executed, an assessor made a statement in the prescribed form,
   i. indicating that, after the power of attorney was executed, the assessor performed an assessment of the grantor's capacity,
   ii. stating the assessor's opinion that, at the time of the assessment, the grantor was capable of personal care and was capable of understanding the effect of the provision and of subsection (4), and
   iii. setting out the facts on which the opinion is based.

(2) **List of provisions —** The provisions referred to in subsection (1) are:

1. A provision that authorizes the attorney and other persons under the direction of the attorney to use force that is necessary and reasonable in the circumstances,
   i. to determine whether the grantor is incapable of making a decision to which the *Health Care Consent Act, 1996* applies,
   ii. to confirm, in accordance with subsection 49 (2), whether the grantor is incapable of personal care, if the power of attorney contains a condition described in clause 49 (1) (b), or
   iii. to obtain an assessment of the grantor's capacity by an assessor in any other circumstances described in the power of attorney.
2. A provision that authorizes the attorney and other persons under the direction of the attorney to use force that is necessary and reasonable in the circumstances to take the grantor to any place for care or treatment, to admit the grantor to that place and to detain and restrain the grantor in that place during the care or treatment.
3. A provision that waives the grantor's right to apply to the Consent and Capacity Board under sections 32, 50 and 65 of the *Health Care Consent Act, 1996* for a review of a finding of incapacity that applies to a decision to which that Act applies.

(3) **Conditions and restrictions —** A provision described in subsection (2) that is contained in a power of attorney for personal care is subject to any conditions and restrictions contained in the power of attorney that are consistent with this Act.

(4) **Revocation —** If a provision described in subsection (2) is contained in a power of attorney for personal care and both of the circumstances described in subsection (1) exist, the power of attorney may be revoked only if, within 30 days before the revocation is executed, an assessor performed an assessment of the grantor's capacity and made a statement in the prescribed form,

(a) indicating that, on a date specified in the statement, the assessor performed an assessment of the grantor's capacity;

(b) stating the assessor's opinion that, at the time of the assessment, the grantor was capable of personal care; and

(c) setting out the facts on which the opinion is based.

(5) **Use of force** — No action lies against an attorney, a police services board, a police officer or any other person arising from the use of force that is authorized by a provision described in subsection (2) that is effective under subsection (1).

[Note: S.O. 1996, c. 2, s. 32(2) provides that if a power of attorney for personal care was accepted for registration under section 50 before March 29, 1996, the power of attorney shall be deemed to contain all the provisions described in subs. 50 (2), as re-enacted by S.O. 1996, c. 2, subs. 32 (1), and both of the circumstances described in subs. 50 (1), as re-enacted by S.O. 1996, c. 2, subs. 32 (1), shall be deemed to exist in respect of each provision.]

[1996, c. 2, s. 32]

51. (1) **Assessment of capacity** — The attorney under a power of attorney for personal care shall, on the request of and on behalf of the grantor, assist in arranging an assessment of the grantor's capacity by an assessor.

(2) **Limit** — Subsection (1) does not require an attorney to assist in arranging an assessment if an assessment has been performed in the six months before the request.

[1996, c. 2, s. 32]

52. (1) **Resignation of attorney** — An attorney under a power of attorney for personal care may resign but, if the attorney has acted under the power of attorney, the resignation is not effective until the attorney delivers a copy of the resignation to,

(a) the grantor;

(b) any other attorneys under the power of attorney;

(c) the person named by the power of attorney as a substitute for the attorney who is resigning, if the power of attorney provides for the substitution of another person; and

(d) unless the power of attorney provides otherwise, the grantor's spouse or partner and the relatives of the grantor who are known to the attorney and reside in Ontario, if the power of attorney does not provide for the substitution of another person or the substitute is not able and willing to act.

(1.1) **Exception** — Clause (1) (d) does not require a copy of the resignation to be delivered to,

(a) the grantor's spouse, if the grantor and the spouse are living separate and apart as a result of a breakdown of their relationship; or

(b) a relative of the grantor, if the grantor and the relative are related only by marriage and the grantor and his or her spouse are living separate and apart as a result of a breakdown of their relationship.

(2) **Notice to other persons** — An attorney who resigns shall make reasonable efforts to give notice of the resignation to persons with whom the attorney previously dealt on behalf of the grantor and with whom further dealings are likely to be required on behalf of the grantor.

[1996, c. 2, s. 33; 2005, c. 5, s. 65]

53. (1) **Termination** — A power of attorney for personal care is terminated,

(a) when the attorney dies, becomes incapable of personal care or resigns, unless,

(i) another attorney is authorized to act under subsection 46 (5), or

(ii) the power provides for the substitution of another person and that person is able and willing to act;

(b) when the court appoints a guardian for the grantor under section 55;

(c) when the grantor executes a new power of attorney for personal care, unless the grantor provides that there shall be multiple powers of attorney for personal care;

(d) when the power of attorney is revoked.

(2) **Execution of revocation** — A revocation shall be in writing and shall be executed in the same way as a power of attorney for personal care.

(3) [Repealed, 1996, c. 2, s. 34]

[1996, c. 2, s. 34]

54. [Repealed, 1996, c. 2, s. 35]

Court-Appointed Guardians of the Person

55. (1) **Court appointment of guardian of the person** — The court may, on any person's application, appoint a guardian of the person for a person who is incapable of personal care and, as a result, needs decisions to be made on his or her behalf by a person who is authorized to do so.

(2) **Prohibition** — The court shall not appoint a guardian if it is satisfied that the need for decisions to be made will be met by an alternative course of action that,

(a) does not require the court to find the person to be incapable of personal care; and

(b) is less restrictive of the person's decision-making rights than the appointment of a guardian.

56. **Procedure, court-ordered appointments** — Part III (Procedure) applies to applications to appoint guardians of the person.

57. (1) **Appointment criteria** — A person who provides health care or residential, social, training or support services to an incapable person for compensation shall not be appointed under section 55 as his or her guardian of the person.

(2) **Exception** — Subsection (1) does not apply to the incapable person's spouse, partner or relative or to the following persons:

1. The incapable person's guardian of property.
2. The attorney for personal care.
3. The attorney under a continuing power of attorney for property.

(2.1) **Exception** — Subsection (1) does not apply to a person if the court is satisfied that there is no other suitable person who is available and willing to be appointed.

(2.2) **P.G.T.** — The court shall not appoint the Public Guardian and Trustee as a guardian under section 55 unless the application proposes the Public Guardian and Trustee as guardian and there is no other suitable person who is available and willing to be appointed.

(3) **Criteria** — Except in the case of an application that is being dealt with under section 77 (summary disposition), the court shall consider,

(a) whether the proposed guardian is the attorney under a continuing power of attorney for property;

(b) the incapable person's current wishes, if they can be ascertained; and

(c) the closeness of the applicant's personal relationship to the incapable person.

(4) **Two or more guardians** — The court may, with their consent, appoint two or more persons as joint guardians of the person or may appoint each of them as guardian in respect of a specified period.

[1996, c. 2, s. 36]

58. (1) **Finding of incapacity** — An order appointing a guardian of the person shall include a finding that the person is incapable in respect of the functions referred to in section 45, or in respect of some of them, and, as a result, needs decisions to be made on his or her behalf by a person who is authorized to do so.

(2) **Contents of order** — An order appointing a guardian may,

(a) make the appointment for a limited period as the court considers appropriate;

(b) impose such other conditions on the appointment as the court considers appropriate.

(3) **Full or partial guardianship** — The order shall specify whether the guardianship is full or partial.

59. (1) **Full guardianship** — The court may make an order for full guardianship of the person only if the court finds that the person is incapable in respect of all the functions referred to in section 45.

(2) **Powers of guardian** — Under an order for full guardianship, the guardian may,

(a) exercise custodial power over the person under guardianship, determine his or her living arrangements and provide for his or her shelter and safety;

(b) be the person's litigation guardian, except in respect of litigation that relates to the person's property or to the guardian's status or powers;

(c) settle claims and commence and settle proceedings on the person's behalf, except claims and proceedings that relate to the person's property or to the guardian's status or powers;

(d) have access to personal information, including health information and records, to which the person could have access if capable, and consent to the release of that information to another person, except for the purposes of litigation that relates to the person's property or to the guardian's status or powers;

(e) on behalf of the person, make any decision to which the *Health Care Consent Act, 1996* applies;

(e.1) make decisions about the person's health care, nutrition and hygiene;

(f) make decisions about the person's employment, education, training, clothing and recreation and about any social services provided to the person; and

(g) exercise the other powers and perform the other duties that are specified in the order.

(3) **Power to apprehend person —** If the guardian has custodial power over the person and the court is satisfied that it may be necessary to apprehend him or her, the court may in its order authorize the guardian to do so; in that case the guardian may, with the assistance of a police officer, enter the premises specified in the order, between 9 a.m. and 4 p.m. or during the hours specified in the order, and search for and remove the person, using such force as may be necessary.

(4) **Matters excluded unless expressly stated —** Unless the order expressly provides otherwise, the guardian does not have power,

(a) [Repealed, 1996, c. 2, s. 37]

(b) to change existing arrangements in respect of custody of or access to a child, or to give consent on the person's behalf to the adoption of a child.

(5) **Same —** If the order provides that the guardian has a power referred to in subsection (4), the order may specify that the power may be exercised from time to time as the need arises.

[1996, c. 2, s. 37]

60. (1) **Partial guardianship —** The court may make an order for partial guardianship of the person for an incapable person if it finds that he or she is incapable in respect of some but not all of the functions referred to in section 45.

(2) **Same —** The order shall specify in respect of which functions the person is found to be incapable.

(3) **Powers of guardian** — Under an order for partial guardianship, the guardian may exercise those of the powers set out in subsections 59 (2), (3), (4) and (5) that are specified in the order.

[1996, c. 2, s. 38]

61. (1) **Variation or substitution of appointment order** — The court may vary an order appointing a guardian of the person under section 55 or substitute another person as guardian, on motion in the proceeding in which the guardian was appointed.

(2) **Who may make motion** — A motion under subsection (1) may be made by the guardian, the applicant in the proceeding in which the guardian was appointed, or any person who was entitled under section 69 to be served with notice of that proceeding.

(3) **Motion to vary** — Subsections 69 (4) to (9) and section 77 apply, with necessary modifications, to a motion to vary an order.

(4) **Motion to substitute** — Subsection 69 (3), subsections 69 (5) to (9), subsection 70 (2) and section 77 apply, with necessary modifications, to a motion to substitute another person as guardian.

[1996, c. 2, s. 39]

62. (1) **Serious adverse effects** — Serious illness or injury, or deprivation of liberty or personal security, are serious adverse effects for the purposes of this section.

(2) **Duty to investigate** — The Public Guardian and Trustee shall investigate any allegation that a person is incapable of personal care and that serious adverse effects are occurring or may occur as a result.

(3) **Extent of investigation** — In conducting an investigation under subsection (2), the Public Guardian and Trustee is not required to take any steps that, in his or her opinion, are unnecessary for the purpose of determining whether an application to the court is required under subsection (3.1).

(3.1) **Application for temporary guardianship** — If, as a result of the investigation, the Public Guardian and Trustee has reasonable grounds to believe that a person is incapable of personal care and that the prompt appointment of a temporary guardian of the person is required to prevent serious adverse effects, the Public Guardian and Trustee shall apply to the court for an order appointing him or her as the incapable person's temporary guardian of the person.

(4) **Notice** — Notice of the application shall be served on the person alleged to be incapable, and his or her attorney for personal care, if known, unless the court dispenses with notice in view of the nature and urgency of the matter.

(5) [Repealed, 1996, c. 2, s. 40]

(6) **Order appointing temporary guardian** — The court may by order appoint the Public Guardian and Trustee as temporary guardian.

(7) **Duration of appointment** — The appointment is valid for a period fixed by the court that does not exceed 90 days.

(8) **Contents of order** — The order shall set out the Public Guardian and Trustee's powers as temporary guardian and any conditions imposed on the guardianship.

(9) **Power of attorney** — The order may suspend the powers of any attorney under a power of attorney for personal care during the term of the temporary guardianship.

(9.1) **Service of order** — If the order was made without notice, it shall be served on the person as soon as possible.

(10) **Power to apprehend person** — If the Public Guardian and Trustee has custodial power over the person and the court is satisfied that it may be necessary to apprehend him or her, the court may authorize the Public Guardian and Trustee to do so; in that case the Public Guardian and Trustee may, with the assistance of a police officer, enter the premises specified in the order, between 9 a.m. and 4 p.m. or during the hours specified in the order, and search for and remove the person, using such force as may be necessary.

(11) **Termination, variation** — On motion by the Public Guardian and Trustee or by the person under guardianship, the court may terminate the guardianship, reduce or extend its term, or otherwise vary the order.

(12) **Duty if no application made** — If the Public Guardian and Trustee conducts an investigation under this section and decides not to make an application under subsection (3.1), the Public Guardian and Trustee shall, within three years,

(a) destroy all information collected during the investigation and during any previous investigations in respect of the person under this section; and

(b) notify the person who was alleged to be incapable that,

(i) an allegation was made that the person was incapable of personal care and that serious adverse effects were occurring or might occur as a result,

(ii) the Public Guardian and Trustee investigated the allegation as required by this Act and decided not to make an application for temporary guardianship, and

(iii) the Public Guardian and Trustee has destroyed all information collected during the investigation.

(13) **Exception** — Subsection (12) does not apply if, within three years after the decision is made not to make an application under subsection (3.1),

(a) another investigation is commenced in respect of the person under this section or section 27; or

(b) the Public Guardian and Trustee becomes the person's guardian of property or guardian of the person.

[1996, c. 2, s. 40]

63. (1) **Termination** — The court may terminate a guardianship created under section 55, on motion in the proceeding in which the guardian was appointed.

(2) **Who may make motion** — A motion under subsection (1) may be made by the guardian, the applicant in the proceeding in which the guardian was appointed, or any person who was entitled under section 69 to be served with notice of that proceeding.

[1996, c. 2, s. 41]

64. **Suspension** — In a motion to terminate a guardianship or temporary guardianship, the court may suspend the powers of the guardian or temporary guardian.

[1996, c. 2, s. 41]

65. **Procedure, termination** — Part III (Procedure) applies to motions to terminate guardianships of the person.

[1996, c. 2, s. 42]

Duties of Guardians of the Person and Attorneys for Personal Care

66. (1) **Duties of guardian** — The powers and duties of a guardian of the person shall be exercised and performed diligently and in good faith.

(2) **Explanation** — The guardian shall explain to the incapable person what the guardian's powers and duties are.

(2.1) **Decisions under *Health Care Consent Act, 1996*** — The guardian shall make decisions on the incapable person's behalf to which the *Health Care Consent Act, 1996* applies in accordance with that Act.

(3) **Other decisions** — The guardian shall make decisions on the incapable person's behalf to which the *Health Care Consent Act, 1996* does not apply in accordance with the following principles:

1. If the guardian knows of a wish or instruction applicable to the circumstances that the incapable person expressed while capable, the guardian shall make the decision in accordance with the wish or instruction.
2. The guardian shall use reasonable diligence in ascertaining whether there are such wishes or instructions.
3. A later wish or instruction expressed while capable prevails over an earlier wish or instruction.
4. If the guardian does not know of a wish or instruction applicable to the circumstances that the incapable person expressed while capable, or if it is impossible to make the decision in accordance with the wish or instruction, the guardian shall make the decision in the incapable person's best interests.

(4) **Best interests** — In deciding what the person's best interests are for the purpose of subsection (3), the guardian shall take into consideration,

(a) the values and beliefs that the guardian knows the person held when capable and believes the person would still act on if capable;

(b) the person's current wishes, if they can be ascertained; and

(c) the following factors:

1. Whether the guardian's decision is likely to,

i. improve the quality of the person's life,

ii. prevent the quality of the person's life from deteriorating, or

iii. reduce the extent to which, or the rate at which, the quality of the person's life is likely to deteriorate.

2. Whether the benefit the person is expected to obtain from the decision outweighs the risk of harm to the person from an alternative decision.

(4.1) **Records of decisions** — The guardian shall, in accordance with the regulations, keep records of decisions made by the guardian on the incapable person's behalf.

(5) **Participation** — The guardian shall encourage the person to participate, to the best of his or her abilities, in the guardian's decisions on his or her behalf.

(6) **Family and friends** — The guardian shall seek to foster regular personal contact between the incapable person and supportive family members and friends of the incapable person.

(7) **Consultation** — The guardian shall consult from time to time with,

(a) supportive family members and friends of the incapable person who are in regular personal contact with the incapable person; and

(b) the persons from whom the incapable person receives personal care.

(8) **Independence** — The guardian shall, as far as possible, seek to foster the person's independence.

(9) **Least restrictive course of action** — The guardian shall choose the least restrictive and intrusive course of action that is available and is appropriate in the particular case.

(10) **Confinement, restraint and monitoring devices** — The guardian shall not use confinement or monitoring devices or restrain the person physically or by means of drugs, and shall not give consent on the person's behalf to the use of confinement, monitoring devices or means of restraint, unless,

(a) the practice is essential to prevent serious bodily harm to the person or to others, or allows the person greater freedom or enjoyment;

(b) [Repealed, 1996, c. 2, s. 43]

(11) **Common law** — Nothing in this Act affects the common law duty of caregivers to restrain or confine persons when immediate action is necessary to prevent serious bodily harm to them or to others.

(12) **Electric shock as aversive conditioning** — The guardian shall not use electric shock as aversive conditioning and shall not give consent on the person's behalf to the use of electric shock as aversive conditioning unless the consent is given to a treatment in accordance with the *Health Care Consent Act, 1996*.

(13) **Research** — Nothing in this Act affects the law relating to giving or refusing consent on another person's behalf to a procedure whose primary purpose is research.

(14) **Sterilization, transplants** — Nothing in this Act affects the law relating to giving or refusing consent on another person's behalf to one of the following procedures:

1. Sterilization that is not medically necessary for the protection of the person's health.
2. The removal of regenerative or non-regenerative tissue for implantation in another person's body.

(15) **Guardianship plan** — A guardian shall act in accordance with the guardianship plan.

(16) **Amendment of plan** — If there is a guardianship plan, it may be amended from time to time with the Public Guardian and Trustee's approval.

(17) [Repealed, 1996, c. 2, s. 43]

(18) [Repealed, 1996, c. 2, s. 43]

(19) **Immunity** — No proceeding for damages shall be commenced against a guardian for anything done or omitted in good faith in connection with the guardian's powers and duties under this Act.

[1996, c. 2, s. 43]

67. Duties of attorney — Section 66, except subsections 66 (15) and (16), applies with necessary modifications to an attorney who acts under a power of attorney for personal care.

[1996, c. 2, s. 44]

68. (1) **Directions from court** — If an incapable person has a guardian of the person or an attorney under a power of attorney for personal care, the court may give directions on any question arising in the guardianship or under the power of attorney.

(2) **Form of request** — A request for directions shall be made,

(a) on application, if no guardian of the person has been appointed under section 55 or 62; or

(b) on motion in the proceeding in which the guardian was appointed, if a guardian of the person has been appointed under section 55 or 62.

(3) **Applicant; moving party** — An application or motion under this section may be made by the incapable person's guardian of the person, attorney under a power of attorney for personal care, dependant, guardian of property or attorney under a continuing power of attorney, by the Public Guardian and Trustee, or by any other person with leave of the court.

(4) **Order** — The court may by order give such directions as it considers to be for the benefit of the person and consistent with this Act.

(5) **Variation of order** — The court may, on motion by a person referred to in subsection (3), vary the order.

[1996, c. 2, s. 44]

Part III

Procedure in Guardianship Applications

69. (0.1) **Service of notice, application to terminate statutory guardianship of property** — Notice of an application to terminate a statutory guardianship of property shall be served on the following persons:

1. The statutory guardian of property.
2. The applicant's guardian of the person, if known.
3. The applicant's attorney for personal care, if known.
4. The Public Guardian and Trustee, if he or she is not the statutory guardian.

(1) **Application to appoint guardian of property** — Notice of an application to appoint a guardian of property shall be served on the following persons, together with the documents referred to in subsection 70 (1), and those referred to in section 72 if applicable:

1. The person alleged to be incapable of managing property.
2. The attorney under his or her continuing power of attorney, if known.
3. His or her guardian of the person, if known.
4. His or her attorney for personal care, if known.
5. The Public Guardian and Trustee.
6. The proposed guardian of property.

(2) **Motion to terminate guardianship of property** — Notice of a motion to terminate a guardianship of property shall be served on the following persons, together with the documents referred to in section 73 if applicable:

1. The person whose property is under guardianship.
2. His or her guardian of the person, if known.
3. His or her attorney for personal care, if known.
4. The Public Guardian and Trustee.
5. The guardian of property.

(3) **Application to appoint guardian of the person** — Notice of an application to appoint a guardian of the person shall be served on the following persons, together with the documents referred to in subsection 70 (2), and those referred to in subsection 71 (1) and section 74 if applicable:

1. The person alleged to be incapable of personal care.
2. The attorney under his or her continuing power of attorney, if known.
3. His or her guardian of property, if known.
4. His or her attorney for personal care, if known.
5. The Public Guardian and Trustee.
6. The proposed guardian of the person.

(4) **Motion to terminate guardianship of the person** — Notice of a motion to terminate a guardianship of the person shall be served on the following persons, together with the documents referred to in section 75 if applicable:

1. The person under guardianship.
2. His or her guardian of property, if known.
3. The attorney under his or her continuing power of attorney, if known.
4. The Public Guardian and Trustee.
5. The guardian of the person.

(5) **Same** — The notice and accompanying documents need not be served on the applicant or moving party.

(6) **Service on family** — The notice and accompanying documents shall also be served on all of the following persons who are known, by ordinary mail sent to the person's last known address:

1. The spouse or partner of the person who is alleged to be incapable of managing property, whose property is under guardianship, who is alleged to be incapable of personal care or who is under guardianship of the person, as the case may be.
2. The person's children who are at least 18 years old, in the case of an application or motion under Part I, or at least 16 years old, in the case of an application or motion under Part II.
3. The person's parents.
4. The person's brothers and sisters who have attained the relevant age referred to in paragraph 2.

(7) **Exception** — Subsection (6) does not require service on a person whose existence or address cannot be ascertained by the use of reasonable diligence.

(8) **Parties** — The parties to the application or motion are the applicant or moving party and the persons served under subsection (0.1), (1), (2), (3) or (4), as the case may be.

(9) **Adding parties** — Any of the following persons is entitled to be added as a party at any stage in the application or motion:

1. A person referred to in paragraph 2 or 3 of subsection (0.1), paragraph 2, 3 or 4 of subsection (1), paragraph 2 or 3 of subsection (2), paragraph 2, 3 or 4 of subsection (3) or paragraph 2 or 3 of subsection (4), as the case may be, who was not served with the notice of application or notice of motion.
2. A person referred to in subsection (6), whether or not served with the notice of application or notice of motion.

(10) [Repealed, 1996, c. 2, s. 45]

(11) [Repealed, 1996, c. 2, s. 45]

[1996, c. 2, s. 45]

70. (1) **Required document application to appoint guardian of property** — An application to appoint a guardian of property shall be accompanied by,

(a) the proposed guardian's consent;

(b) if the proposed guardian is not the Public Guardian and Trustee, a plan of management for the property, in the prescribed form; and

(c) a statement signed by the applicant,

(i) indicating that the person alleged to be incapable has been informed of the nature of the application and the right to oppose the application, and describing the manner in which the person was informed, or

(ii) if it was not possible to give the person alleged to be incapable the information referred to in subclause (i), describing why it was not possible.

(2) **Application to appoint guardian of the person** — An application to appoint a guardian of the person shall be accompanied by,

(a) the proposed guardian's consent;

(b) if the proposed guardian is not the Public Guardian and Trustee, a guardianship plan, in the prescribed form; and

(c) a statement signed by the applicant,

(i) indicating that the person alleged to be incapable has been informed of the nature of the application and the right to oppose the application, and describing the manner in which the person was informed, or

(ii) if it was not possible to give the person alleged to be incapable the information referred to in subclause (i), describing why it was not possible.

[1996, c. 2, s. 46]

71. (1) **Optional document, application to appoint guardian of the person** — An application to appoint a guardian of the person may also be accompanied by one or more statements, each made in the prescribed form by a person who knows the person alleged to be incapable and has been in personal contact with him or her during the twelve months before the notice of application was issued.

(2) **Motion to terminate guardianship of the person** — A motion to terminate a guardianship of the person may be accompanied by one or more statements, each made in the prescribed form by a person who knows the person under guardianship and has been in personal contact with him or her during the twelve months before the notice of motion was filed with the court.

[1996, c. 2, s. 47]

72. (1) **Required documents, summary disposition, application to appoint guardian of property** — If the applicant wishes an application to appoint a guardian of property to be dealt with under section 77 (summary disposition), it shall also be accompanied by two statements made in the prescribed form, one by an assessor and the other by an assessor or by a person who knows the person alleged to be incapable and has been in personal contact with him or her during the twelve months before the notice of application was issued.

(2) **Contents of statements** — Each statement shall,

(a) indicate that its maker is of the opinion that the person is incapable of managing property, and set out the facts on which the opinion is based; and

(b) indicate that its maker can expect no direct or indirect pecuniary benefit as the result of the appointment of a guardian of property.

(3) **Same** — The statement may also indicate that its maker is of the opinion that it is necessary for decisions to be made on the person's behalf by a person who is authorized to do so and, in that case, shall set out the facts on which the opinion is based.

(4) **Assessment** — A statement made by an assessor may be used for the purpose of subsection (1) only if,

(a) the statement indicates that the assessor performed an assessment of the person's capacity and specifies the date on which the assessment was performed; and

(b) the assessment was performed during the six months before the notice of application was issued.

[1996, c. 2, s. 48]

73. (1) **Required documents, summary disposition, motion to terminate guardianship of property** — If the moving party wishes a motion to terminate a guardianship of property to be dealt with under section 77 (summary disposition), it shall be accompanied by two statements made in the prescribed form, one by an assessor and the other by an assessor or by a person who knows the person whose property is under guardianship and has been in personal contact with him or her during the twelve months before the notice of motion was filed with the court.

(2) **Contents of statements** — Each statement shall,

(a) indicate that the maker of the statement is of the opinion that the person is capable of managing property, and set out the facts on which the opinion is based; and

(b) indicate that the maker of the statement can expect no direct or indirect pecuniary benefit as the result of the termination of the guardianship.

(3) **Assessment** — A statement made by an assessor may be used for the purpose of subsection (1) only if,

(a) the statement indicates that the assessor performed an assessment of the person's capacity and specifies the date on which the assessment was performed; and

(b) the assessment was performed during the six months before the notice of motion was filed with the court.

[1996, c. 2, s. 49]

74. (1) **Required documents, summary disposition, application to appoint guardian of the person** — If the applicant wishes an application to appoint a guardian of the person to be dealt with under section 77 (summary disposition), the application shall also be accompanied by two statements, each made in the prescribed form by an assessor.

(2) **Contents of statement** — Each statement shall indicate that its maker is of the opinion that the person is incapable in respect of the functions referred to in section 45 (personal care), or in respect of some of them, and shall set out the facts on which the opinion is based.

(3) **Same** — The statement may also indicate that its maker is of the opinion that the person needs decisions to be made on his or her behalf by a person who is authorized to do so and, in that case, shall set out the facts on which the opinion is based.

(4) **Same** — Each statement shall,

(a) [Repealed, 1996, c. 2, s. 50]

(b) contain an evaluation of the nature and extent of the person's incapacity, setting out the facts on which the evaluation is based.

(5) **Assessment** — A statement may be used for the purpose of subsection (1) only if,

(a) the statement indicates that the assessor performed an assessment of the person's capacity and specifies the date on which the assessment was performed; and

(b) the assessment was performed during the six months before the notice of application was issued.

[1996, c. 2, s. 50]

75. (1) **Required documents, summary disposition, motion to terminate guardianship of the person** — If the moving party wishes a motion to terminate a guardianship of the person to be dealt with under section 77 (summary disposition), the motion shall also be accompanied by two statements, each made in the prescribed form by an assessor.

(2) **Contents of statements** — Each statement shall indicate that its maker is of the opinion that the person is capable of personal care, and shall set out the facts on which the opinion is based.

(3) **Assessment** — A statement may be used for the purpose of subsection (1) only if,

(a) the statement indicates that the assessor performed an assessment of the person's capacity and specifies the date on which the assessment was performed; and

(b) the assessment was performed during the six months before the notice of motion was filed with the court.

[1996, c. 2, s. 51]

76. [Repealed, 1996, c. 2, s. 52]

77. (1) **Summary disposition** — In an application to appoint a guardian of property or guardian of the person or a motion to terminate a guardianship of property or guardianship of the person, the court may, in the circumstances described in subsection (2), make an order without anyone appearing before it and without holding a hearing.

(2) **Same** — The registrar of the court shall submit the notice of application or notice of motion, and the accompanying documents, to a judge of the court if,

(a) in the case of an application, the applicant certifies in writing that,

(i) no person has delivered a notice of appearance,

(ii) the documents required by this Part accompany the application,

(iii) in the case of an application to appoint a guardian of property, at least one of the statements referred to in section 72 indicates that its maker is of the opinion that it is necessary for decisions to be made on the person's behalf by a person who is authorized to do so, and

(iv) in the case of an application to appoint a guardian of the person, at least one of the statements referred to in section 74 indicates that its maker is of the opinion that the person needs decisions to be made on his or her behalf by a person who is authorized to do so;

(b) in the case of a motion, the moving party certifies in writing that,

(i) the documents required by this Part accompany the motion, and

(ii) every person entitled to be served with the notice of motion has filed with the court a statement indicating that they do not intend to appear at the hearing of the motion.

(3) **Order** — On considering the application or motion, the judge may,

(a) grant the relief sought;

(b) require the parties or their counsel to adduce additional evidence or make representations; or

(c) order that the application or motion proceed to a hearing or order the trial of an issue, and give such directions as the judge considers just.

[1996, c. 2, s. 53]

Part IV

Miscellaneous

78. (1) **Right to refuse assessment** — An assessor shall not perform an assessment of a person's capacity if the person refuses to be assessed.

(2) **Information to be provided** — Before performing an assessment of capacity, the assessor shall explain to the person to be assessed,

(a) the purpose of the assessment;

(b) the significance and effect of a finding of capacity or incapacity; and

(c) the person's right to refuse to be assessed.

(3) **Application** — Subsections (1) and (2) do not apply to an assessment if,

(a) the assessment was ordered by the court under section 79; or

(b) a power of attorney for personal care contains a provision that authorizes the use of force to permit the assessment and the provision is effective under subsection 50 (1).

(4) **Use of prescribed form** — An assessor who performs an assessment of a person's capacity shall use the prescribed form in performing the assessment.

(5) **Notice of findings** — An assessor who performs an assessment of a person's capacity shall give the person written notice of the assessor's findings.

[1996, c. 2, s. 54]

79. (1) **Order for assessment** — If a person's capacity is in issue in a proceeding under this Act and the court is satisfied that there are reasonable grounds to believe that the person is incapable, the court may, on motion or on its own initiative, order that the person be assessed by one or more assessors named in the order, for the purpose of giving an opinion as to the person's capacity.

(2) **Same** — The order may require the person,

(a) to submit to the assessment;

(b) to permit entry to his or her home for the purpose of the assessment;

(c) to attend at such other places and at such times as are specified in the order.

(3) **Place of assessment** — The order shall specify the place or places where the assessment is to be performed.

(4) **Same** — If possible, the assessment shall be performed in the person's home.

(5) **Health facility** — An order that specifies a health facility as the place where the assessment is to be performed authorizes the person's admission to the facility for the purpose of the assessment.

80. (1) **Restraining order** — When an order for an assessment has been made, the court may, on motion, make an order restraining a person other than the one whose capacity is in issue from hindering or obstructing the assessment.

(2) [Repealed, 1996, c. 2, s. 55]

(3) **Notice to person** — The party moving for the restraining order shall serve notice of the motion on the person against whom the order is sought.

[1996, c. 2, s. 55]

81. (1) **Order for enforcement of assessment order** — When an order for an assessment has been made, the court may, on motion, order the Public Guardian and Trustee, together with a police officer, to apprehend the person whose capacity is in issue, take him or her into custody and bring him or her to a specified place to be assessed there, if the court is satisfied that,

(a) the assessor named in the first order has made all efforts that are reasonable in the circumstances to assess the person;

(b) the assessor was prevented from assessing the person by the actions of the person or of others;

(c) a restraining order is not appropriate in the circumstances, or has already been used without success; and

(d) there is no less intrusive means of permitting the assessment to be performed than an order under this subsection.

(2) [Repealed, 1996, c. 2, s. 56]

(3) **Duration of order** — The order is valid for seven days.

(4) **Execution of order** — The Public Guardian and Trustee and a police officer may enter the place specified in the order, between 9 a.m. and 4 p.m. or during the hours specified in the order, and may search for and remove the person, using such force as may be necessary.

(5) **Health facility** — An order under subsection (1) that specifies a health facility as the place where the assessment is to be conducted authorizes the person's admission to the facility and his or her detention there, for the purpose of the assessment.

(6) **Restrictions** — The person shall not be held in custody longer than is necessary for the purpose of the assessment, and in any case not for a period exceeding seventy-two hours, and while in custody shall not be confined in a manner that exceeds what is necessary for the purpose of the assessment.

[1996, c. 2, s. 56]

82. (1) **P.G.T.'s powers of entry** — The Public Guardian and Trustee may exercise a right of entry conferred by this section only for the purpose of an investigation required by section 27 or 62.

(2) **Entry to certain premises** — The Public Guardian and Trustee is entitled to enter a facility or controlled-access residence, without a warrant and at any time that is reasonable in the circumstances, if he or she has reasonable grounds to believe that,

(a) the person who is alleged to be incapable is in the premises; and

(b) a meeting with the person is necessary for the purposes of the investigation.

(3) **Controlled-access residences** — The right to enter a controlled-access residence under subsection (2) applies only to the common areas of the premises, including the entryways, hallways, elevators and stairs, and the Public Guardian and Trustee may enter a private dwelling unit in the controlled-access residence without the consent or acquiescence of the occupier only if authorized under subsection (4) or (8).

(4) **Warrant for entry** — A justice of the peace may issue a warrant to the Public Guardian and Trustee for entry to premises if the justice of the peace is satisfied that the person who is alleged to be incapable is in the premises and,

(a) the Public Guardian and Trustee has been prevented from exercising a right of entry to the premises under subsection (2); or

(b) a meeting with the person is necessary for the purposes of the investigation.

(5) **Authority conferred by warrant** — The warrant authorizes the Public Guardian and Trustee to enter the premises specified in the warrant, between 8 a.m. and 8 p.m. or during the hours specified in the warrant, and to remain there for a reasonable time.

(6) **Duration** — A warrant is valid for seven days.

(7) **Police assistance** — The Public Guardian and Trustee may call on a police officer for assistance in executing it.

(8) **Other entry without warrant** — The Public Guardian and Trustee is entitled to enter premises other than premises that he or she is entitled to enter under subsection (2), without a warrant and between 8 a.m. and 8 p.m., if he or she has reasonable grounds to believe that,

(a) the person who is alleged to be incapable is in the premises;

(b) a meeting with the person is necessary for the purposes of the investigation; and

(c) it is impractical, by reason of the location of the premises, to obtain a warrant under subsection (4).

(9) **Meeting** — When the Public Guardian and Trustee exercises a right of entry under this section, he or she is entitled to meet with the person who is alleged to be incapable without interference and in private.

(10) **Obligation to leave premises** — The Public Guardian and Trustee must leave the premises promptly if the person who is alleged to be incapable indicates that he or she does not want to meet with the Public Guardian and Trustee.

(11) **Identification** — A person exercising a right of entry under this section shall, on request, present identification.

(12) **References to P.G.T.** — A reference in this section to the Public Guardian and Trustee includes any person he or she designates for the purpose of this section.

83. (1) **P.G.T.'s access to records** — The Public Guardian and Trustee is entitled to have access, for the purpose of an investigation required by section 27 or 62, to any record relating to the person who is alleged to be incapable that is in the custody or control of,

(a) the person's guardian of property or guardian of the person;

(b) the person's attorney under a power of attorney that confers authority in respect of the person's property or under a power of attorney for personal care;

(c) a member of the College of a health profession as defined in the *Regulated Health Professions Act, 1991*;

(d) a facility;

(e) a person who operates a controlled-access residence;

(f) a bank, loan or trust corporation, credit union or other financial institution;

(g) an administrator of a pension fund;

(h) a real estate broker or agent; or

(i) any other person or class of persons designated by the regulations.

(2) **Exception, solicitor-client privilege** — Subsection (1) does not override any solicitor-client privilege to which a record is subject.

(3) **Exception, law enforcement** — The Public Guardian and Trustee is not entitled to have access to a record or part of a record whose disclosure could reasonably be expected to produce one of the results described in subsection 14 (1) of the *Freedom of Information and Protection of Privacy Act.*

(4) **Rules re access to record** — The following rules apply when the Public Guardian and Trustee is entitled to have access to a record:

1. The Public Guardian and Trustee is entitled to be given access to the record no later than four business days after requesting access.
2. The Public Guardian and Trustee is not entitled to have access to any information in the record that is personal information, as defined in the *Freedom of Information and Protection of Privacy Act*, relating to an individual other than the person who is alleged to be incapable.
3. The Public Guardian and Trustee is not entitled to make a search among the records kept by the person who has custody or control of the record.
4. The Public Guardian and Trustee is entitled to make copies or extracts from the record in any manner that does not damage the record.
5. At the Public Guardian and Trustee's request and within a reasonable time, the person who has custody or control of a record shall provide the Public Guardian and Trustee with photocopies of all or part of the record. The Public Guardian and Trustee shall pay the prescribed amount for any photocopies in excess of twenty pages.
6. If the person who has custody or control of records consents, the Public Guardian and Trustee may remove records for copying.
7. The Public Guardian and Trustee shall give a receipt for the records being removed and shall return them within two business days.
8. Records needed for the current care of the person who is alleged to be incapable shall not be removed.

(5) **Warrant for access to record** — A justice of the peace may issue a warrant for access to a record to the Public Guardian and Trustee if satisfied that,

(a) the Public Guardian and Trustee is entitled to access to the record under this section; and

(b) the Public Guardian and Trustee has been refused access to the record, or has been refused copies and has been refused permission to remove the record for copying.

(6) **Authority conferred by warrant** — The warrant authorizes the Public Guardian and Trustee to,

(a) inspect the record specified in the warrant, between 9 a.m. and 4 p.m. or during the hours specified in the warrant, subject to paragraph 2 of subsection (4);

(b) make copies or extracts from the record in any manner that does not damage the record; and

(c) remove the record, subject to paragraphs 7 and 8 of subsection (4).

(7) **Duration of warrant** — The warrant is valid for seven days.

(8) **Execution** — The Public Guardian and Trustee may call on a police officer for assistance in executing the warrant.

(9) **Clinical record under *Mental Health Act*** — [Repealed, 2004, c. 3, Sched. A, s. 97]

(10) **Other acts** — This section prevails over any other Act.

(11) **References to P.G.T.** — A reference in this section to the Public Guardian and Trustee includes any person he or she designates for the purpose of this section.

[1996, c. 2, s. 57; 2004, c. 3, Sched. A, S. 97]

84. **Statements as evidence** — For the purposes of this Act, a statement in the prescribed form that purports to be signed by its maker is admissible in evidence without proof of his or her signature, office or professional qualifications.

85. (1) **Conflict of laws, formalities** — As regards the manner and formalities of executing a continuing power of attorney or power of attorney for personal care, the power of attorney is valid if at the time of its execution it complied with the internal law of the place where,

(a) the power of attorney was executed;

(b) the grantor was then domiciled; or

(c) the grantor then had his or her habitual residence.

(2) **"Internal law"** — For the purpose of subsection (1), "internal law", in relation to any place, excludes the choice of law rules of that place.

(3) **Revocation** — Subsections (1) and (2) apply with necessary modifications to the revocation of a continuing power of attorney or power of attorney for personal care.

(4) **Legal requirements outside Ontario** — If, under this section or otherwise, a law in force outside Ontario is to be applied in relation to a continuing power of attorney or a power of attorney for personal care, the following requirements of that law shall be treated, despite any rule of that law to the contrary, as formal requirements only:

1. Any requirement that special formalities be observed by grantors answering a particular description.
2. Any requirement that witnesses to the execution of the power of attorney possess certain qualifications.

(5) **Alteration in law** — In determining for the purposes of this section whether or not the execution of a continuing power of attorney or power of attorney for personal care conforms to a particular law, regard shall be had to the formal requirements of that law at the time the power of attorney was executed, but account shall be taken of an alteration of law affecting powers of attorney executed at that time if the alteration enables the power of attorney to be treated as properly executed.

(6) **Application** — This section applies to a continuing power of attorney or power of attorney for personal care executed either in or outside Ontario.

86. (1) **Foreign orders** — In this section,

"foreign order" means an order made by a court outside Ontario that appoints, for a person who is sixteen years of age or older, a person having duties comparable to those of a guardian of property or guardian of the person.

(2) **Resealing** — Any person may apply to the court for an order resealing a foreign order that was made in a province or territory of Canada or in a prescribed jurisdiction.

(3) **Certificate from foreign court** — An order resealing a foreign order shall not be made unless the applicant files with the court,

(a) a copy of the foreign order bearing the seal of the court that made it or a copy of the foreign order certified by the registrar, clerk or other officer of the court that made it; and

(b) a certificate signed by the registrar, clerk or other officer of the court that made the foreign order stating that the order is unrevoked and of full effect.

(4) **Effect of resealing** — A foreign order that has been resealed,

(a) has the same effect in Ontario as if it were an order under this Act appointing a guardian of property or guardian of the person, as the case may be;

(b) is subject in Ontario to any condition imposed by the court that the court may impose under this Act on an order appointing a guardian of property or guardian of the person, as the case may be; and

(c) is subject in Ontario to the provisions of this Act respecting guardians of property or guardians of the person, as the case may be.

87. (1) **Volunteers** — The Public Guardian and Trustee may appoint volunteers to provide advice and assistance under this Act.

(2) **Protection from liability** — No proceeding for damages shall be instituted against a volunteer appointed under this section for any act done in good faith in the execution or intended execution of the volunteer's powers and duties or for any alleged neglect or default in the execution in good faith of the volunteer's powers or duties.

(3) **Same** — Despite subsections 5 (2) and (4) of the *Proceedings Against the Crown Act*, subsection (2) does not relieve the Crown of any liability to which the Crown would otherwise be subject.

[1996, c. 2, s. 58]

88. **Mediation** — The Public Guardian and Trustee may mediate,

(a) a dispute that arises between a person's guardian of property or attorney under a continuing power of attorney and the person's guardian of the person or attorney for personal care, if the dispute arises in the performance of their duties;

(b) a dispute that arises between joint attorneys under a person's continuing power of attorney or power of attorney for personal care, if the dispute arises in the performance of their duties; or

(c) a dispute that arises between joint guardians of property or joint guardians of the person, if the dispute arises in the performance of their duties.

[1996, c. 2, s. 58]

89. (1) **Offence: obstruction** — No person shall hinder or obstruct,

(a) a person who is conducting an assessment ordered under section 79, or is seeking to do so;

(b) a person who is exercising a power of entry conferred by subsection 82 (2), or is seeking to do so.

(2) **Penalty** — A person who contravenes subsection (1) is guilty of an offence and is liable, on conviction, to a fine not exceeding $5,000.

(3) **Exception** — Subsection (1) does not apply to,

(a) the person who is the subject of the order for assessment; or

(b) the person in respect of whom the power of entry is being exercised or is sought to be exercised.

(4) **Offence: restraining order** — A person who contravenes a restraining order made under subsection 80 (1) is guilty of an offence and is liable, on conviction, to a fine not exceeding $5,000.

(5) **Offence: false statement** — No person shall, in a statement made in a prescribed form, assert something that he or she knows to be untrue or profess an opinion that he or she does not hold.

(6) **Penalty** — A person who contravenes subsection (5) is guilty of an offence and is liable, on conviction, to a fine not exceeding $10,000.

(7) **Offence: personal information** — A person who obtains personal information under the authority of a regulation made under subclause 90 (1) (e.4) (ii) and who contravenes a regulation made under clause 90 (1) (e.5) is guilty of an offence and is liable, on conviction, to a fine not exceeding $10,000.

[1996, c. 2, s. 59]

90. (1) **Regulations** — The Lieutenant Governor in Council may make regulations,

(a) prescribing forms;

(b) prescribing facilities for the purpose of the definition of "facility" in subsection 1 (1);

(c) prescribing a fee scale for the compensation of guardians of property and attorneys under continuing powers of attorney, including annual percentage charges on revenue and on capital;

(c.1) prescribing circumstances in which a person's guardian of the person or attorney under a power of attorney for personal care may be compensated from the person's property for services performed as guardian or attorney, and prescribing the amount of the compensation or a method for determining the amount of the compensation;

(c.2) governing the keeping of accounts and other records by attorneys under continuing powers of attorney, attorneys under powers of attorney for personal care, guardians of property and guardians of the person, and requiring them to provide information from the records to persons specified by the regulations;

(c.3) establishing a public record of information relating to guardians of property, guardians of the person, attorneys under continuing powers of attorney or attorneys under powers of attorney for personal care, prescribing the contents of the record, governing the maintenance of the record, requiring persons to provide information for the purpose of the record and governing the disclosure of information from the record;

(d) designating classes of persons, including persons who have successfully completed prescribed courses of training, as being qualified to do assessments of capacity or specific types of assessments of capacity;

(e) prescribing courses of training for assessors;

(e.1) prescribing standards for the performance of assessments of capacity by assessors;

(e.2) regulating the fees that may be charged by assessors;

(e.3) for the purpose of sections 38 and 39 of the *Freedom of Information and Protection of Privacy Act*, authorizing the Public Guardian and Trustee or an institution that has responsibilities related to assessments of capacity to collect personal information, directly or indirectly, for a purpose relating to this Act;

(e.4) authorizing a member of a College as defined in the *Regulated Health Professions Act, 1991* or a person who provides health care or residential, social, training or support services, despite any other Act or the regulations under any other Act, to disclose personal information about a person,

(i) to an assessor, if the information is relevant to an assessment of capacity being performed by the assessor,

(ii) to a person who makes a statement in the prescribed form indicating that the person has made or intends to make an application to appoint a guardian of property or guardian of the person, if the information is relevant to the application, or

(iii) to the Public Guardian and Trustee, if the information is relevant to the making of an allegation described in subsection 27 (2) or 62 (2) or to an investigation being conducted under section 27 or 62;

(e.5) governing the use, disclosure and retention of personal information obtained under the authority of a regulation made under clause (e.4);

(e.6) designating persons or classes of persons from whom the Public Guardian and Trustee may obtain access to records under clause 83 (1) (i);

(f) prescribing an amount per page to be paid for photocopies under paragraph 5 of subsection 83 (4);

(g) prescribing jurisdictions for the purpose of section 86.

(2) **Regulations under cl. (1) (e.4) —** A regulation may not be made under clause (1) (e.4) unless a regulation has been made under clause (1) (e.5).

[1996, c. 2, s. 60; 2004, c. 3, Sched. A, s. 97]

91. **Transition —** Subject to subsections 46 (10) and (11), if a power of attorney for personal care is made in accordance with this Act before this Act comes into force, the power of attorney takes effect when this Act comes into force.

92. (In force provisions).

93. The short title of this Act is the *Substitute Decisions Act, 1992*.

SCHEDULE

Subsection 1 (1) - "Facility"

Alcoholism and Drug Addiction Research Foundation Act

Cancer Act

Charitable Institutions Act

Child and Family Services Act

Community Psychiatric Hospitals Act

Developmental Services Act

General Welfare Assistance Act

Homes for Special Care Act

Homes for the Aged and Rest Homes Act

Independent Health Facilities Act

Mental Health Act

Mental Hospitals Act

Ministry of Community and Social Services Act

Ministry of Correctional Services Act

Ministry of Health Act

Nursing Homes Act

Ontario Mental Health Foundation Act

Private Hospitals Act

Public Hospitals Act

[2001, c. 13, s. 30]

GENERAL

(O. Reg. 26/95)

1. For the purposes of subsection 40 (1) of the Act, a guardian of property or an attorney under a continuing power of attorney shall be entitled, subject to an increase under subsection 40 (3) of the Act or an adjustment pursuant to a passing of the guardian's or attorney's accounts under section 42 of the Act, to compensation of,

(a) 3 per cent on capital and income receipts;

(b) 3 per cent on capital and income disbursements; and

(c) three-fifths of 1 per cent on the annual average value of the assets as a care and management fee.

[O. Reg. 159/00, s. 1]

2. The prescribed amount per page to be paid for photocopies under paragraph 5 of subsection 83 (4) of the Act is 50 cents.

3. (1) An application to replace the Public Guardian and Trustee as statutory guardian of property by a person authorized to apply under subsection 17 (1) of the Act shall be in Form 1.

(2) A management plan required by subsection 17 (3) or clause 70 (1) (b) of the Act shall be in Form 2.

(3) A guardianship plan required by clause 70 (2) (b) of the Act shall be in Form 3.

(4) A request for an assessment of one's own or another person's capacity under subsection 16 (1) of the Act shall be in Form 4.

(5) A statement required by paragraph 1 of subsection 50 (1) of the Act shall be in Form 5.

(6) A statement in support of an application under subsection 71 (1) of the Act shall be in Form 6.

(7) A statement in support of a motion under subsection 71 (2) of the Act shall be in Form 7.

(8) A statement of a person who is not an assessor under section 72 of the Act shall be in Form 8.

(9) A statement of a person who is not an assessor under section 73 of the Act shall be in Form 9.

4. (In force provisions).

[O. Reg. 101/96, s. 1]

REGISTER

(O. Reg.99/96)

1. The Public Guardian and Trustee shall establish and maintain a register of,

(a) guardians of property; and

(b) guardians of the person.

2. The Public Guardian and Trustee shall open a file relating to a person and shall incorporate the file in the register when the first of the following events occurs:

1. The Public Guardian and Trustee becomes the person's statutory guardian of property.
2. The court appoints someone as the person's guardian of property or guardian of the person.

3. (1) A file in the register relating to a person shall contain the following information that is in the possession of the Public Guardian and Trustee:

1. The name and address of the person.
2. The name, address and telephone number of the person's guardian of property, if any, and guardian of the person, if any.
3. For each guardian referred to in paragraph 2, information concerning,
   - i. how the guardian acquired his or her authority,
   - ii. any restrictions on the guardian's authority,
   - iii. with respect to a guardian of the person, whether the authority is full or partial and, if partial, the areas of personal care decision making in which the guardian has authority, and
   - iv. the date that the guardian's authority took effect, terminated or changed.

(2) The Public Guardian and Trustee shall update the information contained in the register whenever he or she receives new information referred to in subsection (1).

4. A guardian of property or guardian of the person shall promptly notify the Public Guardian and Trustee in writing of,

(a) any change in the name, address or telephone number of the guardian; and

(b) any change in the name or address of the person.

5. When the court makes an order relating to the appointment or authority of a guardian of property or guardian of the person, the person who made the application shall promptly send the Public Guardian and Trustee a copy of the order.

6. (1) The Public Guardian and Trustee shall provide information contained in the register under section 3 to any person who requests the information, by telephone or otherwise, if the person identifies by name the person to whom the file relates.

(2) The Public Guardian and Trustee shall not provide any information in response to a request under subsection (1) except as authorized by that subsection.

7. The Public Guardian and Trustee shall inform every guardian about whom information is kept in the register about,

(a) the existence of the register;

(b) the nature of the information kept in the register, as set out in section 3; and

(c) the circumstances, as set out in section 6, under which information from the register may be released.

8. (In force provisions).

ACCOUNTS AND RECORDS OF ATTORNEYS AND GUARDIANS

(O. Reg. 100/96)

Application

1. This Regulation applies to attorneys under continuing powers of attorney, statutory guardians of property, court-appointed guardians of property, attorneys under powers of attorney for personal care and guardians of the person.

Form of Accounts and Records

2. (1) The accounts maintained by an attorney under a continuing power of attorney and a guardian of property shall include,

(a) a list of all the incapable person's assets as of the date of the first transaction by the attorney or guardian on the incapable person's behalf, including real property, money, securities, investments, motor vehicles and other personal property;

(b) an ongoing list of assets acquired and disposed of on behalf of the incapable person, including the date of and reason for the acquisition or disposition and from or to whom the asset is acquired or disposed;

(c) an ongoing list of all money received on behalf of the incapable person, including the amount, date, from whom it was received, the reason for the payment and the particulars of the account into which it was deposited;

(d) an ongoing list of all money paid out on behalf of the incapable person, including the amount, date, purpose of the payment and to whom it was paid;

(e) an ongoing list of all investments made on behalf of the incapable person, including the amount, date, interest rate and type of investment purchased or redeemed;

(f) a list of all the incapable person's liabilities as of the date of the first transaction by the attorney or guardian on the incapable person's behalf;

(g) an ongoing list of liabilities incurred and discharged on behalf of the incapable person, including the date, nature of and reason for the liability being incurred or discharged;

(h) an ongoing list of all compensation taken by the attorney or guardian, if any, including the amount, date and method of calculation;

(i) a list of the assets, and value of each, used to calculate the attorney's or guardian's care and management fee, if any.

(2) An attorney under a continuing power of attorney and a guardian of property shall also keep, together with the accounts described in subsection (1), a copy of the continuing power of attorney, certificate of statutory guardianship or court order constituting the authority of the attorney or guardian, a copy of the management plan, if any, and a copy of any court orders relating to the attorney's or guardian's authority or to the management of the incapable person's property.

3. (1) The records maintained by an attorney under a power of attorney for personal care and a guardian of the person shall include,

(a) a list of all decisions regarding health care, safety and shelter made on behalf of the incapable person, including the nature of each decision, the reason for it and the date;

(b) a copy of medical reports or other documents, if any, relating to each decision;

(c) the names of any persons consulted, including the incapable person, in respect of each decision and the date;

(d) a description of the incapable person's wishes, if any, relevant to each decision, that he or she expressed when capable and the manner in which they were expressed;

(e) a description of the incapable person's current wishes, if ascertainable and if they are relevant to the decision;

(f) for each decision taken, the attorney's or guardian's opinion on each of the factors listed in clause 66 (4) (c) of the Act.

(2) An attorney under a power of attorney for personal care and a guardian of the person shall also keep a copy of the power of attorney for personal care or court order appointing the attorney or guardian, a copy of the guardianship plan, if any, and a copy of any court orders relating to the attorney's or guardian's authority or the incapable person's care.

Confidentiality and Disclosure of Accounts and Records

4. An attorney or guardian shall not disclose any information contained in the accounts and records except,

(a) as required by section 5 or permitted by section 6;

(b) as required by a court order;

(c) as required otherwise under the Act or any other Act; or

(d) as is consistent with or related to his or her duties as attorney or guardian.

5. (1) An attorney under a continuing power of attorney shall give a copy of the accounts and records he or she keeps in accordance with section 2 to any of the following persons who requests it:

1. The incapable person.

2. The incapable person's attorney for personal care or guardian of the person.

(2) A guardian of property shall give a copy of the accounts and records he or she keeps in accordance with section 2 to any of the following persons who requests it:

1. The incapable person.
2. The incapable person's attorney for personal care or guardian of the person.
3. If the Public Guardian and Trustee is the guardian of property, the incapable person's spouse, except a spouse from whom the incapable person is living separate and apart within the meaning of the *Divorce Act* (Canada), or the incapable person's partner, child, parent, brother or sister.
4. The Public Guardian and Trustee, if he or she is not the incapable person's guardian of property or guardian of the person.

(3) An attorney for personal care shall give a copy of the records he or she keeps in accordance with section 3 to any of the following persons who requests it:

1. The incapable person.
2. The incapable person's attorney under a continuing power of attorney or guardian of property.

(4) A guardian of the person shall give a copy of the records he or she keeps in accordance with section 3 to any of the following persons who requests it:

1. The incapable person.
2. The incapable person's attorney under a continuing power of attorney or guardian of property.
3. The Public Guardian and Trustee, if he or she is not the incapable person's guardian of property or of the person.

Retention of Accounts and Records

6. (1) Every attorney and guardian shall retain the accounts and records required by this Regulation until he or she ceases to have authority and one of the following occurs:

1. The attorney or guardian obtains a release of liability from a person who has the authority to give the release.
2. Another person has acquired the authority to manage the incapable person's property or make decisions concerning the incapable person's personal care, as the case may be, and the attorney or guardian delivers the accounts or records to that person.
3. The incapable person has died and the attorney or guardian delivers the accounts or records to the incapable person's personal representative.

4. The attorney or guardian is discharged by the court on a passing of accounts under section 42 of the Act and either the time for appealing the decision relating to the discharge has expired with no appeal being taken or an appeal from the decision relating to the discharge is finally disposed of and the attorney or guardian is discharged on the appeal.
5. A court order is obtained directing the attorney or guardian to destroy or otherwise dispose of the accounts or records.

(2) Subsection (1) applies, with necessary modifications, to former attorneys and guardians.

7. (In force provisions).

CAPACITY ASSESSMENT

(O. Reg. 293/96)

1. (1) A person is qualified to do assessments of capacity if he or she,

(a) satisfies one of the conditions set out in subsection (1.1);

(b) has successfully completed a training course for assessors,

  (i) given or approved by the Attorney General, as described in section 3, or

  (ii) given by the Attorney General under Ontario Regulation 29/95 before this Regulation comes into force; and

(c) is covered by professional liability insurance of not less than $1,000,000.

(1.1) The following are the conditions mentioned in clause (1) (a):

1. Being a member of the College of Physicians and Surgeons of Ontario.
2. Being a member of the College of Psychologists of Ontario.
3. Being a member of the Ontario College of Social Workers and Social Service Workers and holding a certificate of registration for social work.
4. Being a member of the College of Occupational Therapists of Ontario.
5. Being a member of the College of Nurses of Ontario.

(1.2) Until June 30, 2000, being a member of the Ontario College of Certified Social Workers also satisfies the condition set out in paragraph 3 of subsection (1.1).

(2) Despite subsection (1), a person is qualified to do assessments of capacity until the earlier of April 2, 1997 and the termination of the person's agreement with Her Majesty the Queen in right of Ontario concerning his or her designation as an assessor if he or she,

(a) holds a valid certificate of designation as an assessor that was issued before this Regulation comes into force; and

(b) is covered by professional liability insurance of not less than $1,000,000.

[O. Reg. 238/00, s. 1]

2. An assessor shall perform assessments of capacity in accordance with the "Guidelines for Conducting Assessments of Capacity" established by the Attorney General and dated June 7, 1996.

3. The training course required under subclause 1 (1) (b) (i) shall include,

(a) instruction in the *Substitute Decisions Act, 1992*;

(b) instruction in the procedures established by the Attorney General for the conduct of assessments of capacity, as set out in the guidelines referred to in section 2;

(c) instruction in the procedures for determining if a person needs decisions to be made on his or her behalf by a person authorized to do so, as set out in the guidelines referred to in section 2; and

(d) an evaluation of the trainee's mastery of the training at the conclusion of the course.

4. The following forms provided by the Attorney General are prescribed:

1. "Form A: Statement of Assessor - Determination of Capacity/Incapacity or Certificate of Incapacity - Property" for the purpose of subsection 9 (3), subsection 16 (3), section 72 or section 73 of the Act, dated May 30, 1996.
2. "Form B: Statement of Assessor - Determination of Capacity/Incapacity - Personal Care" for the purpose of subsection 49 (2), section 74 or section 75 of the Act, dated March 29, 1996.
3. "Form C: Assessment Form" for the purpose of subsection 78 (4) of the Act, dated May 30, 1996.
4. "Form D: Statement of an Assessor Confirming Capacity" for the purpose of paragraph 2 of subsection 50 (1) of the Act, dated March 29, 1996.
5. "Form E: Statement of an Assessor Confirming Capacity to Revoke a Power of Attorney for Personal Care" for the purpose of subsection 50 (4) of the Act, dated March 29, 1996.

5. (Repeals).

6. (In force provisions).

SUMMARY OF FORMS

FORM	DESCRIPTION
Form 1	Application to Replace the Public Guardian and Trustee as Statutory Guardian of Property by a Person Authorized to Apply under subsection 17(1) 1, 2, 3, 4
Form 2	Management Plan
Form 3	Guardianship Plan
Form 4	Request for Assessment of Capacity under subsection 16(1) of the Act
Form 5	Statement Required under Paragraph 1 of section 50(1) of the Act
Form 6	Optional Statement to Appoint a Guardian of the Person under subsection 71(1) of the Act
Form 7	Optional Statement to Terminate Guardianship of the Person under subsection 71(2) of the Act
Form 8	Statement of a Person who is not an Assessor under section 72 of the Act – Appointment of Guardian of Property by Summary Disposition
Form 9	Statement of a Person who is not an Assessor under section 73 of the Act – Termination of Guardianship of Property by Summary Disposition
Form 18	Application to the Board for Review of a Finding of Incapacity to Manage One's Property under subsection 20.2 (1) of the Act

Power of Attorney for Personal Care
Continuing Power of Attorney for Property
[Note: Forms A-E available only from the Attorney General]

Form A	Statement of Assessor-Determination of Capacity / Incapacity for Certification of Incapacity – Property under subsection 16(3), section 72 or section 73 of the Act
Form B	Statement of Assessor-Determination of Capacity / Incapacity – Personal Care under subsection 49(2), section 74 or 75 of the Act

FORM	DESCRIPTION
Form C	Assessment Form under subsection 78(4) of the Act
Form D	Statement of Assessor Confirming Capacity under subsection 50(1) of the Act
Form E	Statement of Assessor Confirming Capacity to Revoke a Power of Attorney for Personal Care under subsection 50(4) of the Act

FORMS

SUBSTITUTE DECISIONS ACT, 1992 *Form 1*

APPLICATION TO REPLACE THE PUBLIC GUARDIAN AND TRUSTEE AS STATUTORY GUARDIAN OF PROPERTY BY A PERSON AUTHORIZED TO APPLY UNDER SUBSECTION 17(1)1, 2, 3, 4

(Please note: attach additional pages if more space is needed)

Name of Incapable Person (in full): ____________________

(Surname, first and initials)

Address: ____________________

____

Telephone: Residence____________________ Date of Birth: ____________________

(Day, Month, Year)

Your relationship to the incapable person is:

1. spouse * 2. partner ** 3. relative ____________________ (describe relation)

Or, you are a:

4. trust corporation

5. attorney under a continuing power of attorney made prior to the date the Certificate of Incapacity was issued and which does not give the attorney authority over all of the incapable person's property

Attachment(s) required:

if box 4 above is completed, copy of the consent of the incapable person's spouse or partner

if box 5 above is completed, copy of continuing power of attorney

*'Spouse' means a person of the opposite sex,
- (a) to whom the person is married, or
- (b) with whom a person is living in a conjugal relationship outside marriage, if the two persons:
  - (i) have cohabited for at least one year,
  - (ii) are together the parents of a child, or
  - (iii) have together entered into a cohabitation agreement under Section 53 of the *Family Law Act*.

** Two persons are 'partners' if they have lived together for at least one year and have a close personal relationship that is of primary importance in both persons' lives.

1 of 4

Form No. 236

SUBSTITUTE DECISIONS ACT, 1992 ***Form 1***

Please list any other person who is entitled to apply under subsection 17(1) *** who is known to you. Please state whether you have informed each person listed on your application for statutory guardianship and indicate if they have informed you of whether they support or oppose your appointment.

*** Any of the following persons may apply to the Public Guardian and Trustee to replace the Public Guardian and Trustee as an incapable person's statutory guardian of property:

(i) the incapable person's spouse or partner,
(ii) a relative of the incapable person,
(iii) the incapable person's attorney under a continuing power of attorney, if the power of attorney was made before the Certificate of Incapacity was issued and does not give the attorney authority over all of the incapable person's property, or
(iv) a trust corporation within the meaning of the *Loan and Trust Corporations Act*, if the incapable person's spouse or partner consents in writing to the application.

Name	Person(s) Informed Yes/No	Relationship to Incapable Person	Address and Telephone Number	Support or Oppose Application

Applicant's Statement:

1. Have you been in personal contact with the incapable person during the preceding 12-month period?

   Or, if you are a trust corporation, has the incapable person's spouse or partner been in personal contact with the incapable person during the preceding 12-month period?

   Yes No

2. Are you willing to perform all duties required of a guardian in respect of the incapable person's property and do you agree to act in accordance with the Management Plan?

   Yes No

3. To the best of my knowledge and belief, the total approximate value of the property of the incapable person is $______________. Particulars of the assets and their respective approximate value are listed on the attached Management Plan, forming part of this application.
   (If you are a trust corporation, please skip questions 4-8)

4. Is your relationship with the incapable person a friendly one?

   Yes No

5. Have you been found guilty of any offence relating to financial mismanagement under the *Criminal Code*?

2 of 4

Form No. 236

SUBSTITUTE DECISIONS ACT, 1992 ***Form 1***

Yes No

6. Are you an undischarged bankrupt?

Yes No

7. Have you been held liable in a civil proceeding relating to fraud, breach of trust or any other type of financial mismanagement?

Yes No

8. I understand that the Public Guardian and Trustee may refuse my application unless I provide a bond securing the value of the incapable person's property in a form and amount agreeable to the Public Guardian and Trustee of Ontario.

Yes No

NOTE: Attach Management Plan

SUBSECTIONS 89(5) and (6) OF THE *SUBSTITUTE DECISIONS ACT, 1992* PROVIDE:

ss. 89 (5): **NO PERSON SHALL, IN A STATEMENT MADE IN A PRESCRIBED FORM, ASSERT SOMETHING THAT HE OR SHE KNOWS TO BE UNTRUE OR PROFESS AN OPINION THAT HE OR SHE DOES NOT HOLD.**

ss. 89 (6): **A PERSON WHO CONTRAVENES SUBSECTION (5) IS GUILTY OF AN OFFENCE AND IS LIABLE, ON CONVICTION, TO A FINE NOT EXCEEDING $10,000.00**

______________ ______________________________

Date Signature of proposed Statutory Guardian(s) of Property or, if a trust corporation an authorized signing officer

Name (s): ______________________________
(Please Print)

____

Address (es): ______________________________

____

____

Telephone number(s): ______________________________

NOTE: If you are proposing the appointment of two or more persons as joint statutory guardians, please indicate to which applicant the property and accounts, if applicable, and the Certificate of Statutory Guardianship should be delivered if the appointment is made:

Name of proposed statutory guardian of property: ______________________________

Address: ______________________________

____

3 of 4

Form No. 236

SUBSTITUTE DECISIONS ACT, 1992 **Form 1**

Telephone: ____________________

Notice to the Applicants:

1. The personal information contained in your application is collected under the authority of section 17 of the *Substitute Decisions Act, 1992*, and will be used to process your application to replace the Public Guardian and Trustee as statutory guardian of property in accordance with the law and policies of the Office of the Public Guardian and Trustee. Questions about this collection of information should be directed to:

Office of the Public Guardian and Trustee
595 Bay Street, Suite 800
Toronto, Ontario, M5G 2M6
Tel: (416) 314-2800
Attention: Screening Unit

Notice of Fee

The Public Guardian and Trustee charges a fee of **$382.00 plus GST of $26.74** for processing an application for statutory guardianship, under the authority of s.8 of the *Public Guardian and Trustee Act*. This fee will be collected from the incapable person's property at the time the application process is completed or, if insufficient funds are held by the Public Guardian and Trustee, will be payable by the applicant prior to assuance of the certificate of statutory guardianship. In cases where payment of the fee will cause undue financial hardship to the incapable person, it is possible to obtain a waiver of the fee.

4 of 4

Form No. 236

[O.Reg. 101/96, s. 2]

SUBSTITUTE DECISIONS ACT, 1992 *Form 2*

MANAGEMENT PLAN

Note: ***Where the document is completed as part of an application for court appointed guardianship of property, please insert general heading and court file number.***

A. This Management Plan is provided as part of the application made by:

____

(Full names(s) of applicant(s))

to be appointed as guardian of the property of

____

(Full name of person for whom guardianship is sought)

To the best of my knowledge and belief, the assets, liabilities, income and expenditures of

____

(Name of person for whom guardianship is sought)

at this date are stated below. My plans for managing them and the reasons for these plans are as follows:

Complete the parts below that apply to the finances of the person for whom guardianship is sought. Attach additional pages if the space below is insufficient. Where a part does not apply, write 'None' or 'Not Applicable' in the space provided.

B. **LAND:**

Type and address of property or properties	Estimated market value
	TOTAL:

PLAN:

For each of the above noted properties indicate your plans (e.g., sell at market value, lease at market value, other), the anticipated time frame for completing the transactions, if applicable, and your reasons for these plans:

____

____

____

C. **GENERAL HOUSEHOLD ITEMS AND VEHICLES:** (*Give general description for vehicles, list year, model, make.)*

Item	Particulars	Estimated Current Market Value
General Household: Vehicles:		
		TOTAL:

PLAN:

Explain your plans for these items (e.g., retain for use of person for whom guardianship is sought, sell at market value, place in storage, gift, other) and your reasons for these plans:

____

____

____

Form No. 237

1 of 8

D. **VALUABLES** (*including antiques, art, collectibles, jewellery*):

Item	Particulars	Estimated Current Market Value
		TOTAL:

PLAN:
Explain your plans for these items (e.g., sell at market value, place in storage, other) and your reasons for these plans:

____
____
____

E. **SAVINGS AND SAVINGS PLANS** (*include cash, assets in financial institutions, registered retirement or other savings plans, deposit receipts, pension plans etc.*):

Category	Institution	Account Number	Current Amount or Value
			TOTAL:

PLAN:
Explain your plans for the savings described above (e.g., close current accounts and consolidate in a trust account, deposit cash, maintain savings plans, collapse plans as required to meet ongoing expenditures, etc.) and your reasons for these plans:

____
____
____

F. **SECURITIES AND INVESTMENTS** (*include bonds, shares, warrants, options, debentures, notes and any other securities*):

Category	Number	Description	Estimated Current Market Value
			TOTAL:

PLAN:
Explain your plans with respect to the above-noted securities and investments (e.g., maintain in current form, renew as required, convert, redeem, etc.) and your reasons for these plans:

____
____
____

Form No. 237

SUBSTITUTE DECISIONS ACT, 1992 ***Form 2***

G. **ACCOUNTS RECEIVABLE** *(include all debts owing to person for whom guardianship is sought):*

Particulars	Amount
	TOTAL:

PLAN:
Explain your plans regarding collection of the above-noted debts and your reasons for these plans:

____

____

____

H. **BUSINESS INTERESTS:** *(Show any interests owned by the person for whom guardianship is sought in an unincorporated business. An interest in an incorporated business may be shown here or under Securities.)*

Name of Firm or Company	Interest	Estimated Current Value
		TOTAL:

PLAN:
Explain your plans regarding the above-noted business interests (e.g., maintain, dissolve, sell, etc.) and your reasons for these plans:

____

____

____

I. **OTHER PROPERTY:** *(Show any other property owned by the person for whom guardianship is sought and which is not shown above.)*

Category	Particulars	Estimated Current Market Value
		TOTAL:

PLAN:
Explain your plans for the property described above and the reasons for these plans:

____

____

____

Form No. 237

J. **LIABILITIES:** *(Show the debts owed by the person for whom guardianship is sought including personal loans, credit card balances, outstanding bills, income tax owing, etc.)*

Description of Debt	Particulars	Amount of Debt
		TOTAL:

PLAN:
Explain your plans with respect to these debts and the reasons for these plans:

____

____

____

K. **INCOME:** *(Show net income from all sources on an annual basis.)*

Type of Income	Particulars	Approximate Annual Amount
Pension Employment Interest Rental Business Other		
		TOTAL:

PLAN:
Explain your plans for the collection, deposit and allocation of the income described above:

____

____

____

L. **EXPENSES:** (*Describe the expenses, calculated on an annual basis, which you anticipate will be required to be made on behalf of the person for whom guardianship is sought.*)

Expense	Particulars	Approximate Annual Amount
Residential Utilities Recreational/Entertainment Travel Personal Care Support for Dependents Property Maintenance Gifts Loans Charitable Donations Other		
		TOTAL:

Form No. 237

4 of 8

SUBSTITUTE DECISIONS ACT, 1992 *Form 2*

PLAN:

Explain below:

(a) *Whether any of the payments described above are of direct or indirect financial benefit to you, a person you live with or to whom you are related. If so, please explain why these payments are necessary and appropriate:*

____

____

____

(b) *Whether any significant increases or decreases in the above expenditures are anticipated, or whether any additional expenditures are likely. If so, please explain:*

____

____

____

(c) *Whether the expenditures listed above will adequately meet the personal needs and maximize the enjoyment of life of the person for whom guardianship is sought:*

____

____

____

(d) *If you are planning to make gifts, loans or charitable donations, please explain the reasons why you believe these expenditures are appropriate:*

____

____

____

(e) *If payments to dependents, or for their benefit, are required please provide details about the nature of these payments and the reasons for them:*

____

____

____

(f) *Are there any expenditures which others have recommended which you are not planning to make? If so, please explain:*

____

____

____

Form No. 237

5 of 8

SUBSTITUTE DECISIONS ACT, 1992 ***Form 2***

M. **LEGAL PROCEEDINGS:** *(Identify any current legal proceedings relating to property to which he or she is a party including any civil or criminal proceedings.)*

Nature of Legal Proceedings	Status of Proceedings

PLAN:

(a) *Please explain your plans in respect of these proceedings:*

Do you anticipate that legal proceedings may need to be commenced or defended on the person's behalf in respect of his or her property? If so, please explain:

(b) *What arrangements for legal representation for the person have been made or do you propose?*

(c) *Are you aware of any existing court orders or judgments which are relevant to the management of the person's property? If yes, describe or attach copies.*

Yes No If yes, describe: ______________________

N. **ADDITIONAL INFORMATION:**

(a) I have consulted with the person for whom guardianship is sought in making this plan: *(check one)*

Yes No If no, please provide reasons: ______________________

(b) I have consulted with the following other people in preparing this plan:

Form No. 237

6 of 8

SUBSTITUTE DECISIONS ACT, 1992 ***Form 2***

(c) To the best of my knowledge, the person for whom guardianship is sought would not object to any aspect of this management plan: *(check one)*

Yes, would object No, would not object

If yes, please explain: ____________________

____

____

(d) I am aware of my duty to encourage the participation of the person for whom guardianship is sought in decisions I may make and to consult with supportive family and friends and caregivers. My plans to do so are as follows: *(briefly describe)*

____

____

____

(e) I am aware that I would, as guardian of property, be required to make reasonable efforts to determine whether the person for whom guardianship is sought has a will and, if so, what the provisions of the will are and I am entitled to obtain the incapable person's will. My plans to do so are as follows:

____

____

____

(f) I am aware that I am <u>not</u> to dispose of property that I know is subject to a specific testamentary gift in the will of the person for whom guardianship is sought unless the specific testamentary gift is of money or if the disposition of that property is necessary to comply with my duties as guardian of property or to make a gift of the property to the person who would be entitled to it under the will, if the gift is authorized by section 37 of the *Substitute Decisions Act, 1992*.

SUBSECTIONS 32(10) and 32(11) OF THE *SUBSTITUTE DECISIONS ACT, 1992*, PROVIDE:

ss.32(10): A GUARDIAN SHALL ACT IN ACCORDANCE WITH THE MANAGEMENT PLAN.

ss.32(11): IF THERE IS A MANAGEMENT PLAN, IT MAY BE AMENDED FROM TIME TO TIME WITH THE PUBLIC GUARDIAN AND TRUSTEE'S APPROVAL.

SUBSECTIONS 89(5) AND 89(6) of the *SUBSTITUTE DECISIONS ACT, 1992*, PROVIDE:

ss.89(5): NO PERSON SHALL, IN A STATEMENT MADE IN A PRESCRIBED FORM, ASSERT SOMETHING THAT HE OR SHE KNOWS TO BE UNTRUE OR PROFESS AN OPINION THAT HE OR SHE DOES NOT HOLD.

ss.89(6): A PERSON WHO CONTRAVENES SUBSECTION (5) IS GUILTY OF AN OFFENCE AND IS LIABLE, ON CONVICTION, TO A FINE NOT EXCEEDING $10,000.00.

Form No. 237

7 of 8

Date ______________ Signature of proposed Guardian (s) of property ______________

Name (s) (please print) : ______________

Address (es) : ______________

Telephone number (s) : ______________

Form No. 237

[O.Reg. 101/96, s. 2]

SUBSTITUTE DECISIONS ACT, 1992 *Form 3*

GUARDIANSHIP PLAN

Note: Where this document is completed as part of an application for court appointed guardianship of the person, please insert general heading and court file number.

(*Attach additional pages if more space is needed*)

Section I - *Identifying Information*:

A. This plan is for:

____

Name (in full): ______________________________
(Referred to throughout this guardianship plan as 'the person')

Address: ______________________________

____

____

Telephone number: Residence ____________________
Business ____________________

Date of Birth: ______________________________

B. (1) As the proposed guardian of the person (or attorney for personal care) for ______________________________,

I have consulted with the following persons in preparation of this guardianship plan:

the person identified in A.
family members of the person
friends of the person
care providers to the person
the person's guardian of property (attorney under a continuing power of attorney)
others (please specify relationship): ____________________

Section II - *Areas where personal care decision making authority is sought:*

A. I am seeking personal care decision making authority in the following areas: (*mark applicable boxes*)

Health Care
(Including decisions to which the *Health Care Consent Act, 1996* applies)
Nutrition
Shelter/Accommodation
Clothing
Hygiene
Safety

1 of 9

SUBSTITUTE DECISIONS ACT, 1992 ***Form 3***

B. Powers Requiring Specific Court Authorization (*this section is only to be completed by applicants for court-appointed guardianship of the person):*

1. I am asking the court for an order authorizing me to apprehend the person [Section 59 (3)].

   Yes No

2. I am asking the court for an order authorizing me to change existing arrangements in respect of custody of or access to a child, or to give consent on the person's behalf to the adoption of a child [Section 59(4)].

   Yes No

3. a) I am asking the court for an order permitting me to exercise other powers or perform other duties in addition to those set out in the *Substitute Decisions Act, 1992* [Section 59(2)(g)].

   Yes No

   b) If the answer to 3a is yes, please identify the other powers and duties:

   ____
   ____
   ____

C. Notice Regarding Extraordinary Matters:
The law limits or restricts a guardian's authority to make decisions in the following areas relating to personal care:

Sterilization
The law prohibits a substitute decision maker from consenting to non-therapeutic sterilization of a person who is mentally incapable of such a decision. Any proposal to consent on behalf of the person to his or her sterlization as medically necessary for the protection of the person's health must be consistent with the law and should appear in the Guardianship Plan or be the subject of an amendment to the Guardianship Plan prior to consent being given.

Regenerative Tissue Donation
The law restricts the authority of a substitute decision maker regarding decisions to permit regenerative tissue donations by a person who is mentally incapable of such a decision. Any proposal to authorize the removal of regenerative tissue for implantation in another person's body must be consistent with the law and should appear in the Guardianship Plan or be the subject of an amendment to the Guardianship Plan prior to permission being given.

SUBSTITUTE DECISIONS ACT, 1992 *Form 3*

Section III - The plan for personal decision making:

(*Please complete only those sections where decision making authority is sought, and please attach any additional relevant documentation.*)

HEALTH CARE (INCLUDING TREATMENT), NUTRITION AND HYGIENE

Background:

(a) Describe the current status of the health, nutrition and hygiene of the person, including all known health conditions for which treatment is being received or is proposed:

____

____

____

(b) Describe any wishes or instructions made by the person while capable that are known by you and that relate to his/her preferences about health care, treatment, nutrition and hygiene and attach a copy of any written wishes or instructions (e.g., a written advance directive, power of attorney for personal care, living will, etc.):

____

____

____

Plan:

(c) Describe the long-term goals (2-6 years) for decisions under this heading:

____

____

____

(d) Describe the steps you propose to take (within the next 12 months) to achieve the goals under this heading:

____

____

____

(e) Briefly describe your reasons for these plans:

____

____

____

SHELTERING/LIVING ARRANGEMENTS AND SAFETY

Background:

(a) Describe the current status of the person's living arrangements, including any factors relating to safety:

SUBSTITUTE DECISIONS ACT, 1992 **Form 3**

(b) Describe any known wishes or instructions made by the person while capable that relate to his or her preferences about living arrangements and safety issues and attach a copy of any written wishes or instructions:

Plan:

(c) Describe the long-term goals (2-6 years) for decisions under this heading:

(d) Describe the steps you propose to take (within the next 12 months) to achieve the goals under this heading:

(e) Briefly describe your reasons for these plans:

LEGAL PROCEEDINGS

Background:

(a) Describe the current status of any existing or anticipated legal proceedings relating to this person, (including divorce, custody, access, adoption, restraining orders, criminal matters, landlord and tenant matters):

(b) Describe any known wishes or instructions made by the person while capable that relate to his or her preferences about existing or anticipated legal proceedings and attach a copy of any written wishes or instructions:

SUBSTITUTE DECISIONS ACT, 1992 ***Form 3***

(c) If legal proceedings are in progress, describe arrangements for legal representation of the person, if known:

____
____
____

(d) Where there is a guardian of property or attorney under a continuing power of attorney, is he or she aware of the existing or anticipated legal proceedings described in (a)? If so, please describe his or her involvement:

____
____
____

(e) Are you are aware of any existing court orders or judgments against the person? If yes, describe or attach copies:

____
____
____

(f) Is the person on probation or are there pending criminal proceedings in which the person is involved? If so, please provide details:

____
____
____

Plan:

(g) Describe the long-term goals (2-6 years) for decisions under this heading:

____
____
____

(h) Briefly describe your reasons for these plans:

____
____
____

EMPLOYMENT, EDUCATION AND TRAINING

Background:

(a) Is the person employed, or involved in any educational or training programs? If so, please describe current status:

____
____
____

5 of 9

SUBSTITUTE DECISIONS ACT, 1992 ***Form 3***

(b) Describe any known wishes or instructions made by the person while capable that relate to his or her preferences about participation in employment, education or training programs:

____

____

____

Plan:

(c) Describe the long-term goals (2-6 years) for decisions under the heading:

____

____

____

(d) Describe the steps you propose to take (within the next 12 months) to achieve the goals under this heading:

____

____

____

(e) Briefly describe your reasons for these plans:

____

____

____

RECREATIONAL, SOCIAL AND CULTURAL ACTIVITIES

Background:

(a) Describe the activities that the person is involved in (or significant activities that the person was involved in), including hobbies, clubs, affiliations, volunteering:

____

____

____

(b) Describe any known wishes or instructions made by the person while capable that relate to his or preferences about participation in recreational, social and cultural activities:

____

____

____

Plan:

(c) Describe the long-term goals (2-6 years) for decisions under this heading:

____

____

____

6 of 9

SUBSTITUTE DECISIONS ACT, 1992 ***Form 3***

(d) Describe the steps you propose to take (within the next 12 months) to achieve the goals under this heading:

____

____

____

(e) Briefly describe your reasons for these plans:

____

____

____

SOCIAL AND SUPPORT SERVICES

Background:

(a) Describe social and support services received by the person within the past year, including any services currently received:

____

____

____

(b) Describe any known wishes or instructions made by the person while capable that relate to his or her preferences about receipt of social and support services:

____

____

____

Plan:

(c) Describe the long-term goals (2-6 years) for decisions under this heading:

____

____

____

(d) Describe the steps you propose to take (within the next 12 months) to achieve the goals under this heading:

____

____

____

(e) Briefly describe your reasons for these plans:

____

____

____

7 of 9

SUBSTITUTE DECISIONS ACT, 1992 *Form 3*

Section IV - Additional Information:

(a) I have consulted with the person for whom guardianship is sought in making this plan: (*check one*)

Yes No

If no, please provide reasons:

____
____
____

(b) I have consulted with the following other people in preparing this plan: (*please provide full names, addresses, telephone numbers and relationship to the person, of the people you consulted with*)

____
____
____

(c) If consultation did not occur with any of the persons identified in Section I-B (1) above, provide reasons why:

____
____
____

(d) To the best of my knowledge, the person for whom guardianship is sought would not object to any aspect of this guardianship plan: (*check one*)

Yes, would object No, would not object

If yes, please explain:

____
____
____

(e) I am aware of my duty as a guardian of the person to foster the person's independ- ence, to encourage the person's participation in decisions I make on his or her behalf, and to consult with supportive family and friends and caregivers. My plans to do so are as follows: (*briefly describe*)

____
____
____

SUBSTITUTE DECISIONS ACT, 1992 *Form 3*

SUBSECTIONS 66 (15) AND 66 (16) OF THE *SUBSTITUTE DECISIONS ACT, 1992* PROVIDE:

ss.65(15): **A GUARDIAN SHALL ACT IN ACCORDANCE WITH THE GUARDIANSHIP PLAN.**

ss.66(16): **IF THERE IS A GUARDIANSHIP PLAN, IT MAY BE AMENDED FROM TIME TO TIME WITH THE PUBLIC GUARDIAN AND TRUSTEE'S APPROVAL.**

SECTION 67 OF THE *SUBSTITUTE DECISIONS ACT, 1992* PROVIDES:

s.67: **SECTION 66, EXCEPT SUBSECTION 66(15) AND (16), APPLIES WITH NECESSARY MODIFICATIONS TO AN ATTORNEY WHO ACTS UNDER A POWER OF ATTORNEY FOR PERSONAL CARE.**

SUBSECTIONS 89 (5) AND 89 (6) OF THE *SUBSTITUTE DECISIONS ACT, 1992* PROVIDE:

ss.89(5): **NO PERSON SHALL, IN A STATEMENT MADE IN A PRESCRIBED FORM, ASSERT SOMETHING THAT HE OR SHE KNOWS TO BE UNTRUE OR PROFESS AN OPINION THAT HE OR SHE DOES NOT HOLD.**

ss.89(6): **A PERSON WHO CONTRAVENES SUBSECTION (5) IS GUILTY OF AN OFFENCE AND IS LIABLE, ON CONVICTION, TO A FINE NOT EXCEEDING $10,000.002**

____

Date Signature of proposed Guardian(s)/ Attorney(s) for Personal Care

Name(s): ______________________________

Address(es): ______________________________

____

Telephone Number(s): Residence: ________________ Business: ________________

9 of 9

[O.Reg. 101/96, s. 2]

Form 4

Substitute Decisions Act, 1992

REQUEST FOR ASSESSMENT OF CAPACITY UNDER SUBSECTION 16 (1) OF THE ACT

1. I, ____________________, of the ____________________________________ in
(full name) (city, town, etc.)
the _________________________ request that an assessor perform an assessment of
(county, municipality)
__________________________ for the purpose of determining whether the Public
(full name of person to be assessed)
Guardian and Trustee should become my/his/her statutory guardian of property.

Items 2, 3 and 4 are to be completed only if the request is made in respect of another person.

2. I have reason to believe that ____________________________________ of
(full name of person to be assessed)
the _________________ may be incapable of managing property.
(county, municipality)

3. I have made reasonable inquiries and I have no knowledge of the existence of any attorney under a continuing power of attorney that gives the attorney authority over all the property of ________________________________
(full name of person to be assessed)

4. I have made reasonable inquiries and I have no knowledge of any spouse, partner or relative of ____________________________who intends to make
(full name of person to be assessed)
an application under section 22 of the *Substitute Decisions Act, 1992* for the appointment of a guardian of property for him or her.

SUBSECTIONS 89 (5) AND (6) OF THE *SUBSTITUTE DECISIONS ACT, 1992* PROVIDE:

ss. 89(5) : **NO PERSON SHALL, IN A STATEMENT MADE IN A PRESCRIBED FORM, ASSERT SOMETHING THAT HE OR SHE KNOWS TO BE UNTRUE OR PROFESS AN OPINION THAT HE OR SHE DOES NOT HOLD.**

ss. 89(6) : **A PERSON WHO CONTRAVENES SUBSECTION (5) IS GUILTY OF AN OFFENCE AND IS LIABLE, ON CONVICTION, TO A FINE NOT EXCEEDING $10,000.**

Dated ______________________, 19_.

____
(Signature of person making the request)

Name ______________________________

Address ____________________________

Phone Number (include area code) ______________

TO: ________________________
(name of assessor)

[O.Reg. 101/96, s. 2]

Form 5

Substitute Decisions Act, 1992

STATEMENT REQUIRED UNDER PARAGRAPH 1 OF SECTION 50(1) OF THE ACT

1. I, ______________________________, am the grantor of a power of
(insert full name)
attorney for personal care signed on the ____ day of ______________, 19___ that contains one or more of the provisions described in subsection 50(2) of the *Substitute Decisions Act, 1992 ("SDA").*

2. I understand that by including one or more of these provisions I am:
   (i) waiving rights that I would otherwise have by law; and
   (ii) giving to my designated attorney for personal care powers that he or she would not otherwise have.

3. I understand the effect of the provision(s) that I have chosen to include in my power of attorney for personal care.

4. I understand the effect of subsection 50(4) of the *Substitute Decisions Act, 1992* that provides that I cannot revoke this power of attorney for personal care unless I obtain an assessment from an assessor within 30 days before the revocation is signed confirming that I am capable of personal care.

5. I am aware that I cannot be forced to include any of the provisions described in subsection 50(2) of the SDA in my power of attorney for personal care. I am also aware that these provisions will not be effective unless an assessor makes a statement in the prescribed form indicating that he/she performed an assessment of my capacity within 30 days after the power of attorney was executed and that, in the assessor's opinion, at the time of the assessment I was:
   - capable of personal care;
   - capable of understanding the effect of the provision(s) included in my power of attorney;
   - capable of understanding the effect of subsection 50(4) of the *SDA*.

6. I have signed the power of attorney for personal care and this statement of my own free will.

____
Name of grantor (please print)

____
Signature of grantor

____
Date

[O.Reg. 101/96, s. 2]

Form 6

Substitute Decisions Act, 1992

(Court file no.)

ONTARIO COURT
(GENERAL DIVISION)

BETWEEN:

(name)

Applicant

- and -

(name)

Respondent

OPTIONAL STATEMENT TO APPOINT A GUARDIAN OF THE PERSON (under ss. 71 (l) of the *Substitute Decisions Act, 1992)*

I, (full name), of the (city, town, etc.) in the (county, regional municipality, etc.) state that:

1. I know the person alleged to be incapable, (*full name of person*).
2. I have been in personal contact with (*full name of person alleged to be incapable*) during the twelve months before the notice of application to appoint a guardian of the person was issued.
3. (*If desired, set out additional statements in support of the application.*)

(Where more space is required, additional pages may be attached.)

SUBSECTIONS 89 (5) AND (6) OF THE *SUBSTITUTE DECISIONS ACT, 1992* STATE:

NO PERSON SHALL, IN A STATEMENT MADE IN A PRESCRIBED FORM, ASSERT SOMETHING THAT HE OR SHE KNOWS TO BE DNTRUE OR PROFESS AN OPINION THAT HE OR SHE DOES NOT HOLD.

A PERSON WHO CONTRAVENES SUBSECTION (5) IS GUILTY OF AN OFFENCE AND IS LIABLE, ON CONVICTION, TO A FINE NOT EXCEEDING $10,000.

Dated the .... day of .... 19... ....
(signature)

Form 7

Substitute Decisions Act, 1992

(Court file No.)

ONTARIO COURT
(GENERAL DIVISION)

BETWEEN:

(name)

Applicant

- and -

(name)

Respondent

OPTIONAL STATEMENT TO TERMINATE GUARDIANSHIP OF THE PERSON (under subsection 71(2) of the *Substitute Decisions Act, 1992*)

I, (full name), of the (city. town, etc.) in the (county, regional municipality, etc.) state that:

1. I know the person under guardianship, (full name of person).

2. I have been in personal contact with (full name of person) under guardianship) during the twelve months before the motion to terminate the guardianship was filed.

3. (If desired, set out additional statements in support of the motion.)

SUBSECTIONS 89(5) AND (6) OF THE *SUBSTITUTE DECISIONS ACT, 1992* PROVIDE:

ss. 89(5) : NO PERSON SHALL, IN A STATEMENT MADE IN A PRESCRIBED FORM.ASSERT SOMETHING THAT HE OR SHE KNOWS TO BE UNTRUE OR PROFESS AN OPINION THAT HE OR SHE DOES NOT HOLD.

ss. 89(6) : A PERSON WHO CONTRAVENES SUBSECTION (5) IS GUILTY OF AN OFFENCE AND IS LIABLE, ON CONVICTION, TO A FINE NOT EXCEEDING $10.000.00.

Dated the …………… day of ……………………., 19……

……………………………………………
(Signature)

[O. Reg. 101/96, s. 2]

Form 8

Statement of a Person who is not an Assessor under section 72 of the *Substitute Decisions Act, 1992*

APPOINTMENT OF GUARDIAN OF PROPERTY BY SUMMARY DISPOSITION

I, (full name), of the (city, town, etc.), in the (county, regional municipality, etc.) state that:

1. I know (full name of person alleged to be incapable).

2. I have been in personal contact with (full name of person alleged to be incapable) during the twelve months before the notice of application was issued.

3. The notice of application was issued on (day, month, year).

4. I am of the opinion that (full name of person alleged to be incapable) is incapable of managing property.

5. I base my opinion on the following: (Set out the statements of fact in consecutively numbered paragraphs, with each paragraph being confined as far as possible to a particular statement of fact. Give dates wherever possible.)

6. I can expect no direct or indirect pecuniary benefit as the result of the appointment of a guardian of property.

7. (Cross out if not applicable) I am of the opinion that it is necessary for decisions to be made on behalf of (full name of person alleged to be incapable) by a person who is authorized to do so, and I base this opinion on the following: (Set out the statements of fact in consecutively numbered paragraphs, with each paragraph being confined as far as possible to a particular statement of fact. Give dates wherever possible.)

Dated the .... day of ...., 19......

....
(Signature)

[O.Reg. 101/96, s. 2]

Form 9

Statement of a Person who is not an Assessor under section 73 of the *Substitute Decisions Act, 1992*

TERMINATION OF GUARDIANSHIP OF PROPERTY BY SUMMARY DISPOSITION

I, (full name), of the (city, town, etc.), in the (county, regional municipality, etc.) state that:

1. I know (full name of person whose property is under guardianship).

2. I have been in personal contact with (full name of person whose property is under guardianship) during the twelve months before the notice of motion was filed with the court.

3. The notice of motion was filed with the court on (day, month, year).

4. I am of the opinion that (full name of person whose property is under guardianship) is capable of managing property.

5. I base my opinion on the following: (Set out the statements of fact in consecutively numbered paragraphs, with each paragraph being confined as far as possible to a particular statement of fact. Give dates wherever possible.)

6. I can expect no direct or indirect pecuniary benefit as the result of the termination of the guardianship of property.

Dated the .... day of ...., 19......

....
(Signature)

[O.Reg. 101/96, s. 2]

Consent and Capacity Board

Form 18
Substitute Decisions Act

Application to the Board for a Review of a Finding of Incapacity to Manage Property under Subsection 20.2 (1) of the Substitute Decisions Act

My name is: ____________________
(print full name)

I apply to the Board for a hearing to review a finding that I am incapable of managing my property.

Are you currently a patient or resident at a psychiatric, health or residential facility?

☐ **no**
☐ **yes** name, address and telephone no. of facility

____

____

Your home address and telephone number:

____________________ (address) ( ) ____________ (telephone no.)

Name, address, telephone number and fax number of the person who made the original finding of incapacity:

____________________ (name) ____________________ (address)

( ) ____________ (telephone no.) ( ) ____________ (fax no.)

When was that finding made? ____________________

Has there been an assessment of your capacity to manage property within the last six months?

☐ **no**
☐ **yes** name, address telephone and fax numbers of the person who conducted that assessment:

____________________ (name) ____________________ (address)

( ) ____________ (telephone no.) ( ) ____________ (fax no.)

Have you applied to the Board during the past year for a review of a finding regarding your capacity to manage property?

☐ **no**
☐ **yes** If known, provide place and date of last hearing

____________________ (name of place) ____________________ (date)

(Disponible en version française)

3234-04 (99/03)

See reverse
7530-5406

Name and telephone number of your client representative at the office of the Public Guardian and Trustee

______________________ (name) ( ) ______________________ (telephone no.)

Name, address, telephone number and fax number of your lawyer or agent *(if any)*:

______________________ (name) ______________________ (address)

( ) ______________________ (telephone no.) ( ) ______________________ (fax no.)

If someone helped you to fill out this application form, please provide his / her name, address, telephone and fax numbers:

______________________ (name) ______________________ (address)

( ) ______________________ (telephone no.) ( ) ______________________ (fax no.)

______________________ (date) ______________________ (signature)

Collection of this information is for the purpose of conducting a proceeding before this board. It is collected/used for this purpose under the authority of subsection 20.2 of the Substitute Decisions Act. For information about collection practices, contact the office of the Regional Vice-Chair of the Board or call toll free at 1 800 461–2036.

Send this form by fax to the Office of the Regional Vice-Chair of the Board or call toll free at 1 800 461–2036 for assistance.

Form 18 *(page 2)*

3234–04 (99/03) 7530–5406

Power of Attorney for Personal Care

(Made in accordance with the Substitute Decisions Act, 1992)

1. I,______________________________revoke any previous power of attorney for personal
   (Print or type your full name here)

   care made by me and APPOINT:____
   (Print or type the name of the person or persons you appoint here)

   ____

   to be my attorney(s) for personal care in accordance with the *Substitute Decisions Act, 1992.*

   [**Note**: *A person who provides health care, residential, social, training, or support services to the person giving this power of attorney for compensation may not act as his or her attorney unless that person is also his or her spouse, partner, or relative.]*

2. If you have named more than one attorney and you want them to have the authority to act separately, insert the words "jointly and severally" here:

   ____
   (This may be left blank)

3. If the person(s) I have appointed, or any one of them, cannot or will not be my attorney because of refusal, resignation, death, mental incapacity, or removal by the Court, I SUBSTITUTE:

   ____
   (This may be left blank)

   to act as my attorney for personal care in the same manner and subject to the same authority as the person he or she is replacing.

4. I give my attorney(s) the **AUTHORITY** to make any personal care decision for me that I am mentally incapable of making for myself, including the giving or refusing of consent to any matter to which the *Health Care Consent Act, 1996* applies, subject to the *Substitute Decisions Act, 1992*, and any instructions, conditions or restrictions contained in this form.

NOT FOR SALE

5. INSTRUCTIONS, CONDITIONS and RESTRICTIONS
Attach, sign, and date additional pages if required. *(This part may be left blank.)*

____

____

____

____

____

____

____

6. SIGNATURE:________________________________ DATE:______________
(Sign your name here, in the presence of two witnesses.)

ADDRESS: ____
(Insert your current address here.)

7. WITNESS SIGNATURES

*[**Note**: The following people cannot be witnesses: the attorney or his or her spouse or partner; the spouse, partner, or child of the person making the document, or someone that the person treats as his or her child; a person whose property is under guardianship or who has a guardian of the person; a person under the age of 18.]*

Witness #1: *Signature*:________________________ *Print Name*:______________

Address:____

____________________________ *Date*:______________________________

Witness #2: *Signature*:________________________ *Print Name*:______________

Address:____

____________________________ *Date*:______________________________

Continuing Power of Attorney for Property

(Made in accordance with the Substitute Decisions Act,1992)

1. I,____________________________revoke any previous continuing power of attorney
   (Print or type your full name here.)
   for property made by me and **APPOINT**:____________________________________

   ____ to be my attorney(s) for property.
   (Print or type the name of the person or persons you appoint here.)

2. If you have named more than one attorney and you want them to have the authority to act separately, insert the words "jointly and severally" here:____________________
   (This may be left blank.)

3. If the person(s) I have appointed, or any one of them, cannot or will not be my attorney because of refusal, resignation, death, mental incapacity, or removal by the court, **I SUBSTITUTE**: *(This may be left blank.)*

   ____

   to act as my attorney for property with the same authority as the person he or she is replacing.

4. I AUTHORIZE my attorney(s) for property to do on my behalf anything in respect of property that I could do if capable of managing property, except make a will, subject to the law and to any conditions or restrictions contained in this document. I confirm that he/she may do so even if I am mentally incapable.

5. **CONDITIONS AND RESTRICTIONS**
   Attach, sign, and date additional pages if required. *(This part may be left blank.)*

   ____

   ____

   ____

   ____

   ____

   ____

03/96

NOT FOR SALE

6. DATE OF EFFECTIVENESS

Unless otherwise stated in this document, this continuing power of attorney will come into effect on the date it is signed and witnessed.

7. COMPENSATION

Unless otherwise stated in this document, I authorize my attorney(s) to take annual compensation from my property in accordance with the fee scale prescribed by regulation for the compensation of attorneys for property made pursuant to Section 90 of the *Substitute Decisions Act, 1992.*

8. SIGNATURE:________________________________DATE:_______________

(Sign your name in the presence of two witnesses.)

ADDRESS:____

(Insert your full current address here.)

9. WITNESS SIGNATURE

[Note: The following people cannot be witnesses: the attorney or his or her spouse or partner; the spouse, partner, or child of the person making the document, or someone that the person treats as his or her child; a person whose property is under guardianship or who has a guardian of the person; a person under the age of 18.]

Witness #1: *Signature:* ______________________*Print Name:*__________________

*Address:*____

______________________________________*Date:*________________

Witness #2: *Signature:* ______________________*Print Name:*__________________

*Address:*____

______________________________________*Date:*________________

POWERS OF ATTORNEY ACT

(R.S.O. 1990, c. P.20)

Amendments: 1992, c. 32, s. 24; 1993, c. 27, Sched.

1. Definition — In this Act, "attorney" means the donee of a power of attorney or where a power of attorney is given to two or more persons, whether jointly or severally or both, means any one or more of such persons.

[1992, c. 32, s. 24]

2. Form of general power of attorney — A general power of attorney for property is sufficient authority for the donee of the power or, where there is more than one donee, for the donees acting jointly or acting jointly and severally, as the case may be, to do on behalf of the donor anything that the donor can lawfully do by an attorney, subject to such conditions and restrictions, if any, as are contained therein.

[1992, c. 32, s. 24]

3. (1) **Exercise of power after termination —** Where a power of attorney is terminated or revoked or becomes invalid, any subsequent exercise of the power by the attorney is valid and binding as between the donor or the estate of the donor and any person, including the attorney, who acted in good faith and without knowledge of the termination, revocation or invalidity.

(2) **Saving —** Where money is paid in the exercise of a power of attorney to which subsection (1) applies, nothing in subsection (1) affects the right of any person entitled to the money against the person to whom the payment is made, and the person so entitled has the same remedy against the person to whom the payment is made as he, she or it would have had against the person making the payment.

4.-11. [Repealed, 1992, c. 32, s. 24]

FORM 1 [Repealed: 1992, c. 32, s. 24]

HEALTH CARE CONSENT ACT, 1996

COMMENTARY

History and Purpose

The *Health Care Consent Act, 1996* ("HCCA" or "the Act") replaced the former *Consent to Treatment Act, 1992*,[1] which was in force so briefly it really did not have an opportunity to be implemented. Prior to 1995, provisions regarding capacity and consent to treatment were contained in the former *Mental Health Act*.[2] The HCCA is divided into six parts: General, including Purposes and Interpretation (Part I), Treatment (Part II), Admission to Care Facilities (Part III), Personal Assistance Services (Part IV), the Consent and Capacity Board (Part V) and Miscellaneous including Offences (Part VI).

The HCCA is very similar to the precursor legislation, but removes the requirement of independent rights advice to individuals found incapable, other than those in psychiatric facilities. It also includes new provisions regarding capacity to make decisions with respect to long-term care admission, and related provisions for obtaining consent for personal assistance services, defined as ambulation, nutrition, grooming and hygiene, among others, for individuals residing in care facilities, defined as nursing homes and others, but do not include retirement residences in s. 2. The HCCA is also the governing statute that establishes the Consent and Capacity Board.[3]

The Act aims to provide a complete codification of the common law requirements for obtaining informed consent. It also codifies principles of assessing capacity which have developed in Ontario as a result of an exhaustive review of the subject, the Weisstub Enquiry on Mental Competency,[4] undertaken in 1990. In addition, it establishes a statutory regime for substitute decision making on behalf of incapable individuals. The Act establishes a hierarchy of substitute decision makers (SDMs) and prescribes rules for SDMs consenting to or refusing treatment or placement on behalf of incapable persons.

---

[1] *Consent to Treatment Act, 1992*, S.O. 1992, c. 31, proclaimed into force April 3, 1995, as amended, repealed effective March 29, 1996.

[2] *Mental Health Act*, R.S.O. 1980, c. 262; under this Act a physician could obtain a treatment order from the Board's predecessor to administer treatment to incapable psychiatric patients. This provision was repealed with the proclamation of the *Consent to Treatment Act, 1992* in 1995.

[3] s. 73 to 80.

[4] Weisstub, David N., *Enquiry on Mental Competency: Final Report* (Queen's Printer for Ontario: Toronto, 1990).

The HCCA contains a purpose clause[5] identifying the first goal as providing rules with respect to consent to treatment that apply consistently in all settings. Other objectives include facilitating treatment and placement of incapable persons and enhancing the autonomy of individuals for whom treatment or placement is proposed, among others.[6]

Application

Treatment

The provisions of the HCCA apply to treatment decisions wherever and whenever a "treatment" is proposed for an individual. This is not restricted to psychiatric treatment, although a common misconception to this effect exists. As a consequence of independent rights advice being limited to psychiatric facilities, more patients for whom psychiatric treatment is proposed apply to the Consent and Capacity Board for a review of a finding of incapacity than do individuals found incapable with respect to proposed medical treatment. Much of the jurisprudence in the area of consent and capacity law therefore centres on issues of consent for psychiatric medications. However, the principles established by the cases interpreting the provisions of the HCCA apply to any type of treatment proposed. Treatment is essentially defined as anything done for a therapeutic purpose.[7] Any type of intervention a physician considers "treatment" is treatment for purposes of the legislation.[8]

The sections of the Act relating to treatment issues (Part II ss. 8 to 37.1 inclusive) apply within or outside of hospitals or psychiatric facilities. Anyone proposing a treatment for a patient must comply with the rules set out for obtaining consent.[9] All "health practitioners" must comply with the HCCA's rules on consent and capacity. "Health practitioner" is a defined term under the Act and includes, among others, physicians, dentists, chiropractors, nurses, midwives, massage therapists, occupational therapists, psychologists, naturopaths and anyone else so prescribed by Regulation.[10]

---

[5] s. 1.

[6] ss. 1(a) to 1(f).

[7] It includes a course of treatment, plan of treatment or community treatment plan. [s. 2 Interpretation "Treatment".] Community treatment plan has a defined meaning in the *Mental Health Act* as described by s. 33.7 of the MHA and as a required part of a community treatment order under the MHA (the CTO is based on the CTP under s. 33.1(4)(b) of the MHA.).

[8] s. 2 and s. 3 "excluded acts" specifically s. 3(2). For example, the Board has considered "Behaviour Modification Therapies" including "indirect observation (including videotape), intervention assistance and prompting" and "enforcement of targeted behaviour" as "treatment" in one case in these circumstances, see *In re D.W.* TO-04-3842, December 6, 2004.

[9] s. 10-14, especially s. 11 ("elements of consent" and "informed consent").

[10] s. 2.

Admission to Long-Term Care

The provisions regarding admission to a long-term care facility apply in any physical context where a proposal is made to place an individual in a care facility. An individual may be residing in his or her own home or undergoing treatment in a hospital setting when issues arise in relation to the individual's capacity to determine whether admission to a care facility may be necessary.[11] "Care facility" is a defined term under the Act which includes nursing homes. It does not include retirement or group homes.[12] Evaluations of capacity with respect to long-term care admission may only be made by "evaluators" entitled to make this determination. An evaluator may be a speech pathologist, nurse, occupational therapist, physician, physiotherapist, psychologist, or anyone prescribed by Regulation.[13] The evaluator may be, but generally is not, the individual who is proposing the admission. The person who authorizes the admission ultimately is a representative of the Community Care Access Centres (CCACs), the centralized provincial agency which processes all applications for admission to a care facility.

Personal Assistance Services

Provisions governing "personal assistance services"[14] apply only to individuals already residing in long-term care facilities.[15]

Common Ground/Corresponding Provisions under each Part of the Act

The definition of capacity in the Act together with the applicable provisions regarding substitute decision making and applications to the Consent and Capacity Board all apply with necessary modifications to treatment, admission to care facilities and the issue of personal assistance services. Except where otherwise indicated, where reference is made to sections of the Act in relation to treatment, our comments also apply (with necessary modifications) to the corresponding sections in relation to admission and personal assistance services.

Treatment (Part II of the Act)

Consent to Treatment

Generally: Consent as a Precondition to Treatment

Subject to an emergency situation arising under limited circumstances,[16] treatment cannot be given without the necessary consent having been obtained.

---

11 ss. 38 to 54.1 inclusive.

12 s. 2.

13 s. 2.

14 s. 55 to s. 69.1 inclusive

15 s. 2.

16 The exception is in an emergency situation defined as the subject of the proposed treatment currently suffering or at risk of sustaining serious bodily harm if treatment is

The health practitioner must obtain consent either from the patient if the individual is capable, or if incapable, from the person's SDM.[17] The consent must be obtained "in accordance with this Act." Interestingly, although the tribunal established under the Act is named the Consent and Capacity Board, issues of consent do not generally come before the Board for adjudication. If a person complains that treatment was administered without the necessary consent, the remedy lies with the courts by way of civil action in battery or negligence[18] or with the particular governing body of the professional who is alleged to have breached these provisions of the Act. Issues of consent are only tangentially before the Board in very rare applications.[19]

The Act codifies the common law principle of the requirement to obtain informed consent.[20] The consent must relate to the treatment, be informed and given voluntarily without being obtained through misrepresentation or fraud.[21] In addition to the information about the treatment which must be given whenever treatment is proposed,[22] where consent of an SDM is sought on behalf of an incapable person, the health practitioner is also required to provide certain information about the law. Ontario's Court of Appeal has interpreted the requirement to obtain consent "in accordance with this Act"[23] as imposing an affirmative statutory obligation on health practitioners to ensure that SDMs understand the criteria specified in s. 21 of the Act when deciding whether consent to a proposed treatment should be given or refused.[24] Consent to a

---

not administered promptly, but only in limited instances where it is not possible to obtain a consent or refusal either by the person or their SDM in a reasonably timely manner and there is no reason to believe the person does not want the treatment, see s. 25(1), 25(2) and 25(3).

17 s. 10

18 See for example, *Wells (Public Trustee of) v. Paramsothy*, [2000] O.J. No. 2390 (S.C.J.) where the court found a physician liable in negligence for damages suffered by an elderly resident of a nursing home who developed tardive dyskinesia, a permanent debilitating side-effect of neuroleptic treatment, administered without the consent of the individual's SDM even while the patient herself clearly lacked the capacity to consent to her own treatment.

19 For example, s. 35 (Form D) application for directions regarding wishes expressed previously, s. 36 (Form E) application to depart from wishes and s. 37 (Form G) application to determine an SDM's compliance with rules for making decisions on behalf of incapable persons.

20 s. 11, *Reibl v. Hughes* (1980), 114 D.L.R. (3d) 1 (S.C.C.), and *Hopp v. Lepp* (1980), 112 D.L.R. (3d) 67 (S.C.C.).

21 s. 11(1).

22 s. 11(2).

23 s. 10(b).

24 See *M. (A.) v. Benes* (1999), 46 O.R.(3d) 271 (C.A.) at paras 18, 19 and 20, and *T. (I.) v. L. (L.)* (1999), 46 O.R. (3d) 284 (Ont. C.A.).

treatment includes ancillary treatment,[25] some variations or adjustments in the treatment[26] and may be given to a "plan of treatment".[27]

Consent of the Capable Individual

There is no minimum age for capacity to make treatment decisions under the Act. Notwithstanding a common misconception to the contrary, young persons under the age of 16 may be capable of making certain treatment decisions of their own. However, to make treatment decisions for others, an SDM must be 16 years of age or older.[28] Further, although young persons under the age of 16 may determine their own treatment if capable, they cannot expect wishes they express in relation to that treatment to bind an SDM. Only capable wishes expressed in relation to treatment by persons over the age of 16 must be respected at a time of incapacity.[29] While wishes expressed by a young person under 16 must be taken into consideration by the SDM,[30] they do not determine the issue of consent by the SDM.

Capacity is task and time specific. A person may be incapable with respect to some treatments and capable with respect to others[31] or incapable with respect to the same treatment(s) at one time but capable at another.[32] How does a health practitioner determine whether to seek consent from the subject of the proposed treatment or to approach the individual's SDM for the necessary consent? The first basic principle is that there is a presumption of capacity on which the health practitioner may rely, absent reasonable grounds to believe that the individual may be incapable.[33] What are such reasonable grounds? The former *Consent to Treatment Act, 1992*[34] contained the following list of observations which may give a physician reason to question a person's treatment capacity: (1) the person shows evidence of confused or delusional thinking; (2) the person appears unable to

---

[25] s. 23.

[26] s. 12.

[27] s. 13.

[28] s. 20(2)(b).

[29] s. 21(1)1.

[30] s. 21(2)(b).

[31] s. 15(1).

[32] s. 15(2).

[33] s. 4(2), (3). Contrast this to s. 2(2) of the SDA which limits the presumption of capacity to persons who are 16 years of age or more in relation to giving or refusing consent in connection with his or her own personal care (which includes treatment.) This difference has bizarre consequences as follows: If there is a treatment proposed for a young person under the age of 16 the individual is presumed capable regarding treatment if the treatment is proposed under the HCCA's provisions; however, if the identical treatment is proposed as part of the individual's personal care under the SDA, the presumption of capacity does not apply to the young person in relation to making a decision about the treatment.

[34] S.O. 1992, c. 31. Amended by: 1994, c. 27, s. 43 (2); 1996, c. 2, s. 2. Note: Effective March 29, 1996, this Act is repealed by S.O. 1996, c. 2, subsection 2 (2).

make a settled choice about treatment; (3) the person is experiencing severe pain or acute fear or anxiety; (4) the person appears to be severely depressed; (5) the person appears to be impaired by alcohol or drugs; and (6) any other observations which give rise to a concern about the person's capacity, including observations about the person's behaviour or communication.[35] It must be remembered that these observations are not, either independently or cumulatively, determinative of the issue of capacity. They, or any of them, simply may suggest cause for further investigation.

When facing a situation where there are such reasonable grounds to suspect incapacity, how does the health practitioner determine the issue? There are no simple answers to this question. Recently the Supreme Court of Canada examined this issue for the first time and provided some guidance in this complex area.

Capacity

In June 2003, the Supreme Court of Canada released its judgment in *Starson v. Swayze*, [36] the leading case on determining capacity under the Act. In it the SCC followed Ontario's Court of Appeal in equating the common law right to medical self-determination with a section 7 Charter right to liberty and security of the person. [37] The SCC affirmed that "the right to refuse unwanted medical treatment is fundamental to a person's dignity and autonomy. This right is equally important in the context of treatment for mental illness... Unwarranted findings of incapacity severely infringe upon a person's right to self-determination." However, some people are not able to make these decisions and require decision-making in their best interest. Therefore "the Act aims to balance these competing interests of liberty and welfare". [38]

"Capacity" is defined as having both the ability to understand the information that is relevant to making a decision and the ability to appreciate reasonably foreseeable consequences of a decision or lack of decision. [39] A person is not capable of consenting to his or her own treatment (admission etc.) if he or she fails either branch of this test, *i.e.* if there is a demonstrated lack of ability either to understand relevant information or to appreciate consequences of the decision. The ability to understand the information that is relevant to making a treatment decision requires the "cognitive ability to process, retain and understand the relevant information." [40] The ability to appreciate the reasonably foreseeable consequences of the decision or lack of one "requires the patient to be able to apply the relevant information to his or her circumstances, and to be able to weigh

---

[35] O. Reg.19/95 s. 4(4).

[36] [2003] 1 S.C.R. 722.

[37] *Fleming v. Reid* (1991), 4 O.R. (3d) 74 (C.A.), *per* Robins J.A., at 88.

[38] *Starson* at para. 75, Major J. for the majority.

[39] s. 4(1).

[40] *Starson* at para. 78.

the foreseeable risks and benefits of a decision or lack thereof."[41] The *Starson* judgment summarizes the test as follows:

> [A] patient need not agree with the diagnosis of the attending physician in order to be able to apply the relevant information to his or her own circumstances. ... if it is demonstrated that he has a mental "condition", the patient must be able to recognize the possibility that he is affected by that condition. ... As a result, a patient is not required to describe his mental condition as an "illness", or to otherwise characterize the condition in negative terms. Nor is a patient required to agree with the attending physician's opinion regarding the cause of that condition. Nonetheless, if the patient's condition results in him being unable to recognize that he is affected by its manifestations, he will be unable to apply the relevant information to his circumstances, and unable to appreciate the consequences of his decision.[42]

The Act does not require actual appreciation of consequences. There is a distinction between inability and failure that is subtle but important. A person is entitled to disregard a physician's advice regarding treatment, provided the individual retains the ability necessary to make a capable, albeit ill-advised, decision. According to the SCC in *Starson*:

> In practice, the determination of capacity should begin with an inquiry into the patient's actual appreciation of the parameters of the decision being made: the nature and purpose of the proposed treatment; the foreseeable benefits and risks of treatment; the alternative courses of action available; and the expected consequences of not having the treatment. If the patient shows an appreciation of these parameters – regardless of whether he weighs or values the information differently than the attending physician and disagrees with the treatment recommendation – he has the ability to appreciate the decision he makes."... A finding of incapacity is justified only if those reasons demonstrate that the patient's mental disorder prevents him from having the <u>ability</u> to appreciate the foreseeable consequences of the decision.[43]

The Finding of Incapacity

Refusal of the proposed treatment is not incapacity.[44] Refusal to engage in any discussion of the proposed treatment with the health care practitioner is equally not indicative of incapacity, in the event the applicant otherwise demonstrates the ability to understand relevant information and the ability to appreciate consequences as contemplated by the test for capacity.[45]

---

[41] *Ibid.*

[42] *Ibid* at para. 79.

[43] *Ibid* at paras. 80, 81.

[44] *In re NB* CCB January 16, 1992

[45] In re R.K. TO-042229-2289 , July 21, 2004, a 17 year old young woman was found capable regarding treatment based on the fact that she had been requesting information from nursing staff regarding her diagnosis and treatment and attended the hearing with literature provided to her regarding the provisional diagnosis, which she had manifestly reviewed, despite her steadfast refusal to discuss treatment with her physician.

If a health care practitioner does not know the legal test for capacity, there cannot be a valid assessment of capacity before the Board for review and the presumption of capacity has not been rebutted.[46] Where the Board hears testimony from the health care practitioner who made the finding of incapacity and determines that the assessment of capacity was inadequate, the Board will find the individual capable on the presumption of capacity, without hearing from the applicant subject of the assessment.[47]

In the event the Board finds that the finding of incapacity was made during a period of illegal detention of the subject of the assessment of treatment capacity, the Board may, however, find itself without jurisdiction to review the finding of incapacity.[48] Where the subject of an assessment of capacity did not consent to being detained for that assessment and the individual was not properly a "patient" at the time of the assessment, a finding of incapacity made without authority may be a nullity. The Board cannot confirm an unlawful finding of incapacity.[49]

Information the Incapable Person Must Receive Following a Finding of Incapacity

Once a health practitioner makes a finding that an individual is not capable of making his or her own treatment decisions, the finding must be communicated to the subject of the proposed treatment. If the treatment proposed is for an individual in a psychiatric facility, written notice of the finding in the approved form[50] must be provided to the individual[51] and a rights adviser must be notified.[52]

---

[46] *In re AF* HA-05-4585 January 26, 2005 and in the Long Term Care admission context, see *In re SS* TO-05-4570 February 2, 2005 for the same proposition.

[47] For example, where a physician failed to inquire whether the patient accepted the possibility that some condition has affected her mood or behaviour, the patient remains capable. The Starson test requires this threshold question to be asked. See *In re Miss O* TO-05-5075 March 19, 2005.

[48] This approach, to deny the health practitioner "the fruit of a poisonous tree", had once found favour with the Board but had subsequently been rejected for a number of years. It appears to have returned to the Board's jurisprudence as a valid argument for applicants to advance. See *In re SC* OT-05-4952/53 March 11, 2005 and *In re RA* TO-04-0921/22 April 1, 2004.

[49] *In re SC* OT-05-4952/53 March 11, 2005 held that where a Form 1 was not signed by the physcian requesting the assessment, the subsequent Form 3 and finding of incapacity were held to be invalid. On the treatment issue the Board was without jurisdiciton to consider the matter. The Ruling *in Re RA* TO-04-1921/22 April 1, 2005 similarly results from a Form 33 issued during a period of invalid detention due to failure to comply with the Officer in Charge review of certification documents requirement under s. 20(8) of the Mental Health Act.

[50] Form 33 under the MHA; Note: the Board has rejected an argument that the approved form of notice to the patient is inadequate for failure to identify the proposed treatment specifically, see CCB Reasons for Decision in *Re GG*, TO 030202, March 6, 2003.

The rights adviser must promptly meet with the individual and advise him or her of the significance of the finding, the right to apply to the Board for a review of the finding and assist with the application as well as contacting legal counsel for the individual.[53] Outside of psychiatric facilities, the information to be imparted to the person found not capable of consenting to treatment is guided by each professional's governing body. The College of Physicians and Surgeons of Ontario (CPSO) directs physicians to inform the patient of the finding and of the right to apply to the Board.[54]

Litigation of the Issue of Capacity Before the Consent and Capacity Board

Application to Review a Finding of Incapacity (Form A)

A person who "is the subject of a treatment"[55] and does not have a court-appointed guardian of the person under the SDA[56] or a power of attorney for personal care which waives his or her right to a hearing before the Board[57] may

---

51 Failure to provide the Form 33 written notice under the MHA to the individual promptly may result in the finding of incapacity being declared invalid by the Board; see for example, *Re AP*, TO 030577/030578, May 26, 2003.

52 R.R.O. Reg. 741, s. 15(1).

53 R.R.O. 1990, Reg. 741, s. 15(2) and (4); Note: A delay in rights advice may invalidate the finding of incapacity; see for example, May 10, 2003 *Re: N.S.*, SW 03-0159. The delay invalidates the finding, even if the physician notified the rights adviser promptly, if the rights adviser failed to meet with the patient "promptly". What is meant by "prompt" is a factual determination based on context; where a four-day-long weekend intervenes, a five-day delay in the provision of rights advice may not invalidate an involuntary admission (and by analogy a finding of incapacity), see, *Re: M.A.*, TO 04 – 1335, May 4, 2004 (a case relating to rights advice following an involuntary committal.)

54 CPSO guidelines for treatment of incapable patients.

55 The issue of who qualifies as a 'subject of a treatment' is currently under appeal to Superior Court from the Board's Endorsement in *In re KM* TO-05-4261 which required an ongoing relationship between the prescribing physician and the subject of the treatment in order to establish that treatment was still proposed for the individual at the time of the hearing being convened as opposed to the time of the application being made in order to establish jurisdiction to consider the application. This approach leaves the applicant open to prejudice in subjecting the applicant to the possibility of future psychiatric assessment (Form 1) based on Box B criteria available only in respect of those "previously found incapable with respect to their treatment in a psychiatric facility." The Board, in a similar fact situation where no treatment was proposed for the applicant also found itself without jurisdiction, but appeard more focused on the resulting absence of a currently valid finding of incapacity: see *In re PC* PE-05-0471.

56 s. 59, SDA.

57 s. 50(1), SDA.

apply to the Board no more frequently[58] than once every six months for a review of a health practitioner's finding that he or she is incapable with respect to the treatment. Certain other applications[59] that come before the Board include a "deemed application concerning capacity"[60] required to proceed[61] prior to the main application.[62] While the subject of these applications is "deemed to have applied" for a review of the finding of incapacity,[63] this does not necessarily mean that a hearing of the issue of the individual's capacity is mandatory.[64] The Board has not ruled directly on the issue of the legal effect of a waiver of the deemed application. In our opinion, the subject of the treatment should be entitled to take no issue with the finding of incapacity at the time of the hearing of the main application, but choose to make his or her own application on that issue at a later date. In one recent case, however, the Board accepted a waiver from the subject of the treatment, but proceeded to render a decision regarding the deemed

---

[58] s. 32(1), (2), (5). Except with leave under s. 32(6) where there has been a material change in circumstances justifying a reconsideration of the person's capacity. The Board's new Rules of Practice comment on the process now adopted by the Board in relation to leave sought based on a material change of circumstances, see Rule 32 CCB Rules of Practice.

[59] As a result of Bill 68 amendments to the HCCA enacted December 31, 2000 which introduced the "deemed applications".

[60] s. 37.1, In *Conway v. Jacques*, the Superior Court of Justice recently overturned the Board's determination of treatment incapacity, which the Board had based in part on its own assumption that the issue of capacity had been determined on deemed applications in this regard as part of a prior Board hearing to determine an SDM's compliance with s. 21 of the HCCA and related appeals from that Form G application. The Boared erred in law in that the deemed application section was enacted subsequent to the original Form G hearing in relation to Mr. Conway's SDM; See *Conway v. Jac*ques [2005] O.J. No. 400 Ontario S.C. J. February 4, 2005.

[61] Where applicable, *i.e.* there has not been a hearing on the issue within the last six months and the applicant is not waiving the hearing of the issue at the time of the hearing of the application with which the deemed application has been included.

[62] *E.g.* application to appoint a representative for the incapable person under s. 33 and a number of other applications which interpret SDMs' decision making obligations on the incapable person's behalf such as the application for directions regarding a prior capable wish under s. 35, application for permission to depart from a wish under s. 36 and the application under s. 37 for a review of the SDMs' decision making process and determination as to compliance with the rules set out for this purpose under s. 21.

[63] Unless the issue has been determined by the Board in the preceding six months (s. 37.1).

[64] Contrast the "deemed application" provisions under s. 37.1 of the HCCA with the "deemed application" provisions under the *Mental Health Act* (s. 39(4)), which compels a mandatory hearing to inquire into whether the prerequisites for involuntary admission continue to be met on the date of hearing based on the completion of every fourth renewal of a certificate of involuntary admission. Under the MHA provisions, any purported waiver by an involuntary patient of the deemed application or the right to an application is a nullity (s. 35.(5) MHA).

application, in effect estopping the individual from applying for the review of the finding of incapacity in the next six-month[65] period.[66]

Treatment Must Not Commence Pending Determination of the Issue of Capacity

Treatment cannot commence[67] if, before treatment has begun, the health practitioner is informed that the person found incapable intends to apply or has applied to the Board for a review of the finding[68] or to appoint a representative for purposes of making the decision on his or her behalf or another person intends to apply or has applied to be appointed by the Board to make the decision.[69] The physician may, however, continue to administer treatment to the incapable person in the event that treatment had commenced prior to the finding of incapacity being made or before it came to the health practitioner's attention that a hearing of these issues may come before the Board. Once a person has indicated an intent to apply to the Board, however, treatment may only commence in the following circumstances: (1) once 48 hours have elapsed since the health practitioner was informed of the intended application but no application has been made; (2) if the application to the Board has been withdrawn; (3) when the Board has rendered a decision in the matter and no party has indicated an intention to appeal the Board's decision; (4) where a party has indicated an intention to appeal but the time for filing the appeal (seven days) has elapsed without the appeal being filed; or (5) when the appeal from the Board's decision has been finally disposed of.[70]

Who Applies to the Board?

The majority of applicants who challenge a finding of incapacity are individuals who wish to retain the right to refuse recommended treatment. The Board rarely receives an application for a review of a finding of treatment incapacity from an

---

65 In the event the Board feels it is required to review capacity (*i.e.* to enquire) as a prerequisite to appointing an individual as a representative, the individual may still request leave to apply within the six-month period and rely on the fact that (a) he or she requested a waiver of the deemed application and (b) change in circumstances.

66 In *Re AS*, TO 04-1163 and 1164 May 3, 2004, the applicant wished to proceed only with her Form B application to appoint a representative for purposes of making treatment decisions for her. She waived the deemed application only insofar as she was prepared to concede the issue of her incapacity for purposes of affording the Board the jurisdiction to proceed to appoint the representative, on the date of hearing. Her intention was to preserve her right to apply at a later date on the issue of her capacity, an option essentially foreclosed (subject to a potential leave application as described in the note above) by the Board rendering a decision on the issue of capacity.

67 s. 18.

68 s. 32.

69 s. 33(1), (2).

70 s. 33(3).

individual who wishes to receive the recommended treatment. There are a number of reasons for this. First, most individuals who are prepared to accept treatment are equally agreeable to have that decision made by their SDM. Second, while in law, acquiescence to treatment does not mean the person is capable, just as refusal of treatment should not be equated with incapacity, the reality is that assessments of capacity must take into account the individual's ultimate decision about the treatment. In practice, many physicians do not question the capacity of a patient who agrees with their treatment recommendation. In one sense, it is not unreasonable for a physician to presume that his or her patient's compliance with the recommended treatment plan is a capable decision. However, it is clearly problematic if a physician suddenly decides to declare a patient incapable because the individual refuses to continue to take medication rather than because of any change in his condition. Appellate courts have difficulty confirming a finding of incapacity made under these circumstances.[71]

The Proposed Treatment

What is the proposed treatment? At the outset of hearings regarding treatment capacity, this is the first matter which should be ascertained. Generally, the finding of incapacity is framed in relation to a particular class of medications to which the treatment(s) in question belong. For example, a person is often found incapable in relation to anti-psychotic medications or mood stabilizing medications, as opposed to a broader description such as "psychiatric treatment", or the more specific characterization of incapacity with respect to a particular medication such as Lithium. A degree of specificity is required to articulate and clarify what treatment is proposed in order to determine the treatment to which the finding of incapacity applies. Firstly, s. 32 of the Act requires the person to be "the subject of a treatment" in order to apply to the Board to review the finding that he or she is incapable with respect to "the treatment". Secondly, without identifying the treatment, patently unreasonable results could ensue. For instance, an individual may be found not capable with respect to "treatment of a mental disorder" based solely on a treatment proposal at the relevant time confined to psychotherapy. In the event a physician subsequently proposes to treat the mental disorder with electroconvulsive therapy, should an SDM be permitted to consent to this treatment without the individual being afforded a right of review on this issue? Where the risk/benefit analysis in relation to a proposed treatment is significantly different from a previously proposed treatment, the individual's capacity in relation to each treatment should be evaluated independently.

There have been a number of cases heard on appeal from Board hearings confirming incapacity with respect to certain classes of medication which were not specifically addressed during the hearing. In one such case, the court held that

---

[71] See for example, *Boimier v. Swaminath*, [2003] O.J. No. 2848 (S.C.J.), where the court referred the matter back to the Board for rehearing by a different panel and ordered an assessment of the appellant by a different psychiatrist to take place prior to the rehearing.

certain classes of medications in the treatment of mental disorder may qualify as "ancillary treatment" for which no separate finding of incapacity is necessary.[72] The court has also held that the Board appropriately found an individual not capable to make decisions regarding a number of different medications proposed for the same disorder, where there was sufficient evidence before the Board indicating the applicant was unable to appreciate the potential benefit of any medication.[73]

There are great variations in the approach taken by hearing panels of the Board in relation to this issue.[74] On occasion, individuals are found capable with respect to medications to treat side-effects of other medications, even while they are found not capable with respect to the principal treatment.[75] The Board has also recently declined to accede to an applicant's request to appoint a representative for purposes of making all treatment decisions about which he or she may become incapable,[76] notwithstanding that the legislation permits the Board to make this type of order.[77]

---

[72] *Neto v. Klukach*, [2004] O.J. No. 394 (S.C.J.). The court overturned the Board and found the appellant capable with respect to the proposed treatment, but indicated that had the physician proved incapacity regarding mood stabilizers, mild tranquillizers would have constituted ancillary treatment about which the appellant would also have been incapable.

[73] *Paluska v. Cava*, [2001] O.J. No. 4010 (S.C.J.) and *Thompson v. Grant*, [2001] O.J. No. 1778 (S.C.J.)

[74] In *Re AM*, TO 04-1217/1268, April 22, 2004, for example, the Board found the applicant not capable with respect to mood stabilizers only. The Board agreed with the applicant's position that it could not make any finding in relation to capacity respecting antipsychotics, benzodiazepines and anticholinergics, as no assessment specific to these classes of medication had been conducted by the health practitioner proposing the treatment. The Board rejected the doctor's argument that benzodiazepines and anticholinergics are ancillary treatment (notwithstanding that this very position was accepted by Day J. in *Neto v. Klukach* (Ont. SCJ). The AM Board also rejected the doctor's argument (despite the success of this position taken by physicians in *Thompson* and *Paluska*) that she didn't have to do an assessment because the applicant had indicated quite strongly to her from the beginning that he was not interested in psychiatric medications at all and wouldn't change his mind.

[75] See for example, *Re: G.J.*, TO 04-1372/1373 May 20, 2004.

[76] In *Re AS*, TO 04-1163 and 1164, May 3, 2004, the Board chose to limit the appointment of the representative (a friend) to authority to make decisions regarding mood-stabilizers, antipsychotics and hypnotics, even though the Board was aware the result is that decisions regarding any other treatment about which the individual may become incapable will still be made by the highest ranking SDM for her (her mother).

[77] s. 33(5)(c). For an example of the Board acceding to the request to appoint a representative to make any and all decisions in respect of a which an individual may be found not capable in future, see *In re L.F.* TO-04-4244/45 December 20, 2004.

The Board Hearing Regarding Capacity — Role of the Board

The parties to the application are the person found incapable, the health practitioner and any other party the Board may specify.[78] The Board may confirm the finding of incapacity or determine that the person is capable, and in doing so may substitute its own opinion for that of the health practitioner.[79] In *Starson*,[80] the SCC considered the role of the Board in these proceedings and made the following comments:

> The legislative mandate of the Board is to adjudicate solely upon a patient's capacity. The Board's conception of the patient's best interests is irrelevant to that determination... "[a] competent patient has the absolute entitlement to make decisions that any reasonable person would deem foolish" (para. 13). This point was aptly stated by Quinn J. in *Re Koch* (1997), 33 O.R. (3d) 485 (Gen. Div.), at p. 521:
>
>> The right knowingly to be foolish is not unimportant; the right to voluntarily assume risks is to be respected. The State has no business meddling with either. The dignity of the individual is at stake.
>
> In this case, the only issue before the Board was whether Professor Starson was capable of making a decision on the suggested medical treatment. The wisdom of his decision has no bearing on this determination.[81]

Determining Capacity

Major J., writing for the majority, went on to say:

> The law presumes a person is capable to decide to accept or reject medical treatment: s. 4(2) of the Act. At a capacity hearing, the onus is on the attending physician to prove that the patient is incapable. I agree with the Court of Appeal that proof is the civil standard of a balance of probabilities. As a result, patients with mental disorders are presumptively entitled to make their own treatment decisions. Professor D. N. Weisstub, in his Enquiry on Mental Competency: Final Report (1990), at p. 116 (the "Weisstub Report"), notes the historical failure to respect this presumption:
>
>> The tendency to conflate mental illness with lack of capacity, which occurs to an even greater extent when involuntary commitment is involved, has deep historical roots, and even though changes have occurred in the law over the past twenty years, attitudes and beliefs have been slow to change. For

---

[78] s. 32(3).
[79] s. 32(4).
[80] [2003] 1 S.C.R. 722.
[81] *Ibid.* at para. 76.

> this reason it is particularly important that autonomy and self determination be given priority when assessing individuals in this group.
>
> The Board must avoid the error of equating the presence of a mental disorder with incapacity. Here, the respondent did not forfeit his right to self-determination upon admission to the psychiatric facility: see *Fleming v. Reid,* at p. 86. The presumption of capacity can be displaced only by evidence that a patient lacks the requisite elements of capacity provided by the Act.[82]

The facts of the *Starson* case are perhaps unique in that the appellant was an extraordinarily intelligent individual who was able to articulate his position in particularly compelling ways.[83] Because of the rigorous review of the evidence before the Board undertaken by the various levels of court in determining whether the Board's decision was ultimately unreasonable, many subsequent cases on appeal are rather easily distinguished from *Starson*, on their facts.[84] Where it is clear, however, that the Board continues to be inappropriately influenced by its own subjective view of what is in the applicant's best interest, the courts continue to reverse the Board's confirmation of findings of incapacity based on such irrelevant criteria.[85]

The Decision of the Board

The Board, for the most part, confirms physicians' findings of incapacity in relation to treatment, particularly in the psychiatric context. Historically, less than 10 per cent of applicants have been found capable by the Board on the issue of treatment.[86] The Board's decisions are appealable as of right to the SCJ on any question of law or fact or both.[87] Since the Board is an expert tribunal, its decisions are reviewable on a deferential "reasonableness *simpliciter*" standard in relation to factual determinations and on a more stringent standard of correctness in relation to legal issues of statutory interpretation.[88] Very few of these cases are ultimately heard and determined on appeal to the Superior Court; however, many more appeals are commenced without resolution for extended periods of time.

---

82 *Ibid.* at para. 77.

83 *Ibid. Starson v. Swayze* aff'g (2001), 201 D.L.R.(4th) 123 (Ont. C.A.), aff'g (1999), 22 Admin L.R. (3d) 211 (Ont. S.C.J.). It may be worthwhile for the reader to review the lower courts' judgments, particularly the SCJ judgment, for a complete understanding of the facts in this case, on which much of the judgments ultimately turned.

84 See for example *Thompson v. Grant,* [2001] O.J. No. 1778 (S.C.J.); *Paluska v. Cava,* [2001] O.J. No. 4010 (S.C.J.).

85 See for example *Neto v. Klukach,* [2004] O.J. No. 394 (S.C.J.).

86 For statistics in relation to numbers of hearings and outcomes, contact the CCB.

87 s. 80.

88 *Starson* (S.C.C.) at para. 84 and *Daugherty v. Stall* (2002), 48 E.T.R. (2d) 8, [2002] O.J. No. 4715 (S.C.J.).

Since treatment cannot begin until the court disposes of the issue and the person's condition may worsen in the intervening period, physicians often find the delay in commencing treatment very frustrating.

Pending Appeal

Physicians may apply to the court for an order authorizing treatment pending appeal;[89] however, the court must be convinced, among other things, that the person's condition makes treatment necessary before the final disposition of the appeal.[90] These applications are extremely rare. This is perhaps because the cases decided to date indicate the court's reluctance to grant the remedy sought by physicians absent very compelling evidence of the need for treatment. The court is more inclined to expedite the hearing of the appeal without allowing the application for an order permitting treatment. The court's concern is that making the order would have the effect of essentially rendering the individual's appeal moot, if the individual is objecting to the treatment, and the subject matter of the appeal is the person's ongoing refusal to have the treatment.[91]

The Role of the Court on Appeal

The court's role on appeal from the Board is to review the Board's decision on a reasonableness standard.[92] The question the reviewing court asks itself is whether after a somewhat probing examination there is any evidence on which the Board could reasonably have come to its decision.[93]

In the event that a person is found not capable in relation to the treatment proposed and either does not apply to the Board for a review, or the Board or court on appeal finally determines the issue such that the individual is not capable to make his or her own decisions, the health practitioner who proposed the treatment must obtain informed consent, in accordance with the Act, from the individual's SDM.[94]

---

[89] s. 19.

[90] s. 19(2)(d).

[91] *Gunn v. Koczerginski*, [2001] O.J. No. 4479 (S.C.J.) and *Paluska, Jr. v. Cava* (2001), 55 O.R. (3d) 681 (S.C.J.), reversed on other grounds 59 O.R. (3d) 469 (C.A.).

[92] See *T. (I.) v. L. (L.)* (1999), 46 O.R. (3d) 284 (C.A.), affirmed in *Starson* in the SCC at paras. 71 and 84.

[93] *Ibid. T. (I.) v. L. (L.)*, at para. 20.

[94] s. 10, s. 11, s. 20, s. 21 and *M. (A.) v. Benes* (1999), 46 O.R. (3d) 271 (C.A.).

CONSENT ON INCAPABLE PERSON'S BEHALF

Identifying the Appropriate SDM

Hierarchy—SDM identified by the Act

The Act provides a hierarchy of individuals who may give or refuse consent to the proposed treatment on behalf of the incapable person.[95] In the absence of a court-appointed guardian of the person, or an attorney for personal care whose authority includes treatment decisions, an incapable person may apply to the Board to have a representative appointed or another person may apply to be appointed as the representative for the incapable person, provided the incapable person does not object.[96] If there is no guardian, attorney or representative to make the decision, a family member becomes the decision-maker. Spouses (or "partners" including same-sex partners)[97] are highest ranked. Below them (in descending order) are children or parents of the incapable person[98] (equally ranked), an access parent, siblings, and finally any other relative (relative is defined as people related by blood, marriage or adoption.[99]

Other Criteria in Qualifying as SDM

A person described in s. 20(1) may only make the treatment decision if he or she is (1) capable with respect to the treatment, (2) at least 16 years old, is available and willing to make the decision,[100] and no higher ranking individual exists or in the event that such a person does exist, the higher ranking individual either does not otherwise qualify or would not object to the person making the decision.[101]

The Meaning of "Available"

In order to qualify as an "available" SDM, the decision-maker does not have to reside in Ontario or Canada, provided it is possible to obtain the necessary consent or refusal within a reasonable time in the circumstances.[102] The fact that the incapable person may object to their "statutory decision maker" does not disqualify the SDM. It may, however, give rise to the incapable person applying to the Board to have someone else appointed.[103] This is the only option available to the incapable person, even where the person does not object to the particular SDM but has concerns about the way decisions are being made by the SDM. The

[95] s. 20.
[96] s. 33(1), (2), (5), (6).
[97] s. 20(8), (9).
[98] s. 20(1)5.
[99] s. 20(10).
[100] s. 20(2)(a), (b), (d), (e).
[101] s. 20(3), (4).
[102] s. 20(11).
[103] s. 33(1).

Act does not afford any mechanism for the incapable person to question the appropriateness of the SDM's decision-making process on his or her behalf. Although health practitioners have the option of applying to the Board[104] to determine whether an SDM is making decisions according to the principles set out for them under the Act,[105] the incapable person is not entitled to make this type of application. This is a somewhat troubling flaw in the legislative regime and may have Charter implications yet to be tested.

The meaning of "Capable" with respect to SDMs

Identifying the appropriate SDM may be somewhat complicated in rare situations. However, the issue of determining whether an SDM is capable with respect to the treatment is always a difficult one. The SDM is not the health practitioner's patient (generally) and if the health practitioner is of the opinion that the SDM is not capable, is the SDM owed any due process protection? The Act does not appear to contemplate any particular avenue a potential SDM can use to challenge a "finding" that he or she is not capable with respect to the treatment. In fact, there is nothing in the Act preventing a health practitioner from simply moving to the next person in the hierarchy (under s. 20) to obtain consent where the health practitioner believes the higher ranking individual is not capable. What the person passed over may choose to do, however, is apply to the Board to be appointed the representative of the incapable person to make the decision.[106] At the hearing of that application, the Board will need to satisfy itself that the proposed representative is capable, among other things.[107]

---

[104] s. 37.

[105] s. 21.

[106] s. 33(2).

[107] The criteria for the appointment of a representative under s. 33 (6) include (a) that the incapable person does not object, (b) that the proposed representative is over 16 and capable with respect to the treatment and (c) that the appointment is in the incapable person's best interest. Whether the Board's role in these applications (Form B is the incapable person's application to appoint someone and Form C is another person's application to be appointed) is simply to satisfy itself that the proposed representative understands the rules for SDMs' decision making set out under s. 21 or whether the Board must ascertain what decision the proposed representative would make and whether the decision itself is in the incapable person's best interest is still unsettled law. There are Board decisions going both ways, for an example of the former approach see *R.C.*, TO 031142, November 3, 2003 and In *re AS*, TO 04-1163 and 1164, May 3, 2004. For an example of the latter, see *In Re BP*. TO02-21443, 1444, February 4, 2003 and *In Re IA*, LO-O4-0999, 1000, April 9, 2004. In either case, proposed representative's ability to withstand pressure from the incapable person in relation to the decision appears central to the Board's determination regarding the appointment. See *R.C.* TO 031142 November 3, 2003.

The Role of the Public Guardian and Trustee

The Public Guardian and Trustee is the decision maker of last resort and also makes the decision where two or more equally ranked individuals disagree.[108] The Office of the Public Guardian and Trustee has established a specialized Treatment Decisions Unit whose members make decisions on behalf of incapable persons for whom no one else is qualified under s. 20 of the Act or prepared to make the decision.

Principles for giving or refusing consent

The SDM's obligations

The Act sets out the rules for decision making by SDMs on behalf of incapable persons.[109] The incapable person's most recently expressed[110] "prior capable wishes" which apply in the circumstances must be obeyed.[111]

If the SDM does not know of a wish applicable to the circumstances that the incapable person expressed while capable and after attaining 16 years of age, or if it is impossible to comply with the wish, the person shall act in the incapable person's best interests.[112] The Act sets out the factors the SDM must consider when acting in the incapable person's best interest.[113] Where an SDM consents to treatment on behalf of an incapable individual, the SDM may also consent to the incapable person's admission to hospital or a psychiatric facility for purposes of receiving that treatment,[114] except where the incapable person's admission to a psychiatric facility is sought and the individual is over the age of 16 and objects. In that case only court-appointed guardians of the person or attorneys pursuant to a personal care power of attorney which contains the extraordinary powers set out in s. 50 of the SDA can consent.[115]

The health practitioner's obligations

Health practitioners are required to inform SDMs about the rules which govern their decision making on behalf of incapable individuals.[116] Where a health practitioner is aware of prior capable wishes to refuse a treatment, the treatment,

---

[108] s. 20(5),(6).

[109] s. 21.

[110] s. 5(3). The wish may be expressed in any manner — see s. 5(2) including within the body of a power of attorney for personal care or elsewhere in writing or orally or in any other manner after the age of 16 at a time of capacity

[111] s. 21(1)1.

[112] s. 21(1)2.

[113] s. 21(20).

[114] s. 24(1).

[115] s. 24(2).

[116] s. 10 and M. (A) v. Benes (1999), 46 O.R. (3d) 271 (C.A.).

including emergency treatment, cannot be administered.[117] However, in an emergency, the treatment may be administered over an SDM's refusal in the event the health practitioner in the opinion of the SDM did not comply with s. 21.[118] Except in an emergency situation, where a health practitioner forms the opinion that the SDM is not making decisions on behalf of the incapable person in accordance with the provisions of s. 21, the health practitioner may apply to the Board for a determination of the issue.[119] The health practitioner cannot simply ignore the refusal of the SDM and treat the individual or move to the next person under s. 20 to make the decision.

The Role of the Board

The scheme of the Act ensures that in adjudicating issues of consent on behalf of incapable persons, the Board is required, as is the SDM, to consider first and foremost the effect of any prior capable wish expressed by the incapable individual. The previous *Mental Health Act* provisions, which obliged the SDM to obey prior capable wishes, but permitted the Board to order treatment in the best interest of the incapable person (without regard to any prior capable wishes applicable to the circumstances), were the subject of a constitutional challenge brought to the Ontario Court of Appeal in *Fleming v. Reid*.[120] In that case, the Court affirmed the supremacy of prior capable wishes.

Applications Regarding Prior Capable Wishes

Where there is uncertainty in determining whether previously expressed wishes of an incapable person are binding on an SDM in a particular situation, the SDM or the health practitioner who proposes the treatment may apply to the Board for directions in interpreting the wish.[121] Similarly, where the SDM must refuse consent because of the expression of a prior capable wish which applies to the circumstances, the SDM may apply to the Board for permission to depart from the wish or the health practitioner may apply to the Board for permission to accept the SDM's consent despite the wish.[122] The SDM has no recourse to the Board for guidance on how to make decisions in the best interests of the individual, other than the considerations prescribed under s. 21; however, the health practitioner has the option of seeking the Board's directions on whether the SDM is

---

[117] s. 26 and *Malette v. Shulman* (1990), 72 O.R. (2d) 417 (C.A.), a case involving a Jehovah's Witness who was unconscious upon arrival in the emergency room but her purse was found to contain a card instructing against blood transfusion. The court found the physician who transfused her liable for damages for violating clearly stated prior capable wishes.

[118] s. 27.

[119] s. 37.

[120] (1991), 4 O.R. (3d) 74 (C.A.).

[121] s. 35(1).

[122] s. 36(1).

complying with his or her obligations under all of s. 21, including the 'best interests' test.[123] All of these applications contain a deemed application by the incapable person for a review of the finding of incapacity.[124]

Application to Review the SDM's Decision

Only the health practitioner who proposed the treatment may apply to the Board for a determination of the SDM's compliance with s. 21 of the Act.[125] The constitutionality of this provision of the Act was upheld by Ontario's Court of Appeal shortly after the introduction of the Act.[126] The court held that the Board is ideally situated to determine what is in an incapable person's best interests. While an SDM may have more information regarding an incapable person's wishes (be they prior capable wishes, values and beliefs or non-binding wishes),[127] the "best interests" test[128] also involves a risk/benefit analysis about which a medical expert is better informed. The Board's role was seen as one appropriately independent and expert to assist in resolving any tensions between the position of the health practitioner and the SDM, which may arise in these situations.[129]

The parties to this application are the health practitioner who proposed the treatment, the incapable person, the substitute decision-maker and any other person whom the Board specifies.[130] In determining whether the substitute decision-maker complied with section 21, the Board may substitute its opinion for that of the substitute decision-maker.[131] If the Board determines that the substitute decision-maker did not comply with section 21, it may give him or her directions and, in doing so, shall apply section 21.[132] The Board shall specify the time within which its directions must be complied with.[133] If the substitute decision-maker does not comply with the Board's directions within the time specified by the Board, he or she shall be deemed not to meet the requirements of subsection 20 (2)[134] and in that event, any subsequent substitute decision-maker (including

---

[123] s. 37.

[124] s. 37.1.

[125] s. 37(1).

[126] *M. (A.) v. Benes*, (1999), 46 O.R. (3d) 271 (C.A.) and *T. (I.) v. L.(L.)*, (1996), 46 O.R. (3d) 284 (C.A.).

[127] s. 21 (2) (a) and (b).

[128] s. 21 (2) (c).

[129] *M. (A.) v. Benes*, (1999), 46 O.R. (3d) 271 (C.A.); *T. (I.) v. L.(L.)*, (1996) 46 O.R. (3d) 284 (C.A.).

[130] s. 37(2).

[131] s. 37(3).

[132] s. 37(4).

[133] s. 37(5).

[134] s. 37(6).

the PGT) shall[135] comply with the directions given by the Board on the application within the time specified by the Board. The Board's direction to SDMs to consent to the recommended treatment has been upheld in the Court of Appeal for Ontario on three occasions.[136] On one occasion where the Board found the SDMs had not complied with s. 21 in refusing to consent to (what the Board erroneously characterized as) a "Do Not Resuscitate Order" for their mother,[137] the court reversed the Board and in effect reinstated the authority of the SDMs to require ongoing treatment for the incapable person.[138]

Admission to Care Facilities [Part III of the Act]

Impetus Behind the Act — Mini-guardianship

This portion of the Act was enacted in response to frustration with the process of obtaining court-appointed guardianship of the person[139] expressed by family members of elderly individuals who required nursing home placement but refused it. The frustration arose from the considerable time and expense associated with court applications and the uncertainty of whether the court would ultimately grant full guardianship. The resulting provisions under the Act were meant to provide a fast-tracked alternative with access to the immediate remedy afforded by the Board at low or no cost to applicants. However, the incapable person can easily thwart attempts to use the Act as an alternative to guardianship. A common misconception exists that the operation of this part of the Act together with

---

[135] Subject to subsections 37(6.2) and 37(6.3) which allow certain applications by the subsequent SDM other than the PGT where the new SDM knows of prior capable wishes applicable to the circumstances .

[136] *M.(A.) v. Benes*, (1999), 46 O.R. (3d) 271; (C.A.) *T (I.) v. L. (L.)*, (1996) 46 O.R. (3d) 284. See also *Conway v. Jacques*, [2002] O.J. No. 2333 (Ont. C.A.) in which the fact that the subject of the proposed treatment always refused medications proposed while capable was interpreted as a wish not applicable to his current circumstances, because his condition had deteriorated and the medication newly available had fewer side-effects. Considerations of efficacy of newer medication are more appropriately considered, in our view, where permission is sought to consent to a treatment despite a prior capable wish to the contrary, under Form E applications pursuant to s. 36.

[137] In *Re: HJ,* TO-031193, October 8, 2003.

[138] *Scardoni v. Hawryluck*, [2004] O.J. No. 300 (S.C.J.). The court found that the Board had misapprehended the medical evidence and consequently drew incorrect inferences fundamental to determining what was in the best interest of the incapable person. The Board's characterization of the issue as one respecting a "DNR" was incorrect as well. This case is significant because it is the only judicial consideration of the issue of "withdrawing or withholding life support / ICU care"; discussions of what to do in the event of cardiac arrest - ie, whether to provide CPR (the "DNR" issue) - was never properly before the Board. Indeed, the final instruction of the Board to the SDM was clearly to "comply with a treatment plan to withhold or withdraw life-support/ICU care."

[139] See *Substitute Decisions Act, 1992*, s. 59.

decisions of the Board confer custodial powers to SDMs in relation to those persons found incapable with respect to admission to care facilities. This is not the case.

Admission Provisions Mirror the Treatment Provisions under the Act

As indicated above, the provisions of the Act relating to consent and capacity issues arising from a proposal to admit an individual to a care facility essentially adopt, with necessary modifications, the provisions related to treatment.[140] For example, individuals found incapable to make a decision regarding admission also have the right to a review of the finding before the Board once every six months. An SDM is selected according to the same hierarchy and bound by the same rules regarding decision-making on behalf of the incapable person, but for the fact that the prior capable wish, if any, must relate to placement in long-term care. The "best interests" of the individual is, in part, a question of improved "quality of life" (as a result of admission) rather than improvement in the medical or psychiatric condition of the individual (as a result of treatment). Similarly, with limited exceptions,[141] admission to a care facility must not be authorized while there are applications before the Board or the court regarding the issue of capacity and before the issue has been finally determined. Apart from the way the Act is structured, with provisions relating to admission to care mirroring the treatment provisions, there are some differences in the two sections of the Act which are worthwhile to note.

Who Does What?

In the treatment context, the individual who proposes the treatment and makes the determination of incapacity is also the person who requires the necessary consent to the proposed treatment. In the admission context, there is an inevitable division of these three functions among various professionals. The person who makes the finding is not able to admit the individual. Anyone can propose that an individual be admitted to long-term care. However, only certain classes of individuals (evaluators, s. 2) are able to make a legally relevant finding in relation to capacity to make this decision[142], and only representatives of the CCACs can act on the applicable consent on behalf of an incapable person. Applications for admission to a care facility are processed by a centralized agency which determines eligibility of individual applicants for placement, maintains the waiting list of applicants who are deemed eligible, and when a bed becomes

---

[140] ss. 39-54.1.

[141] An exception is a crisis admission where admission is required immediately as a result of a crisis [s. 46(4)]; another exception is admission for a definite period of stay not exceeding 90 days [s. 46(5)].

[142] An inadequate evaluation where the evaluator did not know the test for capacity resulted in a finding that no evaluation took place and the presumption of capacity to make decisions regarding admission to long-term care was reinstated. See In re SS TO-05-4570 February 2, 2005.

available, it is the CCAC which requires the capable applicant or the SDM of the incapable applicant to provide the necessary consent for the admission to occur.

Parties to Board Hearings Regarding Admission

Applications before the Board to review a finding of incapacity in the admission context have one additional statutory party. In addition to the person found incapable who is applying for the review and the evaluator who made the finding, the "person responsible for authorizing admissions to the care facility" is also a party to these proceedings, and the related proceedings regarding appointment of a representative or interpretation of prior capable wishes etc.[143] The CCACs in Ontario are responsible for these decisions. The role of this additional party arises from the fact that in the admission context, the person who makes the finding of incapacity (the evaluator) is not the person who must obtain the necessary consent to authorize the admission. In the treatment context, the health practitioner who makes the finding of incapacity is generally the person who requires consent to the treatment proposed.[144] In the case of a proposed admission, it is the CCAC as the party responsible for authorizing the admission who requires the appropriate consent, and therefore also bears the responsibility for ensuring that consent is given in accordance with the Act. The applications regarding interpretation of prior capable wishes,[145] for permission to depart from such wishes,[146] or to review the decision making of the SDM,[147] may only be brought by the CCAC (or the SDM where applicable) and not the evaluator.

Appeals from Board Decisions regarding Capacity

Board's Decision Unenforceable in Law

Very few appeals are taken from decisions of the Board regarding[148] determinations of capacity to make a decision concerning admission to a care facility. The operation of the Act in relation to admission to care facilities has elsewhere been described as a "toothless tiger" because in essence, these provisions are unenforceable against the individual's will. Absent a court-appointed guardian's

---

143 *E.g.* s. 50(3), 51(4), 54(2).

144 There are rare exceptions to this situation: In one case the Board found that a psychiatrist had the authority to make a finding of incapacity regarding cataract surgery, See *Re: D.K.* (April 26, 1998, C.C.B.), WT-98/097 and WT-98/099. Where there may be disagreement on the issue of capacity between the proposing physician and the physician who ultimately requires the appropriate consent, interesting further issues for discussion arise which fall outside of the scope of this paper.

145 s. 52.

146 s. 53.

147 s. 54.

148 Whether the Board confirms the finding of incapacity or finds the individual capable.

authority to detain the incapable person[149] there are no custodial powers given to an SDM inherent in a decision of the Board confirming incapacity. Without the necessary authority that only court-appointed guardianship may confer, nothing in this Act would permit the actual transfer of the person to the care facility, or to authorize detention of the individual once at the facility, against his or her will.

Practical Reality

Notwithstanding this practical reality, incapable individuals are routinely transferred from hospitals or from their own home to care facilities and detained without any apparent lawful authority. The individuals who find themselves in this situation are those persons who are either too incapacitated to object meaningfully to their detention or simply unable to leave the facility.[150] Those who continue to articulate their refusal to go or to remain in nursing home settings simply have no need for an appeal from a Board decision confirming their incapacity. They are free, through their actions, to defy their SDM's apparent authority to consent to their admission, whether or not entitled by law to make this decision.[151] This is the case certainly where the person retains control of management of his or her own property, since ancillary decisions the SDM is entitled to make when consenting to admission to a care facility on behalf of an incapable person do not include decisions regarding the individual's property.[152] In practice, a finding[153] that the individual is not capable of managing his or her property is often made at the same time as an evaluator determines the person incapable of consenting to admission to a care facility.

---

[149] An argument may be made that an attorney for personal care with the necessary authority may have the ability to detain the individual pursuant to the *Substitute Decisions Act, 1992,* s. 67 which affords attorneys for personal care the same rights and duties as guardians have under s. 66(10)(1) among others. Section 66(10)(1)(a) of the SDA allows the Guardian to consent to confinement, monitoring or restraint if the practice allows the individual greater freedom or enjoyment.

[150] The code to the door is in most nursing homes on the actual door but the person must retain the capacity to make use of this information in order to leave.

[151] In such cases, the only remedy available to the care facility would be (a) provisions of the MHA at s. 15 or s. 16 to cause an assessment or examination of the person, (b) communicating any concerns to the PG & T pursuant to s. 62 of the SDA or (c) assess the resident incapable of personal assistance services and, if necessary to prevent serious bodily harm to the resident or others or to allow the recipient greater freedom, the SDM may consent to restraint, confinement etc. See s. 59(3).

[152] s. 44(3).

[153] Whether made under the MHA if the individual is a patient in a psychiatric facility or under the SDA otherwise.

Cases regarding Admission

Of the handful of cases at the appellate level which consider this part of the Act, *Re Koch*[154] was the first consideration of some of the important issues raised by evaluations of capacity respecting admission to a long-term care facility. The court, in this case, imported some procedural safeguards under the SDA as they related to assessments of an individual's capacity to manage property into evaluations under the HCCA regarding admission to a care facility.[155] The facts of the case were particularly egregious in that the applicant to the Board suffered from multiple sclerosis and was separated from her husband at the time he requested that she be assessed regarding her ability to manage property as well as evaluated with respect to admission to long-term care. Ultimately, the court found the appellant capable in relation to all issues and reversed the Board's finding of incapacity under each application before it.[156] In light of the fact that the matter was disposed of on the substantive issue of capacity, the concerns expressed by Quinn J. in relation to the process undertaken to conduct the assessment and evaluation in question arguably constitute *obiter dicta*.[157]

In another appeal also in Superior Court[158] the court held that a valid finding of incapacity may be made as a result of ongoing evaluation by a psychiatrist of an inpatient under his care. There was no need to notify the subject of the evaluation of the right to refuse the evaluation because a refusal would not have made any difference in this context. The evaluator physician in this case could have made the finding based on his observations of the patient over the course of many weeks and based on his review of the charts, even if the patient refused to discuss the issue of long-term care.

However, the *Koch* judgment, while not necessarily binding on the Board in the procedural safeguards it imports into the Act where those remarks are properly construed as *obiter*, is persuasive in signalling that some protections and due process rights must be afforded individuals where the implications of determinations of capacity have such fundamental impact on the liberty of the person. In *Koch*, Quinn J. also required that meticulous notes be made to support a finding of incapacity resulting from an evaluation again because of the

---

[154] *Re Koch* (1997), 33 O.R. (3d) 485 (Gen. Div.).

[155] In *Re Koch*, the assessment and evaluation were conducted in a manner which, according to Quinn J., breached the natural justice rights of the applicant. The court held that the applicant had the right to be informed of the significance of the finding of incapacity if so made at the end of the evaluation, to have counsel or a friend present during an evaluation, the right to be told that she may refuse the evaluation and the right to refuse to be evaluated.

[156] See also *Bartoszek v. Ontario (Consent and Capacity Board)*, [2002] O.J. No. 3800 (S.C.J.).

[157] The Board takes the view that to the extent the *Koch* judgment would import the right to counsel etc. to HCCA evaluations, it is *obiter* and not binding on the Board, see for *e.g.* In *Re Mrs. I.L.A.*, TO 04-0973, May 16, 2004.

[158] *Heuberger v. Stenn*, [2002] O.J. No. 1285 (Ont.S.C.J.).

importance of the issues at stake for the subject of the evaluation. The Board has subsequently found invalid those evaluations which are not supported by an acceptable level of documentation in support of the outcome of the evaluation.[159]

Personal Assistance Services (Part IV of the Act)

The provisions regarding personal assistance services relate only to "recipients"[160] of such services. "Personal Assistance Service" means assistance with or supervision of hygiene, washing, dressing, grooming, eating, drinking, elimination, ambulation, positioning or any other routine activity of living.[161] The provisions regarding personal assistance services mirror the provisions as set out above in relation to treatment and admission to a care facility. An evaluator (as defined in the Act, being the same classes of persons as for purposes of admission) makes the determination of capacity in relation to personal assistance services. The person who requires the necessary consent to provide personal assistance services, and who therefore takes on the roles and responsibilities of the health care practitioner in the treatment context and the CCAC in the admission context, is the "member of the service provider's staff who is responsible for the personal assistance service."[162]

Of note, the principles for decision making by the SDM contain three additional provisions not seen in either the treatment or the admission sections. The first is a provision prohibiting the SDM from consenting[163] to the use of confinement, monitoring devices or means of restraint, unless the practice is essential to prevent serious bodily harm to the recipient or to others, or allows the recipient greater freedom or enjoyment.[164] The second such provision is the requirement that the SDM shall encourage the recipient to participate, to the best of his or her abilities, in the person's decision concerning the personal assistance service.[165] The third difference is that the Public Guardian and Trustee does not have to make

---

[159] See for example In *re AB*, TO-04 1257, 1260, May 5, 2004.

[160] s. 2 Interpretation, essentially restricted to individuals already residing in a care facility.

[161] s. 2 Interpretation 'personal assistance service' and includes a group of personal assistance services or a plan setting out personal assistance services to be provided to a person, but does not include anything prescribed by the regulations as not constituting a personal assistance service.

[162] See for example s. 67(1) where the SDMs compliance with the rules for decision making are reviewed.

[163] Absent a prior capable wish requiring the consent.

[164] s. 59 (3) which uses exactly the same language as powers granted court-appointed guardians and attorneys for personal care as discussed above in relation to custodial authority to detain individuals in nursing home settings; the difference is that in relation to personal assistance services, the legislation confers the authority in limited circumstances on SDMs for purposes of deciding whether to consent to the personal assistance service, whereas elsewhere only court-appointed guardians of the person or arguably some attorneys for personal care have this type of authority.

[165] s. 59(4).

decisions as SDM of last resort.[166] In relation to personal assistance services then, it would appear, an incapable person may have no SDM since the PG & T appears to have the option of refusing to make this type of decision.

The Consent and Capacity Board (Part V of the Act)

The Act is the governing statute giving rise to the jurisdiction of the Board to adjudicate under the Act, under the *Mental Health Act* and the *Substitute Decisions Act, 1992* as well as limited provisions relating to health records kept in care facilities under the *Long-Term Care Act, 1994*.[167] In this part of the Act, specific provisions governing the membership of the Board and its processes are outlined. The authors' discussion regarding the Board is found as an introduction to the new Rules of Practice of the Board in this consolidation.

Miscellaneous (Part VI)

It is an offence punishable by a fine of up to $10,000 under the Act to falsely assert that one has the necessary authority as an SDM pursuant to the hierarchy set out is s. 20 of the Act,[168] or to misrepresent wishes someone has expressed,[169] or to knowingly act in contravention of prior capable wishes[170] except by permission of the Board.

---

[166] s. 58 (b) provides that the Public Guardian and Trustee "may" make decisions for an individual for whom no one else is available or willing to make the decision, where under s. 20 (treatment) and s. 41 (admission to a care facility), the language used is "shall".

[167] S.O. 1994, c. 26. And effective November 1, 2004, under certain provisions of the *Personal Health Information Protection Act, 2004* regarding capacity in relation to the disclosure of personal health information as well as issues of a person's own access to this type of information, formerly known as the patient's "clinical record" under the MHA.

[168] s. 82.

[169] s. 83.

[170] s. 84.

HEALTH CARE CONSENT ACT, 1996

(S.O. 1996, c. 2)
Schedule A

Amendments: 1998, c. 26, s. 104; 2000, c. 9, ss. 31-48; 2002, c. 18, Sched. A, s. 10; 2004, c. 3, Sched A, s. 84.

Part I

General

1. Purposes — The purposes of this Act are,

(a) to provide rules with respect to consent to treatment that apply consistently in all settings;

(b) to facilitate treatment, admission to care facilities, and personal assistance services, for persons lacking the capacity to make decisions about such matters;

(c) to enhance the autonomy of persons for whom treatment is proposed, persons for whom admission to a care facility is proposed and persons who are to receive personal assistance services by,

  (i) allowing those who have been found to be incapable to apply to a tribunal for a review of the finding,

  (ii) allowing incapable persons to request that a representative of their choice be appointed by the tribunal for the purpose of making decisions on their behalf concerning treatment, admission to a care facility or personal assistance services, and

  (iii) requiring that wishes with respect to treatment, admission to a care facility or personal assistance services, expressed by persons while capable and after attaining 16 years of age, be adhered to;

(d) to promote communication and understanding between health practitioners and their patients or clients;

(e) to ensure a significant role for supportive family members when a person lacks the capacity to make a decision about a treatment, admission to a care facility or a personal assistance service; and

(f) to permit intervention by the Public Guardian and Trustee only as a last resort in decisions on behalf of incapable persons concerning treatment, admission to a care facility or personal assistance services.

2. (1) **Interpretation** — In this Act,

"attorney for personal care" means an attorney under a power of attorney for personal care given under the *Substitute Decisions Act, 1992*;

"Board" means the Consent and Capacity Board;

"capable" means mentally capable, and "capacity" has a corresponding meaning;

"care facility" means,

(a) an approved charitable home for the aged, as defined in the *Charitable Institutions Act*,

(b) a home or joint home, as defined in the *Homes for the Aged and Rest Homes Act*,

(c) a nursing home, as defined in the *Nursing Homes Act*, or

(d) a facility prescribed by the regulations as a care facility;

"community treatment plan" has the same meaning as in the *Mental Health Act*;

"course of treatment" means a series or sequence of similar treatments administered to a person over a period of time for a particular health problem;

"evaluator" means, in the circumstances prescribed by the regulations, a person described in clause (a), (l), (m), (o), (p) or (q) of the definition of "health practitioner" in this subsection or a member of a category of persons prescribed by the regulations as evaluators;

"guardian of the person" means a guardian of the person appointed under the *Substitute Decisions Act, 1992*;

"health practitioner" means,

(a) a member of the College of Audiologists and Speech-Language Pathologists of Ontario,

(b) a member of the College of Chiropodists of Ontario, including a member who is a podiatrist,

(c) a member of the College of Chiropractors of Ontario,

(d) a member of the College of Dental Hygienists of Ontario,

(e) a member of the Royal College of Dental Surgeons of Ontario,

(f) a member of the College of Denturists of Ontario,

(g) a member of the College of Dietitians of Ontario,

(h) a member of the College of Massage Therapists of Ontario,

(i) a member of the College of Medical Laboratory Technologists of Ontario,

(j) a member of the College of Medical Radiation Technologists of Ontario,

(k) a member of the College of Midwives of Ontario,

(l) a member of the College of Nurses of Ontario,

(m) a member of the College of Occupational Therapists of Ontario,

(n) a member of the College of Optometrists of Ontario,

(o) a member of the College of Physicians and Surgeons of Ontario,

(p) a member of the College of Physiotherapists of Ontario,

(q) a member of the College of Psychologists of Ontario,

(r) a member of the College of Respiratory Therapists of Ontario,

(s) a naturopath registered as a drugless therapist under the *Drugless Practitioners Act*, or

(t) a member of a category of persons prescribed by the regulations as health practitioners;

"hospital" means an institution as defined in the *Mental Hospitals Act*, a private hospital as defined in the *Private Hospitals Act* or a hospital as defined in the *Public Hospitals Act*;

"incapable" means mentally incapable, and "incapacity" has a corresponding meaning;

"mental disorder" has the same meaning as in the *Mental Health Act*;

"personal assistance service" means assistance with or supervision of hygiene, washing, dressing, grooming, eating, drinking, elimination, ambulation, positioning or any other routine activity of living, and includes a group of personal assistance services or a plan setting out personal assistance services to be provided to a person, but does not include anything prescribed by the regulations as not constituting a personal assistance service;

"plan of treatment" means a plan that,

(a) is developed by one or more health practitioners,

(b) deals with one or more of the health problems that a person has and may, in addition, deal with one or more of the health problems that the person is likely to have in the future given the person's current health condition, and

(c) provides for the administration to the person of various treatments or courses of treatment and may, in addition, provide for the withholding or withdrawal of treatment in light of the person's current health condition;

"psychiatric facility" has the same meaning as in the *Mental Health Act*;

"recipient" means a person who is to be provided with one or more personal assistance services,

(a) in an approved charitable home for the aged, as defined in the *Charitable Institutions Act*,

(b) in a home or joint home, as defined in the *Homes for the Aged and Rest Homes Act*,

(c) in a nursing home, as defined in the *Nursing Homes Act*,

(d) in a place prescribed by the regulations in the circumstances prescribed by the regulations,

(e) under a program prescribed by the regulations in the circumstances prescribed by the regulations, or

(f) by a provider prescribed by the regulations in the circumstances prescribed by the regulations;

"regulations" means the regulations made under this Act;

"treatment" means anything that is done for a therapeutic, preventive, palliative, diagnostic, cosmetic or other health-related purpose, and includes a course of treatment, plan of treatment or community treatment plan, but does not include,

(a) the assessment for the purpose of this Act of a person's capacity with respect to a treatment, admission to a care facility or a personal assistance service, the assessment for the purpose of the *Substitute Decisions Act, 1992* of a person's capacity to manage property or a person's capacity for personal care, or the assessment of a person's capacity for any other purpose,

(b) the assessment or examination of a person to determine the general nature of the person's condition,

(c) the taking of a person's health history,

(d) the communication of an assessment or diagnosis,

(e) the admission of a person to a hospital or other facility,

(f) a personal assistance service,

(g) a treatment that in the circumstances poses little or no risk of harm to the person,

(h) anything prescribed by the regulations as not constituting treatment.

(2) **Refusal of consent** — A reference in this Act to refusal of consent includes withdrawal of consent.

[2000, c. 9, s. 31]

3. (1) **Meaning of "excluded act"** — In this section,

"excluded act" means,

(a) anything described in clause (b) or (g) of the definition of "treatment" in subsection 2 (1), or

(b) anything described in clause (h) of the definition of "treatment" in subsection 2 (1) and prescribed by the regulations as an excluded act.

(2) **Excluded act considered treatment** — If a health practitioner decides to proceed as if an excluded act were a treatment for the purpose of this Act, this Act and the regulations apply as if the excluded act were a treatment within the meaning of this Act.

4. (1) **Capacity** — A person is capable with respect to a treatment, admission to a care facility or a personal assistance service if the person is able to understand the information that is relevant to making a decision about the treatment, admission or personal assistance service, as the case may be, and able to appreciate the reasonably foreseeable consequences of a decision or lack of decision.

(2) **Presumption of capacity** — A person is presumed to be capable with respect to treatment, admission to a care facility and personal assistance services.

(3) **Exception** — A person is entitled to rely on the presumption of capacity with respect to another person unless he or she has reasonable grounds to believe that the other person is incapable with respect to the treatment, the admission or the personal assistance service, as the case may be.

5. (1) **Wishes** — A person may, while capable, express wishes with respect to treatment, admission to a care facility or a personal assistance service.

(2) **Manner of expression** — Wishes may be expressed in a power of attorney, in a form prescribed by the regulations, in any other written form, orally or in any other manner.

(3) **Later wishes prevail** — Later wishes expressed while capable prevail over earlier wishes.

6. Research, sterilization, transplants — This Act does not affect the law relating to giving or refusing consent on another person's behalf to any of the following procedures:

1. A procedure whose primary purpose is research.
2. Sterilization that is not medically necessary for the protection of the person's health.
3. The removal of regenerative or non-regenerative tissue for implantation in another person's body.

7. Restraint, confinement — This Act does not affect the common law duty of a caregiver to restrain or confine a person when immediate action is necessary to prevent serious bodily harm to the person or to others.

Part II

Treatment

General

8. (1) **Application of Part** — Subject to section 3, this Part applies to treatment.

(2) **Law not affected** — Subject to section 3, this Part does not affect the law relating to giving or refusing consent to anything not included in the definition of "treatment" in subsection 2 (1).

9. Meaning of "substitute decision-maker" — In this Part,

"substitute decision-maker" means a person who is authorized under section 20 to give or refuse consent to a treatment on behalf of a person who is incapable with respect to the treatment.

Consent to Treatment

10. (1) **No treatment without consent** — A health practitioner who proposes a treatment for a person shall not administer the treatment, and shall take reasonable steps to ensure that it is not administered, unless,

(a) he or she is of the opinion that the person is capable with respect to the treatment, and the person has given consent; or

(b) he or she is of the opinion that the person is incapable with respect to the treatment, and the person's substitute decision-maker has given consent on the person's behalf in accordance with this Act.

(2) **Opinion of Board or court governs** — If the health practitioner is of the opinion that the person is incapable with respect to the treatment, but the person is found to be capable with respect to the treatment by the Board on an application for review of the health practitioner's finding, or by a court on an appeal of the Board's decision, the health practitioner shall not administer the treatment, and shall take reasonable steps to ensure that it is not administered, unless the person has given consent.

11. (1) **Elements of consent** — The following are the elements required for consent to treatment:

1. The consent must relate to the treatment.
2. The consent must be informed.
3. The consent must be given voluntarily.
4. The consent must not be obtained through misrepresentation or fraud.

(2) **Informed consent** — A consent to treatment is informed if, before giving it,

(a) the person received the information about the matters set out in subsection (3) that a reasonable person in the same circumstances would require in order to make a decision about the treatment; and

(b) the person received responses to his or her requests for additional information about those matters.

(3) **Same** — The matters referred to in subsection (2) are:

1. The nature of the treatment.
2. The expected benefits of the treatment.
3. The material risks of the treatment.
4. The material side effects of the treatment.
5. Alternative courses of action.
6. The likely consequences of not having the treatment.

(4) **Express or implied** — Consent to treatment may be express or implied.

12. Included consent — Unless it is not reasonable to do so in the circumstances, a health practitioner is entitled to presume that consent to a treatment includes,

(a) consent to variations or adjustments in the treatment, if the nature, expected benefits, material risks and material side effects of the changed treatment are not significantly different from the nature, expected benefits, material risks and material side effects of the original treatment; and

(b) consent to the continuation of the same treatment in a different setting, if there is no significant change in the expected benefits, material risks or material side effects of the treatment as a result of the change in the setting in which it is administered.

13. Plan of treatment — If a plan of treatment is to be proposed for a person, one health practitioner may, on behalf of all the health practitioners involved in the plan of treatment,

(a) propose the plan of treatment;

(b) determine the person's capacity with respect to the treatments referred to in the plan of treatment; and

(c) obtain a consent or refusal of consent in accordance with this Act,

(i) from the person, concerning the treatments with respect to which the person is found to be capable, and

(ii) from the person's substitute decision-maker, concerning the treatments with respect to which the person is found to be incapable.

14. Withdrawal of consent — A consent that has been given by or on behalf of the person for whom the treatment was proposed may be withdrawn at any time,

(a) by the person, if the person is capable with respect to the treatment at the time of the withdrawal;

(b) by the person's substitute decision-maker, if the person is incapable with respect to the treatment at the time of the withdrawal.

Capacity

15. (1) **Capacity depends on treatment —** A person may be incapable with respect to some treatments and capable with respect to others.

(2) **Capacity depends on time —** A person may be incapable with respect to a treatment at one time and capable at another.

16. Return of capacity — If, after consent to a treatment is given or refused on a person's behalf in accordance with this Act, the person becomes capable with respect to the treatment in the opinion of the health practitioner, the person's own decision to give or refuse consent to the treatment governs.

17. Information — A health practitioner shall, in the circumstances and manner specified in guidelines established by the governing body of the health practitioner's profession, provide to persons found by the health practitioner to be incapable with respect to treatment such information about the consequences of the findings as is specified in the guidelines.

18. (1) **Treatment must not begin** — This section applies if,

(a) a health practitioner proposes a treatment for a person and finds that the person is incapable with respect to the treatment;

(b) before the treatment is begun, the health practitioner is informed that the person intends to apply, or has applied, to the Board for a review of the finding; and

(c) the application to the Board is not prohibited by subsection 32 (2).

(2) **Same** — This section also applies if,

(a) a health practitioner proposes a treatment for a person and finds that the person is incapable with respect to the treatment;

(b) before the treatment is begun, the health practitioner is informed that,

(i) the incapable person intends to apply, or has applied, to the Board for appointment of a representative to give or refuse consent to the treatment on his or her behalf, or

(ii) another person intends to apply, or has applied, to the Board to be appointed as the representative of the incapable person to give or refuse consent to the treatment on his or her behalf; and

(c) the application to the Board is not prohibited by subsection 33 (3).

(3) **Same** — In the circumstances described in subsections (1) and (2), the health practitioner shall not begin the treatment, and shall take reasonable steps to ensure that the treatment is not begun,

(a) until 48 hours have elapsed since the health practitioner was first informed of the intended application to the Board without an application being made;

(b) until the application to the Board has been withdrawn;

(c) until the Board has rendered a decision in the matter, if none of the parties to the application before the Board has informed the health practitioner that he or she intends to appeal the Board's decision; or

(d) if a party to the application before the Board has informed the health practitioner that he or she intends to appeal the Board's decision,

(i) until the period for commencing the appeal has elapsed without an appeal being commenced, or

(ii) until the appeal of the Board's decision has been finally disposed of.

(4) **Emergency** — This section does not apply if the health practitioner is of the opinion that there is an emergency within the meaning of subsection 25 (1).

19. (1) **Order authorizing treatment pending appeal** — If an appeal is taken from a Board or court decision that has the effect of authorizing a person to consent to a treatment, the treatment may be administered before the final disposition of the appeal, despite section 18, if the court to which the appeal is taken so orders and the consent is given.

(2) **Criteria for order —** The court may make the order if it is satisfied,

(a) that,

(i) the treatment will or is likely to improve substantially the condition of the person to whom it is to be administered, and the person's condition will not or is not likely to improve without the treatment, or

(ii) the person's condition will or is likely to deteriorate substantially, or to deteriorate rapidly, without the treatment, and the treatment will or is likely to prevent the deterioration or to reduce substantially its extent or its rate;

(b) that the benefit the person is expected to obtain from the treatment outweighs the risk of harm to him or her;

(c) that the treatment is the least restrictive and least intrusive treatment that meets the requirements of clauses (a) and (b); and

(d) that the person's condition makes it necessary to administer the treatment before the final disposition of the appeal.

Consent on Incapable Person's Behalf

20. (1) **List of persons who may give or refuse consent —** If a person is incapable with respect to a treatment, consent may be given or refused on his or her behalf by a person described in one of the following paragraphs:

1. The incapable person's guardian of the person, if the guardian has authority to give or refuse consent to the treatment.
2. The incapable person's attorney for personal care, if the power of attorney confers authority to give or refuse consent to the treatment.
3. The incapable person's representative appointed by the Board under section 33, if the representative has authority to give or refuse consent to the treatment.
4. The incapable person's spouse or partner.
5. A child or parent of the incapable person, or a children's aid society or other person who is lawfully entitled to give or refuse consent to the treatment in the place of the parent. This paragraph does not include a parent who has only a right of access. If a children's aid society or other person is lawfully entitled to give or refuse consent to the treatment in the place of the parent, this paragraph does not include the parent.
6. A parent of the incapable person who has only a right of access.
7. A brother or sister of the incapable person.
8. Any other relative of the incapable person.

(2) **Requirements —** A person described in subsection (1) may give or refuse consent only if he or she,

(a) is capable with respect to the treatment;

(b) is at least 16 years old, unless he or she is the incapable person's parent;

(c) is not prohibited by court order or separation agreement from having access to the incapable person or giving or refusing consent on his or her behalf;

(d) is available; and

(e) is willing to assume the responsibility of giving or refusing consent.

(3) **Ranking** — A person described in a paragraph of subsection (1) may give or refuse consent only if no person described in an earlier paragraph meets the requirements of subsection (2).

(4) **Same** — Despite subsection (3), a person described in a paragraph of subsection (1) who is present or has otherwise been contacted may give or refuse consent if he or she believes that no other person described in an earlier paragraph or the same paragraph exists, or that although such a person exists, the person is not a person described in paragraph 1, 2 or 3 and would not object to him or her making the decision.

(5) **No person in subs. (1) to make decision** — If no person described in subsection (1) meets the requirements of subsection (2), the Public Guardian and Trustee shall make the decision to give or refuse consent.

(6) **Conflict between persons in same paragraph** — If two or more persons who are described in the same paragraph of subsection (1) and who meet the requirements of subsection (2) disagree about whether to give or refuse consent, and if their claims rank ahead of all others, the Public Guardian and Trustee shall make the decision in their stead.

(7) **Meaning of "spouse"** — Subject to subsection (8), two persons are spouses for the purpose of this section if

(a) they are married to each other; or

(b) they are living in a conjugal relationship outside marriage and,

(i) have cohabited for at least one year,

(ii) are together the parents of a child, or

(iii) have together entered into a cohabitation agreement under section 53 of the *Family Law Act*.

(8) **Not spouse** — Two persons are not spouses for the purpose of this section if they are living separate and apart as a result of a breakdown of their relationship.

[2004, c. 3, Sched. A, s. 84 (in force November 1, 2004)]

(9) **Meaning of "partner"** — For the purpose of this section,

"partner" means,

(a) [Repealed, 2004, c. 3, Sched. A, s. 84]

(b) either of two persons who have lived together for at least one year and have a close personal relationship that is of primary importance in both persons' lives.

(10) **Meaning of "relative"** — Two persons are relatives for the purpose of this section if they are related by blood, marriage or adoption.

(11) **Meaning of "available"** — For the purpose of clause (2) (d), a person is available if it is possible, within a time that is reasonable in the circumstances, to communicate with the person and obtain a consent or refusal.

[2002, c. 18, Sched. A, s. 10; 2004, c. 3, Sched. A, s. 84]

21. (1) **Principles for giving or refusing consent** — A person who gives or refuses consent to a treatment on an incapable person's behalf shall do so in accordance with the following principles:

1. If the person knows of a wish applicable to the circumstances that the incapable person expressed while capable and after attaining 16 years of age, the person shall give or refuse consent in accordance with the wish.
2. If the person does not know of a wish applicable to the circumstances that the incapable person expressed while capable and after attaining 16 years of age, or if it is impossible to comply with the wish, the person shall act in the incapable person's best interests.

(2) **Best interests** — In deciding what the incapable person's best interests are, the person who gives or refuses consent on his or her behalf shall take into consideration,

(a) the values and beliefs that the person knows the incapable person held when capable and believes he or she would still act on if capable;

(b) any wishes expressed by the incapable person with respect to the treatment that are not required to be followed under paragraph 1 of subsection (1); and

(c) the following factors:

1. Whether the treatment is likely to,
   i. improve the incapable person's condition or well-being,
   ii. prevent the incapable person's condition or well-being from deteriorating, or
   iii. reduce the extent to which, or the rate at which, the incapable person's condition or well-being is likely to deteriorate.
2. Whether the incapable person's condition or well-being is likely to improve, remain the same or deteriorate without the treatment.
3. Whether the benefit the incapable person is expected to obtain from the treatment outweighs the risk of harm to him or her.
4. Whether a less restrictive or less intrusive treatment would be as beneficial as the treatment that is proposed.

22. (1) **Information** — Before giving or refusing consent to a treatment on an incapable person's behalf, a substitute decision-maker is entitled to receive all the information required for an informed consent as described in subsection 11 (2).

(2) **Conflict** — Subsection (1) prevails despite anything to the contrary in the *Personal Health Information Protection Act, 2004.*

[2004, c. 3, Sched. A, s. 84 (in force November 1, 2004)]

23. Ancillary treatment — Authority to consent to a treatment on an incapable person's behalf includes authority to consent to another treatment that is necessary and ancillary to the treatment, even if the incapable person is capable with respect to the necessary and ancillary treatment.

24. (1) **Admission to hospital, etc.** — Subject to subsection (2), a substitute decision-maker who consents to a treatment on an incapable person's behalf may consent to the incapable person's admission to a hospital or psychiatric facility or to another health facility prescribed by the regulations, for the purpose of the treatment.

(2) **Objection, psychiatric facility** — If the incapable person is 16 years old or older and objects to being admitted to a psychiatric facility for treatment of a mental disorder, consent to his or her admission may be given only by,

(a) his or her guardian of the person, if the guardian has authority to consent to the admission; or

(b) his or her attorney for personal care, if the power of attorney contains a provision authorizing the attorney to use force that is necessary and reasonable in the circumstances to admit the incapable person to the psychiatric facility and the provision is effective under subsection 50 (1) of the *Substitute Decisions Act, 1992*.

Emergency Treatment

25. (1) **Meaning of "emergency"** — For the purpose of this section and section 27, there is an emergency if the person for whom the treatment is proposed is apparently experiencing severe suffering or is at risk, if the treatment is not administered promptly, of sustaining serious bodily harm.

(2) **Emergency treatment without consent: incapable person** — Despite section 10, a treatment may be administered without consent to a person who is incapable with respect to the treatment, if, in the opinion of the health practitioner proposing the treatment,

(a) there is an emergency; and

(b) the delay required to obtain a consent or refusal on the person's behalf will prolong the suffering that the person is apparently experiencing or will put the person at risk of sustaining serious bodily harm.

(3) **Emergency treatment without consent: capable person** — Despite section 10, a treatment may be administered without consent to a person who is apparently capable with respect to the treatment, if, in the opinion of the health practitioner proposing the treatment,

(a) there is an emergency;

(b) the communication required in order for the person to give or refuse consent to the treatment cannot take place because of a language barrier or because the person has a disability that prevents the communication from taking place;

(c) steps that are reasonable in the circumstances have been taken to find a practical means of enabling the communication to take place, but no such means has been found;

(d) the delay required to find a practical means of enabling the communication to take place will prolong the suffering that the person is apparently experiencing or will put the person at risk of sustaining serious bodily harm; and

(e) there is no reason to believe that the person does not want the treatment.

(4) **Examination without consent** — Despite section 10, an examination or diagnostic procedure that constitutes treatment may be conducted by a health practitioner without consent if,

(a) the examination or diagnostic procedure is reasonably necessary in order to determine whether there is an emergency; and

(b) in the opinion of the health practitioner,

(i) the person is incapable with respect to the examination or diagnostic procedure, or

(ii) clauses (3) (b) and (c) apply to the examination or diagnostic procedure.

(5) **Record** — After administering a treatment in reliance on subsection (2) or (3), the health practitioner shall promptly note in the person's record the opinions held by the health practitioner that are required by the subsection on which he or she relied.

(6) **Continuing treatment** — Treatment under subsection (2) may be continued only for as long as is reasonably necessary to find the incapable person's substitute decision-maker and to obtain from him or her a consent, or refusal of consent, to the continuation of the treatment.

(7) **Same** — Treatment under subsection (3) may be continued only for as long as is reasonably necessary to find a practical means of enabling the communication to take place so that the person can give or refuse consent to the continuation of the treatment.

(8) **Search** — When a treatment is begun under subsection (2) or (3), the health practitioner shall ensure that reasonable efforts are made for the purpose of finding the substitute decision-maker, or a means of enabling the communication to take place, as the case may be.

(9) **Return of capacity** — If, after a treatment is begun under subsection (2), the person becomes capable with respect to the treatment in the opinion of the health practitioner, the person's own decision to give or refuse consent to the continuation of the treatment governs.

26. No treatment contrary to wishes — A health practitioner shall not administer a treatment under section 25 if the health practitioner has reasonable grounds to believe that the person, while capable and after attaining 16 years of age, expressed a wish applicable to the circumstances to refuse consent to the treatment.

27. Emergency treatment despite refusal — If consent to a treatment is refused on an incapable person's behalf by his or her substitute decision-maker, the treatment may be administered despite the refusal if, in the opinion of the health practitioner proposing the treatment,

(a) there is an emergency; and

(b) the substitute decision-maker did not comply with section 21.

28. Admission to hospital, etc. — The authority to administer a treatment to a person under section 25 or 27 includes authority to have the person admitted to a hospital or psychiatric facility for the purpose of the treatment, unless the person objects and the treatment is primarily treatment of a mental disorder.

Protection from Liability

29. (1) **Apparently valid consent to treatment** — If a treatment is administered to a person with a consent that a health practitioner believes, on reasonable grounds and in good faith, to be sufficient for the purpose of this Act, the health practitioner is not liable for administering the treatment without consent.

(2) **Apparently valid refusal of treatment** — If a treatment is not administered to a person because of a refusal that a health practitioner believes, on reasonable grounds and in good faith, to be sufficient for the purpose of this Act, the health practitioner is not liable for failing to administer the treatment.

(3) **Apparently valid consent to withholding or withdrawal** — If a treatment is withheld or withdrawn in accordance with a plan of treatment and with a consent to the plan of treatment that a health practitioner believes, on reasonable grounds and in good faith, to be sufficient for the purpose of this Act, the health practitioner is not liable for withholding or withdrawing the treatment.

(4) **Emergency: treatment administered** — A health practitioner who, in good faith, administers a treatment to a person under section 25 or 27 is not liable for administering the treatment without consent.

(5) **Emergency: treatment not administered** — A health practitioner who, in good faith, refrains from administering a treatment in accordance with section 26 is not liable for failing to administer the treatment.

(6) **Reliance on assertion** — If a person who gives or refuses consent to a treatment on an incapable person's behalf asserts that he or she,

(a) is a person described in subsection 20 (1) or clause 24 (2) (a) or (b) or an attorney for personal care described in clause 32 (2) (b);

(b) meets the requirement of clause 20 (2) (b) or (c); or

(c) holds the opinions required under subsection 20 (4),

a health practitioner is entitled to rely on the accuracy of the assertion, unless it is not reasonable to do so in the circumstances.

30. Person making decision on another's behalf — A person who gives or refuses consent to a treatment on another person's behalf, acting in good faith and in accordance with this Act, is not liable for giving or refusing consent.

31. (1) **Admission to hospital, etc.** — Sections 29 and 30, except subsection 29 (4), apply, with necessary modifications, to admission of the incapable person to a hospital, psychiatric facility or other health facility referred to in section 24, for the purpose of treatment.

(2) **Same** — A health practitioner who, in good faith, has a person admitted to a hospital or psychiatric facility under section 28 is not liable for having the person admitted without consent.

Applications to Board

32. (1) **Application for review of finding of incapacity** — A person who is the subject of a treatment may apply to the Board for a review of a health practitioner's finding that he or she is incapable with respect to the treatment.

(2) **Exception** — Subsection (1) does not apply to,

(a) a person who has a guardian of the person, if the guardian has authority to give or refuse consent to the treatment;

(b) a person who has an attorney for personal care, if the power of attorney contains a provision waiving the person's right to apply for the review and the provision is effective under subsection 50 (1) of the *Substitute Decisions Act, 1992*.

(3) **Parties** — The parties to the application are:

1. The person applying for the review.
2. The health practitioner.
3. Any other person whom the Board specifies.

(4) **Powers of Board** — The Board may confirm the health practitioner's finding or may determine that the person is capable with respect to the treatment, and in doing so may substitute its opinion for that of the health practitioner.

(5) **Restriction on repeated applications** — If a health practitioner's finding that a person is incapable with respect to a treatment is confirmed on the final disposition of an application under this section, the person shall not make a new application for a review of a finding of incapacity with respect to the same or similar treatment within six months after the final disposition of the earlier application, unless the Board gives leave in advance.

(6) **Same** — The Board may give leave for the new application to be made if it is satisfied that there has been a material change in circumstances that justifies reconsideration of the person's capacity.

(7) **Decision effective while application for leave pending** — The Board's decision under subsection (5) remains in effect pending an application for leave under subsection (6).

[2000, c. 9, s. 32]

33. (1) **Application for appointment of representative** — A person who is 16 years old or older and who is incapable with respect to a proposed treatment may apply to the Board for appointment of a representative to give or refuse consent on his or her behalf.

(2) **Application by proposed representative** — A person who is 16 years old or older may apply to the Board to have himself or herself appointed as the representative of a person who is incapable with respect to a proposed treatment, to give or refuse consent on behalf of the incapable person.

(3) **Exception** — Subsections (1) and (2) do not apply if the incapable person has a guardian of the person who has authority to give or refuse consent to the proposed treatment, or an attorney for personal care under a power of attorney conferring that authority.

(4) **Parties** — The parties to the application are:

1. The incapable person.
2. The proposed representative named in the application.
3. Every person who is described in paragraph 4, 5, 6 or 7 of subsection 20 (1).
4. The health practitioner who proposed the treatment.
5. Any other person whom the Board specifies.

(5) **Appointment** — In an appointment under this section, the Board may authorize the representative to give or refuse consent on the incapable person's behalf,

(a) to the proposed treatment;

(b) to one or more treatments or kinds of treatment specified by the Board, whenever a health practitioner proposing that treatment or a treatment of that kind finds that the person is incapable with respect to it; or

(c) to treatment of any kind, whenever a health practitioner proposing a treatment finds that the person is incapable with respect to it.

(6) **Criteria for appointment** — The Board may make an appointment under this section if it is satisfied that the following requirements are met:

1. The incapable person does not object to the appointment.
2. The representative consents to the appointment, is at least 16 years old and is capable with respect to the treatments or the kinds of treatment for which the appointment is made.
3. The appointment is in the incapable person's best interests.

(7) **Powers of Board** — Unless the incapable person objects, the Board may,

(a) appoint as representative a different person than the one named in the application;

(b) limit the duration of the appointment;

(c) impose any other condition on the appointment;

(d) on any person's application, remove, vary or suspend a condition imposed on the appointment or impose an additional condition on the appointment.

(8) **Termination —** The Board may, on any person's application, terminate an appointment made under this section if,

(a) the incapable person or the representative requests the termination of the appointment;

(b) the representative is no longer capable with respect to the treatments or the kinds of treatment for which the appointment was made;

(c) the appointment is no longer in the incapable person's best interests; or

(d) the incapable person has a guardian of the person who has authority to consent to the treatments or the kinds of treatment for which the appointment was made, or an attorney for personal care under a power of attorney conferring that authority.

34. (1) **Application with respect to place of treatment —** A person may apply to the Board for a review of a decision to consent on the person's behalf to the person's admission to a hospital, psychiatric facility or other health facility referred to in section 24 for the purpose of treatment.

(2) **Exception —** Subsection (1) does not apply to a decision to consent on the person's behalf to the person's admission to a psychiatric facility as an informal patient, as defined in the *Mental Health Act*, if the person is at least 12 years old but less than 16 years old.

(3) **Admission and treatment despite application —** The decision to admit the person to the hospital, psychiatric facility or health facility may take effect, and the treatment may be administered, even if the person indicates that he or she intends to apply to the Board under subsection (1) or under subsection 13 (1) of the *Mental Health Act* and even if the application to the Board has been made and has not yet been finally disposed of.

(4) **Parties —** The parties to the application are:

1. The person applying for the review.
2. The person who consented to the admission.
3. The health practitioner who proposed the treatment.
4. Any other person whom the Board specifies.

(5) **Considerations —** In reviewing the decision to admit the person to the hospital, psychiatric facility or health facility for the purpose of treatment, the Board shall consider,

(a) whether the hospital, psychiatric facility or health facility can provide the treatment;

(b) whether the hospital, psychiatric facility or health facility is the least restrictive setting available in which the treatment can be administered;

(c) whether the person's needs could more appropriately be met if the treatment were administered in another place and whether space is available for the person in the other place;

(d) the person's views and wishes, if they can be reasonably ascertained; and

(e) any other matter that the Board considers relevant.

(6) **Order** — The Board may,

(a) direct that the person be discharged from the hospital, psychiatric facility or health facility; or

(b) confirm the decision to admit the person to the hospital, psychiatric facility or health facility.

(7) **Restriction on repeated applications** — If the decision to admit the person is confirmed on the final disposition of an application under this section, the person shall not make a new application for a review of the decision to admit within six months after the final disposition of the earlier application, unless the Board gives leave in advance.

(8) **Same** — The Board may give leave for the new application to be made if it is satisfied that there has been a material change in circumstances that justifies reconsideration of the decision to admit.

(9) **Application under *Mental Health Act*** — For the purpose of subsection (7), a final disposition of an application made under section 13 of the *Mental Health Act* shall be deemed to be a final disposition of an application under this section.

35. (1) **Application for directions** — A substitute decision-maker or a health practitioner who proposed a treatment may apply to the Board for directions if the incapable person expressed a wish with respect to the treatment, but,

(a) the wish is not clear;

(b) it is not clear whether the wish is applicable to the circumstances;

(c) it is not clear whether the wish was expressed while the incapable person was capable; or

(d) it is not clear whether the wish was expressed after the incapable person attained 16 years of age.

(1.1) **Notice to substitute decision-maker** — A health practitioner who intends to apply for directions shall inform the substitute decision-maker of his or her intention before doing so.

(2) **Parties** — The parties to the application are:

1. The substitute decision-maker.
2. The incapable person.
3. The health practitioner who proposed the treatment.
4. Any other person whom the Board specifies.

(3) **Directions** — The Board may give directions and, in doing so, shall apply section 21.

[2000, c. 9, s. 33]

36. (1) **Application to depart from wishes —** If a substitute decision-maker is required by paragraph 1 of subsection 21 (1) to refuse consent to a treatment because of a wish expressed by the incapable person while capable and after attaining 16 years of age,

(a) the substitute decision-maker may apply to the Board for permission to consent to the treatment despite the wish; or

(b) the health practitioner who proposed the treatment may apply to the Board to obtain permission for the substitute decision-maker to consent to the treatment despite the wish.

(1.1) **Notice to substitute decision-maker —** A health practitioner who intends to apply under clause (1) (b) shall inform the substitute decision-maker of his or her intention before doing so.

(2) **Parties —** The parties to the application are:

1. The substitute decision-maker.
2. The incapable person.
3. The health practitioner who proposed the treatment.
4. Any other person whom the Board specifies.

(3) **Criteria for permission —** The Board may give the substitute decision-maker permission to consent to the treatment despite the wish if it is satisfied that the incapable person, if capable, would probably give consent because the likely result of the treatment is significantly better than would have been anticipated in comparable circumstances at the time the wish was expressed.

[2000, c. 9, s. 34]

37. (1) **Application to determine compliance with s. 21 —** If consent to a treatment is given or refused on an incapable person's behalf by his or her substitute decision-maker, and if the health practitioner who proposed the treatment is of the opinion that the substitute decision-maker did not comply with section 21, the health practitioner may apply to the Board for a determination as to whether the substitute decision-maker complied with section 21.

(2) **Parties —** The parties to the application are:

1. The health practitioner who proposed the treatment.
2. The incapable person.
3. The substitute decision-maker.
4. Any other person whom the Board specifies.

(3) **Power of Board —** In determining whether the substitute decision-maker complied with section 21, the Board may substitute its opinion for that of the substitute decision-maker.

(4) **Directions —** If the Board determines that the substitute decision-maker did not comply with section 21, it may give him or her directions and, in doing so, shall apply section 21.

(5) **Time for compliance** — The Board shall specify the time within which its directions must be complied with.

(6) **Deemed not authorized** — If the substitute decision-maker does not comply with the Board's directions within the time specified by the Board, he or she shall be deemed not to meet the requirements of subsection 20 (2).

(6.1) **Subsequent substitute decision-maker** — If, under subsection (6), the substitute decision-maker is deemed not to meet the requirements of subsection 20 (2), any subsequent substitute decision-maker shall, subject to subsections (6.2) and (6.3), comply with the directions given by the Board on the application within the time specified by the Board.

(6.2) **Application for directions** — If a subsequent substitute decision-maker knows of a wish expressed by the incapable person with respect to the treatment, the substitute decision-maker may, with leave of the Board, apply to the Board for directions under section 35.

(6.3) **Inconsistent directions** — Directions given by the Board under section 35 on a subsequent substitute decision-maker's application brought with leave under subsection (6.2) prevail over inconsistent directions given under subsection (4) to the extent of the inconsistency.

(7) **P.G.T.** — If the substitute decision-maker who is given directions is the Public Guardian and Trustee, he or she is required to comply with the directions, and subsection (6) does not apply to him or her.

[2000, c. 9, s. 35]

37.1 Deemed application concerning capacity — An application to the Board under section 33, 34, 35, 36 or 37 shall be deemed to include an application to the Board under section 32 with respect to the person's capacity to consent to treatment proposed by a health practitioner unless the person's capacity to consent to such treatment has been determined by the Board within the previous six months.

[2000, c. 9, s. 36]

Part III

Admission to Care Facilities

General

38. Application of Part — This Part applies to admission to a care facility.

39. Definitions — In this Part,

"crisis" means a crisis relating to the condition or circumstances of the person who is to be admitted to the care facility;

"substitute decision-maker" means a person who is authorized under section 41 to give or refuse consent to admission to a care facility on behalf of a person who is incapable with respect to the admission.

Consent on Incapable Person's Behalf

40. (1) **Consent on incapable person's behalf —** If a person's consent to his or her admission to a care facility is required by law and the person is found by an evaluator to be incapable with respect to the admission, consent may be given or refused on the person's behalf by his or her substitute decision-maker in accordance with this Act.

(2) **Opinion of Board or court governs —** If a person who is found by an evaluator to be incapable with respect to his or her admission to a care facility is found to be capable with respect to the admission by the Board on an application for review of the evaluator's finding, or by a court on an appeal of the Board's decision, subsection (1) does not apply.

41. Determining who may give or refuse consent — Section 20 applies, with necessary modifications, for the purpose of determining who is authorized to give or refuse consent to admission to a care facility on behalf of a person who is incapable with respect to the admission.

42. (1) **Principles for giving or refusing consent —** A person who gives or refuses consent on an incapable person's behalf to his or her admission to a care facility shall do so in accordance with the following principles:

1. If the person knows of a wish applicable to the circumstances that the incapable person expressed while capable and after attaining 16 years of age, the person shall give or refuse consent in accordance with the wish.
2. If the person does not know of a wish applicable to the circumstances that the incapable person expressed while capable and after attaining 16 years of age, or if it is impossible to comply with the wish, the person shall act in the incapable person's best interests.

(2) **Best interests —** In deciding what the incapable person's best interests are, the person who gives or refuses consent on his or her behalf shall take into consideration,

(a) the values and beliefs that the person knows the incapable person held when capable and believes he or she would still act on if capable;

(b) any wishes expressed by the incapable person with respect to admission to a care facility that are not required to be followed under paragraph 1 of subsection (1); and

(c) the following factors:

   1. Whether admission to the care facility is likely to,

      i. improve the quality of the incapable person's life,

      ii. prevent the quality of the incapable person's life from deteriorating, or

      iii. reduce the extent to which, or the rate at which, the quality of the incapable person's life is likely to deteriorate.

2. Whether the quality of the incapable person's life is likely to improve, remain the same or deteriorate without admission to the care facility.

3. Whether the benefit the incapable person is expected to obtain from admission to the care facility outweighs the risk of negative consequences to him or her.

4. Whether a course of action that is less restrictive than admission to the care facility is available and is appropriate in the circumstances.

43. (1) **Information** — Before giving or refusing consent on an incapable person's behalf to his or her admission to a care facility, a substitute decision-maker is entitled to receive all the information required in order to make the decision.

(2) **Conflict** — Subsection (1) prevails despite anything to the contrary in the *Personal Health Information Protection Act, 2004.*

[2004, c. 3, Sched. A, s. 84]

44. (1) **Ancillary decisions** — Authority to consent on an incapable person's behalf to his or her admission to a care facility includes authority to make decisions that are necessary and ancillary to the admission.

(2) **Collection and disclosure of information** — A decision concerning the collection and disclosure of information relating to the incapable person is a decision that is necessary and ancillary to the admission, if the information is required for the purpose of the admission and is not personal health information within the meaning of the *Personal Health Information Protection Act, 2004.*

(3) **Exception** — Subsection (1) does not authorize the making of a decision concerning the incapable person's property.

[2004, c. 3, Sched. A, s. 84]

45. Withdrawal of consent — Authority to consent on an incapable person's behalf to his or her admission to a care facility includes authority to withdraw the consent at any time before the admission.

46. (1) **Admission must not be authorized** — This section applies if,

(a) an evaluator finds that a person is incapable with respect to his or her admission to a care facility;

(b) before the admission takes place, the person responsible for authorizing admissions to the care facility is informed that the person who was found to be incapable intends to apply, or has applied, to the Board for a review of the finding; and

(c) the application to the Board is not prohibited by subsection 50 (2).

(2) **Same** — This section also applies if,

(a) an evaluator finds that a person is incapable with respect to his or her admission to a care facility;

(b) before the admission takes place, the person responsible for authorizing admissions to the care facility is informed that,

(i) the incapable person intends to apply, or has applied, to the Board for appointment of a representative to give or refuse consent to the admission on his or her behalf, or

(ii) another person intends to apply, or has applied, to the Board to be appointed as the representative of the incapable person to give or refuse consent to the admission on his or her behalf; and

(c) the application to the Board is not prohibited by subsection 51 (3).

(3) **Same** — In the circumstances described in subsections (1) and (2), the person responsible for authorizing admissions to the care facility shall take reasonable steps to ensure that the person's admission is not authorized and that the person is not admitted,

(a) until 48 hours have elapsed since the person responsible for authorizing admissions to the care facility was first informed of the intended application to the Board without an application being made;

(b) until the application to the Board has been withdrawn;

(c) until the Board has rendered a decision in the matter, if none of the parties to the application before the Board has informed the person responsible for authorizing admissions to the care facility that he or she intends to appeal the Board's decision; or

(d) if a party to the application before the Board has informed the person responsible for authorizing admissions to the care facility that he or she intends to appeal the Board's decision,

(i) until the period for commencing the appeal has elapsed without an appeal being commenced, or

(ii) until the appeal of the Board's decision has been finally disposed of.

(4) **Crisis** — This section does not apply if the person responsible for authorizing admissions to the care facility is of the opinion that the incapable person requires immediate admission to a care facility as a result of a crisis.

(5) **Admission for definite stay** — This section does not apply to a person's admission, or the authorization of a person's admission, to a care facility for a stay of a definite number of days not exceeding 90.

Crisis Admission

47. (1) **Authorization of admission without consent** — Despite any law to the contrary, if a person is found by an evaluator to be incapable with respect to his or her admission to a care facility, the person's admission may be authorized, and the person may be admitted, without consent, if in the opinion of the person responsible for authorizing admissions to the care facility,

(a) the incapable person requires immediate admission to a care facility as a result of a crisis; and

(b) it is not reasonably possible to obtain an immediate consent or refusal on the incapable person's behalf.

(2) **Search** — When an admission to a care facility is authorized under subsection (1), the person responsible for authorizing admissions to the care facility shall ensure that reasonable efforts are made for the purpose of finding the incapable person's substitute decision-maker and obtaining from him or her a consent, or refusal of consent, to the admission.

Protection from Liability

48. (1) **Apparently valid consent to admission** — If the person responsible for authorizing admissions to a care facility admits, or authorizes the admission of, a person to the care facility with a consent that he or she believes, on reasonable grounds and in good faith, to be sufficient for the purpose of this Act, he or she is not liable for admitting the person, or authorizing the person's admission, without consent.

(2) **Apparently valid refusal of admission** — If the person responsible for authorizing admissions to a care facility does not admit, or does not authorize the admission of, a person to the care facility because of a refusal that he or she believes, on reasonable grounds and in good faith, to be sufficient for the purpose of this Act, he or she is not liable for failing to admit the person or failing to authorize the person's admission.

(3) **Crisis admission** — If the person responsible for authorizing admissions to a care facility admits, or authorizes the admission of, a person to the care facility under section 47 in good faith, he or she is not liable for admitting the person, or authorizing the person's admission, without consent.

(4) **Reliance on assertion** — If a person who gives or refuses consent to admission to a care facility on an incapable person's behalf asserts that he or she,

(a) is a person described in subsection 20 (1), as it applies for the purpose of section 41, or an attorney for personal care described in clause 50 (2) (b);

(b) meets the requirement of clause 20 (2) (b) or (c), as it applies for the purpose of section 41; or

(c) holds the opinions required under subsection 20 (4), as it applies for the purpose of section 41,

the person responsible for authorizing admissions to the care facility is entitled to rely on the accuracy of the assertion, unless it is not reasonable to do so in the circumstances.

49. Person making decision on another's behalf — A person who gives or refuses consent on another person's behalf to his or her admission to a care facility, acting in good faith and in accordance with this Act, is not liable for giving or refusing consent.

Applications to Board

50. (1) **Application for review of finding of incapacity** — A person may apply to the Board for a review of an evaluator's finding that he or she is incapable with respect to his or her admission to a care facility.

(2) **Exception** — Subsection (1) does not apply to,

(a) a person who has a guardian of the person, if the guardian has authority to give or refuse consent to the person's admission to a care facility;

(b) a person who has an attorney for personal care, if the power of attorney contains a provision waiving the person's right to apply for the review and the provision is effective under subsection 50 (1) of the *Substitute Decisions Act, 1992*.

(3) **Parties** — The parties to the application are:

1. The person applying for the review.
2. The evaluator.
3. The person responsible for authorizing admissions to the care facility.
4. Any other person whom the Board specifies.

(4) **Subss. 32 (4) to (7) apply** — Subsections 32 (4) to (7) apply, with necessary modifications, to an application under this section.

[2000, c. 9, s. 37]

51. (1) **Application for appointment of representative** — A person who is 16 years old or older and who is incapable with respect to his or her admission to a care facility may apply to the Board for appointment of a representative to give or refuse consent on his or her behalf.

(2) **Application by proposed representative** — A person who is 16 years old or older may apply to the Board to have himself or herself appointed as the representative of a person who is incapable with respect to his or her admission to a care facility, to give or refuse consent on behalf of the incapable person.

(3) **Exception** — Subsections (1) and (2) do not apply if the incapable person has a guardian of the person who has authority to give or refuse consent to the person's admission to a care facility, or an attorney for personal care under a power of attorney conferring that authority.

(4) **Parties** — The parties to the application are:

1. The incapable person.
2. The proposed representative named in the application.
3. Every person who is described in paragraph 4, 5, 6 or 7 of subsection 20 (1), as it applies for the purpose of section 41.
4. The person responsible for authorizing admissions to the care facility.
5. Any other person whom the Board specifies.

(5) **Appointment** — In an appointment under this section, the Board may authorize the representative to give or refuse consent on the incapable person's behalf,

(a) to his or her admission to the care facility; or

(b) to his or her admission to any care facility, or to any of several care facilities specified by the Board, whenever an evaluator finds that the person is incapable with respect to the admission.

(6) **Subss. 33 (6) to (8) apply** — Subsections 33 (6) to (8) apply, with necessary modifications, to an appointment under this section.

52. (1) **Application for directions** — A substitute decision-maker or the person responsible for authorizing admissions to a care facility may apply to the Board for directions if the incapable person expressed a wish with respect to his or her admission to the care facility, but,

(a) the wish is not clear;

(b) it is not clear whether the wish is applicable to the circumstances;

(c) it is not clear whether the wish was expressed while the incapable person was capable; or

(d) it is not clear whether the wish was expressed after the incapable person attained 16 years of age.

(1.1) **Notice to substitute decision-maker** — If the person responsible for authorizing admissions to the care facility intends to apply for directions, the person shall inform the substitute decision-maker of his or her intention before doing so.

(2) **Parties** — The parties to the application are:

1. The substitute decision-maker.
2. The incapable person.
3. The person responsible for authorizing admissions to the care facility.
4. Any other person whom the Board specifies.

(3) **Directions** — The Board may give directions and, in doing so, shall apply section 42.

[2000, c. 9, s. 38]

53. (1) **Application to depart from wishes** — If a substitute decision-maker is required by paragraph 1 of subsection 42 (1) to refuse consent to the incapable person's admission to a care facility because of a wish expressed by the incapable person while capable and after attaining 16 years of age,

(a) the substitute decision-maker may apply to the Board for permission to consent to the admission despite the wish; or

(b) the person responsible for authorizing admissions to the care facility may apply to the Board to obtain permission for the substitute decision-maker to consent to the admission despite the wish.

(1.1) **Notice to substitute decision-maker** — If the person responsible for authorizing admissions to the care facility intends to apply under subsection (1), the person shall inform the substitute decision-maker of his or her intention before doing so.

(2) **Parties** — The parties to the application are:

1. The substitute decision-maker.
2. The incapable person.
3. The person responsible for authorizing admissions to the care facility.
4. Any other person whom the Board specifies.

(3) **Criteria for permission** — The Board may give the substitute decision-maker permission to consent to the admission despite the wish if it is satisfied that the incapable person, if capable, would probably give consent because the likely result of the admission is significantly better than would have been anticipated in comparable circumstances at the time the wish was expressed.

[2000, c. 9, s. 39]

54. (1) **Application to determine compliance with s. 42** — If consent to admission to a care facility is given or refused on an incapable person's behalf by his or her substitute decision-maker, and if the person responsible for authorizing admissions to the care facility is of the opinion that the substitute decision-maker did not comply with section 42, the person responsible for authorizing admissions to the care facility may apply to the Board for a determination as to whether the substitute decision-maker complied with section 42.

(2) **Parties** — The parties to the application are:

1. The person responsible for authorizing admissions to the care facility.
2. The incapable person.
3. The substitute decision-maker.
4. Any other person whom the Board specifies.

(3) **Power of Board** — In determining whether the substitute decision-maker complied with section 42, the Board may substitute its opinion for that of the substitute decision-maker.

(4) **Directions** — If the Board determines that the substitute decision-maker did not comply with section 42, it may give him or her directions and, in doing so, shall apply section 42.

(5) **Time for compliance** — The Board shall specify the time within which its directions must be complied with.

(6) **Deemed not authorized** — If the substitute decision-maker does not comply with the Board's directions within the time specified by the Board, he or she shall be deemed not to meet the requirements of subsection 20 (2), as it applies for the purpose of section 41.

(6.1) **Subsequent substitute decision-maker** — If, under subsection (6), the substitute decision-maker is deemed not to meet the requirements of subsection 20 (2), any subsequent substitute decision-maker shall, subject to subsections

(6.2) and (6.3), comply with the directions given by the Board on the application within the time specified by the Board.

(6.2) **Application for directions** — If a subsequent substitute decision-maker knows of a wish expressed by the incapable person with respect to the admission to a care facility, the substitute decision-maker may, with leave of the Board, apply to the Board for directions under section 52.

(6.3) **Inconsistent directions** — Directions given by the Board under section 52 on a subsequent substitute decision-maker's application brought with leave under subsection (6.2) prevail over inconsistent directions given under subsection (4) to the extent of the inconsistency.

(7) **P.G.T.** — If the substitute decision-maker who is given directions is the Public Guardian and Trustee, he or she is required to comply with the directions, and subsection (6) does not apply to him or her.

[2000, c. 9, s. 40]

54.1 Deemed application concerning capacity — An application to the Board under section 51, 52, 53 or 54 shall be deemed to include an application to the Board under section 50 with respect to the person's capacity to consent to his or her admission to a care facility unless the person's capacity to consent to such admission has been determined by the Board within the previous six months.

[2000, c. 9, s. 41]

Part IV

Personal Assistance Services

General

55. Application of Part — This Part applies to personal assistance services.

56. Meaning of "substitute decision-maker" — In this Part,

"substitute decision-maker" means a person who is authorized under section 58 to make a decision concerning a personal assistance service on behalf of a recipient who is incapable with respect to the service.

Decision on Incapable Recipient's Behalf

57. (1) **Decision on incapable recipient's behalf** — If a recipient is found by an evaluator to be incapable with respect to a personal assistance service, a decision concerning the service may be made on the recipient's behalf by his or her substitute decision-maker in accordance with this Act.

(2) **Opinion of Board or court governs** — If a recipient who is found by an evaluator to be incapable with respect to a personal assistance service is found to be capable with respect to the service by the Board on an application for review of the evaluator's finding, or by a court on an appeal of the Board's decision, subsection (1) does not apply.

58. Determining who may make decision — For the purpose of determining who is authorized to make a decision concerning a personal assistance service on behalf of a recipient who is incapable with respect to the service,

(a) section 20, except subsections 20 (5) and (6), applies with necessary modifications;

(b) if no person described in subsection 20 (1) meets the requirements of subsection 20 (2), the Public Guardian and Trustee may make the decision concerning the personal assistance service; and

(c) if two or more persons who are described in the same paragraph of subsection 20 (1) and who meet the requirements of subsection 20 (2) disagree about the decision to be made concerning the personal assistance service, and if their claims rank ahead of all others, the Public Guardian and Trustee may make the decision in their stead.

59. (1) **Principles for making decision —** A person who makes a decision on an incapable recipient's behalf concerning a personal assistance service shall do so in accordance with the following principles:

1. If the person knows of a wish applicable to the circumstances that the recipient expressed while capable and after attaining 16 years of age, the person shall make the decision in accordance with the wish.
2. If the person does not know of a wish applicable to the circumstances that the recipient expressed while capable and after attaining 16 years of age, or if it is impossible to comply with the wish, the person shall act in the recipient's best interests.

(2) **Best interests —** In deciding what the recipient's best interests are, the person shall take into consideration,

(a) the values and beliefs that the person knows the recipient held when capable and believes he or she would still act on if capable;

(b) any wishes expressed by the recipient with respect to the personal assistance service that are not required to be followed under paragraph 1 of subsection (1); and

(c) the following factors:

1. Whether the personal assistance service is likely to,
   i. improve the quality of the recipient's life,
   ii. prevent the quality of the recipient's life from deteriorating, or
   iii. reduce the extent to which, or the rate at which, the quality of the recipient's life is likely to deteriorate.
2. Whether the quality of the recipient's life is likely to improve, remain the same or deteriorate without the personal assistance service.
3. Whether the benefit the recipient is expected to obtain from the personal assistance service outweighs the risk of harm to him or her.

4. Whether a less restrictive or less intrusive personal assistance service would be as beneficial as the personal assistance service that is the subject of the decision.
5. Whether the personal assistance service fosters the recipient's independence.

(3) **Confinement, monitoring devices, restraint** — Subject to paragraph 1 of subsection (1), the person shall not give consent on the recipient's behalf to the use of confinement, monitoring devices or means of restraint, unless the practice is essential to prevent serious bodily harm to the recipient or to others, or allows the recipient greater freedom or enjoyment.

(4) **Participation** — The person shall encourage the recipient to participate, to the best of his or her abilities, in the person's decision concerning the personal assistance service.

60. (1) **Information** — Before making a decision on an incapable recipient's behalf concerning a personal assistance service, a substitute decision-maker is entitled to receive all the information required in order to make the decision.

(2) **Conflict** — Subsection (1) prevails despite anything to the contrary in the *Personal Health Information Protection Act, 2004*.

[2004, c. 3, Sched. A, s. 84]

61. Change of decision — Authority to make a decision on an incapable recipient's behalf concerning a personal assistance service includes authority to change the decision at any time.

62. Included consent — Unless it is not reasonable to do so in the circumstances, a person who provides a personal assistance service to a recipient is entitled to presume that consent to a personal assistance service includes consent to variations or adjustments in the service, if the nature and risks of the changed service are not significantly different from the nature and risks of the original service.

Protection from Liability

63. (1) **Personal assistance service provided** — If a person provides a personal assistance service to a recipient in accordance with a decision made on the recipient's behalf that the person believes, on reasonable grounds and in good faith, to be sufficient for the purpose of this Act, the person is not liable for providing the personal assistance service without consent.

(2) **Personal assistance service not provided** — If a person does not provide a personal assistance service to a recipient because of a decision made on the recipient's behalf that the person believes, on reasonable grounds and in good faith, to be sufficient for the purpose of this Act, the person is not liable for failing to provide the personal assistance service.

(3) **Reliance on assertion** — If a person who makes a decision on an incapable recipient's behalf concerning a personal assistance service asserts that he or she,

(a) is a person described in subsection 20 (1), as it applies for the purpose of section 58;

(b) meets the requirement of clause 20 (2) (b) or (c), as it applies for the purpose of section 58; or

(c) holds the opinions required under subsection 20 (4), as it applies for the purpose of section 58,

a person who provides a personal assistance service to the recipient is entitled to rely on the accuracy of the assertion, unless it is not reasonable to do so in the circumstances.

64. Person making decision on recipient's behalf — A person who makes a decision on a recipient's behalf concerning a personal assistance service, acting in good faith and in accordance with this Act, is not liable for making the decision.

Applications to Board

65. (1) **Application for review of finding of incapacity** — A recipient may apply to the Board for a review of an evaluator's finding that he or she is incapable with respect to a personal assistance service.

(2) **Exception** — Subsection (1) does not apply to,

(a) a recipient who has a guardian of the person, if the guardian has authority to make a decision concerning the personal assistance service;

(b) a recipient who has an attorney for personal care, if the power of attorney contains a provision waiving the recipient's right to apply for the review and the provision is effective under subsection 50 (1) of the *Substitute Decisions Act, 1992*.

(3) **Parties** — The parties to the application are:

1. The recipient applying for the review.
2. The evaluator.
3. The member of the service provider's staff who is responsible for the personal assistance service.
4. Any other person whom the Board specifies.

(4) **Subss. 32 (4) to (7) apply** — Subsections 32 (4) to (7) apply, with necessary modifications, to an application under this section.

[2000, c. 9, s. 42]

66. (1) **Application for appointment of representative** — A recipient who is 16 years old or older and who is incapable with respect to a personal assistance service may apply to the Board for appointment of a representative to make a decision on his or her behalf concerning the service.

(2) **Application by proposed representative** — A person who is 16 years old or older may apply to the Board to have himself or herself appointed as the representative of a recipient who is incapable with respect to a personal assistance service, to make a decision on behalf of the recipient concerning the service.

(3) **Exception** — Subsections (1) and (2) do not apply if the recipient has a guardian of the person who has authority to make decisions concerning the personal assistance service, or an attorney for personal care under a power of attorney conferring that authority.

(4) **Parties** — The parties to the application are:

1. The recipient.
2. The proposed representative named in the application.
3. Every person who is described in paragraph 4, 5, 6 or 7 of subsection 20 (1), as it applies for the purpose of section 58.
4. The member of the service provider's staff who is responsible for the personal assistance service.
5. Any other person whom the Board specifies.

(5) **Appointment** — In an appointment under this section, the Board may authorize the representative to make a decision on the recipient's behalf,

(a) concerning the personal assistance service; or

(b) concerning any personal assistance service, or any of several personal assistance services or kinds of personal assistance services specified by the Board, whenever a decision is sought concerning that service or a service of that kind and an evaluator finds that the recipient is incapable with respect to it.

(6) **Subss. 33 (6) to (8) apply** — Subsections 33 (6) to (8) apply, with necessary modifications, to an appointment under this section.

67. (1) **Application for directions** — A substitute decision-maker or the member of a service provider's staff who is responsible for the personal assistance service may apply to the Board for directions if the incapable recipient expressed a wish with respect to the personal assistance service, but,

(a) the wish is not clear;

(b) it is not clear whether the wish is applicable to the circumstances;

(c) it is not clear whether the wish was expressed while the recipient was capable; or

(d) it is not clear whether the wish was expressed after the recipient attained 16 years of age.

(1.1) **Notice to substitute decision-maker** — If the member of the service provider's staff responsible for the personal assistance service intends to apply under subsection (1), the member shall inform the substitute decision-maker of his or her intention before doing so.

(2) **Parties** — The parties to the application are:

1. The substitute decision-maker.
2. The recipient.
3. The member of the service provider's staff who is responsible for the personal assistance service.

4. Any other person whom the Board specifies.

(3) **Directions** — The Board may give directions and, in doing so, shall apply section 59.

[2000, c. 9, s. 43]

68. (1) **Application to depart from wishes** — If a substitute decision-maker is required by paragraph 1 of subsection 59 (1) to refuse consent to a personal assistance service because of a wish expressed by the incapable recipient while capable and after attaining 16 years of age,

(a) the substitute decision-maker may apply to the Board for permission to consent to the personal assistance service despite the wish; or

(b) the member of the service provider's staff who is responsible for the personal assistance service may apply to the Board to obtain permission for the substitute decision-maker to consent to the personal assistance service despite the wish.

(1.1) **Notice to substitute decision-maker** — If the member of the service provider's staff who is responsible for the personal assistance service intends to apply under subsection (1), the member shall inform the substitute decision-maker of his or her intention before doing so.

(2) **Parties** — The parties to the application are:

1. The substitute decision-maker.
2. The recipient.
3. The member of the service provider's staff who is responsible for the personal assistance service.
4. Any other person whom the Board specifies.

(3) **Criteria for permission** — The Board may give the substitute decision-maker permission to consent to the personal assistance service despite the wish if it is satisfied that the recipient, if capable, would probably give consent because the likely result of the personal assistance service is significantly better than would have been anticipated in comparable circumstances at the time the wish was expressed.

[2000, c. 9, s. 44]

69. (1) **Application to determine compliance with s. 59** — If a decision concerning a personal assistance service is made on an incapable recipient's behalf by his or her substitute decision-maker and, if the member of the service provider's staff who is responsible for the personal assistance service is of the opinion that the substitute decision-maker did not comply with section 59, the member of the service provider's staff who is responsible for the personal assistance service may apply to the Board for a determination as to whether the substitute decision-maker complied with section 59.

(2) **Parties** — The parties to the application are:

1. The member of the service provider's staff who is responsible for the personal assistance service.

2. The recipient.
3. The substitute decision-maker.
4. Any other person whom the Board specifies.

(3) **Power of Board** — In determining whether the substitute decision-maker complied with section 59, the Board may substitute its opinion for that of the substitute decision-maker.

(4) **Directions** — If the Board determines that the substitute decision-maker did not comply with section 59, it may give him or her directions and, in doing so, shall apply section 59.

(5) **Time for compliance** — The Board shall specify the time within which its directions must be complied with.

(6) **Deemed not authorized** — If the substitute decision-maker does not comply with the Board's directions within the time specified by the Board, he or she shall be deemed not to meet the requirements of subsection 20 (2), as it applies for the purpose of section 58.

(6.1) **Subsequent substitute decision-maker** — If, under subsection (6), the substitute decision-maker is deemed not to meet the requirements of subsection 20 (2), any subsequent substitute decision-maker shall, subject to subsections (6.2) and (6.3), comply with the directions given by the Board on the application within the time specified by the Board.

(6.2) **Application for directions** — If a subsequent substitute decision-maker knows of a wish expressed by the incapable person with respect to the personal assistance service, the substitute decision-maker may, with leave of the Board, apply to the Board for directions under section 67.

(6.3) **Inconsistent directions** — Directions given by the Board under section 67 on a subsequent substitute decision-maker's application brought with leave under subsection (6.2) prevail over inconsistent directions given under subsection (4) to the extent of the inconsistency.

(7) **P.G.T.** — If the substitute decision-maker who is given directions is the Public Guardian and Trustee, he or she is required to comply with the directions, and subsection (6) does not apply to him or her.

[2000, c. 9, s. 45]

69.1 Deemed application concerning capacity — An application to the Board under section 66, 67, 68 or 69 shall be deemed to include an application to the Board under section 65 with respect to the person's capacity to consent to a personal assistance service unless the person's capacity to consent to such service has been determined by the Board within the previous six months.

[2000, c. 9, s. 46]

PART V
Consent and Capacity Board

70. (1) **Consent and Capacity Board** — The board known as the Consent and Capacity Review Board in English and as Commission de révision du consentement et de la capacité in French is continued under the name Consent and Capacity Board in English and Commission du consentement et de la capacité in French.

(2) **Composition** — The members of the Board shall be appointed by the Lieutenant Governor in Council.

(3) **Term and reappointment** — Each member of the Board shall hold office for a term of three years or less, as determined by the Lieutenant Governor in Council, and may be reappointed.

(4) **Remuneration and expenses** — The members of the Board shall be paid the remuneration fixed by the Lieutenant Governor in Council and the reasonable expenses incurred in the course of their duties under this Act.

71. (1) **Chair and vice-chairs** — The Lieutenant Governor in Council shall designate one of the members of the Board as chair and one or more others as vice-chairs.

(2) **Role of chair** — The chair is the chief executive officer of the Board.

(3) **Power to specify qualifications** — The chair may specify qualifications, for the purpose of clause 73 (2) (d), that must be met by members of the Board before they may be assigned to sit alone to deal with particular applications.

(4) **Role of vice-chair** — If the chair is unable to act as such for any reason, the vice-chair (if there are two or more vice-chairs, the one whom the chair designates to replace him or her or, in the absence of a designation, the one who was appointed to the Board first) shall act in the chair's place.

(5) **Same** — A vice-chair also has the powers and duties that the chair delegates to him or her in writing.

71.1 Immunity — No proceeding for damages shall be commenced against the Board, a member, employee or agent of the Board or anyone acting under the authority of the chair of the Board for any act done in good faith in the performance or intended performance of the person's duty or for any alleged neglect or default in the performance in good faith of the person's duty.

[2000, c. 9, s. 47]

72. (1) **Staff** — Such employees as are necessary for the proper conduct of the Board's work may be appointed under the *Public Service Act*.

(2) **Government services and facilities** — The Board shall, if appropriate, use the services and facilities of a ministry or agency of the Government of Ontario.

73. (1) **Assignment of Board members to deal with applications** — The chair shall assign the members of the Board to sit alone or in panels of three or five members to deal with particular applications.

(2) **Qualifications of member sitting alone** — A member of the Board may be assigned to sit alone to deal with an application only if,

(a) throughout the two-year period immediately preceding the assignment, he or she has been a member of the Board or of the review board established by section 37 of the *Mental Health Act*, as it read before the day subsection 20 (23) of the *Consent and Capacity Statute Law Amendment Act, 1992* came into force;

(b) he or she is a member of the Law Society of Upper Canada and has been a member of the Law Society of Upper Canada throughout the ten-year period immediately preceding the assignment;

(c) in the case of an application for a review of a finding of incapacity, he or she has experience that, in the opinion of the chair, is relevant to adjudicating capacity; and

(d) he or she meets all of the other qualifications specified by the chair under subsection 71 (3).

(3) **Panel proceedings** — If a panel is assigned to deal with an application,

(a) the chair shall designate one member of the panel to preside over the hearing to be conducted by the panel in relation to the application; and

(b) a majority of the members of the panel constitutes a quorum.

(4) **Decision of Board** — If a member of the Board is assigned to sit alone to deal with an application, the decision of the member is the decision of the Board, and if a panel is assigned to deal with an application, the decision of a majority of the members of the panel is the decision of the Board.

74. (1) **Disqualification** — A member of the Board shall not take part in the hearing of a matter that concerns a person who is or was the member's patient or client.

(2) **Same** — A member of the Board who is an officer or employee of a hospital or other facility or has a direct financial interest in such a facility shall not take part in the hearing of a matter that concerns a person who is a patient of the facility or who resides in the facility.

75. (1) **Board to fix time and place of hearing** — When the Board receives an application, it shall promptly fix a time and place for a hearing.

(2) **Hearing to begin within seven days** — The hearing shall begin within seven days after the day the Board receives the application, unless the parties agree to a postponement.

(3) **Decision** — The Board shall render its decision and provide each party or the party's counsel or agent with a copy of the decision within one day after the day the hearing ends.

(4) **Reasons** — If, within 30 days after the day the hearing ends, the Board receives a request from any of the parties for reasons for its decision, the Board shall, within two business days after the day the request is received, issue written reasons for its decision and provide each party or the party's counsel or agent with a copy of the reasons.

(5) **Notice of right to request reasons —** The Board shall advise all parties to the application that each party has a right to request reasons for the Board's decision.

(6) **Method of sending decision and reasons —** Despite subsection 18 (1) of the *Statutory Powers Procedure Act*, the Board shall send the copy of the decision and, if reasons are required to be issued under subsection (4), the copy of the reasons,

(a) by electronic transmission;

(b) by telephone transmission of a facsimile; or

(c) by some other method that allows proof of receipt, in accordance with the tribunal's rules made under section 25.1 of the *Statutory Powers Procedure Act*.

(7) **Deemed day of receipt —** Despite subsection 18 (3) of the *Statutory Powers Procedure Act*, if the copy is sent by electronic transmission or by telephone transmission of a facsimile, it shall be deemed to be received on the day that it was sent, unless that day is a holiday, in which case the copy shall be deemed to be received on the next day that is not a holiday.

(8) **Exception —** If a party that acts in good faith does not, through absence, accident, illness or other cause beyond the party's control, receive the copy until a date that is later than the deemed day of receipt, the actual date of receipt governs.

(9) **Meaning of "business day" —** In subsection (4),

"business day" means any day other than Saturday or a holiday.

76. (1) **Examination of documents —** Before the hearing, the parties shall be given an opportunity to examine and copy any documentary evidence that will be produced and any report whose contents will be given in evidence.

(2) **Health record —** The party who is the subject of the treatment, the admission or the personal assistance service, as the case may be, and his or her counsel or agent are entitled to examine and to copy, at their own expense, any medical or other health record prepared in respect of the party, subject to subsections 35 (6) and (7) of the *Mental Health Act* (withholding record of personal health information), subsections 33 (2), (3) and (4) of the *Long-Term Care Act, 1994* (withholding record of personal health information) and subsections 183 (2) to (6) of the *Child and Family Services Act* (withholding record of mental disorder).

[2004, c. 3, Sched. A, s. 84]

77. (1) **Communication re subject-matter of hearing —** The member or members of the Board conducting a hearing shall not communicate about the subject-matter of the hearing directly or indirectly with any party, counsel, agent or other person, unless all the parties and their counsel or agents receive notice and have an opportunity to participate.

(2) **Exception —** However, the member or members of the Board conducting the hearing may seek advice from an adviser independent of the parties, and in

that case the nature of the advice shall be communicated to all the parties and their counsel or agents so that they may make submissions as to the law.

78. Only members at hearing to participate in decision — No member of the Board shall participate in a decision unless he or she was present throughout the hearing and heard the parties' evidence and argument.

79. (1) **Release of evidence** — Within a reasonable time after the final disposition of the proceeding, documents and things put in evidence at the hearing shall, on request, be released to the person who produced them.

(2) **Return of original record** — If an original clinical record respecting a person's care or treatment was put in evidence, it shall be returned to the place from which it was obtained as soon as possible after the final disposition of the proceeding.

80. (1) **Appeal** — A party to a proceeding before the Board may appeal the Board's decision to the Superior Court of Justice on a question of law or fact or both.

(2) **Time for filing notice of appeal** — The appellant shall serve his or her notice of appeal on the other parties and shall file it with the court, with proof of service, within seven days after he or she receives the Board's decision.

(3) **Notice to Board** — The appellant shall give a copy of the notice of appeal to the Board.

(4) **Record** — On receipt of the copy of the notice of appeal, the Board shall promptly serve the parties with the record of the proceeding before the Board, including a transcript of the oral evidence given at the hearing, and shall promptly file the record and transcript, with proof of service, with the court.

(5) **Time for filing appellant's factum** — Within 14 days after being served with the record and transcript, the appellant shall serve his or her factum on the other parties and shall file it, with proof of service, with the court.

(6) **Time for filing respondent's factum** — Within 14 days after being served with the appellant's factum, the respondent shall serve his or her factum on the other parties and shall file it, with proof of service, with the court.

(7) **Extension of time** — The court may extend the time for filing the notice of appeal, the appellant's factum or the respondent's factum, even after the time has expired.

(8) **Early date for appeal** — The court shall fix for the hearing of the appeal the earliest date that is compatible with its just disposition.

(9) **Appeal on the record, exception** — The court shall hear the appeal on the record, including the transcript, but may receive new or additional evidence as it considers just.

(10) **Powers of court on appeal** — On the appeal, the court may,

(a) exercise all the powers of the Board;

(b) substitute its opinion for that of a health practitioner, an evaluator, a substitute decision-maker or the Board;

(c) refer the matter back to the Board, with directions, for rehearing in whole or in part.

[2000, c. 9, s. 48]

81. (1) **Counsel for incapable person** — If a person who is or may be incapable with respect to a treatment, admission to a care facility or a personal assistance service is a party to a proceeding before the Board and does not have legal representation,

(a) the Board may direct the Public Guardian and Trustee or the Children's Lawyer to arrange for legal representation to be provided for the person; and

(b) the person shall be deemed to have capacity to retain and instruct counsel.

(2) **Responsibility for legal fees** — If legal representation is provided for a person in accordance with clause (1) (a) and no certificate is issued under the *Legal Aid Services Act, 1998* in connection with the proceeding, the person is responsible for the legal fees.

(3) **Child in secure treatment program** — If a child who has been admitted to a secure treatment program under section 124 of the *Child and Family Services Act* is a party to a proceeding before the Board, the Children's Lawyer shall provide legal representation for the child unless the Children's Lawyer is satisfied that another person will provide legal representation for the child.

[1998, c. 26, s. 104]

PART VI
Miscellaneous

82. (1) **Offence: false assertion** — No person who gives or refuses consent to a treatment on an incapable person's behalf shall make an assertion referred to in subsection 29 (6), knowing that it is untrue.

(2) **Same** — No person who gives or refuses consent to admission to a care facility on an incapable person's behalf shall make an assertion referred to in subsection 48 (4), knowing that it is untrue.

(3) **Same** — No person who makes a decision concerning a personal assistance service on an incapable recipient's behalf shall make an assertion referred to in subsection 63 (3), knowing that it is untrue.

(4) **Penalty** — A person who contravenes subsection (1), (2) or (3) is guilty of an offence and is liable, on conviction, to a fine not exceeding $10,000.

83. (1) **Offence: misrepresentation of wishes** — No person shall knowingly misrepresent wishes someone has expressed with respect to treatment, admission to a care facility or a personal assistance service.

(2) **Penalty** — A person who contravenes subsection (1) is guilty of an offence and is liable, on conviction, to a fine not exceeding $10,000.

84. (1) **Offence: decision contrary to wishes** — A person who knowingly contravenes paragraph 1 of subsection 21 (1), paragraph 1 of subsection 42 (1) or paragraph 1 of subsection 59 (1) is guilty of an offence and is liable, on conviction, to a fine not exceeding $10,000.

(2) **Exception** — Subsection (1) does not apply if the person acts in accordance with permission given under section 36, 53 or 68 or in accordance with directions given under section 35, 37, 52, 54, 67 or 69.

85. (1) **Regulations** — The Lieutenant Governor in Council may make regulations,

(a) prescribing facilities as care facilities for the purpose of clause (d) of the definition of "care facility" in subsection 2 (1) and providing transitional rules for the application of the Act to such facilities;

(b) for the purpose of the definition of "evaluator" in subsection 2 (1), prescribing categories of persons as evaluators and prescribing the circumstances in which those persons or persons described in clause (a), (l), (m), (o), (p) or (q) of the definition of "health practitioner" in subsection 2 (1) may act as evaluators;

(c) prescribing categories of persons as health practitioners for the purpose of the definition of "health practitioner" in subsection 2 (1);

(d) prescribing things that do not constitute a personal assistance service for the purpose of the definition of "personal assistance service" in subsection 2 (1);

(e) prescribing places, programs, providers and circumstances for the purpose of the definition of "recipient" in subsection 2 (1);

(f) prescribing things that do not constitute treatment for the purpose of the definition of "treatment" in subsection 2 (1);

(g) prescribing excluded acts for the purpose of clause 3 (1) (b);

(h) governing determinations by health practitioners of capacity with respect to treatment and governing determinations by evaluators of capacity with respect to admission to a care facility or a personal assistance service;

(i) prescribing health facilities for the purpose of subsection 24 (1);

(j) regulating the amounts that a person who is entitled to copy medical or other health records under subsection 76 (2) may be charged for copies of the records;

(k) governing the transfer of information between an evaluator and the person responsible for authorizing admissions to a care facility, or between an evaluator and the member of a service provider's staff who is responsible for a personal assistance service;

(l) governing the transfer of information that is relevant to the making of a decision under this Act concerning a treatment, admission to a care facility or a personal assistance service, including regulating the disclosure of such information to the person who is the subject of the decision or to his or her substitute decision-maker and requiring or permitting the disclosure of such information with the consent of the person or his or her substitute decision-maker;

(m) prescribing forms for the purpose of this Act or the regulations.

(2) **Application** — A regulation may be general or specific in its application.

86. [Repealed, 1996, c. 2, Sched. A, s. 86 (2)]

87. (1) **Transition, treatment** — This Act applies to a treatment that is begun after the day this Act comes into force, even if a finding as to capacity was made or consent was given before that day.

(2) **Same** — This Act does not apply to a treatment that is begun on or before the day this Act comes into force.

88. (1) **Transition, admission** — This Act applies to the admission to a care facility of a person who is placed on the waiting list for the facility after the day this Act comes into force, even if a finding as to capacity was made or consent was given before that day.

(2) **Same** — This Act does not apply to the admission to a care facility of a person who is placed on the waiting list for the facility on or before the day this Act comes into force.

(3) **Application of section** — This section does not apply to a care facility described in clause (d) of the definition of "care facility" in subsection 2 (1).

89. Transition, section 19 — Section 19 applies to an appeal commenced before the day this Act comes into force if, on the day this Act comes into force, the appeal has not been finally disposed of and an order authorizing administration of the treatment before the final disposition of the appeal has not been made.

90. (1) **Transition, section 32** — If, on the day this Act comes into force, an application commenced under section 28 of the *Consent to Treatment Act, 1992* has not been finally disposed of,

(a) subsections 32 (3) and (4) of this Act apply to the application;

(b) subsection 32 (2) of this Act does not apply to the application; and

(c) subsection 28 (6) of the *Consent to Treatment Act, 1992*, as it read immediately before the day this Act comes into force, continues to apply to the application.

(2) **Same** — For the purpose of subsection 32 (5) of this Act, a final disposition of the following applications shall be deemed to be a final disposition of an application under section 32 of this Act:

1. An application commenced under section 28 of the *Consent to Treatment Act, 1992* before the day this Act comes into force.
2. An application commenced under section 51 of the *Mental Health Act* before the day subsection 20 (40) of the *Consent and Capacity Statute Law Amendment Act, 1992* came into force.

91. (1) **Transition, section 33 —** If, on the day this Act comes into force, an application commenced under section 29 of the *Consent to Treatment Act, 1992* has not been finally disposed of,

(a) subsections 33 (5) and (6) and clauses 33 (7) (a), (b) and (c) of this Act apply to the application;

(b) subsections 33 (3) and (4) of this Act do not apply to the application; and

(c) subsections 29 (3) and (7) of the *Consent to Treatment Act, 1992*, as they read immediately before the day this Act comes into force, continue to apply to the application.

(2) **Same —** Clause 33 (7) (d) and subsection 33 (8) of this Act apply to an appointment made pursuant to an application commenced under section 29 of the *Consent to Treatment Act, 1992* before the day this Act comes into force.

92. (1) **Transition, section 34 —** If, on the day this Act comes into force, an application commenced under section 32 of the *Consent to Treatment Act, 1992* has not been finally disposed of,

(a) subsections 34 (3), (4), (5) and (6) of this Act apply to the application; and

(b) subsection 34 (2) of this Act does not apply to the application.

(2) **Same —** For the purpose of subsection 34 (7) of this Act, a final disposition of an application commenced under section 32 of the *Consent to Treatment Act, 1992* before the day this Act comes into force shall be deemed to be a final disposition of an application under section 34 of this Act.

93. Transition, section 35 — If, on the day this Act comes into force, an application commenced under section 30 of the *Consent to Treatment Act, 1992* has not been finally disposed of, subsections 35 (2) and (3) of this Act apply to the application if it was commenced by a person who is a substitute decision-maker as defined in Part II of this Act.

94. Transition, section 36 — If, on the day this Act comes into force, an application commenced under section 31 of the *Consent to Treatment Act, 1992* has not been finally disposed of, subsections 36 (2) and (3) of this Act apply to the application if it was commenced by a person who is a substitute decision-maker as defined in Part II of this Act.

95. The short title of this Act is the *Health Care Consent Act, 1996*.

EVALUATORS

(O. Reg. 104/96)

Amended: *O. Reg. 264/00*

1. (1) For the purpose of the definition of "evaluator" in subsection 2 (1) of the Act,

(a) social workers are evaluators;

(b) social workers and persons described in clause (a), (l), (m), (o), (p) or (q) of the definition of "health practitioner" in subsection 2 (1) of the Act may act as evaluators for the purpose of determining whether a person is capable with respect to his or her admission to a care facility and for the purpose of determining whether a person is capable with respect to a personal assistance service.

(2) In this section,

"social worker" means a member of the Ontario College of Social Workers and Social Service Workers who holds a certificate of registration for social work.

[O. Reg. 264/00, s. 2]

2. [Coming into force provisions.]

SUMMARY OF FORMS

FORM	DESCRIPTION
Form A	Application to the Board to Review a Finding of Incapacity under Subsection 32(1), 50(1) or 65(1) of the Act
Form B	Application to the Board to Appoint a Representative under Subsection 33(1), 51(1) or 66(1) of the Act
Form C	Application to the Board to Appoint a Representative under Subsection 33(2), 51(2) or 66(2) of the Act
Form D	Application to the Board for Directions under Subsection 35(1), 52(1) or 67(1) of the Act
Form E	Application to the Board for Permission to Depart from Wishes under Subsection 36(1), 53(1) or 68(1) of the Act
Form F	Application to the Board with Respect to Place of Treatment under Subsection 34(1) of the Act
Form G	Application to the Board to Determine Compliance under Subsection 37(1), 54(1) or 69(1) of the Act
Form H	Application to the Board to Amend the Conditions of or Terminate the Appointment of a Representative under Subsection 33(7) and (8), 51(6) or 66(6) of the Act

Forms

Consent and Capacity Board

Form A
Health Care Consent Act

Application to the Board to Review a Finding of Incapacity under Subsection 32(1), 50(1) or 65(1) of the Act

My name is: ______________________ (print full name) , I apply to the Board for a review of:

☐ an evaluator's finding that I am incapable with respect to my admission to a care facility.

☐ an evaluator's finding that I am incapable with respect to a personal assistance service.

☐ a health practitioner's finding that I am incapable with respect to the following treatment, course of treatment, plan of treatment or community treatment plan:

____

____

Note: An application may only be made if a Health Practitioner or evaluator has made a relevant finding of incapacity.

Please provide the name, address, telephone and fax numbers of the health practitioner or evaluator who made the finding of incapacity:

____

____

Are you currently an in-patient or resident at a health or residential facility?

☐ **no**

☐ **yes** name, address and telephone number of facility

____

____

Your home address and telephone number or other way to contact you:

______________________ (address) ( ) ______________ (telephone no.)

Name, address, telephone number and fax number of your lawyer or agent *(if any)*:

______________ (name) ______________ (address)

( ) ______________ (telephone no.) ( ) ______________ (fax no.)

If this application refers to admission to a care facility, please provide the name, address, telephone and fax numbers of the person responsible for authorizing admissions to the facility:

______________ (name) ______________ (address)

( ) ______________ (telephone no.) ( ) ______________ (fax no.)

(Disponible en version française)

www.ccboard.on.ca

See reverse

7530-5333

2973-04 (00/12)*

HEALTH CARE CONSENT ACT, 1996

If this application refers to a personal assistance service, please provide the name, address, telephone and fax numbers of the staff member responsible for the service:

(name) (address)

( ) (telephone no.) ( ) (fax no.)

If someone helped you to fill out this application form, please provide his / her name, address, telephone and fax numbers:

(name) (address)

( ) (telephone no.) ( ) (fax no.)

Have you applied to the Board during the past year for a review of a finding regarding your capacity to consent to treatment, admission to a long term care facility or personal care services?

☐ no

☐ yes if know, provide place and date of last hearing

(date) (location)

(date) (signature)

Collection of this information is for the purpose of conducting a proceeding before this Board. It is collected/used for this purpose under the authority of subsection 32(1) / 50(1) / 65(1) of the Health Care Consent Act. For information about collection practices, contact the office of the Regional Vice-Chair of the Board or call toll free at 1 800 461–2036.

Send this form by fax to the Office of the Regional Vice-Chair of the Board or call toll free at 1 800 461–2036 for assistance.

For your information

What will happen if I don't apply to the Board? If you have been found incapable of consenting to a treatment, admission to a long term care facility or a personal assistance service, someone else will be asked to make the decision for you. This is usually a close family member. If you have a court-appointed guardian or an attorney for personal care with the authority to make the decision, that person will make it for you.

Who may apply to the Board? Anyone who has been found incapable of consenting to a treatment, admission to a long term care facility or a personal assistance service may apply unless:

- they have either a court-appointed guardian for personal care with authority to make the required decision, or
- they have signed a special kind of power of attorney for personal care in which they waive their right to apply to the Board and which meets specific procedural requirements found in Section 50(1) the Substitute Decision Act.
- may not reapply within six months of a final determination of a previous application except with Board permission.

When & Where will the hearing be? The hearing will be held somewhere close to where you are. It will probably take place within a week after the Board receives your application.

How will the Board make its decision? The Board will base its decision on whether or not it believes that you are:

- able to understand the information that is relevant to making a decision concerning the treatment, admission to a long term care facility or personal assistance service, and
- able to appreciate the reasonable foreseeable consequences of a decision or lack of decision.

Form A *(page 2)*

2973-04 (00/12)* www.ccboard.on.ca 7530-5333

Consent and Capacity Board

Form B
Health Care Consent Act

Application to the Board to Appoint a Representative under Subsection 33(1), 51(1) or 66(1) of the Act

My name is: ____________________
(print full name of patient)

I apply to the Board to have a representative appointed to give or refuse consent on my behalf.

☐ a health practitioner's finding that I am incapable with respect to the following treatment, course of treament, plan of treatment or community treatment plan that has been proposed for me:

____

☐ an evaluator has found that I am not capable with respect to my admission to a care facility.

☐ an evaluator has found that I am not capable with respect to a personal assistance service.

Note: An application may only be made if a health practitioner or evaluator has made a relevant finding of incapacity.

The name of the proposed representative is: ____________________
(print full name of the proposed representative)

His or her address, telephone and fax numbers are:

____
(address)

( ) ____________________ (telephone no.)   ( ) ____________________ (fax no.)

The name of the person who made the finding of incapacity is: ____________________
(print full name of the person)

His or her address and telephone and fax number are:

____
(address)

( ) ____________________ (telephone no.)   ( ) ____________________ (fax no.)

Are you currently an in-patient or resident at a health or residential facility?

☐ **no**

☐ **yes**   provide name, address and telephone number of facility

____

____

Your home address and telephone number or other way to contact you:

____________________ (address)   ( ) ____________________ (telephone no.)

(Disponible en version française)
Form B (page 1)   www.ccboard.on.ca   *See reverse*
2975-04 (00/12)*   7530-5334

HEALTH CARE CONSENT ACT, 1996

You must list your spouse, partner, parent, brothers and sisters and your children. If you are under 18 years old, you must also list any agency or person legally authorised to make treatment decisions on your behalf:

Name	Relationship	Address	Telephone no.
1.			( )
2.			( )
3.			( )
4.			( )
5.			( )

(If further room is required, check here ☐ *and add another sheet)*
If you were unable to provide a complete and accurate list, please explain:

____

WARNING: All persons in the required categories together with correct and complete contact information must be listed unless you are unable to do so and have so indicated. Intentional omissions or misinformation may result in a cost award against you, dismissal of your application or other sanctions.

Name, address, telephone number and fax number of your lawyer or agent *(if any)*:

____________________ (name) ____________________ (address)

( ) ______________ (telephone no.) ( ) ______________ (fax no.)

If this application refers to admission to a care facility, provide the name, address, telephone and fax numbers of the person responsible for authorizing admissions to the facility. (Often, this will be an official from the local Community Care Access Centre.)

____________________ (name) ____________________ (address)

( ) ______________ (telephone no.) ( ) ______________ (fax no.)

If this application refers to a personal assistance service, provide the name, address, telephone and fax numbers of the staff member responsible for the service:

____________________ (name) ____________________ (address)

( ) ______________ (telephone no.) ( ) ______________ (fax no.)

If this application refers to a treatment, provide the name, address, telephone and fax numbers of the health practitioner who proposed it:

____________________ (name) ____________________ (address)

( ) ______________ (telephone no.) ( ) ______________ (fax no.)

If someone helped you to fill out this application form, provide his / her name, and contact information:

____________________ (name) ____________________ (address)

( ) ______________ (telephone no.) ( ) ______________ (fax no.)

I confirm that the proposed representative and I both are at least sixteen years of age.

____________________ (date) ____________________ (signature)

Whenever an application of this type is received, the law provides that the patient is deemed to have applied for a review of his or her capacity to make the relevant decision. This does not apply if the Board has determined this issue of capacity within the previous six months.

Collection of this information is for the purpose of conducting a proceeding before this board. It is collected/used for this purpose under the authority of subsection 33(1) / 51(1) / 66(1) of the Health Care Consent Act. For information about collection practices, contact the office of the Regional Vice-Chair of the Board or call toll free at 1 800 461–2036.

Send this form by fax to the Office of the Regional Vice-Chair of the Board or call toll free at 1 800 461–2036 for assistance.

2975–04 (00/12)* Form B (page 1) www.ccboard.on.ca 7530–5334

Consent and Capacity Board

Form C
Health Care Consent Act

Application to the Board to Appoint a Representative under Subsection 33(2), 51(2) or 66(2) of the Act

My name is: ____________________
(print full name of applicant)

This application is made with respect to ____________________ , a person whom
(print full name of incapable person)

- ☐ an evaluator has found to be incapable with respect to admission to a care facility
- ☐ an evaluator has found to be incapable with respect to a personal assistance service
- ☐ a health practitioner has found to be incapable with respect to the following treatment:

____

☞ **An application may only be made if a health practitioner or an evaluator has made a relevant finding of incapacity.**

I apply to the Board to be appointed a representative for the above named person with respect to this matter.

My home address, telephone and fax numbers are:

____
(address)

( ) ____________________ (telephone no.)   ( ) ____________________ (fax no.)

The name of the person who made the finding of incapacity is: ____________________
(print full name of the person)

His or her address and telephone and fax numbers are:

____
(address)

( ) ____________________ (telephone no.)   ( ) ____________________ (fax no.)

Is the person who has been found incapable with respect to this matter currently an in-patient or resident at a health or residential facility?

- ☐ **no**
- ☐ **yes**   provide name, address and telephone number of facility

____

____

His or her home address and telephone and fax numbers are:

____
(address)

( ) ____________________ (telephone no.)   ( ) ____________________ (fax no.)

See reverse

HEALTH CARE CONSENT ACT, 1996

Name, address, telephone number and fax number of the lawyer or agent *(if any)* for the person who has been found incapable with respect to this matter:

(name) (address)

( ) (telephone no.) ( ) (fax no.)

Name, address, telephone number and fax number of your lawyer or agent *(if any)*:

(name) (address)

( ) (telephone no.) ( ) (fax no.)

You must list the spouse, partner, parent, brothers and sisters and children of the incapable person. If the person is under 18 years old, you must also list any agency or person legally authorised to make treatment decisions on his or her behalf:

Name	Relationship	Address	Telephone no.
1.			( )
2.			( )
3.			( )
4.			( )
5.			( )

(If further room is required, check here ☐ *and add another sheet)*

If you were unable to provide a complete and accurate list, please explain:

WARNING: All persons in the required categories together with correct and complete contact information must be listed unless you are unable to do so and have so indicated. Intentional omissions or misinformation may result in a cost award against you, dismissal of your application or other sanctions.

If this application refers to admission to a care facility, provide the name, address, telephone and fax numbers of the person responsible for authorizing admissions to the facility. (Often, this will be an official from the local Community Care Access Centre.)

(name) (address)

( ) (telephone no.) ( ) (fax no.)

If this application refers to a personal assistance service, provide the name, address, telephone and fax numbers of the staff member responsible for the service:

(name) (address)

( ) (telephone no.) ( ) (fax no.)

If this application refers to a treatment, provide the name, address, telephone and fax numbers of the health practitioner who proposed it:

(name) (address)

( ) (telephone no.) ( ) (fax no.)

I confirm that I am at least sixteen years of age.

(date) (signature)

Whenever an application of this type is received, the law provides that the patient is deemed to have applied for a review of his or her capacity to make the relevant decision. This does not apply if the Board has determined this issue of capacity within the previous six months.

Collection of this information is for the purpose of conducting a proceeding before this board. It is collected/used for this purpose under the authority of subsection 33(2) / 51(2) / 66(2) of the Health Care Consent Act. For information about collection practices, contact the office of the Regional Vice-Chair of the Board or call toll free at 1 800 461-2036.

Send this form by fax to the Office of the Regional Vice-Chair of the Board or call toll free at 1 800 461–2036 for assistance.

www.ccboard.on.ca

Form C (page 2)
2976-04 (00/12)*

7530-5335

Consent and Capacity Board

Form D
Health Care Consent Act

Application to the Board for Directions under Subsection 35(1), 52(1) or 67(1) of the Act

Re: ______________________________ , a person who has been found incapable with respect to:

☐ admission to a care facility
☐ a personal assistance service
☐ the following kind of treatment:
____

Note: An application may only be made if there has been a relevant finding of incapacity.

My name is: ______________________________
(print full name of person)

☐ I am the person's substitute decision maker, or
☐ I am the health care professional who proposed the treatment, or*
☐ I am the Official at the Community Care Access Centre responsible for authorizing admission to the care facility, or*
☐ I am the member of the service provider's staff responsible for providing personal assistance service.*

***Note: Persons in these categories may only bring an application if they have given prior notice to the substitute decision maker of their intention to do so.**

The person named above has previously expressed a wish with respect to this matter but *(mark as many as are applicable)*:

☐ the wish is not clear.
☐ it is not clear if the wish is applicable in the circumstances.
☐ it is not clear if the wish was expressed when the person was capable.
☐ it is not clear if the wish was expressed after the person attained sixteen years of age.

I apply to the Board for directions in this matter.

The name, address, telephone and fax numbers of the substitute decision maker are:

______________________________ (name) ______________________________ (address)

( ) ______________________________ (telephone no.) ( ) ______________________________ (fax no.)

If this application refers to admission to a care facility, provide the name, address, telephone and fax numbers of the person responsible for authorizing admissions to the facility. (This will be an official from the local Community Care Access Centre.)

______________________________ (name) ______________________________ (address)

( ) ______________________________ (telephone no.) ( ) ______________________________ (fax no.)

If this application refers to a personal assistance service, provide the name, address, telephone and fax numbers of the staff member responsible for the service:

______________________________ (name) ______________________________ (address)

( ) ______________________________ (telephone no.) ( ) ______________________________ (fax no.)

(Disponible en version française)

See reverse

2977-04 (00/12)* www.ccboard.on.ca 7530-5336

HEALTH CARE CONSENT ACT, 1996

If this application refers to a treatment, provide the name, address, telephone and fax numbers of the health practitioner who proposed it:

(name) (address)

( ) (telephone no.) ( ) (fax no.)

Is the person who has been found incapable with respect to this matter currently an in-patient or resident at a health or residential facility?

☐ **no**

☐ **yes** provide name, address and telephone number of facility

His or her address and telephone and fax number are:

(address)

( ) (telephone no.) ( ) (fax no.)

Name, address, telephone number and fax number of the lawyer or agent *(if any)* for the person who has been found incapable with respect to this matter:

(name) (address)

( ) (telephone no.) ( ) (fax no.)

Name, address, telephone number and fax number of your lawyer or agent *(if any)*:

(name) (address)

( ) (telephone no.) ( ) (fax no.)

Name, address, telephone number and fax number of your lawyer or agent *(if any)* for the substitute decision maker if you are not the substitute decision maker:

(name) (address)

( ) (telephone no.) ( ) (fax no.)

Whenever an application of this type is received, the law provides that the patient is deemed to have applied for a review of his or her capacity to make the relevant decision. This does not apply if the Board has determined this issue of capacity within the previous six months.

Collection of this information is for the purpose of conducting a proceeding before this board. It is collected/used for this purpose under the authority of subsection 35(1) / 52(1) / 67(1) of the Health Care Consent Act. For information about collection practices, contact the office of the Regional Vice-Chair of the Board or call toll free at 1 800 461-2036.

Send this form by fax to the Office of the Regional Vice-Chair of the Board or call toll free at 1 800 461-2036 for assistance.

2977-04 (00/12)* Form D *(page 2)* www.ccboard.on.ca 7530-5336

Consent and Capacity Board

Form E
Health Care Consent Act

Application to the Board for Permission to Depart from Wishes under Subsection 36(1), 53(1) or 68(1) of the Act

Re: ______________________________ , a person who has been found incapable with respect to:

- ☐ admission to a care facility
- ☐ a personal assistance service
- ☐ the following kind of treatment:

____

Note: **An application may only be made if a health practitioner or evaluator has made a relevant finding of incapacity.**

My name is: ______________________________
(print full name of person)

- ☐ I am the person's substitute decision maker, or
- ☐ I am the health care professional who proposed the treatment, or*
- ☐ I am the Official at the Community Care Access Centre responsible for authorizing admission to the care facility, or*
- ☐ I am the member of the service provider's staff responsible for providing personal assistance service.*

***Note:** **Persons in these categories may only bring an application if they have given prior notice to the substitute decision maker of their intention to do so.**

I apply to the Board for permission to consent to the proposed action despite a contrary wish expressed by the person named above at a time when the person was capable and at least sixteen years of age. I believe that he / she would probably, if capable today, give consent because the likely result of consenting is significantly better than would have been anticipated in comparable circumstances at the time the wish was expressed.

The name, address, telephone and fax numbers of the substitute decision maker are:

______________________________ (name) ______________________________ (address)

( ) ______________________________ (telephone no.) ( ) ______________________________ (fax no.)

If this application refers to admission to a care facility, provide the name, address, telephone and fax numbers of the person responsible for authorizing admissions to the facility:

______________________________ (name) ______________________________ (address)

( ) ______________________________ (telephone no.) ( ) ______________________________ (fax no.)

If this application refers to a personal assistance service, provide the name, address, telephone and fax numbers of the staff member responsible for the service:

______________________________ (name) ______________________________ (address)

( ) ______________________________ (telephone no.) ( ) ______________________________ (fax no.)

If this application refers to a treatment, provide the name, address, telephone and fax numbers of the health practitioner who proposed it:

______________________________ (name) ______________________________ (address)

( ) ______________________________ (telephone no.) ( ) ______________________________ (fax no.)

(Disponible en version française)

See reverse

2978-04 (00/12)*
www.ccboard.on.ca
7530-5337

Is the person who has been found incapable with respect to this matter currently an in-patient or resident at a health or residential facility?

☐ **no**

☐ **yes** provide name, address and telephone number of facility

His or her address and telephone and fax number are:

(address)

(telephone no.) (fax no.)

Name, address, telephone number and fax number of the lawyer or agent *(if any)* for the person who has been found incapable with respect to this matter:

(name) (address)

(telephone no.) (fax no.)

Name, address, telephone number and fax number of your lawyer or agent *(if any)*:

(name) (address)

(telephone no.) (fax no.)

(date) (signature)

Name, address, telephone number and fax number of your lawyer or agent *(if any)* for the substitute decision maker if you are not the substitute decision maker.

(name)

(telephone no.) (fax no.)

(date) (signature)

Whenever an application of this type is received, the law provides that the patient is deemed to have applied for a review of his or her capacity to make the relevant decision. This does not apply if the Board has determined this issue of capacity within the previous six months.

Collection of this information is for the purpose of conducting a proceeding before this board. It is collected/used for this purpose under the authority of subsection 35(1) / 52(1) / 67(1) of the Health Care Consent Act. For information about collection practices, contact the office of the Regional Vice-Chair of the Board or call toll free at 1 800 461–2036.

Send this form by fax to the Office of the Regional Vice-Chair of the Board or call toll free at 1 800 461–2036 for assistance.

Form E *(page 2)*

2978–04 (00/12)* www.ccboard.on.ca 7530–5337

Consent
and Capacity
Board

Form F
Health Care Consent Act

Application to the Board with Respect to Place of Treatment under Subsection 34(1) of the Act

My name is: ______________________________ I apply to the Board for a
(print full name of person)

review of a decision, made on my behalf, to consent to my admission to a hospital, psychiatric facility or other health facility for the purpose of treatment.

A health practitioner has found that I am incapable with respect to the following treatment, course of treatment or plan of treatment:

____

____

and a substitute decision maker has consented to my admission to the following hospital, psychiatric facility or other health facility for the purpose of receiving that treatment, course of treatment or plan of treatment.

Note: An application may only be made if a health practitioner has made a relevant finding of incapacity to consent to a treatment, course of treatment or plan of treatment.

Provide the name, address, telephone and fax numbers of the health practitioner who proposed the treatment:

______________________________ (name) ______________________________ (address)

( ) ______________________________ (telephone no.) ( ) ______________________________ (fax no.)

Name, address, telephone and fax numbers of the substitute decision maker:

______________________________ (name) ______________________________ (address)

( ) ______________________________ (telephone no.) ( ) ______________________________ (fax no.)

Are you currently an in-patient or resident at a health or residential facility?

☐ **no**

☐ **yes** provide name, address and telephone number of facility

____

____

Your home address and telephone number:

______________________________ (address) ( ) ______________________________ (telephone no.)

(Disponible en version française) www.ccboard.on.ca *See reverse*

2980-04 (00/12)* 7530-5338

HEALTH CARE CONSENT ACT, 1996

Name, address, telephone number and fax number of your lawyer or agent *(if any)*:

(name) (address)

( ) (telephone no.) ( ) (fax no.)

If someone helped you to fill out this application form, provide his / her name, address, telephone and fax numbers:

(name) (address)

( ) (telephone no.) ( ) (fax no.)

(date) (signature)

Whenever an application of this type is received, the law provides that the patient is deemed to have applied for a review of his or her capacity to make the relevant decision. This does not apply if the Board has determined this issue of capacity within the previous six months.

Collection of this information is for the purpose of conducting a proceeding before this board. It is collected/used for this purpose under the authority of subsection 34(1) of the Health Care Consent Act. For information about collection practices, contact the office of the Regional Vice-Chair of the Board or call toll free at 1 800 461-2036.

Send this form by fax to the Office of the Regional Vice-Chair of the Board or call toll free at 1 800 461-2036 for assistance.

Form F *(Page 2)*

2980-04 (00/12)* www.ccboard.on.ca 7530-5338

Consent and Capacity Board

Form G
Health Care Consent Act

Application to the Board to Determine Compliance under Subsection 37(1), 54(1) or 69(1) of the Act

This application is made with respect to ______________________ , a person whom
(print full name of incapable person)

- [ ] an evaluator has found to be incapable with respect to admission to a care facility
- [ ] an evaluator has found to be incapable with respect to a personal assistance service
- [ ] a health practitioner has found to be incapable with respect to the following treatment:

____

- **You may only bring an application with regards to a treatment if you are the health practitioner who proposed the treatment.**
- **You may only bring an application with regards to admission to a care facility if you are the official of the Community Care access Centre responsible for authorising the admission.**
- **You may only bring an application with regards to personal assistance if you are the member of the service providers staff responsible for providing the service and only if the person is a resident in a nursing home or home for the aged.**

My name is: ______________________ . I am the
(print full name of applicant)

- [ ] person responsible for authorizing admissions to the care facility
- [ ] staff person responsible for the personal assistance service
- [ ] health practitioner who proposed the treatment

I apply to the Board for a determination as to whether or not the substitute decision-maker in this case has complied with the principles for substitute decision-making as they are set out in the Act.

My address and telephone number(s) are:

____
(address)

( ) ______________ (telephone no.) ( ) ______________ (fax no.)

The name of the substitute decision-maker is: ______________________
(print full name of person)

His or her address, telephone and fax numbers are:

____
(address)

( ) ______________ (telephone no.) ( ) ______________ (fax no.)

Is the person who has been found incapable currently an in-patient or resident at a health or residential facility?

- [ ] **no**
- [ ] **yes** provide name, address and telephone number of facility

____

____

His or her home address and telephone number are:

______________________ (address) ( ) ______________ (telephone no.)

(Disponible en version française)

See reverse
7530-5339

2981-04 (00/12)*

www.ccboard.on.ca

HEALTH CARE CONSENT ACT, 1996

Name, address, telephone number and fax number of the lawyer or agent *(if any)* for the person who has been found incapable with respect to this matter:

(name) (address)

( ) (telephone no.) ( ) (fax no.)

Name, address, telephone number and fax number of your lawyer or agent *(if any):*

(name) (address)

( ) (telephone no.) ( ) (fax no.)

(date) (signature)

Whenever an application of this type is received, the law provides that the patient is deemed to have applied for a review of his or her capacity to make the relevant decision. This does not apply if the Board has determined this issue of capacity within the previous six months.

Collection of this information is for the purpose of conducting a proceeding before this board. It is collected/used for this purpose under the authority of subsection 37(1) / 54(1) / 69(1) of the Health Care Consent Act. For information about collection practices, contact the office of the Regional Vice-Chair of the Board or call toll free at 1 800 461–2036.

Send this form by fax to the Office of the Regional Vice-Chair of the Board or call toll free at 1 800 461–2036 for assistance.

Form G (page two)

2981–04 (00/12)* www.ccboard.on.ca 7530–5339

Consent and Capacity Board

Form H
Health Care Consent Act

Application to the Board to Amend the Conditions of or Terminate the Appointment of a Representative under Subsection 33(7) and (8), 51(6) or 66(6) of the Act

______________________ has been appointed by the Consent and Capacity Board to be
(print full name of representative)

the representative of______________________, for the purpose of making decision with respect to:
(print full name of incapable person)

- ☐ admission to a care facility
- ☐ a personal assistance service
- ☐ the following kind of treatment:

____

Note: Any person may bring this application.

My name is: ______________________ I apply to the Board to
(print full name of applicant)

- ☐ remove a condition imposed on the appointment of the representative named above
- ☐ vary a condition imposed on the appointment of the representative named above
- ☐ suspend a condition imposed on the appointment of the representative named above
- ☐ impose an additional condition on the appointment of the representative named above
- ☐ terminate the appointment of the representative named above

☞ **The Board may only terminate the appointment of a representative if one or more of the following condition are met *(check those that apply)***

- ☐ the incapable person or the representative requests the termination
- ☐ the representative is no longer capable with respect to the matter;
- ☐ the appointment is no longer in the incapable person's best interests; or
- ☐ the incapable person has a guardian of the person or attorney for personal care with the authority to make decision with respect to the matter

My address and telephone number(s) are:

____
(address)

( ) ______________________ (telephone no.)   ( ) ______________________ (fax no.)

The Board-appointed representative's address, telephone and fax numbers are:

____
(address)

( ) ______________________ (telephone no.)   ( ) ______________________ (fax no.)

Is the person who has been found incapable currently an in-patient or resident at a health or residential facility?

- ☐ **no**
- ☐ **yes** provide name, address and telephone number of facility

____

____

(Disponible en version française)   *See reverse*

3232-04 (00/12)*   www.ccboard.on.ca   7530-5404

HEALTH CARE CONSENT ACT, 1996

His or her home address and telephone number are:

______________________ (address) ( ) ______ (telephone no.)

If this application refers to **admission to a care facility**, provide the name, address, telephone and fax numbers of the person responsible for authorizing admissions to the facility. (Often, this will be an official from the local Community Care Access Centre.)

______________________ (name) ______________________ (address)

( ) ______ (telephone no.) ( ) ______ (fax no.)

If this application refers to a **personal assistance service**, provide the name, address, telephone and fax numbers of the staff member responsible for the service:

______________________ (name) ______________________ (address)

( ) ______ (telephone no.) ( ) ______ (fax no.)

If this application refers to a **treatment**, provide the name, address, telephone and fax numbers of the health practitioner who proposed it:

______________________ (name) ______________________ (address)

( ) ______ (telephone no.) ( ) ______ (fax no.)

Name, address, telephone number and fax number of the lawyer or agent *(if any)* for the person who has been found incapable with respect to this matter:

______________________ (name) ______________________ (address)

( ) ______ (telephone no.) ( ) ______ (fax no.)

Name, address, telephone number and fax number of your lawyer or agent *(if any):*

______________________ (name) ______________________ (address)

( ) ______ (telephone no.) ( ) ______ (fax no.)

When and where did the Board appoint the representative?

______________________ (date) ______________________ (city)

______________________ (location)

If possible, please attach a copy of the Board's order/decision from the original hearing.

______________________ (date) ______________________ (signature)

Whenever an application of this type is received, the law provides that the patient is deemed to have applied for a review of his or her capacity to make the relevant decision. This does not apply if the Board has determined this issue of capacity within the previous six months.

Collection of this information is for the purpose of conducting a proceeding before this board. It is collected/used for this purpose under the authority of subsection 37(1) / 54(1) / 69(1) of the Health Care Consent Act. For information about collection practices, contact the office of the Regional Vice-Chair of the Board or call toll free at 1 800 461–2036.

Send this form by fax to the Office of the Regional Vice-Chair of the Board or call toll free at 1 800 461–2036 for assistance.

3232–04 (00/12)* Form H *(page 2)* www.ccboard.on.ca 7530–5404

ADVOCATING FOR CLIENTS*

Nurses who obtain consent have a professional accountability to be satisfied that the client is capable of giving consent. Also, nurses are professionally accountable for acting as client advocates and for helping clients understand the information relevant to making decisions to the extent permitted by the client's capacity. CNO has developed these guidelines to assist nurses to carry out their advocacy role as required by legislation.

1. If the nurse proposing a treatment or evaluating capacity to make an admission or personal assistance service decision determines the client is incapable of making the decision, the nurse informs the client that a substitute decision-maker will be asked to make the final decision. This is communicated in a way that takes into account the particular circumstances of the client's condition and the nurse-client relationship.
2. If there is an indication that the client is uncomfortable with this information, the nurse explores and clarifies the nature of the client's discomfort. If it relates to the finding of incapacity, or to the choice of substitute decision-maker, the nurse informs the client of his/her options to apply to the Consent and Capacity Board for a review of the finding of incapacity, and/or for the appointment of a representative of the client's choice.
3. If there is an indication the client is uncomfortable with the finding of incapacity when the finding was made by another health care practitioner, the nurse explores and clarifies the nature of the client's discomfort. If it relates to the finding of incapacity, or to the choice of substitute decision-maker, the nurse informs the health care practitioner who made the finding of incapacity and discusses appropriate follow-up.
4. The nurse uses professional judgement and common sense to determine whether the client is able to understand the information. For example, a young child or a client suffering advanced dementia is not likely to understand the information. It would not be reasonable in these circumstances for the nurse to inform the client that a substitute decision-maker will be asked to make a decision on his/her behalf.
5. The nurse uses professional judgement to determine the scope of advocacy services to assist the client in exercising his/her options. The nurse documents her/his actions according to CNO's practice standard *Documentation* and agency policy.

---

* College of Nurses of Ontario, *A Guide to Consent* (Toronto, Ontario: College of Nurses of Ontario, revised 2000), App. A. (Previously published as *A Guide to Health Care Consent and Substitute Decisions Legislation for RNs and RPNs* (Toronto, Ontario: College of Nurses of Ontario, June 1996.) Reprinted with permission of the College of Nurses of Ontario.

CONSENT TO MEDICAL TREATMENT*

Policy #1-01

PURPOSE

This policy statement has been developed to help physicians understand the consent to medical treatment process. The statement summarizes obligations faced by physicians under the 1996 Health Care Consent Act (the Act) and sets out College guidelines aimed at assisting physicians to comply with certain requirements of the legislation.

SCOPE

This statement affects all practising physicians who provide health care to patients, regardless of practice setting. This statement does not address the portions of the Act that regulate Admission to Care Facilities and Personal Assistance Services.

It should be noted that the Act does not affect the law relating to consent on another person's behalf with respect to procedures whose primary purpose is research, sterilization that is not medically necessary, and removal of tissue for transplantation. It also does not affect the common law duty of a caregiver to restrain or confine a person when immediate action is necessary to prevent serious bodily harm to that person or others (see sections 6 and 7 of the Act).

When applicable, the physician may wish to consult any policies and procedures developed by his or her hospital or facility in response to the Health Care Consent Act and should consider obtaining legal advice where specific circumstances warrant it.

COLLEGE POLICY

Except in certain emergency situations, as described below, a physician is required to obtain consent from a patient before providing treatment.

---

* Policy #1-01, College of Physicians & Surgeons of Ontario (May/June 2001). Reprinted with permission.

A. NON-EMERGENCY SITUATIONS

Five conditions must be present in order for a consent to treatment to be valid:

> the patient providing the consent must be capable, the consent must be related to the treatment, it must be informed, it must be given voluntarily, and it must not be obtained through misrepresentation or fraud.

The Elements of Consent

1. Patient must have capacity to consent

The physician must determine the patient's capacity to consent to the proposed treatment. Capacity is defined as mental capacity. The physician is entitled to assume that a patient is capable unless there are reasonable grounds to believe otherwise.

The physician may not assume a patient is incapable just because of age, disability or a psychiatric or neurological diagnosis, although such factors may be relevant in the assessment of capacity.

The legislation states:[1]

> *A person is capable with respect to a treatment, admission to a care facility or a personal assistance service if the person is able to understand the information that is relevant to making a decision about the treatment, admission or personal assistance service, as the case may be, and able to appreciate the reasonably foreseeable consequences of a decision or a lack of decision.*

A person who is capable of providing consent is also capable of withdrawing consent to treatment.

Situations in which the person is not capable or in which the physician is unable to communicate with the person because of a language or disability barrier are considered below.

2. Consent must be related to treatment

'Treatment' is defined in the legislation as: *"anything that is done for a therapeutic, preventive, palliative, diagnostic, cosmetic or other health-related purpose, [and] includes a course of treatment or plan of treatment..."* The legislation goes on, however, to set out a number of exclusions to this definition.[2]

---

[1] Direct quotes from the legislation are noted in italics.

[2] Treatment, as defined in the legislation, "*does not include:*

a) the assessment for the purpose of this Act of a person's capacity with respect to a treatment, admission to a care facility or a personal assistance service, the assessment for the purpose of the Substitute Decisions Act, 1992 of a person's capacity to manage property or a person's capacity for personal care, or the assessment of a person's capacity for any other purpose,

The physician may seek consent for a 'course of treatment,' which is defined as *"a series or sequence of similar treatments administered to a person over a period of time for a particular health problem."*

The physician may also choose to establish a 'plan of treatment,' for which he or she can seek consent. According to the Act, 'plan of treatment' means a plan that,

a) *is developed by one or more health practitioners,*
b) *deals with one or more of the health problems that a person has and may, in addition, deal with one or more of the health problems that the person is likely to have in the future given the person's current health condition, and*
c) *provides for the administration to the person of various treatments or courses of treatment and may, in addition, provide for the withholding or withdrawal of treatment in light of the person's current health condition.*

Where there is no significant change in the expected benefits, material risks or material side effects and unless it is unreasonable to do so in the circumstances, the physician may presume that a consent to treatment includes consent to variations or adjustments in the treatment, as well as consent to the continuation of the same treatment in a different setting.

3. Consent must be informed

The patient's decision to consent to (or refuse) treatment must be informed; that is, the patient must receive information about the nature of the proposed treatment, its expected benefits, the material risks,[3] special risks or material side effects associated with it, alternative courses of action and likely consequences of not having the treatment.

The information provided to the patient about such matters must be the information a reasonable person in the same circumstances would require in order to make a decision about the treatment. As well, the person must have received responses to his or her requests for additional information about those matters.

---

b) *the assessment or examination of a person to determine the general nature of the person's condition,*
c) *the taking of a person's health history,*
d) *the communication of an assessment or diagnosis,*
e) *the admission of a person to a hospital or other facility,*
f) *a personal assistance service,*
g) *a treatment that in the circumstances poses little or no risk of harm to the person,*
h) *anything prescribed by the regulations as not constituting treatment."*

Note that for things excluded from the definition of treatment, the common law principles around informed consent still apply; however, if practitioners so choose, they can opt to include the acts described in clauses b), g) and h), above, in the definition of treatment.

[3] Material risks comprise both common risks and serious risks.

4. Consent must be voluntary

This condition is self-explanatory.

5. Consent must not be obtained through fraud or misrepresentation

This condition is self-explanatory.

Evidence of Consent

Although the Act states that consent to treatment may be express or implied, physicians are strongly advised to obtain express consent from the patient and to document the process of doing so.

Physicians should be aware that the critical element of the consent process is the explanation given to the patient and the dialogue between physician and patient around the proposed treatment. Signed consent forms are simply documentary confirmation that the consent process has been followed, and the patient has agreed to the proposed treatment. Documentation of consent discussions in the patient's chart by the physician is also important evidence that the process has been followed.

Incapable Patients

If the physician determines that the person is incapable with respect to consent to treatment in the circumstances, he or she must seek consent from an appropriate substitute decision maker.

The Act sets out the following hierarchy of individuals/agencies who are authorized (subject to the requirements of the legislation) to become substitute decision makers for incapable persons (in decreasing order of authority):

1. Personal care guardian
2. Attorney for personal care
3. Representative appointed by Consent and Capacity Board
4. Spouse or partner
5. Child or parent or individual/agency entitled to give or refuse consent instead of parent
6. Parent with right of access only
7. Brother or sister
8. Any other relative
9. Public Guardian and Trustee

The highest ranking person on this list, if available, capable and willing, is the substitute decision maker for the incapable person.

The substitute decision maker must follow the principles set out in the Act. He or she must follow the most recent wish expressed by the person while capable if the following criteria are met: the person was at least 16 years old at the time, the wish applies to the circumstances, and it is not impossible to comply with the wish.

In the event the substitute does not know of any wish that meets these criteria, he or she must act in the incapable person's best interests. A number of factors must be considered, including the following: any values and beliefs the incapable person held while capable, any wishes the incapable person expressed that are not binding according to the above criteria, and the nature and likely effects of both providing and withholding the proposed treatment.

It is the obligation of the physician to consider whether the substitute decision maker is complying with the principles set out in the Act.

When a physician has determined that a patient is incapable with respect to consent to treatment, the physician is obligated to provide certain information to the patient. The manner and type of information to be provided is set out in the College guidelines that follow.

College guidelines for physicians when treating incapable patients

The following guidelines have been developed by the College to assist physicians in discussions with incapable patients when the emergency provisions of the Act do not apply:

1) The physician must tell the incapable patient that a substitute decision maker will assist the patient in understanding the proposed treatment and will be responsible for making the final decision.
2) The physician should involve the incapable patient, to the extent possible, in discussions with the substitute decision maker.
3) If the patient disagrees with the need for a substitute decision maker because of the finding of incapacity or disagrees with the involvement of the present substitute, the physician must advise the patient of his or her options. These include finding another substitute of the same or more senior rank, and/or applying to the Consent and Capacity Board (the Board) for a review of the finding of incapacity.
4) Physicians are expected to reasonably assist patients if they express a wish to exercise the options outlined above in paragraph 3.

According to the legislation, if the physician is informed that the person he or she believes is incapable either has made or intends to make an application to the Board for representation or for a review of the finding, or if another person either intends to or has applied to the Board to be appointed as a representative, the physician must ensure that treatment is not given:

a) until 48 hours after the physician was first informed of the intent to apply to the Board without an application being made,
b) until the application to the Board has been withdrawn,
c) until the Board makes its decision, if none of the parties informs the physician that they intend to appeal the Board's decision, or
d) if a party to the application before the Board informs the physician that he or she does intend to appeal the Board's decision, until the period for commencing an appeal has elapsed with no appeal having been started, or until the appeal of the Board's decision has been resolved.

Once the physician has identified the substitute decision maker and complied with the requirements applicable to the particular circumstances, the physician must provide the substitute decision maker with the information necessary for that person to make an informed decision as to consent.

Again, all actions should be documented in the patient's chart.

B. EMERGENCY SITUATIONS

The Act states that *"there is an emergency if the person for whom the treatment is proposed is apparently experiencing severe suffering or is at risk, if the treatment is not administered promptly, of sustaining serious bodily harm."*

In emergency situations, the physician must again first make a determination of capacity. If the patient is capable, the physician must seek his or her consent to the treatment proposed.

If the physician determines the patient is not capable with respect to consent to treatment or if the physician is unable to communicate with the patient, the physician must make a reasonable attempt to find the patient's substitute decision maker or a person who can facilitate the communication.

If the substitute decision maker (or an appropriate interpreter) is not readily available, the physician must provide treatment to the patient even though he or she does not yet have the consent, **unless** the physician has reason to believe the person, while capable and over 16 years of age, expressed a wish to refuse consent to treatment in such a situation (for example, a person who, for religious reasons, has indicated that he or she would refuse a blood transfusion).

The physician may also treat the patient if the substitute decision maker refuses to consent to the person's treatment and the physician believes the substitute has not followed the principles set out in the Act for giving or refusing consent on behalf of an incapable person (as discussed earlier).

In these circumstances, the physician is obliged to continue to seek consent from a substitute decision maker or a means to enable communication to take place so as to determine whether the patient consents to the treatment.

It is critical that the physician document his or her actions in the patient's chart.

C. SPECIAL SITUATIONS

Minors

The Act does not identify an age at which minors may exercise independent consent for health care because it is accepted that the capacity to exercise independent judgment for health care decisions varies according to the individual and the complexity of the decision at hand.

Physicians who have concerns about their obligations in such situations should seek advice from the Physician Advisory Service of the College or the appropriate insurance carrier.

Other Special Situations

Physicians may have difficulty knowing how to seek consent to treatment in special situations, for example, those involving the mentally ill or people who refuse certain forms of treatment for religious reasons. In such circumstances, the physician should seek legal advice from the Canadian Medical Protective Association (CMPA) or other insurance carrier, or contact the Physician Advisory Service of the College.

STANDARD OF PRACTICE FOR SOCIAL WORKERS COMMUNICATING POST EVALUATION, A FINDING OF INCAPACITY WITH RESPECT TO ADMISSION TO CARE FACILITIES OR PERSONAL ASSISTANCE SERVICES

PREAMBLE

The following standard of practice for communicating a finding of incapacity with respect to admission to a care facility or personal assistance service has been prepared in the context of the development of standards of professional practice and conduct for the Ontario College of Social Workers and Social Service Workers. This standard of practice is intended to be specific to the social work profession in the province of Ontario.

Registered social workers who evaluate a person and communicate a finding of incapacity with respect to admission to a care facility or personal assistance service are governed by the standards of practice of the social work profession prescribed by the College.

It is recognized that there are variations in the approaches of individual social workers to the evaluation of client capacity to consent to admission to a care facility or a personal assistance service. Also, social workers will vary their methods in response to the demands of each particular situation. Members of the College who hold a certificate of registration for social work will adhere to this standard of practice of the social work profession prescribed by the College.

COMMUNICATION OF A FINDING OF INCAPACITY

1.01 The College member who makes the determination of incapacity will:

(a) Inform the client that a substitute decision-maker will be asked to assist the client and to make final decisions on his or her behalf. The client's right to receive this information should be respected whether or not it is believed he or she is capable of comprehending it. In informing the client regarding the substitute decision-maker, the member will exercise professional judgment and have regard to the particular needs of the client.

(b) If the client disagrees with the need for a substitute decision-maker or disagrees with the involvement of the present substitute, advise the client of his or her options. The member will assist the client if he or she expresses the wish to exercise the options. These options include applying to the Consent and Capacity Board for review of the finding of incapacity and/or finding another substitute of the same or more senior rank.

(c) Help the incapable client participate as far as possible with the substitute decision-maker in planning for himself or herself.

1.02 The member who conducted the evaluation must complete documentation of the finding of incapacity.

May 2000

MENTAL HEALTH ACT

COMMENTARY

OVERVIEW

Application

The *Mental Health Act*[1] ("MHA" or "the Act") governs the involuntary psychiatric assessment[2] and admission[3] of individuals with mental disorder[4] and related issues which arise within[5] psychiatric facilities. It applies only to patients[6] in psychiatric facilities[7] as defined under the Act. The Act and its regulations address many issues which relate to psychiatric patients and the assessment, admission, detention and discharge of these individuals. A process for review of the involuntary status of individuals detained within the facility is also prescribed by the Act. Issues of access to and disclosure of the patient's "personal health information," subject to certain exceptions, are governed by the *Personal Health Information Protection Act*.[8] Management of the individual's property, and the process for issuing community treatment orders also form part of the Act. The Act does not deal with matters of capacity with respect to treatment.[9] The provisions of the *Health Care Consent Act, 1996* apply to patients in psychiatric facilities in that regard.

---

1 R.S.O. 1990, c. M.7, as amended.

2 s. 15.

3 s. 20.

4 "mental disorder" means any disease or disability of the mind, s. 1(1).

5 New community treatment orders and a few other provisions relate to the legal status of individuals outside of psychiatric facilities, but the MHA's provisions do not relate to facilities other than psychiatric facilities as defined in the Act.

6 Defined under s. 1(1) and including application of this Act to individuals detained in psychiatric facilities under Part XX.1 of the *Criminal Code* (Canada) who may be restrained, observed and examined under this Act and provided with treatment under the HCCA, 1996, see. MHA s. 25.

7 "psychiatric facility" means a facility for the observation, care and treatment of persons suffering from mental disorder, and designated as such by the Minister; s. 1(1).

8 MHA, s.35

9 The former *Mental Health Act*, R.S.O. 1980, c. 262 contained provisions regarding treatment issues in relation to psychiatric patients. Those provisions were repealed upon proclamation of the *Consent to Treatment Act, 1992* (now repealed) in April, 1995.

Legislative History: Significant Recent Amendments

Significant amendments were made to the Act in December, 2000,[10] expanding the criteria for involuntary commitment[11] and adding provisions for supervised compulsory treatment while the individual resides in the community.[12] The general thrust of the amendments was reflective of a policy shift from dangerousness criteria only to include commitment based on treatment needs. On May 20, 2004 the *Personal Health Information Protection Act, 2004* received Royal Assent and amendments to the sections of the Act which currently govern access to and disclosure of clinical records in psychiatric facilities took effect November 1, 2004.

Structure of the Act

The main parts of the Act are preceded by a definition section. In considering issues arising under this Act, it is essential to confirm the application of the Act to the particular issue. This often requires revisiting the definition of certain key concepts, such as "patient" and "psychiatric facility." Patients in psychiatric facilities are entitled to certain special protection[13] and enjoy significant due process rights, which are not available to patients in other facilities. A warning to this effect is contained in s. 6 as follows: "Nothing in this Act shall be deemed to affect the rights or privileges of any person except as specifically set out in this Act".

The Act is divided into five parts: Standards [Part I], Hospitalization [Part II] including provisions governing clinical records (now "personal health information"), Estates [Part III], Veterans, etc. [Part IV] and Miscellaneous [Part V.]

Hospitalization — Part II

The Act prescribes under what circumstances an individual may be brought to a psychiatric facility, assessed and admitted against his or her will. The Act also prescribes the criteria for the individual's continued detention within the

---

[10] Bill 68, An Act in Memory of Brian Smith, to amend the *Mental Health Act* and the *Health Care Consent Act, 1996* (Mental Health Legislative Reform, 2000) Amending Statute: 2000, c. 9, s. 1-30;

[11] Committal criteria were broadened by Bill 68: (1) in the case of all individuals subject to certification under the previous Act, by removing the word "imminent" from the ground for certification of "imminent and serious physical impairment"; and, (2) in the case of a special subset of those individuals, by adding the new ground for certification of "substantial mental or physical deterioration" available only in relation to incapable individuals, subject to a host of other criteria also required to be met (see s. 15(1.1) and 20(1.1)).

[12] Community treatment orders (CTOs) s. 33.1.

[13] For example, the requirement to provide prompt rights advice when a patient in a psychiatric facility is found not capable to consent to treatment of a mental disorder, R.R.O. 1990, Reg. 741, s. 15.

psychiatric facility. Before any of that may happen, however, the individual has to arrive at the door of the psychiatric facility.[14]

From Community to the Emergency Room

There are a number of ways a person may attend or be forcibly brought to the psychiatric facility. Although some individuals come on their own or with concerned family members, it is not uncommon for the person to present with police accompaniment, given the many provisions under the Act which authorize police to apprehend and take into custody an individual suffering mental disorder for purposes of transporting the individual to a psychiatric facility for examination or assessment. In addition to the very frequent contact police have with persons with mental disorders as described below, police are necessarily involved in enforcing some provisions of the Act which arise relatively rarely.

Exercise of Police Authority to Apprehend and Transport (Infrequently Arising)

For example, police or correctional staff take the person to the psychiatric facility when a judge makes an order for the examination[15] of an individual who appears before him or an order for the admission[16] of an individual who is in custody and appears before him and appears to suffer from mental disorder. Police also act on the authority of (a) orders for return[17] of patients absent without leave from a psychiatric facility, (b) the minister's order regarding a person coming into Ontario[18], and (c) orders for examination[19] of individuals whose CTO has been terminated for failure to comply with the terms of the order[20] or because consent to the order has been withdrawn.[21]

---

[14] There are two exceptions to the requirement that the Act apply only to "psychiatric facilities." The exceptions are set out in section 18 of the Act. We have included explanatory notes to the actual section (in parentheses): An examination (for purposes of determining whether an application for psychiatric assessment under s. 15 should be completed) under section 16 (justice of the peace's order for psychiatric examination) or 17 (action by police officer) shall be conducted by a physician forthwith after receipt of the person at the place of examination and where practicable the place shall be a psychiatric facility or other health facility.

[15] s. 21.

[16] s. 22.

[17] s. 28(1), Form 9.

[18] s. 32, Form 13.

[19] s. 33.3 (1) and s. 33.4 (3).

[20] s. 33.3 (1).

[21] s. 33.4 (3).

Non-Voluntary Attendance at the Emergency Room (What Most Often Happens)

Other than attending on his or her own voluntarily seeking assessment and/or admission, the most common way a person arrives at the psychiatric facility is in the custody of police. When police bring the individual in, these are the three most likely scenarios. Police officers are acting on the authority granted to them by: (1) the MHA to "take the person in custody to an appropriate place for examination by a physician" under certain circumstances,[22] (2) an order[23] of a justice of the peace[24] to "take the person in custody forthwith to an appropriate place where he or she may be detained for examination by a physician",[25] and (c) an application for a psychiatric assessment[26] signed by a physician to "take the person who is the subject of the application in custody to a psychiatric facility forthwith".[27] The police officer who has an individual in custody under these provisions has a duty to remain at the facility and retain custody of the person until the facility takes custody of him or her.[28]

The provisions of the Act which establish the police's statutory authority, the authority for justices of the peace to order examinations for individuals with mental disorder for purposes of determining whether an assessment is necessary, and the physician's power to apply for a psychiatric assessment each merit a detailed review.

(Independent Statutory) Authority of Police to Act under s. 17

Section 17 of the Act states:

> Where a police officer has reasonable and probable grounds to believe that a person is acting or has acted in a disorderly manner and has reasonable cause to believe that the person:

---

22 s. 17.

23 Valid for a period not to exceed seven days from and including the day that it is made, s. 16 (3).

24 s. 16, Form 2.

25 s. 16(3).

26 Form 1 is "sufficient authority for seven days from and including the day on which it is signed by the physician" s. 15(5).

27 s. 15(5)(a).

28 s. 33, the duty to remain and retain custody is sometimes very onerous for police who may spend endless hours at the psychiatric facility awaiting transfer of custody of the individual to the facility (notwithstanding Reg. 741 s. 7.2, which prescribes a process intended to expedite this transfer) or transporting individuals from one facility to another in the hope of a more efficient determination of the issue of whether the individual will be detained for purposes of an assessment or released. What is not permitted, however, is taking the individual to another psychiatric facility once a physician has examined the person and determined not to complete an application for psychiatric assessment. At that point the authority of police to retain custody of the individual is terminated.

(a) has threatened or attempted or is threatening or attempting to cause bodily harm to himself or herself;

(b) has behaved or is behaving violently towards another person or has caused or is causing another person to fear bodily harm from him or her; or

(c) has shown or is showing a lack of competence to care for himself or herself;[29]

and in addition the police officer is of the opinion that the person is apparently suffering from mental disorder of a nature or quality that likely will result in,

(d) serious bodily harm to the person;

(e) serious bodily harm to another person; or

(f) serious physical impairment of the person,[30]

and that it would be dangerous to proceed under section 16, the police officer may take the person in custody to an appropriate place for examination by a physician.[31]

Prior to the amendments to the Act by Bill 68 in December 2000, police officers could only act under s. 17 in circumstances where they actually observed the individual behaving in ways that "in a normal person would be considered disorderly." The amendment which now allows for action to be taken based on "reasonable and probable grounds to believe the person is acting or has acted in a disorderly manner" arose from a concern that the hands of police to take a person in for examination under the old provisions were tied whenever an individual pulled himself together long enough to meet with the officers, but moments before and after demonstrated behaviour of serious concern.

The possibility of being apprehended based solely on collateral information could leave individuals open to abuse of the provision by third party informants; however, the exercise of police authority under this section is limited to those circumstances where "it would be dangerous to proceed under s. 16." Police may only act under this section if there is not time, under the circumstances, for someone to attend before a justice of the peace and obtain an order for examination (Form 2) by way of sworn information. It is difficult to imagine many scenarios in which police are unable to observe disorderly conduct by the individual and yet the situation is so emergent that it would be "dangerous" to attend before a J.P.

---

[29] These are the "past harm" criteria common to s. 15, s. 16 and s.17 under the Act.

[30] These are the "future harm" criteria common to s. 15, s. 16 and s. 17 although s. 15 and s. 16 have certain additional, broader, criteria applicable in respect of apparently incapable persons only and limited by other prerequisites, as discussed below.

[31] An examination under section 16 or 17 shall be conducted by a physician forthwith after receipt of the person at the place of examination and where practicable the place shall be a psychiatric facility or other health facility, s. 18.

J.P's Order for Examination (Form 2) under s. 16

Anyone[32] can attend before a justice of the peace and request a Form 2 order for examination of an individual[33] believed to be suffering mental disorder. The J.P. does not have to see or speak to the subject of the order sought. The J.P. may make the Order based solely on sworn information presented to the J.P.[34] that the individual satisfies any of the "past harm" criteria[35] and as a result of mental disorder is likely to cause him or herself or another person serious bodily harm or suffer serious physical impairment (the "future harm" test)[36] or satisfies the expanded criteria for an order for examination pursuant to the Bill 68 amendments. The J.P. may make the order if he or she is satisfied on information presented under oath that the individual meets each of the prerequisites of the expanded committal criteria,[37] ie. that the person:

(a) has previously received treatment for mental disorder of an ongoing or recurring nature that, when not treated, is of a nature or quality that likely will result in serious bodily harm to the person or to another person or substantial mental or physical deterioration of the person or serious physical impairment of the person; and

(b) has shown clinical improvement as a result of the treatment,

and in addition based upon the information before him or her the justice of the peace has reasonable cause to believe that the person,

(c) is apparently suffering from the same mental disorder as the one for which he or she previously received treatment or from a mental disorder that is similar to the previous one;

(d) given the person's history of mental disorder and current mental or physical condition, is likely to cause serious bodily harm to himself or herself or to another person or is likely to suffer substantial mental or physical deterioration or serious physical impairment; and

(e) is apparently incapable, within the meaning of the *Health Care Consent Act, 1996*, of consenting to his or her treatment in a psychiatric facility and the consent of his or her substitute decision-maker has been obtained,

---

[32] Although it's commonly thought that only family members can attend before a J.P. and obtain a Form 2, anyone can do this; there is no reason why police officers cannot get a Form 2 themselves in those circumstances where they cannot exercise their s. 17 authority.

[33] On an *ex parte* basis, meaning without notice to the individual.

[34] Information shall be presented in the "prescribed form", s. 16. (4). Reg. 741, s. 7.1 permits information to be presented orally or in writing and prescribes that the information may include documentation or recorded material relevant to the subject matter of the hearing.

[35] See footnote 29 "past harm".

[36] s. 16(1).

[37] s. 16(1.1).

the justice of the peace may issue an order in the prescribed form for the examination of the person by a physician.

J.P.s have the authority to make the order under the expanded criteria. The expanded criteria are not available to police officers under s. 17. However, if the informant is relying on the ground of "substantial mental or physical deterioration" in the expanded criteria, it would be prudent to have documentary evidence in relation to all of the criteria as prescribed. This would include information regarding the subject's "apparent incapacity with respect to treatment" and the fact that the SDM has consented to the treatment in a psychiatric facility. At the very least, if the SDM is not present at the J.P.'s hearing, a letter from the SDM confirming consent should be provided.

Although anyone can obtain a Form 2 from a J.P., in practice, it is most often a concerned family member or community mental health worker. Family are understandably reluctant to do this as there is obvious potential for conflict particularly if the individual first learns of the order when police show up at his or her home. They are also often disappointed to learn that the Form 2 only gets the person to the door of the psychiatric facility. Contrary to a widespread misconception, the order does not authorize detention of the subject once at the facility unless a Form 1 application for psychiatric assessment is then completed by a physician.[38]

Application by a Physician for Psychiatric Assessment (Form 1) under s. 15

Any physician may complete a Form 1 application for psychiatric assessment[39] on essentially any of the same grounds available to a J.P., provided that the physician has reasonable cause to believe and does form the opinion that the criteria for completing such an application exist, and signs the application: (a) within seven days[40] of having personally examined the subject of the application, and (b) after making careful inquiry into all of the facts necessary to form an opinion as to the nature and quality of the mental disorder of the person.[41] Where the J.P. only requires evidence that the subject of the order for examination is "apparently incapable with respect to treatment", the physician who completes the Form 1 must be of the opinion that the person is incapable.

---

[38] Any attempt to admit an individual as an involuntary patient pursuant to a Form 2 order for examination without first completing a Form 1 application for psychiatric assessment will fail unless the individual is admitted voluntarily in the intervening period. The involuntary admission of the individual will be found invalid upon review, see *Dayday v. MacEwan* (1987), 62 O.R. (2d) 588 (Dist. Ct.), on appeal from the decision of the Psychiatric Review Board decided under precursor legislation (MHA R.S.O. 1980), per Matlow D.C.J.

[39] s. 15(1) or s. 15(1.1).

[40] s. 15(4).

[41] s. 15(2).

The truly difficult point of statutory interpretation is whether the physician, before completing a Form 1 on the expanded criteria, needs to ensure that the SDM's consent to the treatment in a psychiatric facility has been obtained subsequent to a finding of incapacity being made. The language of the section favours this interpretation, as opposed to the notion that the physician need only form an "opinion" that the necessary substitute consent has been obtained. If this is the case, however, it is difficult to see how a Form 1 could ever be completed under the expanded criteria for assessment, since the purpose of the assessment is to determine whether the criteria for certification, including under the expanded committal criteria, are present. This would include, presumably, a psychiatric assessment of the individual's capacity to consent to treatment and an inquiry into whether the appropriate necessary consent may, in that event, be obtained from the individual's SDM. On the other hand, it may be argued that a Form 1 under the expanded criteria may be completed if the individual had been found incapable on a previous admission to hospital, and, prior to signing the Form 1, a current consent for treatment in the psychiatric facility may be obtained.

In contrast to the police's statutory authority and the Form 2, a Form 1 signed by a physician does authorize the detention of the subject of the application for a period of up to 72 hours.[42] The 72-hour clock[43] starts running the moment detention at the psychiatric facility for purposes of the assessment commences. Although the subject of an assessment is entitled to written notice [44]of the reasons for the assessment and to be notified of the right to retain and instruct legal counsel without delay,[45] there is no rights advice provided at this stage, nor is there any right to apply to the Board for a review. While the individual is the subject of the Form 1 assessment, he or she is not a patient in the psychiatric facility, but is rather an individual detained for purposes of assessment.[46] If the person has not been admitted as a patient prior to the expiration of the 72-hour

---

[42] s. 15(5)(b); s. 15(5)(a) is the authority to take the person into custody and transport the person to a psychiatric facility. Under s. 15 the place of assessment must be a psychiatric facility, and cannot be another health facility which qualifies under s. 16 and s. 17 for purposes of an examination to determine whether an assessment may be indicated.

[43] The Act does not say "three days" but specifies 72 hours; as a result, the Form 1 prescribed by regulations now has space dedicated to the recording of the times when detention commenced and notice (Form 42) was given to the person of their detention based on the Form 1. This information is necessary for the officer in charge of the facility in order to ascertain exactly when the OIC must release the individual pursuant to s. 20(3) of the Act if, at the expiration of the 72-hour period of assessment, the individual has not been admitted as a patient.

[44] s. 38.1(1).

[45] s. 38.1(2).

[46] In *R v. Webers*, [1994] O.J. No. 2767 (Gen.Div.), the court noted that a "person" who is the subject of a Form 1 assessment does not become a "patient" until she is assessed and a decision is made to admit her either on a voluntary or an involuntary basis.

period of assessment, the officer in charge of the psychiatric facility must discharge the individual.[47]

Inpatient Admission: Who is a Patient in a Psychiatric Facility?

Psychiatric Facility

At one time there were ten provincial psychiatric facilities in Ontario. Today most of these are divested, owned and operated by private entities and no longer governed by Ministry of Health Operational Guidelines previously relating to patient care.[48] As a result, there is not necessarily consistency among the various facilities in the policies and procedures adopted. However, provisions of the Act in relation to the legal status of individuals within psychiatric facilities apply to all such facilities.[49]

The Act also applies to the entire patient population of the remaining provincial and now divested (formerly provincial) psychiatric facilites, whose sole purpose is the care, observation and treatment of individuals with mental disorder. However, psychiatric facilities[50] as defined under the Act, are not limited to these institutions. They include as well most, but not all, general hospitals with psychiatric wards. General hospitals, that are not "psychiatric facilities" for purposes of the Act, do not have the authority to admit or detain individuals as involuntary psychiatric patients. Their physicians do, however, have the ability to complete Form 1 applications for psychiatric assessment (as do all physicians) although the individual's actual assessment must take place elsewhere (ie. in a psychiatric facility).

Patient in a Psychiatric Facility

"Patient" means a person who is under observation, care and treatment in a psychiatric facility.[51] The definition of "outpatient" specifically excludes individuals registered and admitted as a "patient" and a person who is the subject of an application for assessment.[52] An individual becomes a patient in a psychiatric facility in one of three possible ways. The person is admitted either as :

---

[47] s. 20(3).

[48] Although many choose to adopt these guidelines regardless.

[49] s. 7.

[50] s. 1, "psychiatric facility" means a facility for the observation, care and treatment of persons suffering from mental disorder, and designated as such by the Minister; The Minister must maintain a list of psychiatric facilities and make them available to the public [ss.80.2(2) and (3)]. See the website of the Ministry of Health and Long-Term Care for a current list.

[51] s. 1, except for purposes of s. 35 regarding access to and disclosure of records, where patient is defined more broadly and includes out-patients as well as former out-patients

[52] s. 1.

(1) a voluntary patient,[53] (2) an informal patient[54] or (3) an involuntary patient.[55] The legal status of the patient determines the procedure which must be followed in admitting the individual and affects the legal rights of the individual while he or she is a patient. In thinking about the issues which arise under the Act, it is always crucial to ascertain the legal status of the patient at the outset.

Informal and Voluntary Patients – Common Ground

Any person who is believed to be in need of the observation, care and treatment[56] provided in a psychiatric facility may be admitted as an informal or voluntary patient upon the recommendation of a physician.[57] However, wanting to access treatment in a psychiatric facility is no guarantee that a voluntary admission will be granted. Admission to a psychiatric facility may be refused where the immediate needs in the case of the proposed patient are such that hospitalization is not urgent or necessary.[58] Once admitted, nothing in the Act authorizes a psychiatric facility to detain or to restrain an informal or voluntary patient.[59] A person who is a voluntary patient[60] has the legal right to leave the psychiatric facility when he or she chooses to do so. Informal patients (who are over the age of 16) also have this right, provided their admission is not pursuant to the consent of the individual's court-appointed guardian who has custodial

---

[53] s. 20(1)(b).

[54] s. 20(1)(b).

[55] s. 20(1)(c).

[56] Note, the provision does not present the needs of the individual as alternatives, *i.e.* it does not describe the voluntary patient as in need of "observation, care OR treatment" which raises interesting issues as to whether an individual who seeks, accepts or requires only observation and care, but not treatment (*e.g.* Medications) may be admitted as a voluntary patient.

[57] s. 12.

[58] s. 11; how does this section governing where admission may be refused apply in the context of the mandatory language of s. 20(1) (c) which requires a physician to admit an individual as an involuntary patient when the physician is of the opinion that the criteria under either s. 20(1.1) or s. 20(5) are met, when neither of those sections contains any pre-requisite that the feared harm, impairment or deterioration must have a temporal component to it? This raises interesting issues as to the potential for a psychiatric admission being refused to an individual seeking to be admitted voluntarily, because of the absence of urgency to the admission, while someone certifiable under s. 20(1.1) due to a likelihood of suffering only substantial mental deterioration may require admission by operation of statute.

[59] s. 14, On the issue of restraint, see also *Patient Restraints Minimization Act, 2001* (S.O. 2001, c. 16). However, an informal patient's SDM may authorize use of restraint if the SDM is a court-appointed guardian of the person or an attorney for personal care with such authority.

[60] Only an informal patient who is over 16 years of age is free to leave, see discussion on informal patients, below. (NB: voluntary patients of any age may leave the facility of their own accord).

power or his or her attorney pursuant to a power of attorney for personal care with the powers set out in s. 50 of the *Substitute Decisions Act, 1992*.

In order to exercise the right to leave the facility, the patient must be informed that his or her legal status is that of a voluntary or informal patient. Unless the individual is informed of this right to leave, the notion of "voluntariness" becomes essentially meaningless. As a result, the Board's jurisprudence has made it clear that in order to be a bona fide "voluntary" (or informal)[61] patient, a voluntary (or informal) patient must be made aware of his or her legal status as such.[62] Pursuant to the cases on this issue, patients have the right to be so informed in the event that their legal status changes[63] from that of an involuntary patient to either voluntary or informal. This is the case, notwithstanding that the Act does not explicitly require notice to the patient of a change in legal status from involuntary to voluntary or informal.

The Act simply "deems" the legal status of the individual to have changed to "voluntary or informal"[64] as a result of the expiration of a term of involuntary admission.[65] A physician may also continue an individual whose term of involuntary admission has not yet expired, as either a "voluntary or informal" patient by completing the approved form (Form 5). Form 5 does not require the physician to select whether the patient is continued as "voluntary" or "informal." There is no expressed requirement under the Act to file Form 5 or deliver a copy of the form to the patient.[66] However, without some form of communication to the patient of the legal effect of the change in status, the provision allowing for

---

[61] Although Board decisions tend not to address the issue of "informal" patients because it is relatively rare that individuals over 16 are admitted as informal patients to psychiatric facilities (*i.e.* without objection, see discussion below), for purposes of the discussion of legal rights of these individuals in relation to their detention, the terms "voluntary" and "informal" are essentially interchangeable based on the s. 14 prohibition against detention or restraint under the Act of either voluntary or informal patients (excepting the two special circumstances set out in note 59 above.

[62] *Daugherty v. Stall* (2002), 48 E.T.R.(2d) 8, [2002] O.J. No. 4715 (S.C.J.) affirming CCB Reasons for Decision in "A" TO-020721, 22, June 25, 2002, and other Board cases such as, for example, *Re P.P.* TO-030502, May 12, 2003, *Re D.C.* TO-031004, August 27, 2003, and R.C. TO-030502 May 12, 2003.

[63] Whether pursuant to the deeming provision upon expiration of a term of involuntary admission (s. 20(6)) or when changed by a physician prior to the expiration of such a term pursuant to s. 20(7).

[64] This provision [s. 20(6)] does not distinguish between "voluntary" or "informal" in identifying the deemed legal status of the individual whose involuntary status has expired.

[65] s. 20(6).

[66] Contrast these provisions [s. 20(6) and 20(7)] which do not require statutory notice to the individual of a change to voluntary or informal status, with s. 20(3) of the Act which requires the officer in charge of the facility not only to notify but to discharge a patient whose 72-hour period of psychiatric assessment has expired without the admission of the individual to the psychiatric facility as a patient.

the change is meaningless. As a result the Board has read the provision as implying the requirement of notice to the patient.[67] In the case of *Daugherty v. Stall*, the Court has affirmed this interpretation.[68]

The attending physician may also change the legal status of an informal or voluntary patient to that of an involuntary patient[69] by completing and filing with the officer in charge a certificate of involuntary admission, provided the criteria for an involuntary admission are met.[70]

In contrast to the absence of notice requirements under the Act to the patient who has become voluntary or informal, the process of notification the the patient when he or she has become an involuntary patient is prescribed by statute.[71] Not only does the individual receive written notice of the change in status, the reasons for the detention, the right to apply to the Board and the right to retain and instruct legal counsel,[72] but a rights adviser is also promptly notified and must meet promptly with the person to explain the significance of the certification and the right to apply to the Board for a review.[73]

Voluntary Patient

No definition of what is meant by a "voluntary" patient is found in the Act. In *Daugherty* v. *Stall* [74] the court considered this issue[75] and cited with approval the following passage from a decision of the Board[76]: "In order for a person to be considered as a voluntary patient, the person must be in a position to exercise his or her own free will and must have made a capable decision to consent to voluntary status. Except in the case of a person moving from the status of

---

[67] For example, see R.C. TO-030502 May 12, 2003, *Re P.P.* TO-030502, May 12, 2003, and *Re D.C.* TO-031004, August 27, 2003.

[68] *Daugherty v. Stall* (2002), 48 E.T.R.(2d) 8, [2002] O.J. No. 4715 (S.C.J.) affirming CCB Reasons for Decision in "A" TO-020721, 22, June 25, 2002.

[69] s. 19.

[70] *i.e.* Subject to the criteria prescribed for an involuntary admission pursuant to subsections 20 (1.1) or 20.(5).

[71] s. 38(1) states: "An attending physician who completes a certificate of involuntary admission or a certificate of renewal shall promptly give the patient a written notice that complies with subsection (2) and shall also promptly notify a rights adviser". The form of notice as approved by the Minister is the Form 30 notice to the patient.

[72] s. 38(2).

[73] s. 38.(3).

[74] *Daugherty v. Stall*, (2002), 48 E.T.R. (2d) 8 (S.C.J.).

[75] In the context of determining who may be assessed with respect to capacity to manage property under the MHA, and holding that no such assessment may be conducted except in relation to "psychiatric patients", who, if not involuntary, must be a bona fide "voluntary psychiatric patient" and what that means specifically in the setting of a general hospital where the individual is admitted initially and perhaps primarily for purposes of medical treatment.

[76] Referred to in the court's judgment as "P.A.B." but known by the Board as "A", TO-020721, 22 June 25, 2002.

involuntary patient to that of voluntary patient, this consent must be given before the person becomes a voluntary patient." The Court in this case also held that an individual admitted to a hospital for medical reasons can only be considered a voluntary psychiatric patient if certain procedures are followed. First, the patient must be informed that in addition to his or her medical admission, circumstances warrant a psychiatric admission. Second, a voluntary patient must consent to his or her admission as a psychiatric patient. Third, "clearly maintaining records of the person's consent or refusal is a necessary part of the process of protecting patients' rights."

Although a voluntary patient has the legal right to leave the psychiatric facility, as discussed above, in practice exercising this right often appears illusory to voluntary psychiatric patients. One of the criteria for an involuntary admission is that the individual is not suitable to be admitted or continued as a voluntary patient.[77] An argument can be made that if the individual is prepared to stay as a voluntary patient, it is not appropriate or lawful for the physician to hold the individual as an involuntary patient; however, if the individual decides to leave the facility, the physician may well find that the person can no longer be continued as a voluntary patient. If the remaining criteria for an involuntary admission are met, the physician may be justified in completing a certificate of involuntary admission.[78]

Informal Patient

"Informal patient" is defined in the Act.[79] A person over the age of 16 may be admitted to a psychiatric facility as an informal patient only if : (a) the person has been found incapable with respect to the treatment to be provided in the psychiatric facility; (b) the consent of the person's SDM has been obtained pursuant to s. 24 of the HCCA both to the treatment and to the admission of the individual to the psychiatric facility for the purpose of the treatment; and (c) subject to two exceptions,[80] the person is not objecting to the admission.

---

[77] s. 20(1.1)(f) and s. 20(5)(b).

[78] Pursuant to s. 19.

[79] s. 1(1), Definition "informal patient" means a person who is a patient in a psychiatric facility, having been admitted with the consent of another person under section 24 of the *Health Care Consent Act, 1996.*

[80] A person over the age of 16 who is objecting to the admission to a psychiatric facility may still be admitted as an informal patient but only if the person's guardian (under s. 59 of the SDA) or attorney for personal care pursuant to a special form of power of attorney authorizing the use of reasonable necessary force in order to admit the individual (under s. 50 of the SDA) has consented. Section 34(1) of the HCCA permits an application to review the decision of the guardian or attorney to consent to the admission in these circumstances. It is unclear what, if any, legal effect the Board's decision may have in these applications, however, since the authority of the guardian, in any event, may be varied or terminated only by the court.

(a) "Children" Admitted as Informal Minors[81]

Young persons older than 12 but younger than 16 may be admitted to a psychiatric facility as informal patients notwithstanding their objection to the admission, provided the remaining criteria are met. For young persons between the ages of 12 and 16, there is no right to apply for a review of the decision to consent to the admission for purposes of treatment,[82] however, these "informal minors" have the right to apply to the Board to determine whether they are in need of care, observation and treatment in the psychiatric facility. [83] In determining whether the Board should direct that the applicant be discharged from the psychiatric facility or confirm the informal status of the young person,[84] the Board must consider whether there is an available alternative to the psychiatric facility where the child's[85] needs could be more appropriately met.[86]

(b) Informal Patients Over 16

There is no corresponding right of review of an informal admission available to individuals over 16. Presumably, the reason is simply that, subject to two exceptions (the consent of a court-appointed guardian of the person with custodial power or an attorney for personal care with authority granted pursuant to s. 50 of the SDA), those over 16 who object cannot be admitted as informal patients[87] in any event, coupled with the prohibition against detention of informal patients.[88] Nonetheless, there appears to be a laguna in the legislation respecting informal patients over the age of 16 who, while they may not object to the admission, are simply too vulnerable to complain about it. The provision permitting the informal admission of these individuals does not require their consent, rather the absence of an "objection." It is troubling that individuals in this situation can remain potentially indefinitely as informal patients in psychiatric facilities with no provision under the Act for a mandatory review of the issue of whether they are in "need of care, observation and treatment" in the particular psychiatric facility.

---

[81] Children can also be admitted as voluntary or involuntary patients, in addition to admission of them as informal patients (if between 12 and 16) even over their objection.

[82] s. 34(2) of the HCCA bars such an application by children 12 to 16 years of age.

[83] s. 13(1) affords the informal minor the right to apply for a review under this section (Form 25) and the right to be notified by the OIC of the right to apply (Form 27) once every three months; The OIC must notify the Board of the need to schedule a mandatory hearing of this nature every six months that go by without a hearing of the issue (Form 26), see s. 13(2).

[84] s. 13(4), Powers of the Board.

[85] In s. 13, the legislation refers to young person between 12 and 16 years of age as "children".

[86] s. 13(3) Considerations.

[87] HCCA, s. 24.

[88] s. 14.

Involuntary Patients

The Act also prescribes the criteria for an individual's admission as an involuntary patient and for the person's continued detention within the psychiatric facility under s. 20. A person may be admitted as an involuntary patient only if the person is either: (1) a voluntary or informal psychiatric patient[89] or (2) the subject of a psychiatric assessment (under a Form 1 application).[90] Unless the individual's legal status is that of a voluntary or informal patient or the individual is detained under the authority of a Form 1 at the time of completion of a Form 3 certificate, the individual has not been admitted as an involuntary patient in accordance with the Act.[91] All remaining criteria for an involuntary admission must also be met at the time of the completion of the certificate of involuntary admission.[92] An involuntary patient can be detained in a psychiatric facility under a certificate of involuntary admission (Form 3) for a period of not more than two weeks[93] or subsequently under a certificate of renewal (Form 4)[94] for successive periods of not more than one,[95] two[96] or three[97] additional months,[98] provided the criteria for involuntary detention continue to be met.[99]

(a) Substantive Requirements

Box A and Box B Grounds for Involuntary Committal

Effective December 1, 2000, the Act was amended by Bill 68 in a number of ways which had the effect of expanding the criteria for the involuntary

---

[89] s. 19.

[90] s. 20(1)(c).

[91] See for example *Re P.P.* TO-030502, May 12, 2003.

[92] s. 20 (1.1) or s. 20(5).

[93] s. 20(4)(a).

[94] Where a Form 4 purporting to continue the involuntary status of a patient who is the subject of a Form 3 Certificate of Involuntary Admission is signed too early (in this case on the 4th day into the life of the Form 3), it is considered based on a "radically premature and unwarranted opinion as to what the applicant's condition would be ten days hence" (ie. upon expiration of the Form 3), and the Certificate will be rescinded as invalid, see *In re J.W.* OT-05-4954/55/5001 March 18, 2005.

[95] s. 20(4)(b)(i) one additional month pursuant to a first certificate of renewal.

[96] s. 20(4)(b)(ii) two additional months pursuant to a second certificate of renewal.

[97] s. 20(4)(b)(iii) three additional months pursuant to a third or subsequent certificate of renewal.

[98] Detention may continue indefinitely pursuant to certificates of renewal each valid for up to three months, subject to review by the Board at the request of the patient or others or when reviewed mandatorily as discussed below in relation to applications before the Board.

[99] s. 20(4)(b).

admission[100] of persons with mental illness. The grounds which existed under the Act prior to these amendments[101] are the so-called "Box A"[102] grounds. The additional provisions are commonly referred to as the "Box B"[103] grounds, reflecting the design of the various Forms[104] under the Act. Involuntary status means the patient meets the Box A or Box B grounds or both.

Box A – Risk of Serious Harm[105] / Impairment

With the exception of the removal of the requirement of "imminence" in respect of the likelihood of serious physical impairment, s. 20(5) sets out the three grounds for involuntary admission which were the grounds prior to Bill 68.[106] The section provides:

> The attending physician shall complete a certificate of involuntary admission or a certificate of renewal if, after examining the patient, he or she is of the opinion both,
>
> (a) that the patient is suffering from mental disorder of a nature or quality that likely will result in,
>
> (i) serious bodily harm to the patient,
>
> (ii) serious bodily harm to another person, or
>
> (iii) serious physical impairment of the patient,
>
> unless the patient remains in the custody of a psychiatric facility;[107] and

---

100 The Bill 68 amendments also expanded the criteria for examination and psychiatric assessment, as above.

101 With one notable exception, that being the removal of the requirement of "imminence" of anticipated likely serious physical impairment.

102 Criteria under ss. 15(1), 16(1), 17 (police powers) and 20(5).

103 Criteria under ss. 15(1.1), 16(1.1) and 20(1.1).

104 Form 1 (application for psychiatric assessment), Form 2 (order for examination), Form 3 (certificate of involuntary admission) and Form 4 (certificate of renewal) under the Act.

105 The certificate of involuntary admission itself (the Form 3) sets out the Box A criteria in s. 20(5) under the heading "Risk of Serious Harm".

106 Prior to the amendments, s. 20(5) stated: "The attending physician shall not complete a certificate of involuntary admission or a certificate of renewal unless, after he or she has examined the patient, he or she is of the opinion both, ...". The new phrasing contains an obligation on the attending physician to complete a certificate when the grounds are met.

107 Interestingly, while the Box A criteria under s. 20(5) of the Act include a requirement that the risk of serious harm or impairment be likely to occur "unless the patient remains in the custody of a psychiatric facility", this phrase does not appear under the amended expanded committal criteria under Box B in section 20 (1.1).

(b) that the patient is not suitable for admission or continuation as an informal or voluntary patient.

Self-harm versus Harm to Self

The risk of "serious bodily harm to the person" means a risk of suicide or intentional actions of self-harm[108] which is serious in the sense of self-mutilation by severing of digits or limbs or burning one's own body. It is to be contrasted with the ground of "serious physical impairment of the person" which relates to impairment which the individual does not mean to suffer. The impairment the individual is likely to suffer must still be "serious" but results inadvertently from a lack of self-care or from the actions of others based on the individual's behaviour, all due to mental illness. Examples of serious impairment for purposes of this section are malnourishment resulting from a refusal to eat what the individual believes may be poisoned food, frost-bite resulting from the individual's inappropriate attire for the weather, retaliatory action by others in response to provocative behaviour of the individual, or sexual exploitation by others due to the sexually provocative behaviour of the individual.[109]

Removal of the Word "Imminent"
under "Risk of Serious Physical Impairment"

Prior to the Bill 68 amendments, involuntary admission under this ground required a likelihood of the individual suffering ***imminent*** serious physical impairment. Under the amendments, the word "imminent" was removed. The Board continues to interpret these provisions. The new provision has been interpreted[110] as continuing to have a temporal element to it; however one that is "ill defined and flexible."[111] Removal of the requirement of imminence means that it is no longer necessary to establish that the serious physical impairment is likely to occur within a matter of three to four weeks, but within some "reasonable

---

[108] In *L.(C.) v. Hurdalek*, [1997] O.J. No. 2572 (Gen. Div.), the court reversed the Board's finding that the applicant was likely to cause serious bodily harm to herself where the evidence was that she was refusing to eat while in hospital, according to her to protest her committal, according to her physicians because she was waiting for life-saving surgery for a medical condition which did not exist. The evidence did not support certification under the ground of serious bodily harm. Contrast with *Blakely v. Kingston Psychiatric Hospital* [1995] O.J. No. 2847 (Gen. Div.) where the court upheld the Board's confirmation of the involuntary status of the patient on this ground. In this case, the patient had attempted suicide and feared others were trying to kill her.

[109] For a very thorough list of what may constitute "serious physical impairment", see TO-04 1571, *Re: T.W.*, May 18, 2004.

[110] Early on following on the heels of the amendments.

[111] *In the Matter of A.M.E.*, CCB Reasons for Decision (no file number given) March 16, 2001.

period after discharge."[112] The question remains, what is a reasonable period? This issue has yet to receive judicial consideration.

Harm to Others

In order to justify certification on the ground of "serious bodily harm to others[113]", it is not absolutely necessary to prove that the patient had caused others such harm in the past. [114] However, while the Board does not require evidence of a past history of violent conduct, necessarily, the court has overturned a certificate on this ground in the total absence of evidence that the applicant had ever caused serious bodily harm to another person.[115] The courts have interpreted "serious" bodily harm to mean bodily harm that is not merely trifling.[116] And even where there is evidence of a prior incident of the individual causing serious bodily harm to another, past conduct is only one indicia of the likelihood of further similar conduct. The Board considers the issue of risk which exists on the day of hearing, and must consider the evidence in the context of the individual's mental status on that day.[117]

Box B –Patients Incapable of Consenting to Treatment[118]

In essence, Box B contains two grounds of committal not contained in Box A:

1. substantial mental deterioration;
2. substantial physical deterioration.

To rely on these "new grounds", a number of additional criteria must be present. The additional criteria are set out in s. 20(1.1) of the Act. The attending physician shall complete a certificate of involuntary admission or a certificate of renewal if, after examining the patient, he or she is of the opinion that the patient:

> (a) has previously received treatment for mental disorder of an ongoing or recurring nature that, when not treated, is of a nature or quality that likely will result in serious bodily harm to the person or to another person or substantial

---

[112] *Ibid.*

[113] The Board has not settled with issue of whether "serious bodily harm" includes the prospect of psychological harm or whether "serious physician impairment" can encompass the likelihood of such impairment only to the brain of the individual, see the Majority Opinion (in the affirmative) and the Presiding Lawyer Member's Dissent on both issues in *In re C.L.* OT-04-2285 and 2322, August 6, 2004

[114] *Middel v. Adams*, [1993] O.J. No. 2864 (Gen. Div.).

[115] *Dayday v. MacEwan* (1987), 62 O.R. (2d) 588 (Dist. Ct.).

[116] *Ibid.*

[117] *In re D.S.* HA 041939 June 25, 2004, the applicant's involuntary status was rescinded as he was not, on the date of hearing, a "danger", although "he would be to his wife in the near future."

[118] The certificate of involuntary admission (Form 3) itself sets out the Box B criteria under the heading "Patients who are incapable of consenting to treatment and meet the specified criteria."

mental or physical deterioration[119] of the person or serious physical impairment of the person;

(b) has shown clinical improvement as a result of the treatment;[120]

(c) is suffering from the same mental disorder as the one for which he or she previously received treatment or from a mental disorder that is similar to the previous one;[121]

(d) given the person's history of mental disorder and current mental or physical condition, is likely to cause serious bodily harm to himself or herself or to another person or is likely to suffer substantial mental or physical deterioration or serious physical impairment;[122]

---

119 "substantial mental deterioration" may include the concept of "more profoundly symptomatic", See *In Re JB* TO-04-3639 November 17, 2004; however, where the condition of the patient is as bad on the day of hearing as it has ever been, the Board has left open the door to argue that no substantial deterioration is likely from that point forward in the absence of treatment, see In Re AM TO-04-1921 July 26, 2004.

120 The "clinical improvement" experienced in the past must have resulted from the same or similar treatment currently proposed or administered on the occasion of the involuntary admission or its continuation sought to be upheld under Box B. A person who responded well to psychotherapy in the past cannot be certified under Box B when the treatment now proposed is antipsychotic medication and there is no evidence of prior clinical improvement resulting from (or treatment with) this type of medication, see *re CC* TO-04-0267/68 February 17, 2004. See also *In the Matter of E.S.* TO 020892 Aug. 6, 2002 for a related proposition regarding ECT. A single clinical note referencing that the patient "improved somewhat" after a 5 day trial of antipsychotic medication does not meet the evidentiary threshold of "clear, compelling or cogent" for purposes of establishing "clinical improvement", see In re MB TO_04-2343 July 26, 2004.

121 It would appear that the Board does not distinguish as different (for purposes of this section) diagnoses of psychotic versus mood disorders, provided it appears to the Board that the patient has received treatment for a mental disorder in the past and continues at the time of the hearing to require treatment for that disorder (regardless of past diagnoses). Further, the Board appears to consider the proposed treatment as significant in determining whether the patient suffers from a similar mental disorder. If there is "similarity" in the treatment, the conclusion appears to be that the mental disorders must also be "similar." See for example, *in the Matter of GK*, June 26, 2001 (no file number available on Reasons for Decision).

122 In CCB Reasons for Decision In *Re C.M.* June 21, 2001, the Board considered the meaning of "substantial deterioration", indicating that deterioration alone is insufficient. The Board interpreted the meaning of "substantial" in this case by defining "substantial" as "not trivial" but "of substance", "not necessarily catastrophic" but "not fleeting" requiring that the "deterioration" be measured against the "patient's state while being treated."

(e) has been found incapable, within the meaning of the *Health Care Consent Act, 1996*, of consenting to his or her treatment in a psychiatric facility and the consent of his or her substitute decision-maker has been obtained;[123] and

(f) is not suitable for admission or continuation as an informal or voluntary patient.[124]

Additional Box B Criteria

Initially, the amendments of Bill 68 may appear difficult to penetrate. In essence, however, a physician seeking to detain a patient involuntarily under the current regime (Box A and Box B) now has five grounds of committal available:

1. Serious bodily harm to self;
2. Serious bodily harm to another person;
3. Serious physical impairment of self;
4. Substantial mental deterioration;
5. Substantial physical deterioration.

Grounds 1, 2 and 3 may be selected under Box A. If a patient does not meet any of these three grounds, but is likely to suffer (4) substantial mental deterioration or (5) substantial physical deterioration, the patient may be certified under Box B provided the patient meets the additional criteria set out in s. 20(1.1). It is to be noted that these additional criteria do not apply to the Box A grounds.

Given the additional criteria for Box B, a physician's decision to detain a patient involuntarily under Box B rather than Box A would appear reasonable only where the only available grounds for certification are the likelihood of "substantial mental deterioration or substantial physical deterioration." Even in cases where a patient meets all Box B requirements, there would appear to be no rational basis for choosing this alternative for committal when the patient meets any of the three grounds contained in Box A. While "substantial mental deterioration or substantial physical deterioration" is presumably a lower threshold of risk, it is also much more cumbersome given the additional criteria that must be present.

---

[123] Where the required finding of incapacity with respect to "treatment in a psychiatric facility" has not been made or the required consent of the appropriate SDM has not been given prior to the issuance of a certificate of involuntary admission or renewal completed under Box B, that form is "void" and everything that follows with respect to the patient's status as an involuntary patient in hospital is also void. See *In the Matter of DM* TO-01/645 June 12, 2001, In *re GM* TO-03-1123 September 29, 2003 (which revokes the involuntary admission where the SDM consented after the completion of the certificate and rejects an argument that consent by the SDM was given in advance of this admission of the patient, during the last admission; see also In *re XY*, OT 030369/70 November 6, 2003 indicating "blanket consent in advance of the proposal for treatment" is not lawful and cannot be relied upon under Box B.

[124] The onus is on a physician at a hearing to show that the patient is not suitable to be continued as a voluntary patient, see for example In *re T.W.* TO-04 1571 May 18, 2004.

It would appear reasonable that physicians would complete certificates of involuntary admission and renewal under Box A alone until such time as the only remaining available grounds (the fourth and fifth grounds of "substantial mental deterioration or substantial physical deterioration") necessitated completion of a Form 4 (in the case of those patients who also met all the other Box B criteria).

(b) Procedural Requirements

The procedure for admitting (or continuing)[125] an individual as an involuntary patient in a psychiatric facility is clearly set out in the Act. There are a number of key procedural requirements. A physician[126] admits a person as an involuntary patient by completing[127] and filing[128] with the officer in charge a certificate of involuntary admission if the attending physician is of the opinion that the conditions set out in section 20(1.1) or (5) are met.[129] "Forthwith"[130] upon the completion and filing of the certification documents, they must be reviewed[131] by

---

[125] Each of the steps that must be followed in relation to the completion of a Form 3 certificate of involuntary admission must be repeated each time a patient's involuntary status is renewed subject to a Form 4 certificate of renewal, s. 20(4) etc.

[126] The physician who completes a certificate of involuntary admission (Form 3) shall not be the same physician who completed the application for psychiatric assessment under section 15 (Form 1), s. 20 (2).

[127] Pursuant to s. 20(1.1) or s. 20(5) as outlined above.

[128] The Board has issued a number of contradictory reasons in relation to what constitutes "filing" for purposes of this section. Certainly, placing the document on the patient's clinical chart is not sufficient. *In the Matter of P.*, TO-020616, June 13, 2002, C.C.B., the first case of many on this issue. Faxing to a "delegate" of the OIC has been found insufficient in one case (In *re G.M.* TO-03-1123 September 29, 2003) but accepted in another (In *re A.M.* TO-04-0959, April 23, 2004) Evidence of the filing is required to be objectively ascertainable on the clinical chart of the patient prior to the hearing of the issue of an involuntary admission. See *Re: A.M.* TO-04-0543 February 29, 2004.

[129] s. 20.(1)(c).

[130] The requirement to review certification documents forthwith is not met by a three or five day delay, and has been interpreted by the Board as something the legislation contemplates be done on the day of completion of the documents. See for example In *re: N.B.* TO-030723 July 12, 2003, In *re S.S.* TO-030966 August 22, 2003, although "forthwith" should be interpreted in the context of a particular situation See for example In *re M.S.* OT 030416 December 15, 2003. The onus is on the physician to provide the necessary evidence to satisfy the Board that the filing and review took place in a timely manner. See In *re XY*, OT 030369/70, November 6, 2003.

[131] The type of "review" contemplated by this section is interpreted inconsistently by various panels of the Board. No judicial consideration has been brought to bear on the issue. On the one hand, some cases require a substantive review of the certification forms, including the suggestion that the delegate who reviews it (or the OIC him or herself) must be a physician entitled to complete such forms (see In *re S.K.* – currently on appeal—TO-031454, January 4, 2004), as opposed to cases which indicate that this is a clerical review akin to a proofreading function which anyone with training on the

the officer in charge[132] or his or her delegate[133] to ascertain whether they have been completed in compliance with the criteria under the Act.[134] The physician must promptly give the patient a written notice[135]and shall also promptly notify a rights adviser.[136] The rights adviser shall promptly meet with the patient and explain[137] to him or her the significance of the certificate and the right to have it reviewed by the Board.[138]

Failure to follow the required procedure can mean that the Board, upon review of the involuntary status of the individual, will find that the individual was never admitted lawfully as an involuntary patient. The consequence of that finding (whether it leads to a loss of jurisdiction by the Board or a rescission or revocation of the certificate of involuntary admission or renewal), is discussed below.

---

relevant legislation can carry out (See In *re Q* TO-021167 October 8, 2001). The "Q" matter stipulates that the physician who completed the certification document to be reviewed cannot be the delegate of the OIC for purposes of conducting the review.

132 The officer in charge is defined in the Act as the officer who is responsible for the administration and management of a psychiatric facility, s. 1; In *R v. Webers*, [1994] O.J. No. 2767 (Gen.Div.), the court held that the OIC of a psychiatric facility bears the responsibility for putting in place procedures to ensure that physicians and staff within the employ of the facility are carrying out their obligations under the Act in accordance with the Act. In that case there was a failure to deliver a Form 42 notice to a person detained subject to an application for psychiatric assessment.

133 Who the delegate can be is the subject of the same unresolved debate as the one resulting from contradictory decisions of the Board to date on the issue of the type of review contemplated under s. 20(8), see the cases of "Q" and "SK", for examples of the divergent jurisprudence not yet resolved by the courts.

134 s. 20(8) directs the process of reexamination followed by a proper admission if appropriate, or release of the individual, which must result once the OIC notifies a physician that the documents have not been completed appropriately.

135 s. 38(1), the approved form of the written notice which complies with the requirements of s. 38(2) is the Form 30 notice under the Act.

136 s. 38(1). The (Form 30) notice must be delivered "promptly", and a 72-hour delay before the patient receives the notice is not acceptable or "prompt." See *In the Matter of P.P.* TO 030247 & 0336 March 20, 2003.

137 "Explain" is a defined term under s.1(2) as follows: a "rights adviser or other person whom this Act requires to explain a matter satisfies that requirement by explaining the matter to the best of his or her ability and in a manner that addresses the special needs of the person receiving the explanation, whether that person understands it or not."

138 s. 38(3) "promptly"; the requirement is for the rights adviser to meet with the patient "promptly". This requirement is not satisfied just because a physician notifies a rights adviser promptly under s. 38(1); a four-day delay before the patient **receives** the rights advice is not acceptable or "prompt." See *In the Matter of P.P.* TO 030247 & 0336 March 20, 2003.

Leaving the Psychiatric Facility

The Act provides a number of mechanisms by which a patient may leave a psychiatric facility. There is a difference between a "discharge[139]" from hospital, defined in the Act, and an absence with or without leave. The Act stipulates that "a patient shall be discharged from a psychiatric facility when he or she is no longer in need of the observation, care and treatment provided therein."[140] An involuntary patient may leave the psychiatric facility for a designated period of not more than three months under a "leave of absence" authorized by the officer in charge of the facility on the advice of the attending physician.[141] The attending physician and the patient shall comply with such terms and conditions for the leave of absence as the officer in charge may prescribe.[142] The patient's attending physician may also (apparently without the authority of the officer in charge) place the patient on a leave of absence provided that the intention is that the patient shall return to the facility.[143] Provisions for detaining and returning patients who are absent from the psychiatric facility without authorization are prescribed in s. 28.[144] There are also provisions to allow for the transfer of involuntary patients to other psychiatric facilities[145] or to general hospitals[146] for medical treatment. None of these issues come directly before the Board for a review. As a result of the amendments to the Act in December 2000, there is now another means of leaving the psychiatric facility, still subject to certain conditions relating to treatment and follow-up. These new provisions are set out in the Act under community treatment orders.[147]

Community Treatment Orders

Community treatment orders (CTOs) were introduced for the stated purpose of providing "a person who suffers from a serious mental disorder with a comprehensive plan of community-based treatment or care and supervision that is less restrictive than being detained in a psychiatric facility."[148] The intention is to

---

[139] For an interesting Ruling on when a patient has been "discharged" pursuant to the MHA, see In re CM TO-04-2965 September 22, 2004. The Board held that a patient who returned to the facility of her own accord 12 days after going AWOL, had been discharged when her bed was "released" 4 days after leaving the facility, and mail for her was returned to the sender with the word "discharged" written across it by staff; further, the patient was "admitted" upon her return and a fresh Form 1 application for psychiatric assessment had been completed in relation to her.

[140] s. 34(1).

[141] s. 27(2).

[142] s. 27(3).

[143] s. 27(1).

[144] s. 28.

[145] s. 29.

[146] s. 30.

[147] s. 33.1 and related provisions through to 33.9.

[148] s. 33.1(3), the purpose clause.

reduce or eliminate an individual's pattern of improving on medication while in hospital and following discharge deteriorating due to medication non-compliance (the so-called "revolving door syndrome")[149]

To prevent or minimize deterioration due to non-complicance, the CTO provides a mechanism to return the subject of the order to the issuing physician for examination in the event that there are reasonable grounds to suspect non-compliance with treatment.[150] It is not necessary to believe that the individual has caused or suffered any particular harm before police custodial powers may be used to bring the person in for examination. Many physicians and concerned family members of individuals who have a history of serious mental illness are grateful that this type of intervention is permitted prior to the individual deteriorating to the point of meeting the requirements of involuntary admission. For the subjects of CTOs, the fact that they may be forcibly taken to a physician for examination, which may lead to an involuntary admission, simply for failing to take medication as prescribed, is often very troubling. For these reasons, the very topic of CTOs has ignited much emotional and political debate.

Early on after the introduction of the amendments including CTOs, the constitutional validity of the CTO regime was challenged before the Board. In a comprehensive set of reasons for decision, which covers many of the issues raised by the amendments, the Board determined it lacked the requisite jurisdiction to decide Charter questions.[151] However, in light of the recent judgment of the Supreme Court of Canada in *Martin*[152] the matter was once again raised before the Board.[153] On this occasion, where the Board would now have accepted jurisdiction to entertain the Charter challenge to the CTO regime[154], Divisional Court swiftly overturned this determination of the Board, finding that the Board either did not have the ability to determinate questions of law as they related to CTOs, or if wrong on that score, that legislature did not intend for this Board to consider constitutional questions at all, given the practical constraints and tight timelines of its day-to-day operation. [155] There are a number of appeals outstanding from decisions of the Board confirming CTOs, which also challenge the constitutionality of the CTO regime. None has been heard by the court.

The provisions of the Act outlining the procedure and criteria for issuing and terminating CTOs are too cumbersome to set out in detail here. The provisions are

---

149 s. 33.1(3).

150 s. 33.3(1) and in the event that other criteria are met under s. 33.3(2).

151 In *re S.H.*, TO-0115, July 16, 2001.

152 *Nova Scotia (Workers' Compensation Board) v. Martin* [2003] 2 S.C.R. 504 [2003], S.C.J. No. 54.

153 In *re E.S.*, TO-04-1311, was argued over a period of days of hearing before the CCB commencing in June, 2004.

154 In re E.S., TO-04-1311, July 19, 2004, Majority finding jurisdiction, then current Chairman of the CCB sitting as Lawyer Member dissenting.

155 *'Jane Patient" v. the Attorney General of Ontario et al.*, an unreported decision of the Ontario Superior Court of Justice, Divisional Court File No: 439/04 February 21, 2005, on judicial review application of the AG from the CCB, heard December 16, 2004

so complex that there is simply no substitute for reviewing the provisions of the legislation. We can provide only a cursory summary by way of introduction.

Criteria for Issuing or Renewing a CTO

A physician may issue a CTO "for the purpose described in 33.1(3)"[156] if the criteria under section 33.1(4) are met.[157] A CTO can only be issued if the subject had been a patient in a psychiatric facilty on two or more occasions or for a cumulative period of thirty days or longer in the previous three years, or if the individual had been on a CTO previously during the last three years. A community treatment plan[158] must be developed for the person and it is this CTP[159] with which the individual must comply pursuant to the terms of the CTO. The CTP is based on consent between the parties entering into the plan, including the issuing physician and the subject of the CTO (if capable)[160] or his or her SDM (if incapable.) Within 72 hours of entering into the CTP, the physician issuing the order must examine the subject and form the opinion that the individual meets the criteria for the issuance of a Form 1 application for assessment[161] if the individual

---

[156] There is at least one case decided by the CCB where the fact that the subject of the CTO did not fit the description of the 'revolving door patient' (as contemplated by the purpose clause in 33.1 (3)) appeared to influence the Board's decision to revoke the CTO, see In *re R.L.* TO-030767 July 17, 2003.

[157] s. 33.1(1).

[158] The Board has interpreted broadly the types of things that may comprise a CTP; for instance, a condition prescribing where and with whom a subject of a CTO may reside has been affirmed as a valid clause requiring the subject's compliance, see In *re MBG* TO-030685 July 7, 2003.

[159] s. 33.7 sets out the necessary parts of a CTP.

[160] In the event that the capable subject of a CTO withdraws his consent, the Board will revoke the CTO upon review. See in *re R.D.* OT-04-0819 April 25, 2004. Or, in the event the subject of a CTO originally issued pursuant to consent of an SDM is found capable at the hearing of the matter, the CTO is also revoked, see in re RR TO-O4-1562 September 24, 2004. Whether the hearing on the issue of capacity with respect to a CTP proceeds prior to the review of the CTO itself (for an example of this approach see In re KT TO-04-2434 September 6, 2004) or the two applications are heard simultaneously as in R.R. appears to be a question of preference of the hearing panel. The applicant derives substantial benefit from the former approach as in KT, since s/he has the opportunity to appeal the finding on the issue of capacity immediately, thereby staying the implementation of any CTO until the ultimate resolution of the issue by the Court. Where the capacity determination proves dispositive of the CTO issue (ie the applicant is found to be capable), this is also the more efficient way to proceed.

[161] This is the only provision which has received judicial consideration on appeal, to date. In *Haugan v. Whelan*, [2003] O.J. No. 1757, Chilcott J. held that the review standard on legal matters is one of correctness; Interpreting and applying s. 33(1) (4) (c) (ii) criteria for a CTO is a question of law. The Act is clear that a CTO can only issue if the Form 1 criteria are met. In this case, the evidence was that the Form 1 criteria were not met. The Board incorrectly held that it was enough if the patient was on the slippery slope toward meeting the criteria. The Board erred. The CTO was quashed.

is not a patient in a psychiatric facility at the time of the issuance of the order,[162] that the treatment or care and supervision required by the CTO are available in the community and that person is able[163] to comply with the CTP. The physician must consult with all persons named in the CTP and satisfy him or herself that the subject (or SDM if applicable) have consulted with a rights adviser and have been advised of their legal rights. The physician must also secure the necessary consent[164] from the person or his or her SDM, where applicable. In addition, without treatment the subject must be likely, based on his or her history, to cause or suffer one of the harms in the five grounds for committal.[165]

Expiry and Renewal of CTOs

A community treatment order expires six months after the day it is made unless it is renewed or terminated earlier.[166] A community treatment order may be renewed for a period of six months at any time before its expiry and within one month after its expiry.[167] The Board has considered the issue of the expiry and late renewal of CTOs on two occasions with different results.[168]

---

[162] Since the Board reviews whether the criteria are met for issuing or renewing a CTO on the date of hearing, the subject of the CTO must meet the Form 1 criteria on the date of hearing if living in the community at that time. The Board generally confirms CTOs, but for a handful of cases; in one of the very few cases to date where the Board has revoked a CTO (of which we are aware), it did so because the applicant did not meet the Form 1 criteria on the date of hearing See In *re RL* TO-030767 July 17, 2003.

[163] The Board has interpreted this provision to mean that the subject of the CTO is physically able to comply with the CTP, as opposed to considering whether the subject is willing or inclined to comply.

[164] In accordance with the HCCA [s.10 HCCA], so according to s. 21 of the HCCA as prescribed by the Court of Appeal *M. A. v. Benes* (see discussion in the introduction to the HCCA).

[165] 33.1(4)(c)(i) and (iii).

[166] 33.1(11).

[167] 33.1(12).

[168] In *re M.S.*, OT 030431, December 18, 2003, the Board revoked a CTO as "invalid" because it was signed by the issuing physician four days after the expiry of the previous CTO (ie. after the seventh month from the date of issuance of the previous CTO.) On the other hand, in *re E.S.* TO-030503 May 29, 2003, the Board confirmed a CTO signed seven days after the expiry of the previous CTO. In *E.S.* the Board held that each CTO is free-standing and does not depend on the validity of any previous one. The Board also found that the reasons for the delay in completing the CTO under review were explained. The physician had apparently tried to renew the CTO within the renewal period, but was unable to do so because of some difficulty in providing rights advice to the SDM.

Termination of CTOs

The Act provides that CTOs are terminated when consent is withdrawn,[169] when an order for examination is issued due to a suspicion of non-compliance with the order,[170] and upon the physician's determination that the subject is able to live in the community without being subject to the order, based on a request of the person for a review of his condition.[171]

Application to the Board for a CTO Review

A person who is the subject of a CTO, or anyone on his or her behalf, may apply to the Board, each time a CTO is issued or renewed for a review of whether the criteria for issuing or renewing a CTO are met on the date of hearing. Every second renewal results in a mandatory hearing, which the subject cannot waive. The provisions applicable to these applications are set out within s. 39.1 of the Act.[172]

Applications to the Board to Review an Involuntary Admission

Who May Apply and When

An involuntary patient, or any person on his or her behalf, may apply to the Board to inquire into whether or not the prerequisites set out in the Act for admission or continuation as an involuntary patient are met[173] whenever a certificate of involuntary admission[174] or its renewal[175] respecting the patient comes into force.[176] The Minister of Health and the officer in charge of the psychiatric facility where the patient is detained may apply for such a review at any time.[177] A mandatory hearing is held pursuant to a deemed application, which

---

[169] s. 33.4, See In *re R.D.* OT-04-0819, April 25, 2004.

[170] s. 33.3, in the event that a Form 47 order for examination of the individual is issued pursuant to this section, it would appear that the issuing physician has only three choices once the examination is concluded: (1) issue a Form 1 (2) do a new CTO or (3) return the individual to the community without a CTO (see. 33.3(4)). The individual cannot be returned to the community subject to the same CTO pursuant to which he or she was brought in for assessment, as this is not one of the available options, and the CTO has been terminated. See in *re A.S.* TO-04-1163/64, May 3, 2004. Where a Form 47 has been issued, the CTO is revoked. Once issued, a Form 47 cannot be cancelled, see In Re EB OT-04-3958 December 5, 2004.

[171] s. 33.2

[172] In one case, the Board exercised its discretion (notwithstanding that the criteria for issuing the CTO may well have been met on the date of hearing) to revoke a CTO without hearing any evidence on the merits of the application or the CTO, because of delays in the scheduling of the matter. See *Re D.B.* TO-030358 May 21, 2003.

[173] s. 39(1).

[174] s. 39(2)(a).

[175] s. 39(2)(b).

[176] s. 39(2).

[177] s. 39(3).

cannot be waived,[178] by a patient on the completion of a fourth certificate of renewal and on the completion of every fourth certificate of renewal thereafter, unless the patient has already applied when the certificate came into effect.[179]

The Board's Role

On the hearing of an application, the Board shall promptly review the patient's status to determine whether or not the prerequisites set out in the Act for admission as an involuntary patient continue to be met at the time of the hearing of the application.[180]

The Board's Powers

The Board by order may confirm the patient's status as an involuntary patient if the Board determines that the prerequisites set out in the Act for admission as an involuntary patient were met at the time of the hearing of the application.[181] The Board by order shall rescind the certificate if the Board determines that the prerequisites set out in the Act for admission as an involuntary patient were not met at the time of the hearing of the application.[182] The Board has interpreted its discretion to revoke the certificate even if the prerequisites for admission are met at the time of hearing of the application to apply in cases where "something not contemplated by the Act makes it either unjust or inappropriate to confirm"…. "It is ….for rare situations where there are overriding contextual circumstances that make it just to revoke."[183]

---

[178] s. 39(5).

[179] s. 39(4).

[180] s. 41(1) Although it is commonly accepted that a physician respondent before the Board may change the grounds on which he relies for the certification of his or her patient on the date of hearing from the one(s) selected on the certificate of involuntary admission or its renewal which gave rise to the review, there is at least one dissent of a lawyer member of the Board suggesting this is not appropriate or lawful, essentially given the language of the Board's role in determining whether the prerequisites for admission "continue" to be met on the date of hearing. The argument of Mr. Hubbard, lawyer and Presiding Member in *Re H.L.* OT-030447/49 January 19, 2004, raises some fascinating issues regarding the scope of the review before the Board. Although it is also commonly accepted a proposition that the Board is not reviewing the certificate before it per se, but rather the legal status of the individual, there are provisions in the Act which contradict this position. For instance, the Board's decision, if unsatisfied that the prerequisites continue to be met at the hearing, is an order to "rescind the certificate" (see s. 41(3)).

[181] s. 41(2).

[182] s. 41(3).

[183] In *re L.U.* TO-030796, July 11, 2003. In this case the Board declined to exercise its discretion (on the facts before it) but adopted the interpretation offered by counsel for the patient in setting out the scope of the discretionary power under s. 41(2). In the case

The Board's Orders regarding Jurisdiction

There is currently a division among the Board as to the decision or ruling it may make depending on the approach of the individual panel members hearing a matter where issues arise as to the validity of an involuntary admission or its renewal. There has been no appellate judicial consideration of these issues, which is unfortunate as it does have the effect of creating some uncertainty among parties to proceedings before the Board. Judicial guidance on this point would be very helpful to afford consistency and clarity on this important issue.

Some panels of the Board find that the Board is without jurisdiction to consider the issue of an involuntary admission where the pre-requisites for an involuntary admission, which were not met at the time of the hearing, are considered by the members of that particular panel to be "technical", "legal", or "procedural" pre-requisites. These Board panels draw a distinction between situations where, for example, the individual was not a "patient" at the time the Form 3 was completed, or rights advice was not provided in a timely fashion as opposed to determinations considered, by them, more "substantive" in nature, such as for example the evidence does not show that the individual is likely to cause serious bodily harm to another person due to mental disorder. These panels of the Board will, in consequence of finding a "procedural" deficiency, render a ruling that the Board is without jurisdiction in a matter.[184] This approach can become seriously

of *Re: S.T.*, T.O.-03-1221/03-1222 October 23, 2003 (ultimately appealed to Superior Court) the Board declined to even consider exercising this discretionary power, even though the facts were clear that the patient had received treatment during a period when his application for a review of a finding of incapacity to make treatment decisions was pending before the Board (in clear contravention of the prohibition against commencing treatment under these circumstances pursuant to s. 18 of the HCCA) because the prohibition arose under the HCCA rather than the MHA and the Board held it was outside the scope of the issues it may consider under s. 41(2). The court on appeal did not consider the specific point, but appeared to narrowly construe the discretion [see *T. S. v. O'Dea* [2004] O.J. No. 36.] In another case before the Board (*D.B. # 2*, TO-030358 May 21, 2003) regarding CTOs, however, the Board exercised the corresponding discretion to revoke without hearing evidence, and in so doing relied on a case known only as *G.K.* adopted by the Court in *R. v. Webers*, [1994] No. O.J.2767, wherein the Board revoked the involuntary status of an individual based on the "shocking failure" of the physician to provide the individual with a Form 42 notice that she was the subject of a Form 1 application for psychiatric assessment. It may be that this is the power the Board was exercising, without saying so expressly, in the cases of *R.W.* TO-031308 November 2003 and *re SK* – currently on appeal—TO-031454, January 4, 2004 where it was clear on the evidence that the patients had been denied their right to mandatory hearings by a physician who changed their legal status to that of a voluntary patient just before the deemed hearing was to be heard.

[184] See for example In *re GB* TO-04189/90/91 and 040212 February 4, 2004, where the Board goes on to indicate that in situations where it is without jurisdiction due to a "procedural" flaw, the appropriate course of conduct is for a physician to complete a new Form 1 application for psychiatric assessment (an opinion with which many

problematic for the Applicant who finds him or herself without recourse to a hearing of the Board on the so-called "merits" unless and until such time as a subsequent Certificate of Involuntary Admission may be issued.[185] In the last year, declining jurisdiction has been more infrequently seen as the remedy in such situations, but is still seen on occasion.

Other panels of the Board have increasingly held that regardless of the nature of the defect in the involuntary admission or its continuation, whether "legal" or "substantive", the Board's role is to determine whether the pre-requisites are met on the date of hearing. Provided the prerequisites are not met, the Board is mandated to rescind the certificate.[186] This approach has become more commonplace over the course of the last year or so, resulting in marginally greater consistency in the Board's determination of these difficult issues, to the general benefit of the parties, for the reasons described above and exhaustively canvassed in a very recent case before the Board.[187] However, a Decision of the Board simply indicating on its face that the applicant's Certificate of Involuntary Admission has been "rescinded" does not assist the attending physician with the underlying reason for the Board's determination. This can be troubling particularly where objections to all of the pre-requisites under the Act were argued by the applicant or counsel, ie. "substantive" and "procedural" defects were urged on the hearing panel as fatal to the validity of detention.[188]

Appeals To Court

Section 48 of the Act sets out the provisions for appeals to the Court from decisions of the Board regarding involuntary admission. Very few appeals are

---

disagree and one that even commenting on arguably exceeded the Board's jurisdiction; certainly, it is at least obiter) whereas in the event the Board revokes the certificate based on the so-called "substantive merits" of the case, a physician who disagrees with the decision of the Board has no recourse but to appeal the decision

185 Further, at least one Ruling of the Board would suggest that the applicant is not at liberty to determine and instruct counsel on the issue of whether to raise a "procedural" issue as a preliminary matter; rather, the physician is free at any time to complete a "fresh Form 1" depriving the applicant of a hearing in relation to the Certificate of Involuntary Admission or its Continuation in effect at the time of the application being made, see In re JB TO-04-3639 undated, hearing date November 1, 2004.

186 Pursuant to s. 41(3) see for example *G.M.* TO-03-1123 September 29, 2003. For a lengthy and thoughtful consideration of the unsatisfactory nature of the loss of jurisdiction approach, which results in no finality for the parties in practice, and why revocation is the only appropriate determination of these issues, see In *re R.H.* OT-04-0882 March 23, 2004 (albeit decided in the context of the revocation of a finding of incapacity to manage property made under the Act).

187 In re S.C. OT 05-4952 and 4953 March 11, 2005.

188 It may be helpful in such cases if the Board delivered orally its Ruling on any "legal" arguments made as to procedural defects, or, in the alternative, rendered brief Written Reasons for its Decision immediately following the Decision rather than waiting two business days to do so in the event a request for same is made.

launched from the Board to Superior Court on the issue of involuntary admission. While the appeal is pending, the appellant patient continues involuntarily detained without a right of review before the Board. The attending physician must continue to examine the patient at the intervals that would have applied under s. 20 to determine if the requirements for involuntary status continue to be met; however, a Form 7[189] is the certificate which is required to be completed and filed with the Officer in Charge (this certificate does not give rise to a right of review).

It generally takes longer to get an appeal heard before the court than the three-month period of detention pursuant to a third or subsequent certificate of renewal of an involuntary admission. Most often then, it is more sensible for the individual to await the next Board hearing than to appeal. Physician appeals are even more rare, as the certificate revoked by the Board stays in force only for three days after the decision revoking it is rendered in the event that an appeal is taken from the decision, and within that time frame the physician must attend before a Superior Court judge to request a further extension of the certificate pending appeal. The threshold on these motions is high, given that an expert tribunal has just ruled that the prerequisites for involuntary admission were not met, fewer than three days before the hearing of the motion. A more detailed analysis of appeals from the Board in general is provided in this consolidation in the chapter regarding the Board and its practices, procedures and rules.

Estates – Part III[190]

Definition

Incapacity to manage property is not defined in the *Mental Health Act*. The definition set out in the *Substitute Decisions Act, 1992* is accepted for the purposes of the *Mental Health Act*.[191] Section 6 of the *Substitute Decisions Act, 1992* defines incapacity to manage property as follows:

> A person is incapable of managing property if the person is not able to understand information that is relevant to making a decision in the management of his or her property, or is not able to appreciate the reasonably foreseeable consequences of a decision or lack of decision.

The Court of Appeal for Ontario has, on two occasions, considered the issue of capacity to manage property. In *Khan v. St. Thomas Psychiatric Hospital*,[192] the court reversed the Board's confirmation that the appellant was not capable to manage her property.[193] The court concluded that the appellant's liberty to manage

---

189 s. 48(12).

190 Part III, ss. 54 to 60.

191 *Khan v. St. Thomas Psychiatric Hospital* (1992), 7 O.R. (3d) 303 (Ont. C.A.).

192 *Ibid.*

193 The appellant's only income was a comfort allowance of about a hundred dollars a month. Her brother had informed her that she may have inherited a house in Trinidad. She refused to follow up and investigate this information. The Board found the

her very limited income had been taken away solely on the basis of her refusal to investigate the possibility that she might have a more substantial estate. The size of the individual's estate was significant in determining capacity.

In *Lavallie*, decided by the Court of Appeal, October 15, 2000,[194] the court considered the issue of capacity to manage property in the context of an individual, subject to a leave of absence,[195] whose property was placed under statutory guardianship in order to allow the hospital to require that he attend at the hospital each day to pick up a daily stipend of spending money at which time he was given his daily medication. The Court of Appeal confirmed the finding of incapacity. However, the Board has not followed this decision. The Board has held that *Lavallie* predates the *Starson* decision in the Supreme Court of Canada, and paternalism can no longer play any role in determinations of capacity. Whether an individual benefits from medication has no bearing on the issue of capacity to manage property.[196]

Assessment of Capacity

Subject to two exceptions, whenever a patient is admitted to a psychiatric facility, a physician must examine him or her forthwith to determine whether the patient is capable of managing property.[197] The two exceptions are: (1) if the patient's property is under guardianship under the *Substitute Decisions Act, 1992*;[198] or (2) the physician believes on reasonable grounds that the patient has a continuing power of attorney that provides for the management of the patient's property.[199]

After the mandatory examination of the patient's capacity to manage property, the physician must note his or her determination, with reasons, in the patient's clinical record.[200] The finding of incapacity may be found invalid upon review by the Board if this requirement to chart the reasons for the finding is not met.[201]

---

applicant incapable as it related the applicant's refusal to investigate to symptoms of her mental illness. The court reversed the Board, holding that the issue was not whether the appellant owned a house in Trinidad but whether her attitude towards the suggestion made by her brother indicated that she was not capable of managing her estate. The court concluded that the evidence fell short of establishing the appellant's incapacity to manage her estate.

[194] *Lavallie v. Kingston Psychiatric Hospital*, [2000] O.J. No. 3641 (C.A.).

[195] s. 27.

[196] *Re: M.B.G.* TO 030684, July 7, 2003.

[197] s. 54 (1).

[198] s. 54 (6)(a).

[199] s. 54 (6)(b).

[200] s. 54.(3)

[201] *Re A.P.*, TO-04-1405, May 6, 2004 found the applicant capable on the merits after the physician's very summary note of the assessment and his conclusion passed the threshold test regarding the issue of mandatory charting; however, the Board's

A patient's attending physician may also examine him or her at any time to determine whether the patient is capable of managing property.[202] Whether an individual is in fact a patient in a psychiatric facility has been the subject of much discussion.[203]

Certificate of Incapacity

In the event a physician determines a patient not capable of managing property, he or she must issue a certificate of incapacity in the approved form (Form 21) and the officer in charge must transmit the certificate to the Public Guardian and Trustee.[204]

Statutory Guardian of Property

Upon a certificate of incapacity being issued, the Public Guardian and Trustee becomes the person's statutory guardian of property. This authority is contained in s. 15 of the *Substitute Decisions Act, 1992.*

Cancellation of Certificate of Incapacity

The attending physician of a patient with respect to whom a certificate of incapacity has been issued may, after examining the patient, cancel the certificate, in which case the officer in charge must transmit a notice of cancellation in the approved form (Form 23) to the Public Guardian and Trustee.[205]

Notice of Continuance

In the event a certificate of incapacity has been issued with respect to a patient, the attending physician must examine the patient within twenty-one days before discharge from the psychiatric facility to determine whether the patient is incapable of managing property.[206]

In the event the attending physician determines the patient not capable of managing property, he or she must issue a notice of continuance in the approved form (Form 24) and the officer in charge must transmit the notice to the Public Guardian and Trustee.[207] When a patient in respect of whom a certificate of continuance has been completed is discharged from the psychiatric facility, there

---

comments on the issue indicate that an absence of charting is fatal to the validity of a finding under this section.

[202] s. 54(2).

[203] *Daugherty v Stall* (2002), 48 E.T.R., (2d) 8, [2002] O.J. No. 4715 (S.C.J.) affirming *Re:* "A" TO-020721, 22, June 25, 2002, and *Re: R.C.* TO-030502 May 12, 2003.

[204] s. 54(4).

[205] s. 56.

[206] s. 57(1).

[207] s. 57(2).

is a further obligation of the officer in charge to transmit the notice of the discharge to the Public Guardian and Trustee.[208]

Failure to conduct an examination to determine capacity within twenty-one days before discharge as required by the Act or failure to issue a notice of continuance, results in the termination of the statutory guardianship of the Public Guardian and Trustee.[209]

Notice and Rights Advice

A physician who issues a certificate of incapacity to manage property or a certificate of continuance, must promptly advise the patient of the fact[210] and must also promptly notify a rights adviser.[211] The rights adviser must promptly meet with the patient[212] and explain to the patient the significance of the certificate and the right to have the issue of the patient's incapacity to manage property reviewed by the Board.[213]

Physicians who wait until the day of discharge to examine the patient and determine that a notice of continuance should be issued take the risk that the finding of incapacity will not survive a review before the Board. In the event the patient is discharged without receiving rights advice, or notice of the continuance, the Board may hold that due to the failure to comply with these statutory requirements no valid finding was made.[214] Whether the Board's ruling in this type of situation is to revoke the finding[215] or assert that it is without jurisdiction[216]

---

[208] s. 58.

[209] Section 20.3 (1) of the *Substitute Decisions Act, 1992*

[210] The Board has historically held that the failure to deliver to the patient a written notice via a Form 33 (approved form with respect to notification of the finding of incapacity under s. 59 (1) of the Act) under the MHA is fatal to the finding or its continuation, see for example: *S.H.* TO-99/759 and 760 July 24, 1999; however, in a recent case, the Board held that notification to the patient of these findings is not required to be delivered in writing or in the approved form, but may be communicated orally or some other way, see: *Re: A.P.* TO 040596 March 12, 2004.

[211] s. 59(1)

[212] Failure to provide this statutorily required rights advice invalidates the finding or its continuation, see: *Re: A.P.* 040596 March 12, 2004. A substantial delay in delivering rights advice may also result in the finding of incapacity being "void" and the certificate of incapacity being rescinded. See In *re R.H.*, OT-04-0882, March 23, 2004.

[213] s. 59(2).

[214] See *Re: "A"* TO-020721, 22, June 25, 2002 (*"A"), S.H.* TO-99/759 and 760 July 24, 1999 (S.H.) respecting lack of written notice and rights advice; also, respecting the absence of rights advice only: In *re A.P.* CCB File no TO 040596 March 12, 2004

[215] See the discussion in relation to a Form 21 in *Re R.H.* OT-04-0882 March 23, 2004, rescinding the certificate and In *re A.P.*, TO 040596 March 12, 2004, finding the applicant capable.

[216] For example *"A"*, *"S.H."*, above.

to review it, the effect is the same. The ruling terminates the statutory guardianship.

Application for Review

A patient in respect of whom a certificate of incapacity or notice of continuance has been issued may apply in the approved form to have the Board review the issue of his or her capacity to manage property.[217]

Applications to the Board may not be made more frequently than once in every six-month period.[218] This prohibition would not appear to apply in the event a patient requests a review in relation to a notice of continuance notwithstanding a review was held within the preceding six months regarding a certificate of incapacity.

In the event an application is commenced by a patient in respect of whom a notice of continuance was issued, the application may continue to be dealt with by the Board under the provisions of the *Mental Health Act* even after the patient is discharged from the psychiatric facility.[219]

In the event an application is commenced after discharge, the application is subject to the provisions of the *Substitute Decisions Act, 1992*, and a fresh assessment of capacity is required to apply to the Board.[220]

Veterans Etc. – Part IV

This section permits the application of this Act to Ontario psychiatric facilities operated by a department of the Government of Canada pursuant to a special agreement between the Lieutenant Governor, the Minister of Health for Ontario, and the Minister of that department.

Miscellaneous – Part V

Every person who contravenes any provision of this Act or the regulations is guilty of an offence and on conviction is liable to a fine of not more than $25,000.

---

[217] s. 60(1).

[218] s. 60(2).

[219] s. 60(3).

[220] The exception to this rule is that an individual who wants to complain that he or she did not receive the appropriate notice of a finding of incapacity or its continuation or was not provided the mandatory rights advice in relation to either the finding or its continuation while still a patient at the psychiatric facility, or wants to raise an issue that he or she was not a bona fide "patient" in the psychiatric facility at the time the determination of incapacity was made, may apply to the Board even after he or she has been discharged, for a determination of the validity of the finding: See: *"A", S.H. above.*

MENTAL HEALTH ACT

(R.S.O. 1990, c M.7)

Amendments: 1992, c. 32, s. 20; 1993, c. 27, Sched.; 1994, c. 27, s. 43 (2); 1996, c. 2, s. 72; 1997, c. 15, s. 11; 1999, c. 12, Sched. J, s. 33; 2000, c. 9, ss. 1-30; 2001, c. 9, Sched. B, s. 9; 2002, c. 24, Sched. B, s. 25; 2004, c. 3, Sched. A, s. 90.

1. (1) **Definitions —** In this Act,

"attending physician" means a physician to whom responsibility for the observation, care and treatment of a patient has been assigned;

"Board" means the Consent and Capacity Board continued under the *Health Care Consent Act, 1996*;

"community treatment plan" means a plan described in section 33.7 that is a required part of a community treatment order;

"Deputy Minister" means the deputy minister of the Minister;

"health practitioner" has the same meaning as in the *Health Care Consent Act, 1996*;

"informal patient" means a person who is a patient in a psychiatric facility, having been admitted with the consent of another person under section 24 of the *Health Care Consent Act, 1996*;

"involuntary patient" means a person who is detained in a psychiatric facility under a certificate of involuntary admission or a certificate of renewal;

"local board of health" has the same meaning as board of health in the *Health Protection and Promotion Act*;

"medical officer of health" has the same meaning as in the *Health Protection and Promotion Act*;

"mental disorder" means any disease or disability of the mind;

"mentally competent" [Repealed, 2004, c. 3, Sched. A, s. 90]

"Minister" means the Minister of Health and Long-Term Care or such other member of the Executive Council as the Lieutenant Governor in Council designates;

"Ministry" means the Ministry of the Minister;

"officer in charge" means the officer who is responsible for the administration and management of a psychiatric facility;

"out-patient" means a person who is registered in a psychiatric facility for observation or treatment or both, but who is not admitted as a patient and is not the subject of an application for assessment;

"patient" means a person who is under observation, care and treatment in a psychiatric facility;

"personal health information" has the same meaning as in the *Personal Health Information Protection Act, 2004*;

"physician" means a legally qualified medical practitioner and, when referring to a community treatment order, means a legally qualified medical practitioner who meets the qualifications prescribed in the regulations for the issuing or renewing of a community treatment order;

"plan of treatment" has the same meaning as in the *Health Care Consent Act, 1996*;

"prescribed" means prescribed by the regulations;

"psychiatric facility" means a facility for the observation, care and treatment of persons suffering from mental disorder, and designated as such by the Minister;

"psychiatrist" means a physician who holds a specialist's certificate in psychiatry issued by The Royal College of Physicians and Surgeons of Canada or equivalent qualification acceptable to the Minister;

"record of personal health information", in relation to a person, means a record of personal health information that is compiled in a psychiatric facility in respect of the person;

"regulations" means the regulations made under this Act;

"restrain" means place under control when necessary to prevent serious bodily harm to the patient or to another person by the minimal use of such force, mechanical means or chemicals as is reasonable having regard to the physical and mental condition of the patient;

"rights adviser" means a person, or a member of a category of persons, qualified to perform the functions of a rights adviser under this Act and designated by a psychiatric facility, the Minister or by the regulations to perform those functions, but does not include,

(a) a person involved in the direct clinical care of the person to whom the rights advice is to be given, or

(b) a person providing treatment or care and supervision under a community treatment plan;

"senior physician" means the physician responsible for the clinical services in a psychiatric facility;

"substitute decision-maker", in relation to a patient, means the person who would be authorized under the *Health Care Consent Act, 1996* to give or refuse consent to a treatment on behalf of the patient, if the patient were incapable with respect to the treatment under that Act, unless the context requires otherwise;

"treatment" has the same meaning as in the *Health Care Consent Act, 1996*.

[1992, c. 32, s. 20; 1996, c. 2, s. 72; 2000, c. 9, s. 1]

(2) **Meaning of "explain"** — A rights adviser or other person whom this Act requires to explain a matter satisfies that requirement by explaining the matter to the best of his or her ability and in a manner that addresses the special needs of the person receiving the explanation, whether that person understands it or not.

2.-5. [Repealed: 1992, c. 32, s. 20]

6. Effect of Act on rights and privileges — Nothing in this Act shall be deemed to affect the rights or privileges of any person except as specifically set out in this Act.

Part I

Standards

7. Application of Act — This Act applies to every psychiatric facility.

8. Conflict — Every psychiatric facility has power to carry on its undertaking as authorized by any Act, but, where the provisions of any Act conflict with the provisions of this Act or the regulations, the provisions of this Act and the regulations prevail.

9. (1) **Advisory officers** — The Minister may designate officers of the Ministry or appoint persons who shall advise and assist medical officers of health, local boards of health, hospitals and other bodies and persons in all matters pertaining to mental health and who shall have such other duties as are assigned to them by this Act or the regulations.

(2) **Powers** — Any such officer or person may at any time, and shall be permitted so to do by the authorities thereat, visit and inspect any psychiatric facility, and in so doing may interview patients, examine books, records and other documents relating to patients, examine the condition of the psychiatric facility and its equipment, and inquire into the adequacy of its staff, the range of services provided and any other matter he or she considers relevant to the maintenance of standards of patient care.

10. Provincial aid — The Minister may pay psychiatric facilities provincial aid in such manner, in such amounts and on such conditions as he or she considers appropriate.

[1997, c. 15, s. 11]

Part II

Hospitalization

11. Where admission may be refused — Despite this or any other Act, admission to a psychiatric facility may be refused where the immediate needs in the case of the proposed patient are such that hospitalization is not urgent or necessary.

12. Admission of informal or voluntary patients — Any person who is believed to be in need of the observation, care and treatment provided in a psychiatric facility may be admitted thereto as an informal or voluntary patient upon the recommendation of a physician.

13. (1) **Child as informal patient** — A child who is twelve years of age or older but less than sixteen years of age, who is an informal patient in a psychiatric facility and who has not so applied within the preceding three months may apply in the approved form to the Board to inquire into whether the child needs observation, care and treatment in the psychiatric facility.

(2) **Application deemed made** — Upon the completion of six months after the later of the child's admission to the psychiatric facility as an informal patient or the child's last application under subsection (1), the child shall be deemed to have applied to the Board in the approved form under subsection (1).

(3) **Considerations** — In determining whether the child needs observation, care and treatment in the psychiatric facility, the Board shall consider,

(a) whether the child needs observation, care and treatment of a kind that the psychiatric facility can provide;

(b) whether the child's needs can be adequately met if the child is not an informal patient in the psychiatric facility;

(c) whether there is an available alternative to the psychiatric facility in which the child's needs could be more appropriately met;

(d) the child's views and wishes, where they can be reasonably ascertained; and

(e) any other matter that the Board considers relevant.

(4) **Powers of Board** — The Board by an order in writing may,

(a) direct that the child be discharged from the psychiatric facility; or

(b) confirm that the child may be continued as an informal patient in the psychiatric facility.

(5) **No limitation** — Nothing in this section prevents a physician from completing a certificate of involuntary admission in respect of the child.

(6) **Panels of three or five members** — Despite subsection 73 (1) of the *Health Care Consent Act, 1996*, the chair shall assign the members of the Board to sit in panels of three or five members to deal with applications under this section.

(7) **Procedure** — Subsection 39 (6) and section 42 of this Act and clause 73 (3) (a), subsection 73 (4) and sections 74 to 80 of the *Health Care Consent Act, 1996* apply to an application under this section, with necessary modifications.

[1992, c. 32, s. 20; 1996, c. 2, s. 72; 2000, c. 9, s. 2]

14. Informal or voluntary patient — Nothing in this Act authorizes a psychiatric facility to detain or to restrain an informal or voluntary patient.

15. (1) **Application for psychiatric assessment** — Where a physician examines a person and has reasonable cause to believe that the person,

(a) has threatened or attempted or is threatening or attempting to cause bodily harm to himself or herself;

(b) has behaved or is behaving violently towards another person or has caused or is causing another person to fear bodily harm from him or her; or

(c) has shown or is showing a lack of competence to care for himself or herself,

and if in addition the physician is of the opinion that the person is apparently suffering from mental disorder of a nature or quality that likely will result in,

(d) serious bodily harm to the person;

(e) serious bodily harm to another person; or

(f) serious physical impairment of the person,

the physician may make application in the prescribed form for a psychiatric assessment of the person.

(1.1) **Same** — Where a physician examines a person and has reasonable cause to believe that the person,

(a) has previously received treatment for mental disorder of an ongoing or recurring nature that, when not treated, is of a nature or quality that likely will result in serious bodily harm to the person or to another person or substantial mental or physical deterioration of the person or serious physical impairment of the person; and

(b) has shown clinical improvement as a result of the treatment,

and if in addition the physician is of the opinion that the person,

(c) is apparently suffering from the same mental disorder as the one for which he or she previously received treatment or from a mental disorder that is similar to the previous one;

(d) given the person's history of mental disorder and current mental or physical condition, is likely to cause serious bodily harm to himself or herself or to another person or is likely to suffer substantial mental or physical deterioration or serious physical impairment; and

(e) is incapable, within the meaning of the *Health Care Consent Act, 1996*, of consenting to his or her treatment in a psychiatric facility and the consent of his or her substitute decision-maker has been obtained,

the physician may make application in the prescribed form for a psychiatric assessment of the person.

(2) **Contents of application** — An application under subsection (1) or (1.1) shall set out clearly that the physician who signs the application personally examined the person who is the subject of the application and made careful inquiry into all of the facts necessary for him or her to form his or her opinion as to the nature and quality of the mental disorder of the person.

(3) **Idem** — A physician who signs an application under subsection (1) or (1.1),

(a) shall set out in the application the facts upon which he or she formed his or her opinion as to the nature and quality of the mental disorder;

(b) shall distinguish in the application between the facts observed by him or her and the facts communicated to him or her by others; and

(c) shall note in the application the date on which he or she examined the person who is the subject of the application.

(4) **Signing of application** — An application under subsection (1) or (1.1) is not effective unless it is signed by the physician within seven days after he or she examined the person who is the subject of the examination.

[2000, c. 9, s. 3]

(5) **Authority of application** — An application under subsection (1) or (1.1) is sufficient authority for seven days from and including the day on which it is signed by the physician,

(a) to any person to take the person who is the subject of the application in custody to a psychiatric facility forthwith; and

(b) to detain the person who is the subject of the application in a psychiatric facility and to restrain, observe and examine him or her in the facility for not more than 72 hours.

16. (1) **Justice of the peace's order for psychiatric examination** — Where information upon oath is brought before a justice of the peace that a person within the limits of the jurisdiction of the justice,

(a) has threatened or attempted or is threatening or attempting to cause bodily harm to himself or herself;

(b) has behaved or is behaving violently towards another person or has caused or is causing another person to fear bodily harm from him or her; or

(c) has shown or is showing a lack of competence to care for himself or herself,

and in addition based upon the information before him or her the justice of the peace has reasonable cause to believe that the person is apparently suffering from mental disorder of a nature or quality that likely will result in,

(d) serious bodily harm to the person;

(e) serious bodily harm to another person; or

(f) serious physical impairment of the person,

the justice of the peace may issue an order in the prescribed form for the examination of the person by a physician.

(1.1) **Same** — Where information upon oath is brought before a justice of the peace that a person within the limits of the jurisdiction of the justice,

(a) has previously received treatment for mental disorder of an ongoing or recurring nature that, when not treated, is of a nature or quality that likely will result in serious bodily harm to the person or to another person or substantial mental or physical deterioration of the person or serious physical impairment of the person; and

(b) has shown clinical improvement as a result of the treatment,

and in addition based upon the information before him or her the justice of the peace has reasonable cause to believe that the person,

(c) is apparently suffering from the same mental disorder as the one for which he or she previously received treatment or from a mental disorder that is similar to the previous one;

(d) given the person's history of mental disorder and current mental or physical condition, is likely to cause serious bodily harm to himself or herself or to another person or is likely to suffer substantial mental or physical deterioration or serious physical impairment; and

(e) is apparently incapable, within the meaning of the *Health Care Consent Act, 1996*, of consenting to his or her treatment in a psychiatric facility and the consent of his or her substitute decision-maker has been obtained,

the justice of the peace may issue an order in the prescribed form for the examination of the person by a physician.

(2) **Idem** — An order under this section may be directed to all or any police officers of the locality within which the justice has jurisdiction and shall name or otherwise describe the person with respect to whom the order has been made.

(3) **Authority of order** — An order under this section shall direct, and, for a period not to exceed seven days from and including the day that it is made, is sufficient authority for any police officer to whom it is addressed to take the person named or described therein in custody forthwith to an appropriate place where he or she may be detained for examination by a physician.

(4) **Manner of bringing information before justice** — For the purposes of this section, information shall be brought before a justice of the peace in the prescribed manner.

[2000, c. 9, s. 4]

17. Action by police officer — Where a police officer has reasonable and probable grounds to believe that a person is acting or has acted in a disorderly manner and has reasonable cause to believe that the person,

(a) has threatened or attempted or is threatening or attempting to cause bodily harm to himself or herself;

(b) has behaved or is behaving violently towards another person or has caused or is causing another person to fear bodily harm from him or her; or

(c) has shown or is showing a lack of competence to care for himself or herself, and in addition the police officer is of the opinion that the person is apparently suffering from mental disorder of a nature or quality that likely will result in,

(d) serious bodily harm to the person;

(e) serious bodily harm to another person; or

(f) serious physical impairment of the person,

and that it would be dangerous to proceed under section 16, the police officer may take the person in custody to an appropriate place for examination by a physician.

[2000, c. 9, s. 5]

18. Place of psychiatric examination — An examination under section 16 or 17 shall be conducted by a physician forthwith after receipt of the person at the place of examination and where practicable the place shall be a psychiatric facility or other health facility.

19. Change from informal or voluntary patient to involuntary patient — Subject to subsections 20 (1.1) and (5), the attending physician may change the status of an informal or voluntary patient to that of an involuntary patient by completing and filing with the officer in charge a certificate of involuntary admission.

[2000, c. 9, s. 6]

20. (1) **Duty of attending physician** — The attending physician, after observing and examining a person who is the subject of an application for assessment under section 15 or who is the subject of an order under section 32,

(a) shall release the person from the psychiatric facility if the attending physician is of the opinion that the person is not in need of the treatment provided in a psychiatric facility;

(b) shall admit the person as an informal or voluntary patient if the attending physician is of the opinion that the person is suffering from mental disorder of such a nature or quality that the person is in need of the treatment provided in a psychiatric facility and is suitable for admission as an informal or voluntary patient; or

(c) shall admit the person as an involuntary patient by completing and filing with the officer in charge a certificate of involuntary admission if the attending physician is of the opinion that the conditions set out in subsection (1.1) or (5) are met.

(1.1) **Conditions for involuntary admission** — The attending physician shall complete a certificate of involuntary admission or a certificate of renewal if, after examining the patient, he or she is of the opinion that the patient,

(a) has previously received treatment for mental disorder of an ongoing or recurring nature that, when not treated, is of a nature or quality that likely will result in serious bodily harm to the person or to another person or substantial mental or physical deterioration of the person or serious physical impairment of the person;

(b) has shown clinical improvement as a result of the treatment;

(c) is suffering from the same mental disorder as the one for which he or she previously received treatment or from a mental disorder that is similar to the previous one;

(d) given the person's history of mental disorder and current mental or physical condition, is likely to cause serious bodily harm to himself or herself or to another person or is likely to suffer substantial mental or physical deterioration or serious physical impairment;

(e) has been found incapable, within the meaning of the *Health Care Consent Act, 1996*, of consenting to his or her treatment in a psychiatric facility and the consent of his or her substitute decision-maker has been obtained; and

(f) is not suitable for admission or continuation as an informal or voluntary patient.

(2) **Physician who completes certificate of involuntary admission** — The physician who completes a certificate of involuntary admission pursuant to clause (1) (c) shall not be the same physician who completed the application for psychiatric assessment under section 15.

(3) **Release of person by officer in charge** — The officer in charge shall release a person who is the subject of an application for assessment under section 15 or who is the subject of an order under section 32 upon the completion of 72 hours of detention in the psychiatric facility unless the attending physician has released the person, has admitted the person as an informal or voluntary patient or has admitted the person as an involuntary patient by completing and filing with the officer in charge a certificate of involuntary admission.

(4) **Authority of certificate** — An involuntary patient may be detained, restrained, observed and examined in a psychiatric facility,

(a) for not more than two weeks under a certificate of involuntary admission; and

(b) for not more than,

(i) one additional month under a first certificate of renewal,

(ii) two additional months under a second certificate of renewal, and

(iii) three additional months under a third or subsequent certificate of renewal,

that is completed and filed with the officer in charge by the attending physician.

(5) **Conditions for involuntary admission** — The attending physician shall complete a certificate of involuntary admission or a certificate of renewal if, after examining the patient, he or she is of the opinion both,

(a) that the patient is suffering from mental disorder of a nature or quality that likely will result in,

(i) serious bodily harm to the patient,

(ii) serious bodily harm to another person, or

(iii) serious physical impairment of the patient,

unless the patient remains in the custody of a psychiatric facility; and

(b) that the patient is not suitable for admission or continuation as an informal or voluntary patient.

(6) **Change of status, where period of detention has expired** — An involuntary patient whose authorized period of detention has expired shall be deemed to be an informal or voluntary patient.

(7) **Idem, where period of detention has not expired** — An involuntary patient whose authorized period of detention has not expired may be continued as an informal or voluntary patient upon completion of the approved form by the attending physician.

(8) **Examination of certificate by officer in charge** — Forthwith following completion and filing of a certificate of involuntary admission or of a certificate of renewal, the officer in charge or his or her delegate shall review the certification documents to ascertain whether or not they have been completed in compliance with the criteria outlined in this Act and where, in his or her opinion, the documents are not properly completed, the officer in charge shall so inform the attending physician and, unless the person is re-examined and released or admitted in accordance with this section, the officer in charge shall release the person.

[2000, c. 9, s. 7]

21. (1) **Judge's order for examination** — Where a judge has reason to believe that a person who appears before him or her charged with or convicted of an offence suffers from mental disorder, the judge may order the person to attend a psychiatric facility for examination.

(2) **Senior physician's report** — Where an examination is made under this section, the senior physician shall report in writing to the judge as to the mental condition of the person.

22. (1) **Judge's order for admission** — Where a judge has reason to believe that a person in custody who appears before him or her charged with an offence suffers from mental disorder, the judge may, by order, remand that person for admission as a patient to a psychiatric facility for a period of not more than two months.

(2) **Senior physician's report** — Before the expiration of the time mentioned in such order, the senior physician shall report in writing to the judge as to the mental condition of the person.

23. Condition precedent to judge's order — A judge shall not make an order under section 21 or 22 until he or she ascertains from the senior physician of a psychiatric facility that the services of the psychiatric facility are available to the person to be named in the order.

24. Contents of senior physician's report — Despite this or any other Act or any regulation made under any other Act, the senior physician may report all or any part of the information compiled by the psychiatric facility to any person where, in the opinion of the senior physician, it is in the best interests of the person who is the subject of an order made under section 21 or 22.

25. Detention under the *Criminal Code* (Canada) — Any person who is detained in a psychiatric facility under Part XX.1 of the *Criminal Code* (Canada) may be restrained, observed and examined under this Act and provided with treatment under the *Health Care Consent Act, 1996*.

[2000, c. 9, s. 8]

26. (1) **Communications to and from patients** — Except as provided in this section, no communication written by a patient or sent to a patient shall be opened, examined or withheld, and its delivery shall not in any way be obstructed or delayed.

(2) **Where communication may be withheld** — Where the officer in charge or a person acting under his or her authority has reasonable and probable cause to believe,

(a) that the contents of a communication written by a patient would,

(i) be unreasonably offensive to the addressee, or

(ii) prejudice the best interests of the patient; or

(b) that the contents of a communication sent to a patient would,

(i) interfere with the treatment of the patient, or

(ii) cause the patient unnecessary distress,

the officer in charge or a person acting under his or her authority may open and examine the contents thereof and, if any condition mentioned in clause (a) or (b), as the case may be, exists, may withhold such communication from delivery.

(3) **Exceptions** — Subsection (2) does not apply to a communication written by a patient to, or appearing to be sent to a patient by,

(a) a barrister and solicitor;

(b) a member of the Board; or

(c) a member of the Assembly.

[1992, c. 32, s. 20]

27. (1) **Leave of absence** — The attending physician may, subject to subsection (3), place a patient on a leave of absence from the psychiatric facility for a designated period of not more than three months if the intention is that the patient shall return to the facility.

(2) **Same** — The officer in charge may, upon the advice of the attending physician, place a patient on a leave of absence from the psychiatric facility for a designated period of not more than three months.

(3) **Terms and conditions** — The attending physician and the patient shall comply with such terms and conditions for the leave of absence as the officer in charge may prescribe.

(4) **Exception —** This section does not authorize the placing of a patient on a leave of absence where he or she is subject to detention otherwise than under this Act.

[2000, c. 9, s. 9]

28. (1) **Unauthorized absence —** Where a person who is subject to detention is absent without leave from a psychiatric facility, a police officer or any other person to whom the officer in charge has issued an order for return shall make reasonable attempts to return the person and may, within one month after the absence becomes known to the officer in charge, return the person to the psychiatric facility or take the person to the psychiatric facility nearest to the place where the person is apprehended.

(2) **Detention during return —** A patient who is being returned under subsection (1) may be detained in an appropriate place in the course of his or her return.

(3) **Period of detention upon return —** For the purposes of this Act, a patient who is returned under subsection (1) may be detained for the remainder of the period of detention to which he or she was subject when his or her absence became known to the officer in charge.

(4) **Where not returned —** Where a patient is not returned within one month after his or her absence became known to the officer in charge, he or she shall, unless subject to detention otherwise than under this Act, be deemed to be discharged from the psychiatric facility.

(5) **Prohibitions —** No person shall do or omit to do any act for the purpose of aiding, assisting, abetting or counselling a patient in a psychiatric facility to be absent without authorization.

[2000, c. 9, s. 10]

29. (1) **Transfer of patients from one facility to another —** Upon the advice of the attending physician, the officer in charge of a psychiatric facility may, if otherwise permitted by law and subject to arrangements being made with the officer in charge of another psychiatric facility, transfer a patient to such other psychiatric facility upon completing a memorandum of transfer in the approved form.

(1.1) **Transfer of records from one facility to another —** The officer in charge of the psychiatric facility from which the patient is transferred may transfer the patient's record of personal health information to the officer in charge of the psychiatric facility to which the patient is transferred.

(2) **Authority to detain —** Where a patient is transferred under subsection (1), the authority to detain him or her continues in force in the psychiatric facility to which he or she is so transferred.

[2000, c. 9, s. 11; 2004, c. 3, Sched. A, s. 90]

30. (1) **Treatment in public hospital —** Upon the advice of the attending physician that a patient requires hospital treatment that cannot be supplied in the psychiatric facility, the officer in charge may, if otherwise permitted by law, transfer the patient to a public hospital for such treatment and return him or her to the psychiatric facility upon the conclusion thereof.

(2) **Powers of superintendent** — Where a patient is transferred under subsection (1), the superintendent of the public hospital has, in addition to the powers conferred upon him or her by the Act under which the hospital operates, the powers under this Act of an officer in charge of a psychiatric facility in respect of the custody and control of the patient.

31. Transfer of patients to institutions outside Ontario — Where it appears to the Minister,

(a) that a patient in a psychiatric facility has come or been brought into Ontario from elsewhere and his or her hospitalization is the responsibility of another jurisdiction; or

(b) that it would be in the best interests of a patient in a psychiatric facility to be hospitalized in another jurisdiction,

the Minister may, upon compliance in Ontario with necessary modifications with the laws respecting hospitalization in such other jurisdiction, by warrant in the approved form authorize his or her transfer thereto.

[2000, c. 9, s. 12]

32. (1) **Mentally disordered person coming into Ontario** — Where the Minister has reasonable cause to believe that there may come or be brought into Ontario a person suffering from mental disorder of a nature or quality that likely will result in,

(a) serious bodily harm to the person; or

(b) serious bodily harm to another person,

unless the person is placed in the custody of a psychiatric facility, the Minister by an order in the prescribed form may authorize any one to take the person in custody to a psychiatric facility and the order is authority to admit, detain, restrain, observe and examine the person in the psychiatric facility.

(2) **Delegation of Minister's powers** — The Minister may, in writing, delegate his or her powers under subsection (1) to the Deputy Minister or to any officer or officers of the Ministry subject to such limitations, conditions and requirements as the Minister may set out in the delegation.

33. Duty to remain and retain custody — A police officer or other person who takes a person in custody to a psychiatric facility shall remain at the facility and retain custody of the person until the facility takes custody of him or her in the prescribed manner.

[2000, c. 9, s. 14]

33.1 (1) **Community treatment order** — A physician may issue or renew a community treatment order with respect to a person for a purpose described in subsection (3) if the criteria set out in subsection (4) are met.

(2) **Same** — The community treatment order must be in the prescribed form.

(3) **Purposes** — The purpose of a community treatment order is to provide a person who suffers from a serious mental disorder with a comprehensive plan of community-based treatment or care and supervision that is less restrictive than being detained in a psychiatric facility. Without limiting the generality of the foregoing, a purpose is to provide such a plan for a person who, as a result of his or her serious mental disorder, experiences this pattern: The person is admitted to a psychiatric facility where his or her condition is usually stabilized; after being released from the facility, the person often stops the treatment or care and supervision; the person's condition changes and, as a result, the person must be re-admitted to a psychiatric facility.

(4) **Criteria for order** — A physician may issue or renew a community treatment order under this section if,

(a) during the previous three-year period, the person,

(i) has been a patient in a psychiatric facility on two or more separate occasions or for a cumulative period of 30 days or more during that three-year period, or

(ii) has been the subject of a previous community treatment order under this section;

(b) the person or his or her substitute decision-maker, the physician who is considering issuing or renewing the community treatment order and any other health practitioner or person involved in the person's treatment or care and supervision have developed a community treatment plan for the person;

(c) within the 72-hour period before entering into the community treatment plan, the physician has examined the person and is of the opinion, based on the examination and any other relevant facts communicated to the physician, that,

(i) the person is suffering from mental disorder such that he or she needs continuing treatment or care and continuing supervision while living in the community,

(ii) the person meets the criteria for the completion of an application for psychiatric assessment under subsection 15 (1) or (1.1) where the person is not currently a patient in a psychiatric facility,

(iii) if the person does not receive continuing treatment or care and continuing supervision while living in the community, he or she is likely, because of mental disorder, to cause serious bodily harm to himself or herself or to another person or to suffer substantial mental or physical deterioration of the person or serious physical impairment of the person,

(iv) the person is able to comply with the community treatment plan contained in the community treatment order, and

(v) the treatment or care and supervision required under the terms of the community treatment order are available in the community;

(d) the physician has consulted with the health practitioners or other persons proposed to be named in the community treatment plan;

(e) subject to subsection (5), the physician is satisfied that the person subject to the order and his or her substitute decision-maker, if any, have consulted with a rights adviser and have been advised of their legal rights; and

(f) the person or his or her substitute decision-maker consents to the community treatment plan in accordance with the rules for consent under the *Health Care Consent Act, 1996*.

(5) **Exception** — Clause (4) (e) does not apply to the person subject to the order if the person himself or herself refuses to consult with a rights adviser and the rights adviser so informs the physician.

(6) **Content of order** — A community treatment order shall indicate,

(a) the date of the examination referred to in clause (4) (c);

(b) the facts on which the physician formed the opinion referred to in clause (4) (c);

(c) a description of the community treatment plan referred to in clause (4) (b); and

(d) an undertaking by the person to comply with his or her obligations as set out in subsection (9) or an undertaking by the person's substitute decision-maker to use his or her best efforts to ensure that the person complies with those obligations.

(7) **Protection from liability, substitute decision-maker** — The substitute decision-maker who, in good faith, uses his or her best efforts to ensure the person's compliance and believes, on reasonable grounds, that the person is in compliance is not liable for any default or neglect of the person in complying.

(8) **Legal advice** — The person who is being considered for a community treatment order, or who is subject to such an order, and that person's substitute decision-maker, if any, have a right to retain and instruct counsel and to be informed of that right.

(9) **Obligations of person** — If a person or his or her substitute decision-maker consents to a community treatment plan under this section, the person shall,

(a) attend appointments with the physician who issued or renewed the community treatment order, or with any other health practitioner or other person referred to in the community treatment plan, at the times and places scheduled from time to time; and

(b) comply with the community treatment plan described in the community treatment order.

(10) **To whom copies of order and plan to be given** — The physician who issues or renews a community treatment order under this section shall ensure that a copy of the order, including the community treatment plan, is given to,

(a) the person, along with a notice that he or she has a right to a hearing before the Board under section 39.1;

(b) the person's substitute decision-maker, where applicable;

(c) the officer in charge, where applicable; and

(d) any other health practitioner or other person named in the community treatment plan.

(11) **Expiry of order** — A community treatment order expires six months after the day it is made unless,

(a) it is renewed in accordance with subsection (12); or

(b) it is terminated earlier in accordance with section 33.2, 33.3 or 33.4.

(12) **Renewals** — A community treatment order may be renewed for a period of six months at any time before its expiry and within one month after its expiry.

(13) **Subsequent plans** — Upon the expiry or termination of a community treatment order, the parties may enter into a subsequent community treatment plan if the criteria set out in subsection (4) are met.

[2000, c. 9, s. 15]

33.2 (1) **Early termination of order pursuant to request** — At the request of a person who is subject to a community treatment order or of his or her substitute decision-maker, the physician who issued or renewed the order shall review the person's condition to determine if the person is able to continue to live in the community without being subject to the order.

(2) **Same** — If the physician determines, upon reviewing the person's condition, that the circumstances described in subclauses 33.1 (4) (c) (i), (ii) and (iii) no longer exist, the physician shall,

(a) terminate the community treatment order;

(b) notify the person that he or she may live in the community without being subject to the community treatment order; and

(c) notify the persons referred to in clauses 33.1 (10) (b), (c) and (d) that the community treatment order has been terminated.

[2000, c. 9, s. 15]

33.3 (1) **Early termination of order for failure to comply** — If a physician who issued or renewed a community treatment order has reasonable cause to believe that the person subject to the order has failed to comply with his or her obligations under subsection 33.1 (9), the physician may, subject to subsection (2), issue an order for examination of the person in the prescribed form.

(2) **Conditions for issuing order for examination** — The physician shall not issue an order for examination under subsection (1) unless,

(a) he or she has reasonable cause to believe that the criteria set out in subclauses 33.1 (4) (c) (i), (ii) and (iii) continue to be met; and

(b) reasonable efforts have been made to,

(i) locate the person,

(ii) inform the person of the failure to comply or, if the person is incapable within the meaning of the *Health Care Consent Act, 1996*, inform the person's substitute decision-maker of the failure,

(iii) inform the person or the substitute decision-maker of the possibility that the physician may issue an order for examination and of the possible consequences; and

(iv) provide assistance to the person to comply with the terms of the order.

(3) **Return to physician** — An order for examination issued under subsection (1) is sufficient authority, for 30 days after it is issued, for a police officer to take the person named in it into custody and then promptly to the physician who issued the order.

(4) **Assessment on return** — The physician shall promptly examine the person to determine whether,

(a) the physician should make an application for a psychiatric assessment of the person under section 15;

(b) the physician should issue another community treatment order where the person, or his or her substitute decision-maker, consents to the community treatment plan; or

(c) the person should be released without being subject to a community treatment order.

[2000, c. 9, s. 15]

33.4 (1) **Early termination of order on withdrawal of consent** — A person who is subject to a community treatment order, or his or her substitute decision-maker, may withdraw his or her consent to the community treatment plan by giving the physician who issued or renewed the order a notice of intention to withdraw consent.

(2) **Duty of physician** — Within 72 hours after receipt of the notice, the physician shall review the person's condition to determine if the person is able to continue to live in the community without being subject to the order.

(3) **Order for examination** — If the person subject to the community treatment order fails to permit the physician to review his or her condition, the physician may, within the 72-hour period, issue in the prescribed form an order for examination of the person if he or she has reasonable cause to believe that the criteria set out in subclauses 33.1 (4) (c) (i), (ii) and (iii) continue to be met.

(4) **Return to physician** — An order for examination issued under subsection (3) is sufficient authority, for 30 days after it is issued, for a police officer to take the person named in it into custody and then promptly to the physician who issued the order.

(5) **Assessment on return** — The physician shall promptly examine the person to determine whether,

(a) the physician should make an application for a psychiatric assessment of the person under section 15;

(b) the physician should issue another community treatment order where the person, or his or her substitute decision-maker, consents to the community treatment plan; or

(c) the person should be released without being subject to a community treatment order.

[2000, c. 9, s. 15]

33.5 (1) **Accountability** — A physician who issues or renews a community treatment order, or a physician who is appointed under subsection (2), is responsible for the general supervision and management of the order.

(2) **Appointment of other physician** — If the physician who issues or renews a community treatment order is absent or, for any other reason, is unable to carry out his or her responsibilities under subsection (1) or under section 33.2, 33.3 or 33.4, the physician may appoint another physician to act in his or her place, with the consent of that physician.

(3) **Responsibility, named providers** — A person who agrees to provide treatment or care and supervision under a community treatment plan shall indicate his or her agreement in the plan and is responsible for providing the treatment or care and supervision in accordance with the plan.

(4) **Responsibility of other persons** — All persons named in a community treatment plan, including the person subject to the plan and the person's substitute decision-maker, if any, are responsible for implementing the plan to the extent indicated in it.

[2000, c. 9, s. 15]

33.6 (1) **Protection from liability, issuing physician** — If the physician who issues or renews a community treatment order or a physician appointed under subsection 33.5 (2) believes, on reasonable grounds and in good faith, that the persons who are responsible for providing treatment or care and supervision under a community treatment plan are doing so in accordance with the plan, the physician is not liable for any default or neglect by those persons in providing the treatment or care and supervision.

(2) **Same, other persons involved in treatment** — If a person who is responsible for providing an aspect of treatment or care and supervision under a community treatment plan believes, on reasonable grounds and in good faith, that a person who is responsible for providing another aspect of treatment or care and supervision under the plan is doing so in accordance with the plan, the person is not liable for any default or neglect by that person in providing that aspect of treatment or care and supervision.

(3) **Same, physician** — If a person who is responsible for providing an aspect of treatment or care and supervision under a community treatment plan believes, on reasonable grounds and in good faith, that the physician who issued or renewed the community treatment order or a physician appointed under subsection 33.5 (2) is providing treatment or care and supervision in accordance with the plan, the person is not liable for any default or neglect by the physician in providing the treatment or care and supervision.

(4) **Reports** — The physician who issues or renews a community treatment order or a physician appointed under subsection 33.5 (2) may require reports on the condition of the person subject to the order from the persons who are responsible for providing treatment or care and supervision under the community treatment plan.

[2000, c. 9, s. 15]

33.7 Community treatment plans — A community treatment plan shall contain at least the following:

1. A plan of treatment for the person subject to the community treatment order.
2. Any conditions relating to the treatment or care and supervision of the person.
3. The obligations of the person subject to the community treatment order.
4. The obligations of the substitute decision-maker, if any.
5. The name of the physician, if any, who has agreed to accept responsibility for the general supervision and management of the community treatment order under subsection 33.5 (2).
6. The names of all persons or organizations who have agreed to provide treatment or care and supervision under the community treatment plan and their obligations under the plan.

[2000, c. 9, s. 15]

33.8 No limitation — Nothing in sections 33.1 to 33.7 prevents a physician, a justice of the peace or a police officer from taking any of the actions that they may take under section 15, 16, 17 or 20.

[2000, c. 9, s. 15]

33.9 (1) **Review** — The Minister shall establish a process to review the following matters:

1. The reasons that community treatment orders were or were not used during the review period.
2. The effectiveness of community treatment orders during the review period.
3. Methods used to evaluate the outcome of any treatment used under community treatment orders.

(2) **First review** — The first review must be undertaken during the third year after the date on which subsection 33.1 (1) comes into force.

(3) **Subsequent reviews** — A review must be completed every five years after the first review is completed.

(4) **Report** — The Minister shall make available to the public for inspection the written report of the person conducting each review.

[2000, c. 9, s. 15]

34. (1) **Discharge of patients** — A patient shall be discharged from a psychiatric facility when he or she is no longer in need of the observation, care and treatment provided therein.

(2) **Exception** — Subsection (1) does not authorize the discharge into the community of a patient who is subject to detention otherwise than under this Act.

34.1 Conflict — Where there is a conflict between the *Personal Health Information Protection Act, 2004* and section 35 or 35.1 of this Act or any provision of this Act relating to the issuance or renewal of a community treatment order or the treatment, care or supervision of a person in accordance with a community treatment plan, the provisions of this Act apply.

[2004, c. 3, Sched. A, s. 90]

35. (1) **Personal health information** — In this section,

"patient" includes former patient, out-patient, former out-patient and anyone who is or has been detained in a psychiatric facility.

(2) **Disclosure, etc., for purpose of detention or order** — The officer in charge of a psychiatric facility may collect, use and disclose personal health information about a patient, with or without the patient's consent, for the purposes of,

(a) examining, assessing, observing or detaining the patient in accordance with this Act; or

(b) complying with Part XX.1 (Mental Disorder) of the *Criminal Code* (Canada) or an order or disposition made pursuant to that Part.

(3) **Disclosure to Board** — In a proceeding before the Board under this or any other Act in respect of a patient, the officer in charge shall, at the request of any party to the proceeding, disclose to the Board the patient's record of personal health information.

(4) **Disclosure of record** — The officer in charge may disclose or transmit a person's record of personal health information to or permit the examination of the record by,

(a) a physician who is considering issuing or renewing, or who has issued or renewed, a community treatment order under section 33.1;

(b) a physician appointed under subsection 33.5 (2);

(c) another person named in the person's community treatment plan as being involved in the person's treatment or care and supervision upon the written request of the physician or other named person; or

(d) a prescribed person who is providing advocacy services to patients in the prescribed circumstances.

(4.1) ***Substitute Decisions Act, 1992*** — The officer in charge shall disclose or transmit a clinical record to, or permit the examination of a clinical record by, a person who is entitled to have access to the record under section 83 of the *Substitute Decisions Act, 1992.*

(4.2) [Repealed, 1996, c. 2, s. 72]

(5) **Disclosure pursuant to summons** — Subject to subsections (6) and (7), the officer in charge or a person designated in writing by the officer in charge shall disclose, transmit or permit the examination of a record of personal health information pursuant to a summons, order, direction, notice or similar requirement in respect of a matter in issue or that may be in issue in a court of competent jurisdiction or under any Act.

(6) **Statement by attending physician** — Where the disclosure, transmittal or examination of a record of personal health information is required by a summons, order, direction, notice or similar requirement in respect of a matter in issue or that may be in issue in a court of competent jurisdiction or under any Act and the attending physician states in writing that he or she is of the opinion that the disclosure, transmittal or examination of the record of personal health information or of a specified part of the clinical record,

(a) is likely to result in harm to the treatment or recovery of the patient; or

(b) is likely to result in,

(i) injury to the mental condition of a third person, or

(ii) bodily harm to a third person,

no person shall comply with the requirement with respect to the record of personal health information or the part of the record of personal health information specified by the attending physician except under an order made by the court or body before which the matter is or may be in issue after a hearing from which the public is excluded and that is held on notice to the attending physician.

(7) **Matters to be considered by court or body** — On a hearing under subsection (6), the court or body shall consider whether or not the disclosure, transmittal or examination of the record of personal health information or the part of the record of personal health information specified by the attending physician,

(a) is likely to result in harm to the treatment or recovery of the patient; or

(b) is likely to result in,

(i) injury to the mental condition of a third person, or

(ii) bodily harm to a third person,

and for the purpose the court or body may examine the record of personal health information, and, if satisfied that such a result is likely, the court or body shall not order the disclosure, transmittal or examination unless satisfied that to do so is essential in the interests of justice.

(8) **Return of clinical record to officer in charge** — Where a clinical record is required pursuant to subsection (5) or (6), the clerk of the court or body in which the clinical record is admitted in evidence or, if not so admitted, the person to whom the clinical record is transmitted shall return the clinical record to the officer in charge forthwith after the determination of the matter in issue in respect of which the clinical record was required.

(8.1) [Repealed, 2004, c. 3, Sched. A, s. 90]

(9) **Disclosure in proceeding** — No person shall disclose in a proceeding in any court or before any body any information in respect of a patient obtained in the course of assessing or treating the patient, or in the course of assisting in his or her assessment or treatment, or in the course of employment in the psychiatric facility, except,

(a) where the patient is mentally capable within the meaning of the *Personal Health Information Protection Act, 2004*, with the patient's consent;

(b) where the patient is not mentally capable, with the consent of the patient's substitute decision-maker within the meaning of the *Personal Health Information Protection Act, 2004*; or

(c) where the court or, in the case of a proceeding not before a court, the Divisional Court determines, after a hearing from which the public is excluded and that is held on notice to the patient or, if the patient is not mentally capable, the patient's substitute decision-maker referred to in clause (b), that the disclosure is essential in the interests of justice.

(10) **Board proceedings** — Subsection (9) does not apply to a proceeding before the Board under this or any other Act, or to an appeal from a decision of the Board.

(11) **Other proceedings** — Subsection (9) does not apply to a proceeding before a court or any other body that is commenced by or on behalf of a patient and that relates to the assessment or treatment of the patient in a psychiatric facility.

(12) [Repealed, 2004, c. 3, Sched. A, s. 90]

[1992, c. 32, s. 20; 1996, c. 2, s. 72; 2000, c. 9, s. 16; 2004, c. 3, Sched. A, s. 90]

35.1 (1) **Consultation permitted** — Despite any other Act or the regulations made under any other Act, a physician who is considering issuing or renewing a community treatment order with respect to a person may consult with a member of a regulated health profession or of the Ontario College of Social Workers and Social Service Workers or any other person to determine whether the order should be issued or renewed.

(2) **Sharing of information** — Despite any other Act or the regulations made under any other Act, a member of a regulated health profession acting within the scope of practice of his or her profession or a member of the Ontario College of Social Workers and Social Service Workers or any other person named in a community treatment plan as participating in the treatment or care and supervision of a person who is subject to the order may share information with each other relating to the person's mental or physical condition for the purpose of treating, caring for and supervising the person in accordance with the plan.

(3) **Disclosure** — Except as provided in subsection (1), no person shall disclose the fact that a person is being considered for or is subject to a community treatment order without the consent of the person or the person's substitute decision-maker.

(4) **Prohibition** — A person who receives personal information under subsection (1) or (2) shall not disclose that information except in accordance with this section.

(5) **Definition** — In this section,

"regulated health profession" means a health profession set out in Schedule 1 of the *Regulated Health Professions Act, 1991.*

[2000, c. 9, s. 17]

36. Patient access to clinical record — Despite subsection 90 (12) of Schedule A to the *Health Information Protection Act, 2004*, this section, as it read immediately before that subsection came into force, continues to apply to a request for access that a patient made under this section before that subsection came into force.

[1992, c. 32, s. 20; 1996, c. 2, s. 72; 2000, c. 9, s. 18; 2004, c. 3, Sched. A, s. 90]

36.1 [Repealed, 2004, c. 3, Sched. A, s. 90]

36.2 [Repealed, 2004, c. 3, Sched. A, s. 90]

36.3 [Repealed, 2004, c. 3, Sched. A, s. 90]

37. [Repealed, 1992, c. 32, s. 20]

38. (1) **Notice of certificate** — An attending physician who completes a certificate of involuntary admission or a certificate of renewal shall promptly give the patient a written notice that complies with subsection (2) and shall also promptly notify a rights adviser.

(2) **Contents of notice to patient** — The written notice given to the patient shall inform the patient,

(a) of the reasons for the detention;

(b) that the patient is entitled to a hearing before the Board; and

(c) that the patient has the right to retain and instruct counsel without delay.

(3) **Rights adviser** — The rights adviser shall promptly meet with the patient and explain to him or her the significance of the certificate and the right to have it reviewed by the Board.

(4) [Repealed, 2004, c. 3, Sched. A, s. 90]

(5) [Repealed, 2004, c. 3, Sched. A, s. 90]

(6) **Notice of child's right** — Whenever a child has a right to apply to the Board under section 13, the officer in charge shall promptly give the child a written notice of the fact that indicates the child is entitled to a hearing before the Board, and shall also promptly notify a rights adviser.

(7) **Rights adviser** — The rights adviser shall promptly meet with the child and explain to him or her the right to apply to the Board under section 13.

(8) **Exception** — Subsections (3) and (7) do not apply if the person himself or herself refuses to meet with the rights adviser.

(9) **Assistance** — At the person's request, the rights adviser shall assist him or her in making an application to the Board and in obtaining legal services.
[1992, c. 32, s. 20; 2004, c. 3, Sched. A, s. 90]

38.1 (1) **Notice of application or order** — The attending physician of a person who is the subject of an application for assessment under section 15 or an order under section 32 shall promptly give the person a written notice of the application or order.

(2) **Same** — The notice shall state the reasons for the detention and shall indicate that the person has the right to retain and instruct counsel without delay.
[1992, c. 32, s. 20]

39. (1) **Application for review by patient, etc.** — An involuntary patient, or any person on his or her behalf, may apply to the Board in the approved form to inquire into whether or not the prerequisites set out in this Act for admission or continuation as an involuntary patient are met.

(2) **When application may be made** — In addition to the applications under subsection (4), an application under subsection (1) may be made,

(a) when a certificate of involuntary admission respecting the patient comes into force; or

(b) when any certificate of renewal respecting the patient comes into force.

(3) **Application for review by Minister, etc.** — An application under subsection (1) may be made at any time by the Minister, the Deputy Minister or the officer in charge in respect of any involuntary patient.

(4) **Where notice deemed to have been given** — On the completion of a fourth certificate of renewal and on the completion of every fourth certificate of renewal thereafter, the patient shall be deemed to have applied in the approved form under subsection (1) to the Board unless he or she has already applied under clause (2) (b).

(5) **Waiver** — A waiver by an involuntary patient of an application or of the right to an application mentioned in subsection (4) is a nullity.

(5.1) **Panels of three or five members** — Despite subsection 73 (1) of the *Health Care Consent Act, 1996*, the chair shall assign the members of the Board to sit in panels of three or five members to hear applications under this section.

(6) **Composition and quorum of panels** — The following rules apply with respect to the composition and quorum of panels of the Board that hear applications under this section:

1. A three-member panel shall consist of a psychiatrist, a lawyer and a third person who is neither a psychiatrist nor a lawyer. Despite clause 73 (3) (b) of the *Health Care Consent Act, 1996*, all the members of the panel are required to make up the quorum.

2. A five-member panel shall include one or two psychiatrists and one or two lawyers. The other member or members shall be persons who are neither psychiatrists nor lawyers. A majority of the members of the panel

constitutes a quorum. A psychiatrist, a lawyer and a member who is neither a psychiatrist nor a lawyer are required to make up the quorum.

(7) **Procedure** — Clause 73 (3) (a), subsection 73 (4) and sections 74 to 80 of the *Health Care Consent Act, 1996* apply to an application under this section, with necessary modifications.

[1992, c. 32, s. 20; 1996, c. 2, s. 72; 2000, c. 9, s. 21]

39.1 (1) **Application for review by person subject to community treatment order** — A person who is subject to a community treatment order, or any person on his or her behalf, may apply to the Board in the approved form to inquire into whether or not the criteria for issuing or renewing a community treatment order set out in subsection 33.1 (4) are met.

(2) **When application may be made** — An application under subsection (1) may be made each time a community treatment order is issued or renewed under section 33.1.

(3) **Deemed application** — When a community treatment order is renewed for the second time and on the occasion of every second renewal thereafter, the person shall be deemed to have applied to the Board in the approved form under subsection (1) unless an application has already been made under that subsection.

(4) **Notice to Board** — When a physician renews a community treatment order for the second time and on the occasion of every second renewal thereafter, he or she shall give notice of the renewal to the Board in the approved form.

(5) **Waiver** — A waiver by the person who is subject to the community treatment order of an application or of the right to an application mentioned in subsection (3) is a nullity.

(6) **Review of community treatment order** — On the hearing of an application, the Board shall promptly review whether or not the criteria for issuing or renewing the community treatment order set out in subsection 33.1 (4) are met at the time of the hearing of the application.

(7) **Confirm or revoke order** — The Board may, by order, confirm the issuance or renewal of the community treatment order if it determines that the criteria mentioned in subsection (6) are met at the time of the hearing, but, if the Board determines that those criteria are not met, it shall revoke the community treatment order.

(8) **Application of order** — An order of the Board under subsection (7) applies to the community treatment order in force immediately before the making of the Board's order.

(9) **Parties** — The physician who issues or renews the community treatment order, the person subject to it or any other person who has required the hearing and such other persons as the Board may specify are parties to the hearing before the Board.

(10) **Procedure** — Subsections 39 (5.1), (6) and (7) apply to an application under this section with necessary modifications.

[2000, c. 9, s. 22]

40. Hearing deemed abandoned — Except as provided in subsection 48 (6) or (11), where an appeal is taken against a certificate of involuntary admission or a certificate of renewal and the time period for the certificate under subsection 20 (4) expires before a decision is rendered, the appeal shall be deemed to be abandoned whether or not the certificate is renewed.

41. (1) **Review of admission or renewal** — On the hearing of an application, the Board shall promptly review the patient's status to determine whether or not the prerequisites set out in this Act for admission as an involuntary patient continue to be met at the time of the hearing of the application.

(2) **Confirming order** — The Board by order may confirm the patient's status as an involuntary patient if the Board determines that the prerequisites set out in this Act for admission as an involuntary patient were met at the time of the hearing of the application.

(3) **Rescinding order** — The Board by order shall rescind the certificate if the Board determines that the prerequisites set out in this Act for admission as an involuntary patient were not met at the time of the hearing of the application.

(4) **Application of order** — An order of the Board confirming or rescinding a certificate applies to the certificate of involuntary admission or the certificate of renewal in force immediately before the making of the order.
[1992, c. 32, s. 20]

42. Parties — The attending physician, the patient or other person who has required the hearing and such other persons as the Board may specify are parties to the proceedings before the Board.

43. Counsel for patient under 16 — If a patient who is less than 16 years old is a party to a proceeding before the Board under section 13 or 39 and does not have legal representation,

(a) the Board may direct the Children's Lawyer to arrange for legal representation to be provided for the patient; and

(b) the patient shall be deemed to have capacity to retain and instruct counsel.

[1996, c. 2, s. 72]

44.-47. [Repealed, 1992, c. 32, s. 20]

48. (1) **Appeal to court** — A party to a proceeding under this Act before the Board may appeal the Board's decision to the Superior Court of Justice on a question of law or fact or both.

(2) [Repealed, 1992, c. 32, s. 20]

(3) **Same** — Section 80 of the *Health Care Consent Act, 1996* applies to the appeal.

(4) [Repealed, 1992, c. 32, s. 20]

(5) **Extension of discontinued certificate** — Where an appeal is taken against a decision by the Board to discontinue a certificate of involuntary admission, a certificate of renewal or an extension of a certificate, the certificate shall continue

in effect for a period of three clear days excluding Saturday and holidays, following the decision of the Board.

(6) **Extension of certificate for appeal** — Where, before a certificate of involuntary admission, a certificate of renewal or an extension of a certificate expires, a party to the appeal other than the patient or the person acting on the patient's behalf makes a motion to the court for an extension of the certificate beyond the time period for the certificate under subsection 20 (4), the court may by order extend the effectiveness of the certificate.

(7) **Authority of extension** — An extension of a certificate under subsection (6) is effective,

(a) for the next period of time provided for renewal of the certificate under subsection 20 (4) or any shorter period set by the court;

(b) until the certificate is rescinded;

(c) until the party appealing withdraws the appeal; or

(d) until the attending physician confirms under subsection (12) that the patient does not meet the criteria set out in subsection 20 (1.1) or (5),

whichever first occurs.

(8) **Renewal of certificate** — Subject to subsection 20 (1.1) and (5), when a patient or a person acting on the patient's behalf withdraws an appeal, a physician may complete and file a renewal of the certificate that was under appeal.

(9) **Authority of certificate** — A renewal of a certificate under subsection (8) is effective for the next period of time provided for under subsection 20 (4).

(10) **Evidence for extension** — The court shall not grant an extension of the certificate under subsection (6) to a party other than the patient or the person acting on the patient's behalf unless the court is satisfied that there are reasonable and probable grounds to believe that the patient's condition would justify the completion and filing of a certificate of renewal.

(11) **Effectiveness of certificate** — Where an appeal is taken from a decision of the Board to confirm a certificate of involuntary admission or a certificate of renewal, the certificate is effective until,

(a) the certificate is confirmed or rescinded by the court;

(b) the certificate is rescinded by the attending physician;

(c) forty-eight hours after notice is given to the attending physician that the party appealing has withdrawn the appeal; or

(d) the attending physician confirms under subsection (12) that the patient does not meet the criteria set out in subsection 20 (1.1) or (5).

(12) **Examination** — Despite subsections (1) to (10), the attending physician shall examine the patient at the intervals that would have applied under section 20 and shall complete and file with the officer in charge a statement in writing as to whether or not the patient meets the criteria set out in subsection 20 (1.1) or (5).

(13)-(18) [Repealed, 1992, c. 32, s. 20]

[1992, c. 32, s. 20; 1993, c. 27, Sched., 1996, c. 2, s. 72; 1999, c. 12, Sched. J, s. 33; 2000, c. 9, s. 23]

49. (1) **Psychosurgery** — Psychosurgery shall not be administered to an involuntary patient, to a person who is incapable of giving or refusing consent to psychosurgery on his or her own behalf for the purposes of the *Health Care Consent Act, 1996*, or to a person who is remanded or detained in a psychiatric facility pursuant to the *Criminal Code* (Canada).

(2) **Same** — Psychosurgery is any procedure that, by direct or indirect access to the brain, removes, destroys or interrupts the continuity of histologically normal brain tissue, or that inserts indwelling electrodes for pulsed electrical stimulation for the purpose of altering behaviour or treating psychiatric illness, but does not include neurological procedures used to diagnose or treat organic brain conditions, intractable physical pain or epilepsy, if these conditions are clearly demonstrable.

[1992, c. 32, s. 20; 1996, c. 2, s. 72]

50. Application to Board — If a patient or another person on a patient's behalf gives or transmits to the officer in charge an application to the Board under this or any other Act, the officer in charge shall promptly transmit the application to the Board.

51. [Repealed, 1992, c. 32, s. 20]

52. [Repealed, 1992, c. 32, s. 20]

53. (1) **Documentation of use of restraint** — The use of restraint on a patient shall be clearly documented in the patient's record of personal health information by the entry of a statement that the patient was restrained, a description of the means of restraint and a description of the behaviour of the patient that required that the patient be restrained or continue to be restrained.

(2) **Chemical restraint** — Where a chemical restraint is used, the entry shall include a statement of the chemical employed, the method of administration and the dosage.

[2004, c. 3, Sched. A, s. 90]

Part III

Estates

54. (1) **Examination on admission to determine capacity** — Forthwith on a patient's admission to a psychiatric facility, a physician shall examine him or her to determine whether the patient is capable of managing property.

(2) **Examination at other times** — A patient's attending physician may examine him or her at any time to determine whether the patient is capable of managing property.

(3) **Clinical record** — After an examination under subsection (1) or (2), the physician shall note his or her determination, with reasons, in the patient's record of personal health information.

(4) **Certificate of incapacity** — If the physician determines that the patient is not capable of managing property, he or she shall issue a certificate of incapacity

in the approved form, and the officer in charge shall transmit the certificate to the Public Guardian and Trustee.

(5) **Same —** If the circumstances are such that the Public Guardian and Trustee should immediately assume management of the patient's property, the officer in charge (or the physician who examined the patient, if the officer in charge is absent) shall notify the Public Guardian and Trustee of the matter as quickly as possible.

(6) **Exception —** This section does not apply if,

(a) the patient's property is under guardianship under the *Substitute Decisions Act, 1992*; or

(b) the physician believes on reasonable grounds that the patient has a continuing power of attorney under that Act that provides for the management of the patient's property.

[1992, c. 32, s. 20; 2000, c. 9, s. 24; 2001, c. 9, Sched. B, s. 9; 2004, c. 3, Sched. A, s. 90]

55. Financial statement — When a certificate of incapacity is issued, the officer in charge shall forthwith transmit a financial statement in the approved form to the Public Guardian and Trustee.

[1992, c. 32, s. 20; 2000, c. 9, s. 26]

56. Cancellation of certificate — The attending physician of a patient with respect to whom a certificate of incapacity has been issued may, after examining the patient for that purpose, cancel the certificate, and the officer in charge shall transmit a notice of cancellation in the approved form to the Public Guardian and Trustee.

57. (1) **Examination before discharge to determine capacity —** Within twenty-one days before the discharge from the psychiatric facility of a patient with respect to whom a certificate of incapacity has been issued, the attending physician shall examine him or her to determine whether the patient is capable of managing property.

(2) **Notice of continuance —** If the attending physician determines that the patient is not capable of managing property, he or she shall issue a notice of continuance in the approved form, and the officer in charge shall transmit the notice to the Public Guardian and Trustee.

[1992, c. 32, s. 20; 2000, c. 9, s. 27]

58. Notice of discharge — When a patient in respect of whom a certificate of continuance has been issued is discharged from the psychiatric facility, the officer in charge shall transmit notice of the fact to the Public Guardian and Trustee.

[1992, c. 32, s. 20]

59. (1) **Advice to patient, notice to rights adviser —** A physician who issues a certificate of incapacity or a certificate of continuance shall promptly advise the patient of the fact and shall also promptly notify a rights adviser.

(2) **Meeting with rights adviser —** The rights adviser shall promptly meet with the patient and explain to him or her the significance of the certificate and

the right to have the issue of the patient's capacity to manage property reviewed by the Board.

(3) **Exception** — Subsection (2) does not apply if the patient himself or herself refuses to meet with the rights adviser.

(4) **Assistance** — At the patient's request, the rights adviser shall assist him or her in making an application to the Board and in obtaining legal services.

[1992, c. 32, s. 20]

60. (1) **Application to Board for review** — A patient in respect of whom a certificate of incapacity or a notice of continuance has been issued may apply in the approved form to have the Board review the issue of his or her capacity to manage property.

(2) **Procedure** — Except that applications may be made not more frequently than once in any six-month period, section 42 of this Act and sections 73 to 80 of the *Health Care Consent Act, 1996* apply to an application under subsection (1), with necessary modifications.

(3) **Patient discharged** — If an application is commenced under this section by a patient in respect of whom a notice of continuance has been issued, the application may continue to be dealt with by the Board even after the patient is discharged from the psychiatric facility.

[1992, c. 32, s. 20; 1996, c. 2, s. 72; 2000, c. 9, s. 28]

61-76. [Repealed, 1992, c. 32, s. 20]

Part IV

Veterans, etc.

77. Agreement with Government of Canada authorized — The Lieutenant Governor in Council may authorize an agreement between Her Majesty the Queen in right of Ontario represented by the Minister and Her Majesty the Queen in right of Canada represented by the Minister of any department of the Government of Canada that is from time to time charged with the observation, care and treatment of persons who are suffering from a mental disorder whereunder that department may establish, operate, maintain, control and direct in Ontario psychiatric facilities within the meaning of this Act for the observation, care and treatment of such persons, and where such an agreement is made, it may provide that the provisions of Parts II and III of this Act and the relevant regulations, or any of them, apply with necessary modifications.

Part V

Miscellaneous

78. [Repealed, 2002, c. 24, Sched. B, s. 25]

79. Certain actions barred — No action lies against any psychiatric facility or any officer, employee or servant thereof for a tort of any patient.

80. Offence — Every person who contravenes any provision of this Act or the regulations is guilty of an offence and on conviction is liable to a fine of not more than $25,000.

80.1 Forms — The Minister may establish forms and require their use and may require the use of forms approved by the Minister.

[2000, c. 9, s. 29]

80.2 (1) **Power of Minister to designate** — The Minister may designate and classify psychiatric facilities, and exempt any psychiatric facility or class of psychiatric facility from the application of any provision of the regulations made under clause 81 (1) (b).

(2) **List** — The Minister shall maintain a list of psychiatric facilities and their classifications, and of any exemptions from the application of any provision of the regulations made under clause 81 (1) (b).

(3) **Same** — The list referred to in subsection (2) shall be available for public inspection from the Ministry.

[2000, c. 9, s. 29]

81. (1) **Regulations** — The Lieutenant Governor in Council may make regulations,

(a) [Repealed, 2000, c. 9, s. 30]

(b) in respect of psychiatric facilities or any class thereof,

(i) providing for the creation, establishment, construction, alteration, renovation and maintenance thereof,

(ii) prescribing the accommodation, facilities, equipment and services thereof,

(iii) providing for the government, management, conduct, operation, use and control thereof,

(iv) providing for the officers and employees and prescribing their qualifications,

(v) prescribing the forms, records, books, returns and reports to be made and kept in that respect and the period for which the psychiatric facility involved shall retain each, and providing for returns, reports and information to be furnished to the Ministry;

(c) prescribing additional duties of officers designated and persons appointed under subsection 9 (1);

(d) [Repealed, 1997, c. 15, s. 11]

(e) exempting any psychiatric facility or class thereof from the application of Part II;

(f) classifying patients, and limiting the classes of patients that may be admitted to any psychiatric facility or class thereof;

(f.1) prescribing the manner in which information may be brought before a justice of the peace for the purposes of section 16;

(g) respecting taking custody of persons under section 33, the examination and detention of persons and the admission, detention, leave of absence, absence without authorization, transfer, discharge and placement of patients;

(g.1) respecting and governing community treatment orders, including the qualifications required for issuing such orders, additional duties of physicians who issue or renew such orders, additional duties of physicians who consent to an appointment under subsection 33.5 (2) and additional duties of persons who agree to provide treatment or care and supervision under a community treatment plan;

(g.2) designating persons or categories of persons who may review community treatment order documents to ascertain whether or not they have been completed in compliance with the criteria set out in this Act and prescribing additional duties of such persons;

(g.3) designating persons or categories of persons who may agree to provide treatment or care and supervision under a community treatment plan under subsection 33.5 (3) and prescribing the qualifications or requirements that a person must meet before he or she provides such treatment or care and supervision;

(h) governing designations by psychiatric facilities or the Minister of persons or categories of persons to perform the functions of a rights adviser under this Act and governing the revocation of such designations, including,

  (i) requiring, permitting or prohibiting designations and revocations,

  (ii) prescribing who may make designations and revocations on behalf of a psychiatric facility,

  (iii) prescribing qualifications or requirements that a person must meet before he or she may be designated by a psychiatric facility and qualifications or requirements that a person must meet before he or she may be designated by the Minister, and

  (iv) prescribing obligations in relation to the provision of information about designations and revocations that have been made;

(h.1) designating persons or categories of persons as rights advisers and prescribing the qualifications or requirements that a person must meet before he or she may provide rights advice pursuant to clause 33.1 (4) (e);

(h.2) requiring that a physician who determines that a patient is incapable of consenting to the collection, use or disclosure of personal health information promptly,

  (i) give the patient a written notice that sets out the advice that the regulation specifies with respect to the patient's rights, and

  (ii) notify a rights adviser;

(h.3) requiring the rights adviser mentioned in clause (h.2) to give the patient the explanations that the regulation specifies and governing the content of the explanations;

(i) respecting the manner in which rights advisers must carry out their obligations under this Act or the regulations;

(j) prescribing and governing the obligations of health practitioners, rights advisers, psychiatric facilities and others in relation to the provision of information about rights, and assistance in exercising rights, to persons who have been admitted to a psychiatric facility as patients and who are either incapable, within the meaning of the *Health Care Consent Act, 1996*, with respect to treatment of a mental disorder or are incapable, within the meaning of the *Personal Health Information Protection Act, 2004*, with respect to personal health information including prescribing,

(i) the information or assistance that must be given,

(ii) the categories of persons who must be given the information or assistance,

(iii) the circumstances in which the information or assistance must be given,

(iv) the persons by whom the information or assistance must be given, and

(v) the manner and time in which the information or assistance must be given;

(j.1) prescribing and governing the obligations of health practitioners, rights advisers, health facilities and others in relation to the provision of information about rights, and assistance in exercising rights, to persons who are subject to community treatment orders and to their substitute decision-makers, including,

(i) the information or assistance that must be given,

(ii) the categories of persons who must be given the information or assistance,

(iii) the circumstances in which the information or assistance must be given,

(iv) the persons by whom the information or assistance must be given; and

(v) the manner and time in which the information or assistance must be given;

(k) governing the transfer of information among those involved in the process of providing persons with information about their rights and among those involved in the process of implementing a community treatment plan;

(k.1) regulating the timing of the treatment of a person in a psychiatric facility or subject to a community treatment order, if the person must be provided with information about his or her rights or if the person exercises, or indicates an intention to exercise, any of his or her rights;

(k.2) [Repealed, 2004, c. 3, Sched. A, s. 90]

(k.3) governing the use, disclosure and retention of personal information obtained from the disclosure, transmission or examination of a record of personal health information under subsection 35 (4)

(k.4) prescribing a person and circumstances for the purpose of clause 35 (4) (d);

(l) exempting any psychiatric facility or class thereof from the application of Part III;

(m) prescribing forms and providing for their use;

(n) respecting any matter necessary or advisable to carry out effectively the intent and purpose of this Act.

(2) [Repealed, 2000, c. 9, s. 30]

[1992, c. 32, s. 20; 1996, c. 2, s. 72; 1997, c. 15, s. 11; 2000, c. 9, s. 30; 2004, c. 3, Sched. A, s. 90]

GENERAL

(R.R.O. 1990, Reg. 741)

1. In this Regulation,

"psychiatric facility" means a facility that the Minister designates as such under section 80.2 of the Act.

[O. Reg. 616/00, s. 1]

Standards

2. Plans and specifications for the creation, establishment, construction, alteration or renovation of a psychiatric facility shall be submitted to the Minister for approval.

3. [Repealed, O. Reg. 616/00, s. 2]

4. (1) Unless exempted therefrom by the Minister under subsection 80.2 (1) of the Act, every psychiatric facility shall offer a program that includes the following essential services:

1. In-patient services.
2. Out-patient services.
3. Day care services.
4. Emergency services.
5. Consultative and educational services to local agencies.

(2) Any alteration in the program of a psychiatric facility that limits or restricts any of the essential services listed in subsection (1) shall be submitted to the Minister for approval.

(3) The list of psychiatric facilities designated by the Minister, their classifications, as well as any exemption from the requirement to provide the essential services mentioned in subsection (1), is available on the Internet through the web site of the Ministry of Health and Long-Term Care.

[O. Reg. 616/00, s. 3; 331/04, s. 1]

5. The observation, care and treatment of patients of a psychiatric facility shall be under the direction and supervision of a psychiatrist except at the Woodstock General Hospital and the St. Joseph's Care Group, Westmount St. Site, in Thunder Bay.

[O. Reg. 616/00, s. 4]

Returns

6. (1) The Minister may require a psychiatric facility to furnish any returns, reports and information that the Minister may consider necessary from time to time.

(2) A psychiatric facility shall comply with a requirement of the Minister under subsection (1).

[R.R.O. 1990, Reg. 741, s. 6; 331/04, s. 3]

Application of Parts II and III of Act

7. The psychiatric facilities designated by the Minister as belonging to the class of facilities not required to provide in-patient services are exempt from the application of,

(a) Part II of the Act, except sections 35 and 35.1; and

(b) Part III of the Act.

[O. Reg. 616/00, s. 5; 331/04, s. 3]

Bringing Information Before Justice under Section 16

7.1 For the purposes of section 16 of the Act, information on oath may be brought before a justice of the peace orally or in writing, and may include documents and other recorded materials relevant to the subject matter of the proceeding.

[O. Reg. 616/00, s. 6]

Taking into Custody by Facility

7.2 (1) Where a person is taken to a psychiatric facility under section 33 of the Act, the officer in charge or his or her delegate shall ensure that a decision is made as soon as is reasonably possible as to whether or not the facility will take custody of the person.

(2) The staff member or members of the psychiatric facility responsible for making the decision shall consult with the police officer or other person who has taken the person in custody to the facility.

(3) A staff member designated for this purpose shall communicate with the police officer or other person about any delays in the making of the decision.

(4) Where a decision is made to take the person into custody, the designated staff member shall promptly inform the police officer or other person of the decision.

[O. Reg. 616/00, s. 6]

Community Treatment Orders

7.3 A physician is qualified to issue or renew a community treatment order if he or she is,

(a) a psychiatrist;

(b) a physician who practises in the area of mental health; or

(c) a physician who is an employee or staff member of a psychiatric facility.

[O. Reg. 616/00, s. 6]

7.4 Where a physician issues an order for examination under subsection 33.3 (1) or 33.4 (3), the physician shall ensure that the police,

(a) have complete and up-to-date information about the name, address and telephone number of the physician responsible for completing the examination required under the order and, if the information changes, shall provide the police with the changed information; and

(b) are immediately notified if the person subject to the order voluntarily attends for the examination or, for any other reason, the order is revoked prior to its expiry date.

[O. Reg. 616/00, s. 6]

Absence Without Authorization

8. (1) Where the absence without authorization of a patient who is subject to detention in a psychiatric facility becomes known to the officer in charge, he or she shall forthwith issue an order for return in the approved form and notify the appropriate law enforcement authorities.

(2) Where the officer in charge has issued an order for return and has notified the appropriate law enforcement authorities, he or she shall notify those authorities forthwith if the patient returns or if the patient does not return and is deemed discharged from the facility under subsection 28 (4) of the Act.

[O. Reg. 616/00, s. 7]

Board

9. The officer in charge shall complete and transmit to the Board a notice in the approved form of the filing of a fourth certificate of renewal or a subsequent fourth certificate of renewal respecting a patient.

[O. Reg. 15/95, s. 2; O. Reg. 616/00, s. 8]

10. Every psychiatric facility in respect of which the Board has jurisdiction shall provide applications for review and envelopes pre-addressed to the Board having jurisdiction and an application and envelope shall be furnished forthwith to any person who requests them.

[O. Reg. 15/95, s. 3]

11. [Repealed, O. Reg. 15/95, s. 4]

12. [Repealed, O. Reg. 616/00, s. 9]

Forms

13. (1) An application under subsection 15 (1) or (1.1) of the Act shall be in Form 1.

(2) An order under subsection 16 (1) or (1.1) of the Act shall be in Form 2.

(3) A certificate of involuntary admission shall be in Form 3.

(4) A certificate of renewal shall be in Form 4.

(5) An order under subsection 21 (1) of the Act shall be in Form 6.

(6) An order under subsection 22 (1) of the Act shall be in Form 8.

(7) An order to admit a person coming into Ontario under subsection 32 (1) of the Act shall be in Form 13.

(8) A community treatment order under subsection 33.1 (2) of the Act shall be in Form 45.

(9) An order for examination under subsection 33.3 (1) or 33.4 (3) of the Act shall be in Form 47.

(10) Where the Minister approves a form and requires its use under section 80.1 of the Act, the form shall be available on the Internet through the website of the Ministry of Health and Long-Term Care.

[O. Reg. 616/00, s. 10; 331/04, s. 4]

Rights Advice

14. (1) The Minister shall designate one or more persons or categories of persons to perform the functions of a rights adviser under the Act in each psychiatric facility designated as an institution under the *Mental Hospitals Act* and may revoke such a designation.

(2) A psychiatric facility that is not an institution under the *Mental Hospitals Act* shall designate one or more persons or categories of persons to perform the functions of a rights adviser under the Act in the facility.

(3) A psychiatric facility acting under subsection (2) may designate a person or persons or a category of persons designated by the Minister under subsection (1) but on doing so the facility shall inform the Minister of the designation.

(4) A psychiatric facility may revoke a designation made under subsection (3).

(5) A designation or revocation by a psychiatric facility shall be made on its behalf by the officer in charge.

[O. Reg. 616/00, s. 11]

14.1 The Minister shall designate one or more persons or categories of persons to perform the functions of a rights adviser under the Act with respect to a person who is being considered for the issuance or renewal of a community treatment order where the person is not a patient in a psychiatric facility and may revoke such a designation.

[O. Reg. 616/00, s. 11]

14.2 Only persons who meet the following requirements may be designated to perform the functions of a rights adviser under the Act whether in a psychiatric facility or with respect to a person who is being considered for the issuance or renewal of a community treatment order:

1. The person must be knowledgeable about the rights to apply to the Board provided under the Act, the *Health Care Consent Act, 1996*, and the *Personal Health Information Protection Act, 2004*;
2. The person must be knowledgeable about the workings of the Board, how to contact the Board and how to make applications to the Board.
3. The person must be knowledgeable about how to obtain legal services.
4. The person must have the communications skills necessary to perform effectively the functions of a rights adviser under the Act.
5. The person must have successfully completed a training course for rights advisers approved by the Minister and have been certified as having completed such a course.

[O. Reg. 616/00, s. 11; 331/04, s. 5]

14.3 (1) A physician who is considering issuing or renewing a community treatment order for a person under section 33.1 of the Act shall give notice of his or her intention in the approved form to the person, the person's substitute decision-maker, if any, and to a rights adviser.

(2) A rights adviser who receives notice under subsection (1) shall promptly,

(a) provide rights advice to the person unless the person refuses the provision of rights advice;

(b) provide rights advice to the person's substitute decision-maker, if any.

(3) The rights adviser shall explain to the person and the substitute decision-maker, if any, the requirements for the issuance or renewal of a community treatment order, the significance of such an order, including any obligations that the person or the substitute decision-maker may be required to meet under the order.

(4) Where a rights adviser who receives notice under subsection (1) believes that it is in the best interest of the person to receive rights advice from another rights adviser, he or she shall ensure that a second rights adviser provides such advice.

(5) Where a rights adviser provides rights advice to the person and the substitute decision-maker, if any, the rights adviser shall promptly provide confirmation of that fact to the physician in the approved form.

(6) Where a person refuses the provision of rights advice, the rights adviser shall promptly provide confirmation of that fact to the physician in the approved form.

[O. Reg. 616/00, s. 11]

Rights Advice for Patients Found Incapable with Respect to Treatment of a Mental Disorder

15. (1) If a person who has been admitted to a psychiatric facility as a patient is 14 years old or older and if the person's attending physician proposes treatment of a mental disorder of the person and finds that the person is incapable with respect to the treatment within the meaning of the *Health Care Consent Act, 1996*, the attending physician shall ensure that,

(a) the person is promptly given a written notice indicating that he or she has been found by the attending physician to be incapable with respect to the treatment; and

(b) a rights adviser is promptly notified of the finding of incapacity.

(2) A rights adviser who is notified of a finding of incapacity shall promptly meet with the person who has been found incapable and shall explain to the person the significance of the finding and the right to apply to the Board under the *Health Care Consent Act, 1996* for a review of the finding.

(3) Subsection (2) does not apply if the person who has been found incapable refuses to meet with the rights adviser.

(4) At the request of the person who has been found incapable, the rights adviser shall assist him or her in applying to the Board under the *Health Care Consent Act, 1996* for a review of the finding and in obtaining legal services.

(5) This section does not apply if,

(a) the person has a guardian of the person appointed under the *Substitute Decisions Act, 1992* who has authority to give or refuse consent to the treatment;

(b) the person has an attorney under a power of attorney for personal care given under the *Substitute Decisions Act, 1992*, the power of attorney contains a provision waiving the person's right to apply to the Board for a review of the finding of incapacity and the provision is effective under subsection 50 (1) of the *Substitute Decisions Act, 1992*;

(c) the person is in a coma, is unconscious, is semi-conscious or is unable to communicate comprehensibly despite reasonable efforts to understand the person; or

(d) the attending physician is of the opinion that there is an emergency within the meaning of subsection 25 (1) of the *Health Care Consent Act, 1996*.

(6) If a rights adviser has met with a person who was admitted to a psychiatric facility and was found incapable with respect to a treatment of a mental disorder,

and if the rights adviser has provided the person with the explanation required by subsection (2), this section does not apply to any subsequent finding of incapacity made in respect of the person during his or her stay in the facility pursuant to that admission, whether the subsequent finding is made in relation to the same treatment or a different treatment.

[O. Reg. 103/96, s. 3]

Rights Advice for Patients Determined Incapable of Consenting to the Collection, Use or Disclosure of Personal Health Information under the Personal Health Information Protection Act, 2004

15.1 (1) If a person who has been admitted to a psychiatric facility as a patient is 14 years old or older and if the officer in charge of the psychiatric facility determines that the person is incapable of consenting to a collection, use or disclosure of personal health information within the meaning of the *Personal Health Information Protection Act, 2004*, the officer in charge of the psychiatric facility shall ensure that,

(a) the person is promptly given a written notice indicating that he or she has been determined, by the officer in charge, incapable of consenting to the collection, use or disclosure of his or her personal health information; and

(b) a rights adviser is promptly notified of the determination of incapacity.

(2) A rights adviser who is notified of a determination of incapacity shall promptly meet with the person who has been determined to be incapable and shall explain to the person the significance of the determination and the right to apply to the Board for a review of the determination under subsection 22 (3) of the *Personal Health Information Protection Act, 2004* and, where the patient is 16 years old or older, that the patient has the right to apply to the Board for appointment of a representative as set out in subsection 27 (1) of that Act.

(3) Subsection (2) does not apply if the person who has been determined to be incapable refuses to meet with the rights adviser.

(4) At the request of the person who has been determined to be incapable, the rights adviser shall assist him or her in applying to the Board for a review of the determination, for appointment of a representative or in obtaining legal services.

(5) This section does not apply if,

(a) the person has a guardian of the person or a guardian of property appointed under the *Substitute Decisions Act, 1992* who has authority, on behalf of the person, to give or refuse consent to the collection, use or disclosure of personal health information;

(b) the person has an attorney under a power of attorney for personal care given under the *Substitute Decisions Act, 1992*, the power of attorney contains a provision waiving the person's right to apply to the Board for a review of the determination of incapacity and the provision is effective under subsection 50 (1) of that Act;

(c) the person is in a coma, is unconscious, is semi-conscious or is unable to communicate comprehensibly despite reasonable efforts to understand the person; or

(d) the attending physician is of the opinion that there is an emergency.

(6) If a rights adviser has met with a person who was admitted to a psychiatric facility and was determined to be incapable of consenting to the collection, use or disclosure of personal health information, and if the rights adviser has provided the person with the explanation required by subsection (2), this section does not apply to any subsequent determination of incapacity with respect to collection, use or disclosure of personal health information made in respect of the person during his or her stay in the facility pursuant to that admission.

[O. Reg. 331/04, s. 6]

Explanation by Rights Advisers

16. (1) A rights adviser fulfils his or her obligation under this Regulation to explain a matter to a person if the rights adviser explains the matter to the best of his or her ability and in a manner that addresses the person's special needs, even if the person does not understand the explanation.

(2) In circumstances other than those described in subsections 14.3 (5) and (6), where a rights adviser is required to explain a matter to a person under the Act, he or she shall provide confirmation that the explanation has been given to the attending physician or the officer in charge, as the case may be, in the approved form.

[O. Reg. 103/96, s. 3; O. Reg. 616/00, s. 12]

SCHEDULES 1-5 Repealed: O. Reg. 616/00, s. 13.

GRANTS

(R.R.O. 1990, Reg. 742)

1. Where provincial aid is paid under the Act, it shall be paid in accordance with this Regulation.

Part I

Operating Grant Assistance

2. (1) Subject to subsection (3), provincial aid in the form of operating grant assistance to a psychiatric facility shall not exceed an amount equivalent to the reasonable cost as determined by the Minister of providing,

(a) general maintenance, including light, heat and power;

(b) administration;

(c) depreciation on furniture, equipment and apparatus;

(d) patient care including salaries, supplies and equipment, including the expense of,

- (i) the office of the officer-in-charge,
- (ii) radiology and laboratory examinations,
- (iii) patient records,
- (iv) dietary services,
- (v) housekeeping, and
- (vi) the laundry;

(e) depreciation on buildings owned by the psychiatric facility or depreciation on leasehold improvements to buildings leased by the psychiatric facility other than those buildings or improvements for which capital grant assistance has been paid by the Minister under Part II;

(f) interest due or payable on debts incurred by a psychiatric facility other than long term debts on all or part of the actual cost of a building project for which capital grant assistance has been paid by the Minister under Part II; and

(g) rental payments made by a psychiatric facility for the use of real property.

(2) Subject to subsection (3) and despite subsection (1), a psychiatric facility may be paid provincial aid in addition to the provincial aid paid under subsection (1), not to exceed an amount equivalent to a reasonable allowance as determined by the Minister representing a return on funds expended by the psychiatric facility to acquire assets other than funds expended to finance all or part of the actual cost

of a building project for which capital grant assistance has been paid by the Minister under Part II.

(3) There shall be deducted from the provincial aid payable to a psychiatric facility under subsections (1) and (2) the following revenue received by the psychiatric facility,

(a) 75 per cent of all money received from charitable and benevolent organizations and individual endorsements and bequests for purposes ordinarily a part of the routine operations of the psychiatric facility; and

(b) all other money received by the psychiatric facility from any source other than operating grant assistance received under subsection (1).

3. (1) Every psychiatric facility shall annually prepare and submit to the Minister a budget estimate of the costs and revenue referred to in section 2 including particulars of the services it proposes to offer and the estimated costs thereof.

(2) A psychiatric facility may submit an amendment to the budget estimate supplied to the Minister under subsection (1).

4. (1) Operating grant assistance paid under section 2 may be paid in monthly instalments in advance, subject to final adjustments upon the receipt of annual financial statements audited by a licensed public accountant for the period during which advance payments have been made.

(2) The annual financial statements referred to in subsection (1) shall be supplied by a psychiatric facility within a reasonable time of a written request by the Minister being received by the psychiatric facility and the financial statements shall include particulars of the revenue referred to in subsection 2 (3).

5. Operating grant assistance may be paid under section 2 in respect of non-residential treatment and urban re-entry programs.

Part II

Capital Grant Assistance

6. In this Part,

"approved cost" means that portion of the actual cost of a building project of a psychiatric facility approved by the Minister, and includes,

(a) fees that are approved by the Minister and paid to an architect for his or her services and the services of his or her consulting engineers,

(b) fees that are approved by the Minister for consultants, other than those paid through the architect,

(c) necessary equipment and furnishings and the installation thereof,

(d) land surveys and soil tests, and

(e) necessary paving and sodding,

but does not include,

(f) initial supplies,

(g) financing charges,

(h) working capital and pre-opening expenses,

(i) contingency allowances,

(j) landscaping, gardens, works of art, murals, busts, statues and similar decorations, or

(k) facilities for ancillary revenue-producing operations;

"balance of the cost" means the remainder after deducting the amount of the grant from the actual cost of the building project;

"building project" means,

(a) the acquisition of existing buildings and alterations or additions thereto,

(b) the construction of a new building or buildings excluding demolition of existing buildings and other clearance of site, and

(c) the renovation or alteration of existing buildings.

7. The amount of capital grant assistance that may be paid by the Minister shall be two-thirds of the approved cost of the building project.

8. Despite section 7, the amount of capital grant assistance that may be paid by the Minister shall be the full approved cost of the building project where the project is undertaken solely to provide services for children in the following psychiatric facilities:

1	Hamilton	Chedoke Child and Family Care Centre
2	Ottawa	Royal Ottawa Hospital Regional Children's Centre
3	Sudbury	Sudbury Algoma Hospital Regional Children's Centre
4	Windsor	Western Hospital Centre

9. (1) An application for capital grant assistance shall be made to the Minister and shall set out such information as the Minister may require.

(2) An application for capital grant assistance shall be accompanied by a preliminary sketch plan in triplicate showing any existing buildings acquired or proposed to be acquired for the purpose of the building project and the alterations necessary thereto or showing the new construction, additions or alterations, as the case may be.

(3) No tenders shall be called for any proposed new construction, additions or alterations until the Minister is satisfied and so advises in writing that the total funds required for the completion of the building project, including capital grant assistance, will be available.

10. No capital grant assistance shall be paid unless,

(a) the building project has been approved by the Minister;

(b) the applicant undertakes that it will not, without the consent of the Minister,

(i) sell, mortgage or otherwise dispose of the psychiatric facility or any part thereof,

(ii) use the psychiatric facility for any other purpose than that for which the grant is made, or

(iii) make any alterations or additions to any building forming part of the psychiatric facility; and

(c) in the case of a non-profit organization, the non-profit organization undertakes to pay the balance of the cost of the project.

11. (1) Capital grant assistance shall be paid as follows:

1. One-fifth when the contract for the building project is signed.
2. One-tenth when one-eighth of the work is completed.
3. One-tenth when one-quarter of the work is completed.
4. One-tenth when three-eighths of the work is completed.
5. One-tenth when one-half of the work is completed.
6. One-tenth when five-eighths of the work is completed.
7. One-tenth when three-quarters of the work is completed.
8. One-tenth when seven-eighths of the work is completed.
9. The balance when the work is completed to the satisfaction of the Minister.

(2) No payment shall be made under subsection (1) unless a member of the Ontario Association of Architects certifies or the Minister is otherwise satisfied that the proper proportion of the work has been completed.

SUMMARY OF FORMS

Form 1	- Application by Physician for Psychiatric Assessment (Regulated)
Form 2	- Order for Examination under Section 16 (Regulated)
Form 3	- Certificate of Involuntary Admission (Regulated)
Form 4	- Certificate of Renewal (Regulated)
Form 5	- Change to Informal or Voluntary Status Subsection 20(7) of the Act (Approved)
Form 6	- Order for Attendance for Examination Subsection 21(1) of the Act, (Regulated)
Form 7	- Confirmation by Attending Physician of Continued Involuntary Status under Subsection 48(12) of the Act (Approved)
Form 8	- Order for Admission, Subsection 22(1) of the Act (Regulated)
Form 9	- Order for Return, Subsection 28(1) of the Act (Approved)
Form 10	- Memorandum of Transfer, Subsection 29(1) of the Act (Approved)
Form 11	- Transfer to a Public Hospital, Subsection 30(1) of the Act (Approved)
Form 12	- Warrant for Transfer from Ontario to Another Jurisdiction
Form 13	- Order to Admit a Person Coming into Ontario (Regulated) [Note: Form 13 is a "View only" form; see http://www.health.gov.on.ca/english/public/forms/form_menus/mental_fm.html]
Form 15	- Statement by Attending Physician under Subsection 35(6) of the Act (Approved)
Form 16	- Application to the Board to Review a Patient's Involuntary Status under Subsection 39(1) of the Act (Approved)
Form 17	- Notice to the Board of the Need to Schedule a Mandatory Review of a Patient's Involuntary Status under Subsection 39(4) of the Act (Approved)
Form 18	- Application to the Board to Review a Finding of Incapacity to Manage Property under section 60 of the Act (Approved)
Form 21	- Certificate of Incapacity to Manage One's Property under Subsection 54(4) of the Act (Approved)
Form 22	- Financial Statement - Section 55 of the Act (Approved)
Form 23	- Notice of Cancellation of Certificate of Incapacity to Manage One's Property under Section 56 of the Act (Approved)
Form 24	- Notice of Continuance of Certificate of Incapacity to Manage One's Own Property under Subsection 57(2) of the Act (Approved)
Form 25	- Application to the Board to Review the Status of an Informal Patient who is a Child between 12 and 15 Years of Age under Subsection 13(1) of the Act (Approved)
Form 26	- Notice to the Board of the Need to Schedule a Mandatory Review of the Status of an Informal Patient who is a Child between 12 and 15 Years of Age under Subsection 13(2) of the Act (Approved)

Form 27 - Notice by Officer-in-Charge to a Child who is between 12 and 15 Years of Age, who is an Informal Patient under Subsection 38(6) of the Act (Approved)

Form 28 - Request to Examine or to Copy Clinical Record under Subsections 36(2) and (16) of the Act (Approved)

Form 29 - Application to the Board to Withhold All or Part of the Clinical Record under Subsection 36(4) of the Act (Approved)

Form 30 - Notice to Patient under Subsection 38(1) of the Act (Approved)

Form 31 - Application to the Board to Review a Patient's Competency to Examine/Disclose his or her Clinical Record under Subsection 36(14) of the Act (Approved)

Form 33 - Notice to Patient under Subsections 38(4) and 59(1) of the Act and under Clause 15(1) (a) of Regulation 741 (Approved)

Form 36 - Notice under Subsection 36.1(4) of the Act of Right to Appoint a Representative (Approved)

Form 40 - Notice to Patient of Right to Apply to the Board for an Appointment of a Representative under Subsection 36.2(2) of the Act (Approved)

Form 41 - Application to the Board to Appoint a Representative under Subsection 36.2(1) of the Act (Approved)

Form 42 - Notice to Person under Subsection 38.1 of the Act of Application for Psychiatric Assessment under Section 15 or an Order under Section 32 of the Act (Approved)

Form 44 - Appointment of a Representative under Subsection 36.1 of the Act

Form 45 - Community Treatment Order (Regulated)

Form 46 - Notice to Person of Issuance or Renewal of Community Treatment Order (Section 33.1(10)) (Approved)

Form 47 - Order for Examination Sections 33.3(1) and 33.4(3) of the Act (Regulated)

Form 48 - Application to Board to Review Community Treatment Order (s. 39.1(1)) and Notice to Board by Physician of Need to Schedule Mandatory Review of Community Treatment Order (s. 39.1(4)) (Approved)

Form 49 - Notice of Intention to Issue or Renew Community Treatment Order (section 33.1(4), section 33.1(8)) (Approved)

Form 50 - Confirmation of Rights Advice (Approved)

- Request for Correction in Clinical Record under section 36 of the *Mental Health Act*

- Statement of Disagreement with Clinical Record under Section 36 of the *Mental Health Act*.

Ministry of Health

Form 1
Mental Health Act

Application by Physician for Psychiatric Assessment

Name of physician ______________________ (print name of physician)

Physician address ______________________ (address of physician)

Telephone number ( ) ______________ Fax number ( ) ______________

On ____________ (date) I personally examined ______________________ (print full name of person)

whose address is ______________________ (home address)

*You may only sign this **Form 1** if you have personally examined the person within the past seven days. In deciding if a Form 1 is appropriate, you must complete **either** Box A (serious harm test) **or** Box B (persons who are incapable of consenting to treatment and meet the specified criteria test) below.*

Box A – Section 15(1) of the Mental Health Act
Serious Harm Test

The Past / Present Test *(check one or more)*

I have reasonable cause to believe that the person:

☐ has threatened or is threatening to cause bodily harm to himself or herself
☐ has attempted or is attempting to cause bodily harm to himself or herself
☐ has behaved or is behaving violently towards another person
☐ has caused or is causing another person to fear bodily harm from him or her; or
☐ has shown or is showing a lack of competence to care for himself or herself

I base this belief on the following information *(you may, as appropriate in the circumstances, rely on any combination of your own observations and information communicated to you by others.)*
My own observations:

Facts communicated to me by others:

The Future Test *(check one or more)*

I am of the opinion that the person is apparently suffering from mental disorder of a nature or quality that likely will result in:

☐ serious bodily harm to himself or herself,
☐ serious bodily harm to another person,
☐ serious physical impairment of himself or herself

6427–41 (00/12) *(Disponible en version française)* *See reverse* 7530–4972

MENTAL HEALTH ACT

Box A – Section 15(1) of the Mental Health Act
Serious Harm Test *(continued)*

I base this opinion on the following information *(you may, as appropriate in the circumstances, rely on any combination of your own observations and information communicated to you by others.)*

My own observations:

Facts communicated by others:

Box B – Section 15(1.1) of the Mental Health Act
Patients who are Incapable of Consenting to Treatment and Meet the Specified Criteria

Note: The patient *must* meet the criteria set out in *each* of the following conditions.

I have reasonable cause to believe that the person:

1. Has previously received treatment for mental disorder of an ongoing or recurring nature that, when not treated, is of a nature or quality that likely will result in one or more of the following: *(please indicate one or more)*
   - ☐ serious bodily harm to himself or herself,
   - ☐ serious bodily harm to another person,
   - ☐ substantial mental or physical deterioration of himself or herself, or
   - ☐ serious physical impairment of himself or herself;

AND

2. Has shown clinical improvement as a result of the treatment.

AND

I am of the opinion that the person,

3. Is incapable, within the meaning of the *Health Care Consent Act, 1996,* of consenting to his or her treatment in a psychiatric facility and the consent of his or her substitute decision-maker has been obtained;

AND

4. Is apparently suffering from the same mental disorder as the one for which he or she previously received treatment or from a mental disorder that is similar to the previous one;

(Disponible en version française)

6427-41 (00/12) 7530-4972

Box B – Section 15(1.1) of the Mental Health Act
Patients who are Incapable of Consenting to Treatment and Meet the Specified Criteria
(continued)

AND

5. Given the person's history of mental disorder and current mental or physical condition, is likely to: *(choose one or more of the following)*

- ☐ cause serious bodily harm to himself or herself, or
- ☐ cause serious bodily harm to another person, or
- ☐ suffer substantial mental or physical deterioration, or
- ☐ suffer serious physical impairment

I base this opinion on the following information *(you may, as appropriate in the circumstances, rely on any combination of your own observations and information communicated to you by others.)*

My own observations:

Facts communicated by others:

I have made careful inquiry into all the facts necessary for me to form my opinion as to the nature and quality of the person's mental disorder. I hereby make application for a psychiatric assessment of the person named.

Today's date ______________________ Today's time ______________________

Examining physician's signature ______________________
(signature of physician)

This form authorizes, for a period of 7 days including the date of signature, the apprehension of the person named and his or her detention in a psychiatric facility for a maximum of 72 hours.

For Use at the Psychiatric Facility

Once the period of detention at the psychiatric facility begins, the attending physician should note the date and time this occurs and must promptly give the person a Form 42.

______________________ ______________________
(Date and time detention commences) (signature of physician)

______________________ ______________________
(Date and time Form 42 delivered) (signature of physician)

(Disponible en version française)

6427-41 (00/12) 7530-4972

MENTAL HEALTH ACT

Ministry of Health

Form 2
Mental Health Act

Order for Examination under Section 16

To the police officers of Ontario.

Whereas information upon oath has been brought before me, a justice of the peace in and for the province of Ontario

by ____________________
(print full name of person bringing information)

of ____________________
(address of person bringing information)

in respect of ____________________
(print full name or other description of person to be examined)

of ____________________
(home address, if known)

Part A or Part B must be completed

Part A – Subsection 16 (1)

Information has been brought before me that such person

☐ has threatened or attempted or is threatening or attempting to cause bodily harm to himself or herself;

☐ has behaved or is behaving violently towards another person or has caused or is causing another person to fear bodily harm from him or her; or

☐ has shown or is showing a lack of competence to care for himself or herself.

In addition based upon the information before me I have reasonable cause to believe that the person is apparently suffering from mental disorder of a nature or quality that likely will result in,

☐ serious bodily harm to the person;

☐ serious bodily harm to another person, or

☐ serious physical impairment of the person.

Part B – Subsection 16 (1.1)

Information has been brought before me that such person

a) has previously received treatment for mental disorder of an ongoing or recurring nature that, when not treated, is of a nature or quality that likely will result in serious bodily harm to the person or to another person or substantial mental or physical deterioration of the person or serious physical impairment of the person; and

b) has shown clinical improvement as a result of the treatment;

In addition based upon the information before me I have reasonable cause to believe that the person,

c) is apparently suffering from the same mental disorder as the one for which he or she previously received treatment or from a mental disorder that is similar to the previous one;

6428–41 (00/12) 7530–4973

Part B *(continued)*

d) given the person's history of mental disorder and current mental or physical condition, is likely to

☐ cause serious bodily harm to himself or herself;
☐ cause serious bodily harm to another person,
☐ suffer substantial mental or physical deterioration of the person, or
☐ suffer serious physical impairment of the person; and

e) is apparently incapable within the meaning of the *Health Care Consent Act*, 1996 of consenting to his or her treatment in a psychiatric facility and the consent of his or her substitute decision-maker has been obtained.

Now therefore, I order you, the said police officers, or any of you, to take the said person in custody forthwith to an appropriate place for examination by a physician.

____
(date of signature)

____
(Municipality where order signed)

____
(signature of Justice of the Peace)

____
(print name of Justice of the Peace)

6428-41 (00/12) 7530-4973

Notes for Applicant / Informant

1. You may wish to provide your telephone number on this form so that you can be contacted by the police or the examining physician after this order is issued. This is entirely voluntary. ***You are not required to give this information for the order to be issued or for the order to be legally valid.***

____________________ (print name)   ____________________ (telephone number)

2. You may wish to seek legal advice concerning this order, including the effect of this order and your legal rights.

3. You may wish to inform the police, the examining physician and/or an appropriate health care professional of the evidence you gave to the justice of peace, if you consider it appropriate in all the circumstances to do so. If you decide to do so, please use the space provided below. Use the back of this form if necessary. ***You are not required to give this information for the order to be issued or for the order to be legally valid.***

6428-41 (00/12)   7530-4973

Ministry of Health

Form 3
Mental Health Act

Certificate of Involuntary Admission

Name of patient ______________________ (print name of patient)

Name of physician ______________________ (print name of physician)

Name of psychiatric facility ______________________ (name of psychiatric facility)

Date of examination ______________ (date)

I hereby certify that the following three pieces of information are correct:

1. I personally examined the patient on the date set out above.
2. I am of the opinion that the patient named above is not suitable for voluntary or informal status.
3. Complete one or more boxes as appropriate.

☐ I am of the opinion that the patient named above meets the criteria set out in Box A. *(please complete Box A below)*

☐ I am of the opinion that the patient named above meets each of the criteria set out in Box B. *(please complete Box B below)*

Box A – Risk of Serious Harm

Note: Check one or more boxes as appropriate.

The patient is suffering from mental disorder of a nature or quality that likely will result in:

☐ serious bodily harm to the patient,

☐ serious bodily harm to another person

☐ serious physical impairment of the patient

unless he or she remains in the custody of a psychiatric facility.

Box B – Patients who are Incapable of Consenting to Treatment and Meet the Specified Criteria

Note: The patient *must* meet *all* of the following five criteria.

1. The patient has been found incapable, within the meaning of the *Health Care Consent Act, 1996* of consenting to his or her treatment in a psychiatric facility and the consent of his or her substitute decision-maker has been obtained.
2. The patient has previously received treatment for mental disorder of an ongoing or recurring nature that, when not treated, is of a nature or quality that likely will result in one or more of the following: *(please indicate one or more)*

☐ serious bodily harm to the patient,

☐ serious bodily harm to another person,

☐ substantial mental or physical deterioration of the patient, or

☐ serious physical impairment of the patient;

(Disponible en version française)

See reverse.

6429-41 (00/12) 7530-4974

MENTAL HEALTH ACT

Box B – Patients who are Incapable of Consenting to Treatment and Meet the Specified Criteria *(continued)*

3. The patient has shown clinical improvement as a result of the treatment.

4. The patient is suffering from the same mental disorder as the one for which he or she previously received treatment or from a mental disorder that is similar to the previous one.

5. Given the person's history of mental disorder and current mental or physical condition, is likely to: *(please indicate one or more)*

☐ cause serious bodily harm to himself or herself, or
☐ cause serious bodily harm to another person, or
☐ suffer substantial mental or physical deterioration, or
☐ suffer serious physical impairment

(Date of signature) (signature of attending physician)

Notes

1) This certificate is valid for *14 calendar days*, including the day upon which it was signed.

2) The following actions must be taken promptly after this form is signed:

a) The signing physician must give the patient a properly executed Form 30 notice and notify a rights adviser.

b) The rights adviser must meet with the patient and explain to him or her the significance of the certificate and the right to have it reviewed by the Consent and Capacity Board.

(Disponible en version française)

6429–41 (00/12) 7530–4974

Ministry of Health

Form 4
Mental Health Act

Certificate of Renewal

Name of patient ______________________
(print name of patient)

Name of physician ______________________
(print name of physician)

Name of psychiatric facility ______________________
(name of psychiatric facility)

Date of examination ______________________
(date)

The person's status at the psychiatric facility is that he/she is

☐ an involuntary patient subject to a Certificate of Involuntary Admission which expires on

______________________ or
(date)

☐ an involuntary patient subject to an existing Certificate of Renewal which expires on

____
(date)

You must complete one or more of Box A or Box B for this form to be valid.

Box A

You must be satisfied that both criteria are met.

I am of the opinion that

1. The patient is suffering from mental disorder of a nature or quality that likely will result in:
(choose one or more of the following)

☐ serious bodily harm to the patient,

☐ serious bodily harm to another person,

☐ serious physical impairment of the patient,

unless he or she remains in the custody of a psychiatric facility; and

2. The patient is not suitable for continuation as an informal or voluntary patient.

MENTAL HEALTH ACT

(Disponible en version française)

See reverse

6430-41 (00/12)

7530-4975

Box B

You must be satisfied that all six criteria are met.

I am of the opinion that

1. the patient has been found incapable, within the meaning of the *Health Care Consent Act, 1996* of consenting to his or her treatment in a psychiatric facility and the consent of his or her substitute decision-maker has been obtained,

AND

2. the patient has previously received treatment for mental disorder of an ongoing or recurring nature that, when not treated, is of a nature or quality that likely will result in *(choose one or more of the following)*

   ☐ serious bodily harm to the patient,

   ☐ serious bodily harm to another person,

   ☐ substantial mental or physical deterioration of the patient, or

   ☐ serious physical impairment of the patient,

AND

3. has shown clinical improvement as a result of the treatment,

AND

4. is suffering from the same mental disorder as the one for which he or she previously received treatment or from a mental disorder that is similar to the previous one,

AND

5. given the patient's history of mental disorder and current mental or physical condition, is likely to *(choose one or more of the following)*

   ☐ cause serious bodily harm to himself or herself,

   ☐ cause serious bodily harm to another person,

   ☐ suffer substantial mental or physical deterioration,

   ☐ suffer serious physical impairment;

AND

6. the patient is not suitable for continuation as an informal or voluntary patient.

This is a ____________________ Certificate of Renewal.

This certificate is effective on the date that it is signed and expires on ____________________
(Date) (day / month / year)

____________________ (Date of signature)

____________________ (signature of attending physician)

(Disponible en version française)

6430-41 (00/12) 7530-4975

Ministry of Health

Form 5
Mental Health Act

Change to Informal or Voluntary Status Subsection 20(7) of the Act

I, ______________________________ the undersigned
(print name of physician)

attending physician, hereby terminate the involuntary status of

____
(print full name of patient)

____
(print name of psychiatric facility)

who shall now be continued as an informal or voluntary patient.

I last examined the patient on ______________ .
(date)

The most recent Certificate of Involuntary Admission or Certificate Renewal with regards to this patient was signed on ______________ .
(date)

The decision to terminate the involuntary status of the patient is based on the following factors:

____

Date ______________________________
(day / month / year)

____
(signature of attending physician)

1972–41 (00/12)* 7530–4538

MENTAL HEALTH ACT

Ministry of Health

Form 6
Mental Health Act

Order for Attendance for Examination
Subsection 21(1) of the Act

In the ______________ (name of court) held at ______________ (address)

____

TO ______________ (name of psychiatric facility)

WHEREAS ______________ (name of person in full)

______________ (address)

Strike out inapplicable words | is charged with / has been convicted of ______________ (offence)

contrary to section ______________ of the ______________;

AND WHEREAS he/she has appeared before me and I have reason to believe that he/she suffers from mental disorder;

AND WHEREAS I have ascertained from

______________ (name of senior physician, as defined in the Act)

the senior physician of ______________ (name of psychiatric facility)

that the services of the said psychiatric facility are available to the above-named person;

I HEREBY ORDER that the above-named person attend, by appointment, the said psychiatric facility for examination;

______________ (Judge)

Date ______________ (day / month / year)

1970-41 (00/12)*  7530-4539

Ministry of Health

Form 7
Mental Health Act

Confirmation by Attending Physician of Continued Involuntary Status under Subsection 48(12) of the Act

To: ______________________ (name of officer-in-charge) of ______________________ (name of psychiatric facility)

I, ______________________ (name of physician), am the attending physician of

______________________ (name of involuntary patient) who is detained at this facility

under the authority of a Form ____________ (Form 3 or 4) under the *Mental Health Act.*

The patient's involuntary status was ______________________ (confirmed or rescinded) by the Board on

______________________ (date of decision) (day / month / year) and the ______________________ (patient or physician) is appealing this decision.

I hereby confirm that I examined ______________________ (name of patient) on ____________ (date).

Part A and/or Part B must be completed

Part A

I am of the opinion that

a) the patient is suffering from mental disorder of a nature or quality that likely will result in,

- ☐ serious bodily harm to the patient,
- ☐ serious bodily harm to another person,
- ☐ serious physical impairment of the patient,

unless the patient remains in the custody of a psychiatric facility; and

b) that the patient is not suitable for admission or continuation as an informal or voluntary patient.

Part B

I am of the opinion that

a) the patient has previously received treatment for mental disorder of an ongoing or recurring nature that, when not treated, is of a nature or quality that likely will result in

- ☐ serious bodily harm to the patient,
- ☐ serious bodily harm to another person,
- ☐ substantial mental or physical deterioration of the patient, or
- ☐ serious physical impairment of the patient,

b) has shown clinical improvement as a result of the treatment;

c) is suffering from the same mental disorder as the one for which he or she previously received treatment or from a mental disorder that is similar to the previous one;

1977-41 (00/12) 7530-4540

MENTAL HEALTH ACT

Part B *(continued)*

d) given the patient's history of mental disorder and current mental or physical condition, the patient is likely to

☐ cause serious bodily harm to himself or herself,

☐ cause serious bodily harm to another person,

☐ suffer substantial mental or physical deterioration, or

☐ suffer serious physical impairment;

e) the patient has been found incapable, within the meaning of the Health Care Consent Act, 1996 of consenting to his or her treatment in a psychiatric facility and the consent of his or her substitute decision-maker has been obtained; and

f) the patient is not suitable for admission or continuation as an informal or voluntary patient.

This confirmation is effective on the ____________________ (day / month / year) and will expire on the ____________________ (day / month / year)

Date ______________________________ (day / month / year)

______________________________ (signature of attending physician)

______________________________ (print name of attending physician)

1977-41 (00/12) 7530-4540

Ministry of Health

Form 8
Mental Health Act

Order for Admission
Subsection 22(1) of the Act

In the ______________________ held at ______________________
(name of court) (address)

____

TO the Peace Officers in the ______________________ of ______________________

AND TO ____
(name of psychiatric facility)

WHEREAS ____
(name of person in full)

____
(address)

is a person in custody charged with ____
(offence)

contrary to section ______________ of the ______________________________;

AND WHEREAS he/she has appeared before me and I have reason to believe that he/she suffers from mental disorder;

AND WHEREAS I have ascertained from

____
(name of senior physician, as defined in the Act)

the senior physician of ____
(name of psychiatric facility)

that the services of the said psychiatric facility are available to the above-named person;

I HEREBY ORDER that the above-named person be remanded for admission as a patient to the said psychiatric facility for a period of not more than

____;

AND I FURTHER ORDER and direct you, the said Peace Officers, or any of you, to convey him/her to the said psychiatric facility;

AND I AUTHORIZE you, the authorities at the said psychiatric facility, to admit him/her in accordance with this order.

____
(Judge)

Date ____
(day / month / year)

1980–41 (00/12)* 7530–4541

MENTAL HEALTH ACT

Ministry of Health

Form 9
Mental Health Act

Order for Return
Subsection 28(1) of the Act

To: ______________________________

AND TO all or any Police Officers in the Province of Ontario.

WHEREAS ______________________________ is subject to detention as
(print full name of patient)

____

____

and is absent from ______________________________
(name of psychiatric facility)

AND WHEREAS the absence of such person without authorization became known to me on

______________________________ .
(date)

NOW THEREFORE I hereby direct and authorize you, or any of you, to return such person to the said psychiatric facility or to the psychiatric facility nearest to the place where such person is apprehended;

AND in the course of returning such person, you are authorized to detain such person in an appropriate place.

THIS ORDER shall have force until ______________________________ .
(date)

____
(Officer-in-Charge)

____
(print name of Officer-in-Charge)

____
(psychiatric facility)

Date ______________________________
(day / month / year)

6431–41 (00/12)* 7530–4976

Ministry of Health

Form 10
Mental Health Act

Memorandum of Transfer Subsection 29(1) of the Act

Upon the advice of his/her attending physician, I ______________________
(print name)

officer-in-charge of ______________________
(psychiatric facility)

hereby transfer ______________________
(print full name of patient)

____
(home address)

to ______________________
(psychiatric facility)

arrangements having been made with the officer-in-charge of that facility.

NOTE: The following portion of this memorandum **must** be completed:

Check A,B, or C

☐ A. The patient is an informal or voluntary one.

☐ B. The patient is the subject of an application for assessment. *(A copy of the document authorizing detention is attached to this memorandum).*

☐ C. The patient is an involuntary one. *(A copy of the document authorizing detention is attached to this memorandum).*

Check D,E, or F

☐ D. The property of the patient is under the management of an attorney under a power of attorney for property.

☐ E. The property of the patient is under the management of the Public Guardian and Trustee. *(attach a Certificate of Incapacity to Manage Property)*

☐ F. The property of the patient is under the management of a court appointed guardian *(other than the Public Guardian and Trustee)*

____
(name of attorney or court appointed guardian)

____
(signature of officer-in-charge)

Date ______________________
(day / month / year)

6432-41 (00/12)* 7530-4977

MENTAL HEALTH ACT

Ministry of Health

Form 11
Mental Health Act

Transfer to a Public Hospital
Subsection 30(1) of the Act

Upon the advice of his/her attending physician that

____
(name of patient in full)

____
(home address)

requires hospital treatment that cannot be supplied in this facility, I,

____

officer-in-charge of ______________________________
(psychiatric facility)

hereby transfer the said patient to ______________________________
(name of public hospital)

for such treatment.

Note:
Where the patient is subject to detention, a copy of the document authorizing such detention must accompany this document.

____
(signature of officer-in-charge)

Date ______________________________
(day / month / year)

1978–41 (00/12)* 7530–4544

Form 12

Mental Health Act

Warrant for Transfer from Ontario to Another Jurisdiction

TO ____

WHEREAS it appears to me that ______________________________
(name of patient in full)

____
(home address)

who is now a patient in ______________________________
(psychiatric facility)

has come or has been brought into Ontario from ______________________, and

(strike out inapplicble clause)

(a) his/her hospitalization is the responsibility of ______________.
(name of jurisdiction)

or

(b) it would be in his/her best interests to be hospitalized in

____
(name of jurisdiction)

AND WHEREAS the laws respecting hospitalization in ______________
(name of jurisdiction)

have been complied with, with necessary modifications.

NOW THEREFORE I hereby authorize you, the said ______________
to transfer him/her to ______________________________
(place of transfer)

____
(Minister of Health)

Date ____
day/month/year

Form 13

Order to Admit a Person Coming into Ontario

[Note: Form 13 is a "View only" form; see http://www.health.gov.on.ca/english/public/forms/form_menus/mental_fm.html]

Ministry of Health

Form 15
Mental Health Act

Statement by Attending Physician under Subsection 35(6) of the Act

I, ______________________________
(print name of physician)

am of the opinion that the disclosure, transmittal or examination of the clinical record or the following part of the clinical record, namely

____

____

compiled in ______________________________
(name of psychiatric facility)

in respect of ______________________________
(print full name of patient)

is likely to result in

- ☐ harm to the treatment or recovery of the said patient, or
- ☐ injury to the mental condition of a third person, or
- ☐ bodily harm to a third person.

____
(signature of physician)

Date ______________________________
(day / month / year)

6435–41 (00/12)*

7530–4980

Consent and Capacity Board

Form 16
Mental Health Act

Application to the Board to Review a Patient's Involuntary Status under Subsection 39(1) of the Act

Part I This section must be completed by all applicants

I, ____________________
(print full name of applicant)

apply to the Board for a hearing to determine whether or not ____________________
(print full name of patient)

who is a patient at ____________________
(name of psychiatric facility)

☐ is suffering from a mental disorder of a nature or quality that will likely result in serious bodily harm to the patient or another person or serious physical impairment of the patient, unless he or she remains as an involuntary patient in the custody of a psychiatric facility; or

☐ has previously received treatment for mental disorder of an ongoing or recurring nature that, when not treated, is of a nature or quality that likely will result in serious bodily harm to the patient, serious bodily harm to another person, substantial mental or physical deterioration of the patient, or serious physical impairment of the patient; has shown clinical improvement as a result of the treatment; is suffering from the same mental disorder as the one for which he or she previously received treatment or from a mental disorder that is similar to the previous one; given the patient's history of mental disorder and current mental or physical condition, the patient is likely to cause serious bodily harm to himself or herself, cause serious bodily harm to another person, suffer substantial mental or physical deterioration, or suffer serious physical impairment; the patient has been found incapable, within the meaning of the Health Care Consent Act, 1996 of consenting to his or her treatment in a psychiatric facility and the consent of his or her substitute decision-maker has been obtained; and the patient is not suitable for admission or continuation as an informal or voluntary patient.

____________________ (date) ____________________ (signature of applicant)

Part II This information is not required but will assist us in scheduling the hearing
(provide only information where known)

If the applicant is someone other than the patient, please provide an address and telephone number:

____________________ (address) ( ) ____________________ (telephone no.)

Please provide the name, telephone and fax numbers and any other information that will assist us in contacting the patient's attending physician:

____________________ (name) ( ) ____________________ (telephone no.) ( ) ____________________ (fax no.)

Name, telephone and fax numbers of a hospital official who may assist in arranging the hearing:

____________________ (name) ( ) ____________________ (telephone no.) ( ) ____________________ (fax no.)

6436-41 (00/12)* 7530-4981

MENTAL HEALTH ACT

Part II **This information is not required but will assist us in scheduling the hearing**
(provide only information where known) continued

Name, telephone and fax numbers of a lawyer or agent for the patient:

______________________ ( ) ______________ ( ) ______________
(name) (telephone no.) (fax no.)

Name, telephone and fax numbers of a lawyer or agent for the patient's attending physician:

______________________ ( ) ______________ ( ) ______________
(name) (telephone no.) (fax no.)

Send this form by fax to the Regional Office of the Board or call toll free at 1–800–461–2036 for assistance

6436–41 (00/12)* 7530–4981

Consent and Capacity Board

Form 17
Mental Health Act

Notice to the Board of the Need to Schedule a Mandatory Review of a Patient's Involuntary Status under Subsection 39(4) of the Act

Part I This section must be completed by all applicants

____
(name of psychiatric facility)

____
(print full name of patient)

A fourth certificate of renewal or a subsequent fourth certificate of renewal for the above-named patient was filed on the following date:

______________ ______________
(date) (signature of officer-in-charge)

Part II This information is not required but will assist us in scheduling the hearing
(provide only information where known)

Please provide the name, telephone and fax numbers and any other information that will assist us in contacting the patient's attending physician:

______________ ( ) ______________ ( ) ______________
(name) (telephone no.) (fax no.)

____

____

Name, telephone and fax numbers of a hospital official who may assist in arranging the hearing:

______________ ( ) ______________ ( ) ______________
(name) (telephone no.) (fax no.)

Name, telephone and fax numbers of a lawyer or agent for the patient:

______________ ( ) ______________ ( ) ______________
(name) (telephone no.) (fax no.)

Name, telephone and fax numbers of a lawyer or agent for the patient's attending physician:

______________ ( ) ______________ ( ) ______________
(name) (telephone no.) (fax no.)

Send this form by fax to the Regional Office of the Board or call toll free at 1–800–461–2036 for assistance

January 1, 1995

7219–41 (97/04)*

7530–4698

MENTAL HEALTH ACT

Consent and Capacity Board

Form 18
Mental Health Act

Application to the Board to Review a Finding of Incapacity to Manage Property under section 60 of the Act

Part I This section must be completed by all applicants

I, ______________________________
(print full name of patient)

apply to the Board for a hearing to determine whether or not I am capable of managing my property.

I am a patient at ______________________________
(name of psychiatric facility)

______________________ ______________________
(date) (signature of applicant)

Part II This information is not required but will assist us in scheduling the hearing
(provide only information where known)

Please provide the name, telephone and fax numbers and any other information that will assist us in contacting your attending physician:

______________________ ( ) ______________ ( ) ______________
(name) (telephone no.) (fax no.)

____

____

Name, telephone and fax numbers of a hospital official who may assist in arranging the hearing:

______________________ ( ) ______________ ( ) ______________
(name) (telephone no.) (fax no.)

Name, telephone and fax numbers of your lawyer or agent:

______________________ ( ) ______________ ( ) ______________
(name) (telephone no.) (fax no.)

Name, telephone and fax numbers of lawyer or agent for your attending physician:

______________________ ( ) ______________ ( ) ______________
(name) (telephone no.) (fax no.)

Send this form by fax to the Regional Office of the Board or call toll free at 1-800-461-2036 for assistance

6437-41 (96/03) 7530-4982

Forms 19 and 20 [Repealed, O. Reg. 15/95, s. 6]

Ministry
of
Health

Form 21
Mental Health Act

Certificate of Incapacity to Manage One's Property under Subsection 54(4) of the Act

Re: ____
(print full name of patient admitted to the psychiatric facility)

of ____
(home address)

I, ____
(print name of physician)

of ____
(name of psychiatric facility)

state that:

1. I examined the above-named patient on ______________________
(date) (day / mnth / year)

2. I observed the following facts indicating incapacity:

____

____

3. The following facts, if any, indicating incapacity were communicated to me by others:

____

____

4. I certify that the above-named patient is incapable to manage his/her property

______________________ (date) (day / mnth / year)

______________________ (signature of physician)

Note: *The physician shall promptly advise the patient of the certificate of incapacity by giving the patient a Form 33 and shall notify a right adviser.*

This form only applies in respect of a patient admitted to a psychiatric facility and not to an out-patient. Section 1 defines a "patient" as a person under observation, care and treatment in a psychiatric facility.

"Out-patient" means a person who is registered in a psychiatric facility for observation or treatment, or both but who is not admitted as a patient and is not the subject of an application for assessment.

A "psychiatric facility" means a facility for the observation, care and treatment of persons suffering from mental disorder and designated as such by the Minister.

6440-41 (00/12)*

7530-4985

MENTAL HEALTH ACT

Ministry of Health / Ministère de la Santé

Form 22
Mental Health Act
Formule nº 22
Loi sur la santé mentale

Financial Statement
Section 55 of the Act

État des finances
Article 55 de la Loi

1. Name of patient in full/Nom et prénoms du/de la malade :

2. Sex/Sexe :

3. Psychiatric facility/Établissement psychiatrique :

4. Residence *(street and number or lot and concession)*/Résidence *(numéro et rue ou lot et concession)* :

   (Municipality)/(Municipalité) :

   (County, etc. or district)/(Comté, etc. ou district) :

5. Length of residence in this municipality/Durée de résidence dans cette municipalité :

6. Date of birth/Date de naissance :

7. Place of birth/Lieu de naissance :

8. Citizenship/Citoyenneté :

9. Occupation/Profession :

10. Marital status/État matrimonial :

11. If married, give name and address of husband or wife/Si le/la malade est marié(e), nom et adresse du mari ou de l'épouse :

12. If not married, give name and address of spouse or partner, if applicable:
    Si le/la malade n'est pas marié(e), nom et adresse du conjoint ou partenaire, le cas échéant :

13. Give the name and address of next of kin:
    Nom et adresse du plus proche parent :

14. Give the names and ages of any dependants whom the patient has to support
    Nom et âge des personnes à la charge du/de la malade, le cas échéant :

15. Give patient's/Renseignements à l'égard du/de la malade :

    1. Social Insurance Number/Numéro d'assurance sociale :

    2. Health Card number/Numéro de carte Santé

6441-41 (00/12)* 7530-4986

3. If other medical insurance plan, state name of company and contract number
Si le/la malade est protégé(e) par un autre régime d'assurance-maladie, donner le nom de la compagnie et le numéro de la police :

4. Old Age Security Number/Numéro – sécurité de la vieillesse :

16. Name and address of employer/Nom et adresse de l'employeur :

Real Estate/Biens Immeubles

17. Property of patient, and mortgages or charges on same, if any;
Biens du/de la malade et hypothèques ou charges, le cas échéant, le grevant :

1. Number of lot, concession, township and county, etc.
Numéro du lot, concession, canton et comté, etc. :
2. Number of acres/Nombre d'acres :
3. Leasehold or freehold/Tenure à bail ou tenure franche :
4. Name and address of mortgagee, if any/Nom et adresse du créancier hypothécaire, le cas échéant :
5. Market value of property/Valeur marchande du bien :

18. If property of the patient has been rented, give the following information
Si le bien du/de la malade a été loué, donner les renseignements suivants :

1. Name of tenant/Nom du/de la locataire :
2. Particulars of tenancy, such as length and terms of lease
Détails relatifs à la location, (durée, conditions du bail) :
3. Is the lease in writing?/Le bail est-il par écrit?
4. If so, in whose possession is the document?/Si oui, personne en possession du document :
5. Give the address of such person/Adresse de cette personne :
6. To whom has the rent been paid?/Personne à qui a été versé le loyer :
7. To what date has the rent been paid?/Date jusqu' à laquelle le loyer a été payé :

19. **Life, accident, disability and income protection insurance**
Assurance-vie, accident, invalidité et protection du revenu

Name of the Company or Society Nom de la compagnie ou de la société	Number of Policy or Certificate Numéro de la police ou du certificat	Amount of insurance Montant de l'assurance	In whose possession is the policy? Qui est en possession de la police?	Is this group insurance? *(state yes or no)* S'agit-il d'une assurance collective? *oui ou non*

6441-41 (00/12)*

MENTAL HEALTH ACT

20. **Pension or superannuation/Retraite**
If patient receives pension or superannuation, etc., give particulars;
Si le/la malade touche des prestations de retraite, etc., donner des précisions :

Personal Estate/Biens Meubles

21. **Cash on hand, in bank accounts and safety deposits;**
Encaisse, dépôts bancaires et sommes dans des coffrets de sûreté :

1. Give name and address of person who is in possession of the cash:
Nom et adresse de la personne en possession de l'encaisse :
2. What is the amount?/Montant :
3. If deposited in a bank, give the name and address of the branch
Nom et adresse de la succursale bancaire où se trouvent les dépôts, le cas échéant :
4. In whose possession is the bank book?/Personne en possession du livret de banque :
5. State the amount in the bank account/Montant des dépôts bancaires :
6. If joint account, give name and address of joint owner:
S'il s'agit d'un compte en commun, nom et adresse de l'autre titulaire du compte :
7. If patient has a safety deposit box, give the location, name and address of person in possession of the keys;
Si le/la malade a un coffret de sûreté, emplacement du coffret et nom et adresse de la personne en possession des clés :

22. **Stocks, bonds and similar investments**
Actions, obligations et placements semblables

Name of security Nom de la valeur	Par value Montant nominal	In whose possession Personne qui en a la possession

23. **Personal property** *(give approximate values)*
Biens meubles *(valeur approximative)*

1. Farm implements/Instruments aratoires :
2. Stock in trade/Stock :
3. Livestock/Bétail :
4. Farm produce/Produits de la ferme :
5. Motor vehicles/Véhicules automobiles :
6. Other property or income *(if any)*/Autres biens ou revenus *(le cas échéant)* :

6441-41 (00/12)* 7530-4986

24. **Money secured by mortgage/Sommes d'argent garanties par une hypothèque**

1. Give the name and address of the mortgagors who have borrowed money from the patient, setting out in detail separately each mortgage:
   Nom et adresse des débiteurs hypothécaires qui ont emprunté de l'argent du/de malade *(donner des précisions relativement à chaque hypothèque) :*

2. State in whose possession the mortgages are, and the address of such person:
   Nom et adresse de la personne en possession des hypothèques :

25. **Book debts and promissory notes owing to the patient**
Comptes débiteurs et billets dus au/à la malade

1. Give the names and addresses of debtors/Nom et adresse des débiteurs :

2. State in whose possession the notes are, and the address of such person:
   Nom et adresse de le personne en possession des billets :

26. **Liabilities, if any, other than mortgage debts**
Dettes, le cas échéant, sauf les dettes hypothécaires

27. Does the patient have a will? ☐ yes/oui ☐ no/non
Le malade a-t-il(elle) un testament
If so, state in whose possession it is, and the address of such person.
Si oui, nom et adresse de la personne en possession du testament :

28. Does the patient have a power of attorney for property? ☐ yes/oui ☐ no/non
Le/la malade a-t-il/elle donné une procuration relative à ses biens?
If so, state whose possession it is, and the address of such person.
Si oui, nom et adresse de la personne qui en est possession.

29. Any other information relevant to the administration of the patient's financial affairs
Tout autre renseignement concernant la gestion des avoirs financiers du/de la malade

____
(Signature of the person completing the form/Signature de la personne qui a rempli la formule)

____
(print name of the person completing the form
Nom en caractères d'imprimerie de la personne qui a rempli la formule)

____
(address)/adresse)

____
(relationship to patient)/(Lien avec le/la malade)

Date/Fait le ____________________
(day / month / year / jour / mois / année)

6441-41 (00/12)*

Ministry of Health

Form 23
Mental Health Act

Notice of Cancellation of Certificate of Incapacity to Manage One's Property under Section 56 of the Act

Re: ______________________________
(print full name of patient)

of ______________________________
(home address)

I, ______________________________
(print name of physician)

of ______________________________
(name of psychiatric facility)

state that:

1. I examined the above-named patient on ______________________________
(day / month / year)

2. I hereby cancel the certificate of incapacity issued in respect of the above-named patient on

______________________________ ______________________________
(day / month / year) (signature of physician)

Note: The Officer-in-Charge shall transmit the notice of cancellation to the Public Guardian and Trustee.

6442-41 (00/12)* 7530-4987

Ministry
of
Health

Form 24
Mental Health Act

Notice of Continuance of Certificate of Incapacity to Manage One's Property under Subsection 57(2) of the Act

Re: ______________________________
(print full name of patient)

of ______________________________
(home address)

I, ______________________________
(print name of physician)

of ______________________________
(name of psychiatric facility)

state that:

1. I examined the above-named patient on ______________________________
(day / month / year)

2. I observed the following facts indicating incapacity:

____

____

3. The following facts, if any, indicating incapacity were communicated to me by others:

____

____

4. I am of the opinion that the above-named patient will not, upon discharge, be capable to manage his/her property.

______________________________ (day / month / year)

______________________________ (signature of physician)

Note:

1. *The physician shall promptly advise the patient of the notice of continuance by giving the patient a Form 33 and shall notify a right adviser.*

2. *The Officer-in-Charge shall transmit the Notice of Continuance to the Public Guardian and Trustee.*

6443–41 (00/12)*

7530–4988

MENTAL HEALTH ACT

Consent and Capacity Board

Form 25
Mental Health Act

Application to the Board to Review the Status of an Informal Patient who is a Child between 12 and 15 Years of Age under Subsection 13(1) of the Act

Part I This section must be completed by all applicants

My name is ____________________
(print full name of patient)

I am between 12 and 15 years old. ____________________
(date of birth, if known)

____
(home address)

I am an informal patient at ____________________
(name of psychiatric facility)

I have not applied for a review of my informal status during the last three months.

I apply to the Board for a hearing to determine whether I need observation, care and treatment in this psychiatric facility.

____________________ ____________________
(date) (signature of applicant)

Part II This information is not required but will assist us in scheduling the hearing
(provide only information where known)

Please provide the name, telephone and fax numbers and any other information that will assist us in contacting your attending physician:

____________________ ( ) ____________ ( ) ____________
(name) (telephone no.) (fax no.)

____

____

Name, telephone and fax numbers of a hospital official who may assist in arranging the hearing:

____________________ ( ) ____________ ( ) ____________
(name) (telephone no.) (fax no.)

Name, telephone and fax numbers of your lawyer or agent:

____________________ ( ) ____________ ( ) ____________
(name) (telephone no.) (fax no.)

Name, telephone and fax numbers of a lawyer or agent for the patient's attending physician:

____________________ ( ) ____________ ( ) ____________
(name) (telephone no.) (fax no.)

Send this form by fax to the Regional Office of the Board or call toll free at 1–800–461–2036 for assistance January 1, 1995

1065–41 (96/12)* 7530–4153

Consent and Capacity Board

Form 26
Mental Health Act

Notice to the Board of the Need to Schedule a Mandatory Review of the Status of an Informal Patient who is a Child between 12 and 15 Years of Age under Subsection 13(2) of the Act

Part I This section must be completed by all applicants

____
(name of psychiatric facility)

Name of patient ______________________________ ______________________
(print full name of patient) (date of birth, if known)

The Board is hereby notified that six months have passed since the later of the patient's admission or the patient's last application to the Board to review his or her informal status. The Board is required to conduct an inquiry as to whether the patient requires further observation, care and treatment in this facility.

Date of the later of the patient's admission or last application.

______________________ ______________________________
(date) (signature of officer-in-charge)

Part II This information is not required but will assist us in scheduling the hearing
(provide only information where known)

Please provide the name, telephone and fax numbers and any other information that will assist us in contacting the patient's attending physician:

______________________ ( ) ______________ ( ) ______________
(name) (telephone no.) (fax no.)

____

____

Name, telephone and fax numbers of a hospital official who may assist in arranging the hearing:

______________________ ( ) ______________ ( ) ______________
(name) (telephone no.) (fax no.)

Name, telephone and fax numbers of your lawyer or agent:

______________________ ( ) ______________ ( ) ______________
(name) (telephone no.) (fax no.)

Name, telephone and fax numbers of a lawyer or agent for the patient's attending physician:

______________________ ( ) ______________ ( ) ______________
(name) (telephone no.) (fax no.)

Send this form by fax to the Regional Office of the Board or call toll free at 1–800–461–2036 for assistance

1066–41 (96/03) 7530–4193

MENTAL HEALTH ACT

Ministry of Health

Form 27
Mental Health Act

Notice by Officer-in-Charge to a Child who is between 12 and 15 Years of Age, who is an Informal Patient under Subsection 38(6) of the Act

To: ______________________________ ______________________________
(print name of the child between 12 and 15 years of age inclusive who is an informal patient) (date of birth, where available)

of ______________________________
(home address)

This is to inform you that as a child between 12 and 15 years inclusive who is an informal patient in

______________________________ you, or someone on your behalf,
(print name of psychiatric facility)

have the right to apply to the Board under section 13 of the *Mental Health Act*.
You may apply for such a hearing by completing Form 25 (attached)

Upon such application, an inquiry as to whether you need to stay in this psychiatric facility for observation, care and treatment will be held.

______________________________ ______________________________
(date) (signature of officer-in-charge)

____
(print name of officer-in-charge)

After you receive this notice, a person called a "rights adviser" shall meet with you to inform you as to your rights and help you in applying for a hearing if that is what you wish to do.

For further information or assistance with anything mentioned in this notice, please contact

______________________________ ______________________________
(print name(s) of appropriate staff member(s)) (telephone number)

***Note:** The Officer-in-charge shall promptly notify a rights adviser.*

January 1, 1995

1067–41 (95/01)* 7530–4242

Ministry of Health

Form 28
Mental Health Act

Request to Examine or to Copy Clinical Record under Subsections 36(2) and (16) of the Act

To: Officer-in-charge of ______________________
(print name of psychiatric facility)

Re: ______________________
(print full name of patient)

____
(date of birth, where available)

I, ______________________
(print full name of applicant)

request to examine or to copy the clinical record compiled with regard to

____
(print full name of patient)

____
(signature of witness)

____
(signature of applicant)

____
(if other than the patient, state relationship to patient)

Date ______________________
(day / month / year)

1068–41 (00/12)* 7530–4249

MENTAL HEALTH ACT

Consent and Capacity Board

Form 29
Mental Health Act

Application to the Board to Withhold All or Part of the Clinical Record under Subsection 36(4) of the Act

____
(print name of psychiatric facility)

I, ______________________________ , the officer-in-charge of
(print name of officer-in-charge)

______________________________ , having been advised by
(print name of psychiatric facility)

______________________________ that disclosure of the clinical record of
(print name of attending physician)

______________________________ is likely to result in,
(print name of patient)

☐ (a) serious harm to the treatment or recovery of the patient while in treatment at the psychiatric facility;
or

☐ (b) serious physical harm or serious emotional harm to another person,

hereby apply for authority to withhold all/part of the clinical record.

____
(signature of officer-in-charge)

____
(signature of witness)

Date ______________________________

1072–41 (00/12) 7530–4251

Ministry of Health

Form 30
Mental Health Act

Notice to Patient under Subsection 38(1) of the Act

To: ______________________________
(print name of patient)

of ______________________________
(home address)

This is to inform you that you are being detained under the authority of a

Under Section 20
- ☐ Certificate of Involuntary Admission *(Form 3)*

  or
- ☐ Certificate of Renewal *(Form 4)*

which expires on ______________________________
(date of expiry)

I completed this certificate on ______________________________
(date)

Part A and/or Part B must be completed

Part A

I am of the opinion that

a) you are suffering from mental disorder of a nature or quality that likely will result in,

- ☐ serious bodily harm to yourself;
- ☐ serious bodily harm to another person,
- ☐ serious physical impairment of you,

unless you remain in the custody of a psychiatric facility; and

b) that you are not suitable for admission or continuation as an informal or voluntary patient.

Part B

I am of the opinion that

a) you have previously received treatment for mental disorder of an ongoing or recurring nature that, when not treated, is of a nature or quality that likely will result in

- ☐ serious bodily harm to yourself,
- ☐ serious bodily harm to another person,
- ☐ substantial mental or physical deterioration of you, or
- ☐ serious physical impairment of you;

b) you have shown clinical improvement as a result of the treatment;

c) you are suffering from the same mental disorder as the one for which you previously received treatment or from a mental disorder that is similar to the previous one;

(Disponible en version française)

See reverse.

1076-41 (00/12)* 7530-4275

Part B ***(continued)***

d) given your history of mental disorder and current mental or physical condition, you are likely to

☐ cause serious bodily harm to yourself,
☐ cause serious bodily harm to another person,
☐ suffer substantial mental or physical deterioration, or
☐ suffer serious physical impairment;

e) you have been found incapable, within the meaning of the Health Care Consent Act, 1996 of consenting to your treatment in a psychiatric facility and the consent of your substitute decision-maker has been obtained; and

f) you are not suitable for admission or continuation as an informal or voluntary patient.

If you wish to challenge your detention, you have the right to a hearing before the Board. You may apply for a hearing by completing Form 16 (attached).

_______________________ (date)

_______________________ (signature of attending physician)

_______________________ (print name of attending physician)

_______________________ (print name of psychiatric facility)

After you receive this notice, a person called a "rights adviser" will meet with you to inform you as to your rights and help you in applying for a hearing if that is what you wish to do.
You have the right to retain and instruct a lawyer without delay.

For further information or assistance with anything mentioned in this notice, please contact

_______________________ (print name of appropriate staff member(s))

_______________________ (telephone number)

_______________________ (print name of psychiatric facility)

Note: The attending physician who completes a Certificate of Involuntary Admission or a Certificate of Renewal, shall promptly notify a rights adviser.

_______________________ (date and time rights adviser notified)

1076-41 (00/12)* 7530-4275

Consent and Capacity Board

Form 31
Mental Health Act

Application to the Board to Review a Patient's Competency to Examine/Disclose his or her Clinical Record under Subsection 36(14) of the Act

Part I This section must be completed by all applicants

My name is ____________________
(print full name of patient)

____
(home address)

I am a patient at ____________________
(name of psychiatric facility)

I, apply to the Board for a hearing to determine whether or not I am mentally competent

Check appropriate box(es)

☐ to examine my clinical record

☐ to consent to the disclosure of my clinical record

____________________ (date) ____________________ (signature of applicant)

Part II This information is not required but will assist us in scheduling the hearing
(provide only information where known)

Please provide the name, telephone and fax numbers and any other information that will assist us in contacting your attending physician:

____________________ (name) ( ) __________ (telephone no.) ( ) __________ (fax no.)

____

____

Name, telephone and fax numbers of a hospital official who may assist in arranging the hearing:

____________________ (name) ( ) __________ (telephone no.) ( ) __________ (fax no.)

Name, telephone and fax numbers of your lawyer or agent:

____________________ (name) ( ) __________ (telephone no.) ( ) __________ (fax no.)

Name, telephone and fax numbers of a lawyer or agent for your attending physician:

____________________ (name) ( ) __________ (telephone no.) ( ) __________ (fax no.)

Send this form by fax to the Regional Office of the Board or call toll free at 1–800–461–2036 for assistance January 1, 1995

1084–41 (96/12)* 7530–4283

Form 32 [Repealed, O. Reg. 15/95, s. 6]

MENTAL HEALTH ACT

Ministry of Health

Form 33
Mental Health Act

Notice to Patient under Subsection 59(1) of the Act and under Clauses 15(1) (a) and 15.1(a) of Regulation 741

To: ______________________________
(print name of patient)

of ______________________________
(home address)

This is to inform you that on ______________________________
(date of determination)

I, ______________________________ , have made a determination
(print name of physician)

that you

Check appropriate box(es):	*Form patient uses to challenge findings:*
1. ☐ are not mentally capable to consent to the collection, use or disclosure of personal health information within the meaning of the *Personal Health Information Protection Act*, 2004	1. Form P-1
2. ☐ are not mentally capable to manage your property	2. Form 18
3. ☐ are not mentally capable to consent to treatment of a mental disorder ("treatment" within the meaning of the *Health Care Consent Act*)	3. Form A

Check where appropriate:

1. ☐ A certificate of incapacity to manage property has been issued	1. Form 21
2. ☐ A certificate of continuance has been issued	2. Form 24

If you wish to challenge this (these) determination(s), you have the right to a hearing before the Board. You may apply for a hearing by completing the relevant form noted above.

Application forms are available from a Rights Adviser, this facility and the regional offices of the Board.

______________________ (date)

______________________ (signature of physician)

______________________ (print name of physician)

______________________ (print name of psychiatric facility)

(Disponible en version française)

See reverse.

1088-41 (04/11)*

©Queen's Printer for Ontario, 2004

7530-4324

After you receive this notice, a person called a "rights adviser" will meet with you to inform you as to your rights and help you in applying for a hearing if that is what you wish to do.

For further information or assistance with anything mentioned in this notice, please contact

_______________________________ _______________________
(print name(s) of appropriate staff member(s)) (telephone number)

____
(print name of psychiatric facility)

Note: *The physician shall promptly notify a rights adviser.*

____
(date and time rights adviser notified)

1088-41 (04/11)* ©Queen's Printer for Ontario, 2004 7530-4324

Forms 34 and 35 [Repealed, O. Reg. 15/95, s. 6]

Ministry of Health

Form 36
Mental Health Act

Notice under Subsection 36.1(4) of the Act of Right to Appoint a Representative

To: ______________________________
(name of patient)

You have the right to appoint someone to give or refuse consent on your behalf to access or disclosure of your clinical record in a psychiatric facility under the ***Mental Health Act.***

If you do not appoint someone and you become mentally incompetent to consent, a substitute decision maker will serve in this capacity.

Once appointed, your representative has the right to:

(a) have access to, examine and copy your clinical record; and

(b) authorize the disclosure of your clinical record to other persons.

You may revoke the appointment, in writing, at any time while you are mentally competent to appoint a representative.

Appointment forms are available at ______________________________
(name the psychiatric facility)

For more information, contact ______________________________
(name of person at facility)

Date ____________________ (day / month / year) ______________________________ (signature of attending physician)

____
(print name of attending physician)

1202-41 (00/12)* 7530-4368

Forms 37 - 39 [Repealed, O. Reg. 15/95, s. 6]

Ministry of Health

Form 40
Mental Health Act

Notice to Patient of Right to Apply to the Board for an Appointment of a Representative under Subsection 36.2(2) of the Act

To: ______________________________
(name of patient)

of ______________________________
(home address)

This is to inform you that on ______________________________ ,
(date of determination) (day / month / year)

I, ______________________________ have made a determination
(name of attending physician)

that you are not mentally competent to appoint a representative to give or refuse consent on your behalf to access or disclosure of your clinical record.

To my knowledge, you did not appoint a representative for these purposes when you were mentally competent to do so.

This is to notify you that you have the right to apply to the Board for the appointment of a representative to give or refuse such consent. You may apply for a hearing before the Board by completing a Form 41.

Copies of Form 41 are available at this facility and the regional offices of the Board.

You have the right to suggest to the Board who you want to be appointed as your representative.

______________________ (date)

______________________ (signature of attending physician)

______________________ (print name of attending physician)

______________________ (name of psychiatric facility)

Once appointed, your representative has the right to:

(a) have access to, examine and copy your clinical record; and

(b) authorize the disclosure of your clinical record to others.

1781–41 (00/12)*

7530–4573

MENTAL HEALTH ACT

Consent and Capacity Board

Form 41
Mental Health Act

Application to the Board to Appoint a Representative under Subsection 36.2(1) of the Act

Part I This section must be completed by all applicants

I apply to the Board to appoint a representative to give or refuse consent to access or disclosure of my clinical record.

My name is ______________________________
(print full name of patient)

____
(home address)

I am a patient at ______________________________
(name of psychiatric facility)

The name of the proposed representative is: ______________________________
(name of proposed representative)

The address and telephone number of the proposed representative are:

______________________________ ( ) ____________
(address) (telephone no.)

This appointment is subject to the following conditions and restrictions, if any:

____

____

____

____

____

____

______________________________ ______________________________
(date) (signature of applicant)

(Disponible en version française) *See reverse.*

1786-41 (96/04)* 7530-4609

Part II This information is not required but will assist us in scheduling the hearing
(provide only information where known)

Please provide the name, telephone and fax numbers and any other information that will assist us in contacting your attending physician:

________________ ( ) ________ ( ) ________
(name) (telephone no.) (fax no.)

____

____

Name, telephone and fax numbers of a hospital official who may assist in arranging the hearing:

________________ ( ) ________ ( ) ________
(name) (telephone no.) (fax no.)

Name, telephone and fax numbers of your lawyer or agent:

________________ ( ) ________ ( ) ________
(name) (telephone no.) (fax no.)

Name, telephone and fax numbers of a lawyer or agent for your attending physician:

________________ ( ) ________ ( ) ________
(name) (telephone no.) (fax no.)

Send this form by fax to the Regional Office of the Board or call toll free at 1–800–461–2036 for assistance.

MENTAL HEALTH ACT

1786–41 (96/04)* 7530–4609

Ministry of Health

Form 42
Mental Health Act

Notice to Person under Subsection 38.1 of the Act of Application for Psychiatric Assessment under Section 15 or an Order under Section 32 of the Act

Part I *(complete only if appropriate)*

To: ______________________________ (name of person)

of ______________________________ (home address)

This is to inform you that ______________________________ (name of physician)

examined you on ______________________ (date of examination) (day / month / year) and has made an application for you to have a psychiatric assessment.

Part A and/or Part B must be completed

Part A

That physician has certified that he/she has reasonable cause to believe that you have:

Check Box(es)

☐ threatened or attempted or are threatening or attempting to cause bodily harm to yourself;

☐ behaved or are behaving violently towards another person or have caused or are causing another person to fear bodily harm from you; or

☐ shown or are showing a lack of competence to care for yourself.

and that you are suffering from a mental disorder of a nature or quality that likely will result in:

Check Box(es)

☐ serious bodily harm to yourself;

☐ serious bodily harm to another person; or

☐ serious physical impairment of you.

Part B

That physician has certified that he/she has reasonable cause to believe that you:

a) have previously received treatment for mental disorder of an ongoing or recurring nature that, when not treated, is of a nature or quality that likely will result in

☐ serious bodily harm to yourself,

☐ serious bodily harm to another person,

☐ substantial mental or physical deterioration of you, or

☐ serious physical impairment of you;

b) have shown clinical improvement as a result of the treatment;

c) are suffering from the same mental disorder as the one for which you previously received treatment or from a mental disorder that is similar to the previous one;

(Disponible en version française)

See reverse

1787-41 (00/12)*

7530-4627

Part B ***(continued)***

d) given your history of mental disorder and current mental or physical condition, you are likely to

- ☐ cause serious bodily harm to yourself,
- ☐ cause serious bodily harm to another person,
- ☐ suffer substantial mental or physical deterioration, or
- ☐ suffer serious physical impairment;

e) have been found incapable, within the meaning of the Health Care Consent Act, 1996 of consenting to your treatment in a psychiatric facility and the consent of your substitute decision-maker has been obtained; and

f) you are not suitable for admission or continuation as an informal or voluntary patient.

The application is sufficient authority to hold you in custody in this hospital for up to 72 hours.

You have the right to retain and instruct a lawyer without delay.

________________ (date) ________________ (signature of attending physician)

Part II *(complete only if appropriate)*

To: ________________ (name of person)

of ________________ (home address)

This is to inform you that ________________ (name of Minister of Health and Long-Term Care)

Minister of Health and Long-Term Care for the Province of Ontario, has reasonable cause to believe that you are suffering from mental disorder of a nature or quality that likely will result in:

Check Box(es)

- ☐ serious bodily harm to yourself; or
- ☐ serious bodily harm to another person.

unless you are placed in the custody of a psychiatric facility and has by Order dated

________________ (date of order) (day / month / year), authorized your custody in a psychiatric facility for up to 72 hours.

You have the right to retain and instruct a lawyer without delay.

________________ (date) ________________ (signature of attending physician)

1787-41 (00/12)* 7530-4627

Form 43 - [Repealed, O. Reg. 15/95, s. 6]

Ministry of Health

Form 44
Mental Health Act

Appointment of a Representative under Subsection 36.1 of the Act

You have the right to appoint someone to give or refuse consent on your behalf to access or disclosure of your clinical record in a psychiatric facility under the ***Mental Health Act.***

Once appointed, your representative has the right to:

(a) have access to, examine and copy your clinical record; and

(b) authorize the disclosure of your clinical record to other persons.

To: ______________________ of ______________________
(name of officer-in-charge) (name of psychiatric facility)

where applicable, or **To whom it may concern**

I, ______________________, of ______________________
(name of person appointing representative) (home address)

hereby appoint ______________________ to be my representative.
(name of representative)

My relationship with my representative is: ______________________
(please specify relationship)

My representative's date of birth is: ______________________
(date of birth)

My representative's address is: ______________________

and his/her telephone number is: *(home)* ______________________

(work) ______________________

This appointment is subject to the following conditions and restrictions, if any:

Date ______________________
(day / month / year)

______________________ ______________________
(signature of witness) (signature of person)

______________________ ______________________
(print name of witness) (print name of person)

1797-41 (00/12)* 7530-4750

Ministry of Health

Form 45
Mental Health Act

Community Treatment Order

Part 1 – To be Filled Out by Examining Physician

Name of person ______________________
(print name of patient)

Name of physician ______________________
(print name of physician)

Name of substitute decision-maker *(if applicable)* ______________________
(print name of substitute decision-maker)

Name of psychiatric facility *(if applicable)* ______________________
(name of psychiatric facility)

Date of examination ______________________
(date)

This community treatment order for the above named person is the:

☐ first for this person ☐ ______________ renewal
(no. of times CTO has been renewed)

Date of issue of previous community treatment order *(if applicable)* ______________________
(date)

Date of expiry of previous community treatment order *(if applicable)* ______________________
(date)

During the previous three year period, the person named above:

☐ has been a patient in a psychiatric facility on two or more separate occasions or for a cumulative period of 30 days or more during that three year period, OR

☐ has been the subject of a previous community treatment order.

Criteria for Community Treatment Order

(Note: All the criteria set out below must be met for this order to be valid)

I am of the opinion that

a) the person is suffering from mental disorder such that he or she needs continuing treatment or care and continuing supervision while living in the community, AND

b) if the person does not receive continuing treatment or care and continuing supervision while living in the community, he or she is likely, because of mental disorder, to: (choose one or more of the following)

☐ cause serious bodily harm to himself or herself, OR
☐ cause serious bodily harm to another person, OR
☐ suffer substantial mental deterioration of the person, OR
☐ suffer substantial physical deterioration of the person OR
☐ suffer serious physical impairment of the person,

AND

c) the person is able to comply with the community treatment plan contained in the community treatment order, AND

(Disponible en version française) *See reverse*

3760-41 (00/12) 7530-5576

MENTAL HEALTH ACT

d) the treatment or care and supervision required under the terms of the community treatment order are available in the community, AND

e) If the person is not currently a patient in a psychiatric facility, the person meets the criteria for the completion of an application for psychiatric assessment under subsection 15(1) or (1.1).

The facts on which I formed the above opinion are as follows:

Rights Advice

Note: The person and his or her substitute decision–maker, if applicable, must receive rights advice before the order is issued.

I am satisfied that the substitute decision-maker of the person, if applicable, has consulted with a rights adviser and been advised of his or her legal rights, AND

I am satisfied that the person:

☐ has consulted with a rights adviser and been advised of his or her legal rights, or

☐ has not consulted with a rights adviser because he or she has refused to consult a rights adviser.

Community Treatment Plan

Note: A copy of the community treatment plan must be attached to this order.

I am satisfied that a community treatment plan has been devised for the person.

I have consulted with all the persons named in the community treatment plan.

I am satisfied that:

☐ the person OR

☐ the person's substitute decision-maker, if the person is incapable, consents to the community treatment plan.

The community treatment plan for the person is

(Describe the community treatment plan. Use back of this form if necessary. The community treatment plan must be attached to this order.)

(Disponible en version française)

3760–41 (00/12) 7530–5576

Part 2 – To be Filled Out by the Person or the Person's Substitute Decision-Maker

Undertaking of Person or Person's Substitute Decision-Maker
(to be completed by the person or the person's substitute decision maker, if applicable)

I am

☐ the person named above. I promise to comply with all my obligations as set out in the community treatment plan, OR

☐ the person's substitute decision-maker. I promise to use my best efforts to ensure that the person named above complies with all the obligations as set out in the community treatment plan.

By my signature at the bottom of this order, I signify that I consent to the community treatment plan, and I consent to, and am assuming my undertakings as stated in, the community treatment plan.

Part 3 – Time in Force – To be Completed by the Examining Physician

This community treatment order is in force for 6 months, including the day upon which it is signed, and expires at midnight on the ________________ unless it is terminated at an earlier date.
(date) (day / month / year)

Part 4 – Patient Right to Apply to Consent and Capacity Board

A person who is subject to a community treatment order, or any person on his or her behalf, may apply to the Board using a ***Form 48*** to inquire into whether or not the criteria for issuing or renewing this community treatment order have been met.

Signed at ____
(name of psychiatric facility, or name of place [eg. doctor's office, hospital] where community treatment order signed)

________________________ (Date)

________________________ (signature of physician)

________________________ (signature of person)

________________________ (signature of substitute decision-maker) *(if applicable)*

Notes:

The following actions must be taken by the physician who signs this order immediately after the order is signed:

1. A copy of this order, including the community treatment plan must be given to:
   a) the person,
   b) the person's substitute decision-maker, if applicable,
   c) the officer in charge of a psychiatric facility, if applicable,
   d) any other health practitioner or other person named in the community treatment plan.
2. A notice in the approved form ***(Form 46)*** must be given to the person that he or she is entitled to a hearing before the Consent and Capacity Board.

3760-41 (00/12) 7530-5576

MENTAL HEALTH ACT

Ministry of Health

Form 46
Mental Health Act

Notice to Person of Issuance or Renewal of Community Treatment Order (Section 33.1(10))

TO: ______________________________
(print full name of person)

of: ______________________________
(print home address of person)

This is to inform you that you are subject to a community treatment order completed on ______________________
(date community treatment order signed)

The community treatment order expires on ______________________
(date community treatment order expires)

If you wish to challenge the community treatment order, you have a right to a hearing before the Consent and Capacity Board.

You have a right to retain and instruct counsel about the community treatment order at any time after it is issued or renewed.

You may apply for a hearing by completing a ***Form 48*** which is attached to this notice.

Date ______________________
(day / month / year)

______________________ (signature of physician)

______________________ (print name of physician)

______________________ (name of psychiatric facility) (if applicable)

Notes

1. A community treatment order may be issued or renewed for not more than 6 months.
2. A person who is subject to a community treatment order, or any person on his or her behalf, may apply to the Board in the approved form (Form 48) to inquire into whether or not the criteria for issuing or renewing a community treatment order in subsection 33.1(4) of the Mental Health Act are met.
3. An application to the Board may be made each time a community treatment order is issued or renewed.

3762-41 (00/12)* 7530-5580

Ministry of Health

Form 47
Mental Health Act

Order for Examination Sections 33.3(1) and 33.4 (3) of the Act

To the police officers of Ontario

WHEREAS ______________________________
(print name of person subject to a community treatment order)

of ______________________________
(address of person subject to community treatment order)

is subject to a community treatment order issued or renewed on ______________
(date of order)

by ______________________________
(name of issuing or renewing physician)

of ______________________________ and
(business address of issuing or renewing physician)

WHEREAS such person has

☐ failed to attend appointments or comply with treatment in accordance with ss.33.1(9) of the *Mental Health Act*, or

☐ failed to permit ______________________ to review his/her condition,
(name of iphysician)

in accordance with ss.33.4 (2) of the *Mental Health Act*, and

WHEREAS I have reasonable cause to believe that such person

(i) is suffering from mental disorder such that he/she needs continuing treatment or care and continuing supervision while living in the community;

(ii) meets the criteria for the completion of a Form 1 [an application for psychiatric assessment under ss.15 (1) or (1.1) of the *Mental Health Act*] and is not currently a patient in a psychiatric facility; and

(iii) if the person does not receive continuing treatment or care and continuing supervision while living in the community, he/she is likely, because of mental disorder, to *(choose one or more of the following)*

☐ cause serious bodily harm to himself / herself

☐ cause serious bodily harm to another person

☐ suffer substantial mental or physical deterioration of the person

☐ suffer serious physical impairment of the person.

Now therefore, I hereby issue this Order for Examination for any of you to take such person in custody forthwith to ______________________________
(address of physician, agency or psychiatric facility where the person will be examined)

for an examination by me or by a physician named below appointed to carry out this responsibility in accordance with ss. 33.5 (2) of the *Mental Health Act*.

____
(name of physician, agency or psychiatric facility responsible for examination of the person)

This order is in force for 30 days after the date upon which it is issued and will expire at midnight on ______________
(date order will expire)

Dated at ______________________ on ______________
(name of municipality / city / town) (date) (day / month / year)

______________________ ______________________
(signature of physician) (print name of physician)

3761-41 (00/12) 7530-5577

MENTAL HEALTH ACT

Notes:

1. The physician who issues an order for examination shall ensure that the police have complete and up-to-date information about the name, address and telephone number of the physician responsible for completing the examination required under an order for examination and shall ensure that the police have such information at all times that the order for examination is in force.
2. The physician who issues an order for examination shall ensure that the police are immediately notified if the person who is subject to the order for examination voluntarily attends for an examination or, for any other reason, the order for examination is cancelled prior to its expiry date.
3. The police may need a physical description of the person named in your Order for Examination so that the person may be located and returned to you for an examination. Please use the space below to provide the police with relevant information about the person's physical description.
4. The police may ask you for information about the person's physical description, in addition to the information you have provided below.

3761-41 (00/12) 7530-5577

Ministry of Health

Form 48
Mental Health Act

Application to Board to Review Community Treatment Order (s.39.1(1) and Notice to Board by Physician of Need to Schedule Mandatory Review of Community Treatment Order (s.39.1(4))

Part 1 – To be Completed by the Person Subject to a Community Treatment Order or Another Person on his or her Behalf

My name is: ____________________

My home address is: ____________________

My telephone number is: (   ) ____________________

My lawyer's or agent's name (if any) is: ____________________

My lawyer's or agent's address is: ____________________

My lawyer's or agent's telephone number is: (   ) ____________________

I apply to the Board for a review of a community treatment order issued or renewed under section 33.1(4) for:

____________________ (myself) or ____________________ (name of person on community treatment order)

The community treatment order was issued or renewed on ____________________ (date) (day / month / year)

and has been renewed *(to be best of my knowledge)* __________ times.

Name of physician who issued or renewed the community treatment order:

____________________ (name)

Address of physician who issued or renewed the community treatment order:

____________________ (address)

Telephone number of physician who issued or renewed the community treatment order:

(   ) ____________________ (telephone no.)

____________________ (signature) ____________________ (date)

(Disponible en version française)

See reverse

3763-41 (00/12)* 7530-5584

MENTAL HEALTH ACT

Part 2 – To be Completed by the Physician

This section must be completed every time a community treatment order is renewed for the second time and on the occasion of every second renewal thereafter.

Name of physician: ____________________

Name of psychiatric facility *(if applicable)*: ____________________

Telephone number where physician can be reached: (____) ____________________

Fax number of physician: (____) ____________________

Lawyer or agent for physician *(if applicable)*: ____________________

Telephone number where lawyer or agent for physician can be reached *(if applicable)*: (____) ____________________

Name of person subject to community treatment order: ____________________

Address of person: ____________________

Telephone number where person can be reached: (____) ____________________

Fax number of person *(if applicable)*: (____) ____________________

Name of person's lawyer or agent *(if known)*: ____________________

Telephone number of person's lawyer or agent *(if known)*: (____) ____________________

A second renewal (or second renewal thereafter) of the person's community treatment order was made on the following date ____________________
(day / month / year)

To the best of my knowledge, the person or another person on his or her behalf has not applied for a review of his or her community treatment order.

Ministry of Health

Form 49
Mental Health Act

Notice of Intention to Issue or Renew Community Treatment Order (section 33.1(4), section 33.1(8))

Part 1 – Notice of Intention to Issue or Renew a Community Treatment Order

TO: ______________________________________
(print full name of person)

I am considering issuing or renewing a community treatment order (Form 45) for you.

During the previous three year period you

☐ have been a patient in a psychiatric facility on two or more separate occasions or for a cumulative period of 30 days or more during that three year period, OR

☐ have been the subject of a previous community treatment order

Part 2 – Capacity to Consent to Treatment Proposed in a Community Treatment Plan

On ______________________ a determination was made that you are incapable
date (day / month / year)

with respect to giving or refusing consent to a proposed community treatment plan.

Your substitute decision-maker under the *Health Care Consent Act* is ______________________
(name of substitute decision-maker)

Your substitute decision-maker will also receive notice that I am considering issuing or renewing a community treatment order for you.

Part 3 – Community Treatment Plan

A community treatment plan must be developed with you or with your substitute decision-maker (where applicable) and any other health practitioners or persons involved in your treatment or care and supervision.

A copy of the community treatment plan developed for you is attached to this notice.

During the 72 hours ***prior to*** entering into the community treatment plan, I examined you and am of the opinion that:

1. You are suffering from mental disorder such that you need continuing treatment or care and continuing supervision while living in the community, AND
2. You meet the criteria for the completion of an application for psychiatric assessment, if you are not currently a patient in a psychiatric facility, AND
3. If you do not receive continuing treatment or care and continuing supervision while living in the community, you are likely, because of mental disorder, to cause serious bodily harm to yourself or another person or to suffer substantial mental or physical deterioration of yourself or serious physical impairment of yourself, AND
4. You are able to comply with the community treatment plan contained in the community treatment order, AND
5. The treatment or care and supervision required under the terms of the community treatment order are available in the community.

3764-41 (00/12) 7530-5581

Part 4 – Rights Advice and Right to Counsel

TO: ____
(print full name of person)

AND TO: ____
(print name of substitute decision-maker, if applicable)

You are entitled to consult a rights adviser before a community treatment order can be issued or renewed.

A rights adviser will receive notice of the physician's intention to issue or renew a community treatment order and will contact you for the purpose of providing you with rights advice.

You have the right to retain and instruct counsel about the proposed community treatment order before it is issued or renewed and to retain and instruct counsel about the community treatment order at any time after it is issued or renewed.

Date of issue ____________________
(day / month / year)

____
(physician's business address)

____
(name of psychiatric facility if applicable)

____________________ ____________________
(signature of physician) (print name of physician)

Notes

1. The rights adviser shall explain to the person and the substitute decision-maker, if any, the requirements for the issuance or renewal of a community treatment order, the significance of such an order, including any obligations that the person or substitute decision-maker may be required to meet under the order.
2. Where a rights adviser believes that it is in the best interests of the person to receive rights advice from another rights adviser, he or she shall ensure that a second rights adviser provides such advice.
3. Where a rights adviser provides rights advice to the person and the substitute decision-maker, if any, the rights adviser shall provide confirmation of this fact to the physician in ***Form 50***.
4. Where a person refuses the provision of rights advice, the rights adviser shall provide confirmation of that fact to the physician in ***Form 50***.

3764-41 (00/12) 7530-55l

Ministry of Health

Form 50
Mental Health Act

Confirmation of Rights Advice

Please print all information.

Part 1 – To be Completed by the Rights Adviser of a Person Every Time Rights Advice is Given

My name is: ______________________________
(first name) (last name)

I am qualified and certified pursuant to the regulations under the *Mental Health Act* to be a rights adviser.

Name of person receiving rights advice ______________________________
(first name) (last name)

Person's date of birth *(if known)*: ______________________________

Name of person's substitute decision-maker *(if applicable)*: ______________________________
(first name) (last name)

Name of psychiatric facility where person is a patient *(if applicable)*: ______________________________
(name of psychiatric facility) (city)

Name of person's attending physician *(if applicable)*: ______________________________
(first name) (last name)

On ______________________________ , at approximately______________ o'clock,
date (day / month / year)

I approached the person named above for the purpose of providing him or her with rights advice on the following issue(s): *(check all that apply)*

- ☐ Form 3 – Notice of Certificate of Involuntary Admission
- ☐ Form 4 – Notice of Certificate of Renewal
- ☐ Form 21 – Certificate of Incapacity re: Property
- ☐ Form 24 – Notice of Continuance re: Property
- ☐ Form 27 – Notice of Right to a Review of Informal Status
- ☐ Form 33 – Not Mentally Competent to Examine your Clinical Record
- ☐ Form 33 – Not Mentally Competent to Consent to Disclosure of your Clinical Record
- ☐ Form 33 – Not Mentally Capable to Consent to Treatment of Mental Disorder under the Health Care Consent Act ***(please complete Part 2)***
- ☐ Form 49 – Notice of Intention to Issue Community Treatment Order ***(please complete Part 3)***

(Disponible en version française)

See reverse

3766-41 (00/12)

7530-5583

____
(print name of person receiving rights advice)

Part 2 – Incapacity with Respect to Treatment

The person: *(check all that apply)*

☐ refused to meet with me or was unable to communicate with me.

☐ received rights advice and the person ***did not*** indicate a wish to apply to the Consent and Capacity Board to review the finding of incapacity with respect to treatment.

☐ received rights advice and the person ***did*** indicate a wish to apply to the Consent and Capacity Board to review the finding of incapacity with respect to treatment.

☐ received rights advice and the person applied to the Consent and Capacity Board to review the finding of incapacity with respect to treatment.

Note regarding section 18 of the Health Care Consent Act: *if before the treatment of an incapable patient has begun, the health practitioner is notified that the patient intends to apply to the Board, then the health practitioner shall not begin the treatment and shall take reasonable steps to ensure that the treatment is not begun until 48 hours have elapsed since the health practitioner was first notified of the intended application without the application being made.*

Part 3 – Confirmation of Rights Advice – Community Treatment Order

This part must be completed every time a physician gives Notice of the Intention to Issue or Renew a Community Treatment Order (Form 49).

Check all that apply:

☐ I provided rights advice to the person named above who is subject to a community treatment order.

☐ I provided rights advice to the person's substitute decision-maker named above *(if applicable).*

☐ The person named above refused to let me provide him or her with rights advice.

☐ I believe that it is in the best interest of the person named above to receive rights advice from another rights adviser and pursuant to subsection 14.3 (4) of Regulation 741 under the *Mental Health Act*, I have taken steps to ensure that a second rights adviser provides such advice.

☐ I received notice from a rights adviser pursuant to subsection 14.3 (4) of Regulation 741under the *Mental Health Act* that it is in the best interest of the person named above to receive rights advice from another rights adviser and

- ☐ I provided rights advice to the person named above.
- ☐ The person named above refused to let me provide him or her with rights advice.

Note: *The rights adviser shall explain to the person and the substitute decision-maker, if any, the requirements for the issuance or renewal of a community treatment order, the significance of such an order, including any obligations that the person or the substitute decision-maker may be required to meet under the order. A second rights adviser who receives notice under subsection 14.3(4) of Regulation 741 under the Mental Health Act must complete a separate Form 50.*

______________________________ ______________________________
Date of signature (day / month / year) (signature of rights adviser)

Ministry of Health and Long-Term Care
Ministère de la Santé et des Soins de longue durée

Request for Correction in Clinical Record under Section 36 of the *Mental Health Act*

Demande de correction du dossier clinique en vertu de l'article 36 de la *Loi sur la santé mentale*

To: Officer in Charge of/Destinataire : Dirigeant(e) responsable de

____
(name of psychiatric facility/nom de l'établissement psychiatrique)

I,/Je soussigné(e), ______________________________
(print full name of person/écrire vos nom et prénom en lettres moulées)

of/de ______________________________
(address/adresse)

hereby request that the following information be corrected in the clinical record of
demande par la présente que les renseignements suivants soient corrigés sur le dossier clinique de

______________________________ Casebook no. Nº de recueil ______________
(name of patient/nom du patient/de la patiente)

Information in Clinical Record Renseignement figurant dans le dossier clinique	Correct information Renseignement correct

____
(signature)

Date/Fait le ______________________________
(day / month / year / jour / mois / année)

For hospital use only/Réservé à l'hôpital

☐ have been made in full/a été intégralement corrigé

☐ no action taken/n'a pas été suivi d'effet

☐ have not been made *(a Statement of Disagreement has been forwarded for completion)*
n'a pas été corrigé (une Déclaration de désaccord a été envoyée pour y inscrire la correction)

☐ have been made in part *(specify)*/a été partiellement corrigé *(précisér)*

______________________________ ______________________________
(date) (processed by/traité par)

1468–41 (99/08)* 7530–4746

MENTAL HEALTH ACT

Ministry of Health
and Long-Term Care

Ministère de la Santé
et des Soins de longue durée

Statement of Disagreement with Clinical Record under Section 36 of the *Mental Health Act*

Déclaration de désaccord avec le dossier clinique en vertu de l'article 36 de la *Loi sur la santé mentale*

To: Officer in Charge of/Destinataire : Dirigeant(e) responsable de ____________________
(name of psychiatric facility/nom de l'établissement psychiatrique)

I,/Je soussigné(e), ____________________
(print full name of person/écrire vos nom et prénom en lettres moulées)

of/de ____________________
(address/adresse)

hereby state that I disagree with the information contained in the clinical record of
déclare par la présente être en désaccord avec les renseignements contenus dans le dossier clinique de

____________________ Casebook no. Nº de recueil ____________________
(name of patient/nom du patient/de la patiente)

and hereby require that this "Statement of Disagreement" be attached to the above clinical record with respect to a correction or corrections requested but not made.
et demande que la présente *"Déclaration de désaccord"* soit annexée au dossier clinique susmentionné parce que la ou les corrections demandées n'ont pas été effectuées.

Information in Clinical Record Renseignement figurant dans le dossier clinique	Disagreement/Preferred information Désaccord/Renseignement corrigé

____
(signature)

Date/Fait le ____________________
(day / month / year / jour / mois / année)

1469-41 (99/08)* 7530-4747

PERSONAL HEALTH INFORMATION PROTECTION ACT, 2004

COMMENTARY

As of November 1, 2004, access and consent to the disclosure, use and collection of personal health information is governed by the *Personal Health Information Protection Act*. The Act applies to personal health information that is collected, used or disclosed by custodians. Personal health information, subject to specific exceptions,[1] includes oral or written information about the individual, if the information: (a) relates to the individual's physical or mental health, including family health history; (b) relates to the provision of health care, including the identification of persons providing health care; (c) is a plan of service for individuals requiring long-term care; (d) relates to payment or eligibility for health care; (e) relates to the donation of body parts or bodily substances or is derived from the testing or examination of any such parts or substances; (f) is the individual's health number; or (g) identifies an individual's Substitute Decision Maker[2].

A health information custodian is a listed individual or organization that, as a result of their powers or duties, has custody or control of personal health information.[3] Examples of health information custodians include: (a) health care practitioners, including doctors, nurses, pharmacists, psychologists and dentists; (b) hospitals; (c) psychiatric facilities; (d) pharmacies; (e) laboratories; (f) nursing homes and long-term care facilities; (g) retirement homes and homes for special care; (h) community care access centres; (i) ambulance services; (j) boards of health; (k) the Minister of Health and Long-Term Care; and (l) entities prescribed by regulation that are not defined as health information custodians but are permitted to collect personal health information from health information custodians for the purposes of health planning and management[4].

Capacity to Consent to Collection, Use, or Disclosure of Personal Health Information

An individual may access their personal health information or consent to the collection, use or disclosure of their personal health information, provided they are mentally capable of doing so.[5] Mentally capable is defined in the Act as: (a) the ability to understand the information that is relevant to deciding whether to

---

1 PHIPA, s.4
2 PHIPA, s.4
3 PHIPA, s.3
4 PHIPA, s.3
5 PHIPA, s.21

consent to the collection, use or disclosure, as the case may be; and (b) the ability to appreciate the reasonably foreseeable consequences of giving, not giving, withholding, or withdrawing consent.[6] In the event an individual is assessed not capable of consenting to the collection, use or disclosure of personal health information, the individual has a right to apply to the Consent and Capacity Board for a review of the determination, unless there is a person who is entitled to act as the substitute decision maker for the individual in relation to treatment, admission to a care facility, or personal assistance service under the provisions of the *Health Care Consent Act*.[7] There is very little guidance set out in the Act in relation to the information a health information custodian must provide to an individual determined not capable (i.e. there is no requirement for rights advice, notice of the finding or the right to apply to have the finding reviewed). The Act only states that provided it is reasonable in the circumstances, the individual must be provided with information about the consequences of the determination of incapacity, including the information, if any, that is prescribed. To date, the Act has no regulations prescribing any information to be provided.[8]

Refusal of Access and Disclosure on Grounds Other Than Incapacity

Although an individual may have the capacity to access or consent to the collection, use or disclosure of their personal health information, a health information custodian may refuse access to the personal health information in those circumstances set out in the Act, including a reasonable expectation that granting the access could (a) result in risk of serious harm to the treatment or recovery of the individual or risk of bodily harm to the individual or another person, (b) lead to the identification of a person who is required by law to provide information and the record to the custodian, or (c) lead to the identification of a person who provided information and the record to the custodian explicitly or implicitly in confidence if the custodian considers it appropriate in the circumstances that the name of the person be kept confidential.[9] It is to be noted that prior to November 1, 2004, the provisions of the *Mental Health Act* applied to health records maintained in a psychiatric facility. In circumstances where health records maintained in a psychiatric facility were refused to a patient or former patient based on a risk of serious harm to the treatment or recovery to the individual or risk of bodily harm to the individual or another person, the psychiatric facility was required under the MHA to apply to the Consent and Capacity Board for permission to withhold the record. The Board, after reviewing the record and convening a Hearing to hear submissions, would then make a decision. This is no longer the case. The provisions of PHIPA allow the custodian to withhold the record without applying to the Consent and Capacity Board. Although there is a requirement that the health information custodian give written

[6] PHIPA, s.21

[7] PHIPA, s.21(3)

[8] PHIPA, s 22(2)

[9] PHIPA, s 52

notice to the individual of the refusal to provide access, the written notice in certain circumstances, may simply state that the custodian is refusing to confirm or deny the existence of any record.[10] In such a case, the individual may make a complaint about the refusal to the Commissioner under Part VI of the Act.[11]

Manner of Access

An individual may exercise a right of access to a record of personal health information by making a written request to the health information custodian that has custody or control of the information.[12] There is no specific form prescribed by the Act. Within thirty days of the request (which period may be extended for a further period of thirty days) the health information custodian must make the record available to the individual for examination and, at the request of the individual, provide a copy of the record to the individual, and if reasonably practical, an explanation of any term, quote or abbreviation used in the record.[13]

In the event the custodian refuses the request based on the incapacity of the individual, the custodian is only required to provide the information required by section 22(2) of the Act. In the event the custodian refuses the request on grounds other than incapacity, the custodian must provide a written notice in accordance with s. 54(1)(c) and (d) of the Act.

Disclosure Without Consent

The Act allows a health information custodian to disclose personal health information without consent to health care practitioners, long–term care service providers, and persons who operate health care facilities, programs and services if: (a) the disclosure is reasonable necessary for the provision of health care; (b) it is not reasonably possible to obtain consent in a timely way; and (c) the individual has not instructed the custodian not to make the disclosure.[14] In addition, a health information custodian may disclose personal health information without consent: (a) for the purpose of contacting a relative, friend or potential substitute decision maker of the individual, if the individual is injured, incapacitated or ill and unable to give consent personally;[15] (b) if the custodian believes on reasonable ground that the disclosure is necessary for the purpose of eliminating or reducing a significant risk of serious bodily harm to a person or a group of persons;[16] (c) for the purpose of determining, assessing, or confirming capacity under the *Health Care Consent Act*, the *Substitute Decisions Act*, or *Personal Health Information Protection Act*;[17] and (d) for the purpose of legal proceedings.[18]

---

[10] PHIPA s.54(1)(d)

[11] PHIPA, s. 54(8)

[12] PHIPA, s. 53

[13] PHIPA, s. 54(1)(a)

[14] PHIPA, s. 38(1)

[15] PHIPA, s. 38(1)(c)

[16] PHIPA. s. 40(1)

[17] PHIPA, s. 43(1)(a)

Appointment of Representative

An individual who is sixteen years of age or older and who is determined to be incapable of consenting to the collection, use or disclosure of personal health information, may apply to the Consent and Capacity Board for the appointment of a representative.[19] In addition, an individual, other than the incapable person, may apply to the Board to be appointed as a representative.[20] These applications may not be made if the individual to whom the health information relates has a guardian of the person, a guardian of property, an attorney for personal care, or an attorney for property who has authority to give or refuse consent to the collection, use or disclosure.[21] Such an application gives rise to a deemed application to review whether or not the individual to whom the personal health information relates, is capable of consenting to the collection, use or disclosure as the case may be.[22] It remains to be determined whether or not a deemed application will proceed if the application to review capacity would otherwise be prohibited by virtue of the incapable person having a SDM for the purposes of the HCCA.[23]

Application to Determine Compliance

If a substitute decision maker, on behalf of an incapable individual, gives, withholds, or withdraws a consent to a collection, use or disclosure of personal health information about the individual or provides an express instruction under s. 37(1)(a), s. 38(1)(a) or s. 50(1)(e) and if the custodian is of the opinion that the SDM has not complied with the factors to be considered for consent under s. 24, the custodian may apply to the Consent and Capacity Board for a determination as to whether the SDM is acting in compliance with the Act.[24] This application gives rise to a deemed application to review a finding of incapacity.[25] Whether such a deemed application would proceed if the application would otherwise be prohibited by virtue of s. 22(3) of the Act has yet to be determined. There is no provision in the Act allowing the incapable person to make a similar application to determine compliance.

Correction to Record of Personal Health Information

If a health information custodian has granted an individual access to a record of his or her personal health information and if the individual believes that the record is inaccurate or incomplete for the purposes for which the custodian has collected

---

[18] PHIPA, s. 41(1)
[19] PHIPA s.27(1)
[20] PHIPA, s.27(2)
[21] PHIPA, s. 27(3)
[22] Ontario Regulation 329/04, s.9
[23] PHIPA, a.22(3)
[24] PHIPA, S.24(2)
[25] Ontario Regulation 329/04, s.9

or used the information, the individual may request in writing that the custodian correct the record.[26]

The procedure for requesting the correction and the obligations of the health care custodian are set out in s. 55 of the Act. There is a duty to correct the information if the individual demonstrates, to the satisfaction of the custodian, that the record is incomplete or inaccurate.

In the event the health custodian refuses the request for a correction, a Notice of Refusal must be given setting out the reasons for the refusal and informing the individual that they are entitled to: (a) prepare a concise Statement of Disagreement that sets out the correction that the health information custodian has refused to make; (b) require that the health information custodian attach the Statement of Disagreement as part of the records that it holds of the individual's personal health information, and disclose the Statement of Disagreement whenever the custodian discloses information to which the statement relates; (c) require that the health information custodian make all reasonable efforts to disclose the Statement of Disagreement to any person who would have been notified under clause (10)(c) if the custodian had granted the request to correction; and (d) make a complaint about the refusal to the Commissioner.[27]

Access To Personal Health Information for Purposes of Hearings Before the Consent and Capacity Board

The *Health Care Consent Act* allows a party to a hearing before the Consent and Capacity Board to be given an opportunity before the hearing to examine and copy any documentary evidence that will be produced and any reporter whose contents will be given in evidence.[28] This Act also entitles a party who is the subject of the treatment, the admission, or the personal assistance services as the case may be, and his or her counsel, to examine and copy, at their own expense, any medical or other health record prepared in respect of the party, subject to certain provisions of the *Mental Health Act*, the *Long-Term Care Act* and the *Child and Family Services Act*.[29]

[26] PHIPA, s.55

[27] PHIPA, s.55(11)

[28] HCCA, s.76(1)

[29] HCCA, s.76(2)

PERSONAL HEALTH INFORMATION PROTECTION ACT, 2004

(S.O. 2004, c. 3, Sched. A)

Part I
Interpretation and Application

Purposes, Definitions and Interpretation

1. Purposes — The purposes of this Act are,

(a) to establish rules for the collection, use and disclosure of personal health information about individuals that protect the confidentiality of that information and the privacy of individuals with respect to that information, while facilitating the effective provision of health care;

(b) to provide individuals with a right of access to personal health information about themselves, subject to limited and specific exceptions set out in this Act;

(c) to provide individuals with a right to require the correction or amendment of personal health information about themselves, subject to limited and specific exceptions set out in this Act;

(d) to provide for independent review and resolution of complaints with respect to personal health information; and

(e) to provide effective remedies for contraventions of this Act.

2. Definitions — In this Act,

"agent", in relation to a health information custodian, means a person that, with the authorization of the custodian, acts for or on behalf of the custodian in respect of personal health information for the purposes of the custodian, and not the agent's own purposes, whether or not the agent has the authority to bind the custodian, whether or not the agent is employed by the custodian and whether or not the agent is being remunerated;

"Assistant Commissioner" means the Assistant Commissioner for Personal Health Information appointed under the *Freedom of Information and Protection of Privacy Act*;

"attorney for personal care" means an attorney under a power of attorney for personal care made in accordance with the *Substitute Decisions Act, 1992*;

"attorney for property" means an attorney under a continuing power of attorney for property made in accordance with the *Substitute Decisions Act, 1992*;

"Board" means the Consent and Capacity Board constituted under the *Health Care Consent Act, 1996*;

"capable" means mentally capable, and "capacity" has a corresponding meaning;

"collect", in relation to personal health information, means to gather, acquire, receive or obtain the information by any means from any source, and "collection" has a corresponding meaning;

"Commissioner" means the Information and Privacy Commissioner appointed under the *Freedom of Information and Protection of Privacy Act*;

"disclose", in relation to personal health information in the custody or under the control of a health information custodian or a person, means to make the information available or to release it to another health information custodian or to another person, but does not include to use the information, and "disclosure" has a corresponding meaning;

"guardian of property" means a guardian of property or a statutory guardian of property under the *Substitute Decisions Act, 1992*;

"guardian of the person" means a guardian of the person appointed under the *Substitute Decisions Act, 1992*;

"health care" means any observation, examination, assessment, care, service or procedure that is done for a health-related purpose and that,

(a) is carried out or provided to diagnose, treat or maintain an individual's physical or mental condition,

(b) is carried out or provided to prevent disease or injury or to promote health, or

(c) is carried out or provided as part of palliative care,

and includes,

(d) the compounding, dispensing or selling of a drug, a device, equipment or any other item to an individual, or for the use of an individual, pursuant to a prescription, and

(e) a community service that is described in subsection 2 (3) of the *Long-Term Care Act, 1994* and provided by a service provider within the meaning of that Act;

"health care practitioner" means,

(a) a person who is a member within the meaning of the *Regulated Health Professions Act, 1991* and who provides health care,

(b) a person who is registered as a drugless practitioner under the *Drugless Practitioners Act* and who provides health care,

(c) a person who is a member of the Ontario College of Social Workers and Social Service Workers and who provides health care, or

(d) any other person whose primary function is to provide health care for payment;

"health information custodian" has the meaning set out in section 3;

"health number" means the number, the version code or both of them assigned to an insured person within the meaning of the *Health Insurance Act* by the General Manager within the meaning of that Act;

"incapable" means mentally incapable, and "incapacity" has a corresponding meaning;

"individual", in relation to personal health information, means the individual, whether living or deceased, with respect to whom the information was or is being collected or created;

"information practices", in relation to a health information custodian, means the policy of the custodian for actions in relation to personal health information, including,

(a) when, how and the purposes for which the custodian routinely collects, uses, modifies, discloses, retains or disposes of personal health information, and

(b) the administrative, technical and physical safeguards and practices that the custodian maintains with respect to the information;

"Minister" means the Minister of Health and Long-Term Care;

"partner" means either of two persons who have lived together for at least one year and have a close personal relationship that is of primary importance in both persons' lives;

"person" includes a partnership, association or other entity;

"personal health information" has the meaning set out in section 4;

"prescribed" means prescribed by the regulations made under this Act;

"proceeding" includes a proceeding held in, before or under the rules of a court, a tribunal, a commission, a justice of the peace, a coroner, a committee of a College within the meaning of the *Regulated Health Professions Act, 1991*, a committee of the Board of Regents continued under the *Drugless Practitioners Act*, a committee of the Ontario College of Social Workers and Social Service Workers under the *Social Work and Social Service Work Act, 1998*, an arbitrator or a mediator;

"quality of care information" has the same meaning as in the *Quality of Care Information Protection Act, 2004*;

"record" means a record of information in any form or in any medium, whether in written, printed, photographic or electronic form or otherwise, but does not include a computer program or other mechanism that can produce a record;

"relative" means either of two persons who are related to each other by blood, marriage or adoption;

"research" means a systematic investigation designed to develop or establish principles, facts or generalizable knowledge, or any combination of them, and includes the development, testing and evaluation of research;

"researcher" means a person who conducts research;

"research ethics board" means a board of persons that is established for the purpose of approving research plans under section 44 and that meets the prescribed requirements;

"spouse" means either of two persons who,

(a) are married to each other, or

(b) live together in a conjugal relationship outside marriage and,

(i) have cohabited for at least one year,

(ii) are together the parents of a child, or

(iii) have together entered into a cohabitation agreement under section 53 of the *Family Law Act*,

unless they are living separate and apart as a result of a breakdown of their relationship;

"substitute decision-maker" has the meaning set out in section 5;

"use", in relation to personal health information in the custody or under the control of a health information custodian or a person, means to handle or deal with the information, subject to subsection 6 (1), but does not include to disclose the information, and "use", as a noun, has a corresponding meaning.

3. (1) **Health information custodian** — In this Act,

"health information custodian", subject to subsections (3) to (11), means a person or organization described in one of the following paragraphs who has custody or control of personal health information as a result of or in connection with performing the person's or organization's powers or duties or the work described in the paragraph, if any:

1. A health care practitioner or a person who operates a group practice of health care practitioners.
2. A service provider within the meaning of the *Long-Term Care Act, 1994* who provides a community service to which that Act applies.
3. A community care access corporation within the meaning of the *Community Care Access Corporations Act, 2001*.
4. A person who operates one of the following facilities, programs or services:

   i. A hospital within the meaning of the *Public Hospitals Act*, a private hospital within the meaning of the *Private Hospitals Act*, a psychiatric facility within the meaning of the *Mental Health Act*, an institution within the meaning of the *Mental Hospitals Act* or an independent health facility within the meaning of the *Independent Health Facilities Act*.

   ii. An approved charitable home for the aged within the meaning of the *Charitable Institutions Act*, a placement co-ordinator described in subsection 9.6 (2) of that Act, a home or joint home within the meaning of the *Homes for the Aged and Rest Homes Act*, a placement co-ordinator described in subsection 18 (2) of that Act, a nursing home within the meaning of the *Nursing Homes Act*, a placement co-ordinator described in subsection 20.1 (2) of that Act or a care home within the meaning of the *Tenant Protection Act, 1997*.

iii. A pharmacy within the meaning of Part VI of the *Drug and Pharmacies Regulation Act.*

iv. A laboratory or a specimen collection centre as defined in section 5 of the *Laboratory and Specimen Collection Centre Licensing Act.*

v. An ambulance service within the meaning of the *Ambulance Act.*

vi. A home for special care within the meaning of the *Homes for Special Care Act.*

vii. A centre, program or service for community health or mental health whose primary purpose is the provision of health care.

5. An evaluator within the meaning of the *Health Care Consent Act, 1996* or an assessor within the meaning of the *Substitute Decisions Act, 1992.*

6. A medical officer of health or a board of health within the meaning of the *Health Protection and Promotion Act.*

7. The Minister, together with the Ministry of the Minister if the context so requires.

8. Any other person prescribed as a health information custodian if the person has custody or control of personal health information as a result of or in connection with performing prescribed powers, duties or work or any prescribed class of such persons.

(2) **Interpretation, officer in charge —** For the purposes of subparagraph 4 i of the definition of "health information custodian" in subsection (1), the officer in charge of an institution within the meaning of the *Mental Hospitals Act* shall be deemed to be the person who operates the institution.

(3) **Exceptions —** Except as is prescribed, a person described in any of the following paragraphs is not a health information custodian in respect of personal health information that the person collects, uses or discloses while performing the person's powers or duties or the work described in the paragraph, if any:

1. A person described in paragraph 1, 2 or 5 of the definition of "health information custodian" in subsection (1) who is an agent of a health information custodian.

2. A person who is authorized to act for or on behalf of a person that is not a health information custodian, if the scope of duties of the authorized person does not include the provision of health care.

3. The Minister when acting on behalf of an institution within the meaning of the *Freedom of Information and Protection of Privacy Act* or the *Municipal Freedom of Information and Protection of Privacy Act* that is not a health information custodian.

(4) **Other exceptions —** A health information custodian does not include a person described in one of the following paragraphs who has custody or control of personal health information as a result of or in connection with performing the work described in the paragraph:

1. An aboriginal healer who provides traditional healing services to aboriginal persons or members of an aboriginal community.

2. An aboriginal midwife who provides traditional midwifery services to aboriginal persons or members of an aboriginal community.

3. A person who treats another person solely by prayer or spiritual means in accordance with the tenets of the religion of the person giving the treatment.

(5) **Multiple facilities** — Subject to subsection (6) or an order of the Minister under subsection (8), a health information custodian that operates more than one facility described in one of the subparagraphs of paragraph 4 of the definition of "health information custodian" in subsection (1) shall be deemed to be a separate custodian with respect to personal health information of which it has custody or control as a result of or in connection with operating each of the facilities that it operates.

(6) **Single custodian** — Despite subsection (5), the following persons shall be deemed to be a single health information custodian with respect to all the functions described in the applicable paragraph, if any:

1. A person who operates a hospital within the meaning of the *Public Hospitals Act* and any of the facilities, programs or services described in paragraph 4 of the definition of "health information custodian" in subsection (1).

2. A community care access corporation that provides a community service within the meaning of subsection 2 (3) of the *LongITerm Care Act, 1994* and acts as a placement co-ordinator as described in subsection 9.6 (2) of the *Charitable Institutions Act*, subsection 18 (2) of the *Homes for the Aged and Rest Homes Act* or subsection 20.1 (2) of the *Nursing Homes Act*.

3. Health information custodians or facilities that are prescribed.

(7) **Application to act as one custodian** — A health information custodian that operates more than one facility described in one of the subparagraphs of paragraph 4 of the definition of "health information custodian" in subsection (1) or two or more health information custodians may apply to the Minister, in a form approved by the Minister, for an order described in subsection (8).

(8) **Minister's order** — Upon receiving an application described in subsection (7), the Minister may make an order permitting all or some of the applicants to act as a single health information custodian on behalf of those facilities, powers, duties or work that the Minister specifies, subject to the terms that the Minister considers appropriate and specifies in the order, if the Minister is of the opinion that it is appropriate to make the order in the circumstances, having regard to,

(a) the public interest;

(b) the ability of the applicants to provide individuals with reasonable access to their personal health information;

(c) the ability of the applicants to comply with the requirements of this Act; and

(d) whether permitting the applicants to act as a single health information custodian is necessary to enable them to effectively provide integrated health care.

(9) **Scope of order —** In an order made under subsection (8), the Minister may order that any class of health information custodians that the Minister considers to be situated similarly to the applicants is permitted to act as a single health information custodian, subject to the terms that the Minister considers appropriate and specifies in the order, if the Minister is of the opinion that it is appropriate to so order, having regard to,

(a) the public interest;

(b) the ability of the custodians that are subject to the order made under this subsection to provide individuals with reasonable access to their personal health information;

(c) the ability of the custodians that are subject to the order made under this subsection to comply with the requirements of this Act; and

(d) whether permitting the custodians that are subject to the order made under this subsection to act as a single health information custodian is necessary to enable them to effectively provide integrated health care.

(10) **No hearing required —** The Minister is not required to hold a hearing or to afford to any person an opportunity for a hearing before making an order under subsection (8).

(11) **Duration —** Subject to subsection (12), a health information custodian does not cease to be a health information custodian with respect to a record of personal health information until complete custody and control of the record, where applicable, passes to another person who is legally authorized to hold the record.

(12) **Death of custodian —** If a health information custodian dies, the following person shall be deemed to be the health information custodian with respect to records of personal health information held by the deceased custodian until custody and control of the records, where applicable, passes to another person who is legally authorized to hold the records:

1. The estate trustee of the deceased custodian.
2. The person who has assumed responsibility for the administration of the deceased custodian's estate, if the estate does not have an estate trustee.

4. (1) **Personal health information —** In this Act,

"personal health information", subject to subsections (3) and (4), means identifying information about an individual in oral or recorded form, if the information,

(a) relates to the physical or mental health of the individual, including information that consists of the health history of the individual's family,

(b) relates to the providing of health care to the individual, including the identification of a person as a provider of health care to the individual,

(c) is a plan of service within the meaning of the *Long-Term Care Act, 1994* for the individual,

(d) relates to payments or eligibility for health care in respect of the individual,

(e) relates to the donation by the individual of any body part or bodily substance of the individual or is derived from the testing or examination of any such body part or bodily substance,

(f) is the individual's health number, or

(g) identifies an individual's substitute decision-maker.

(2) **Identifying information** — In this section,

"identifying information" means information that identifies an individual or for which it is reasonably foreseeable in the circumstances that it could be utilized, either alone or with other information, to identify an individual.

(3) **Mixed records** — Personal health information about an individual includes identifying information about the individual that is not personal health information described in subsection (1) but that is contained in a record that contains personal health information described in that subsection about the individual.

(4) **Exception** — Personal health information does not include identifying information contained in a record that is in the custody or under the control of a health information custodian if,

(a) the identifying information contained in the record relates primarily to one or more employees or other agents of the custodian; and

(b) the record is maintained primarily for a purpose other than the provision of health care or assistance in providing health care to the employees or other agents.

5. (1) **Substitute decision-maker** — In this Act,

"substitute decision-maker", in relation to an individual, means, unless the context requires otherwise, a person who is authorized under this Act to consent on behalf of the individual to the collection, use or disclosure of personal health information about the individual.

(2) **Decision about treatment** — A substitute decision-maker of an individual within the meaning of section 9 of the *Health Care Consent Act, 1996* shall be deemed to be a substitute decision-maker of the individual in respect of the collection, use or disclosure of personal health information about the individual if the purpose of the collection, use or disclosure is necessary for, or ancillary to, a decision about a treatment under Part II of that Act.

(3) **Admission to a care facility** — A substitute decision-maker of an individual within the meaning of section 39 of the *Health Care Consent Act, 1996* shall be deemed to be a substitute decision-maker of the individual in respect of the collection, use or disclosure of personal health information about the individual if the purpose of the collection, use or disclosure is necessary for, or ancillary to, a decision about admission to a care facility under Part III of that Act.

(4) **Personal assistance services** — A substitute decision-maker of an individual within the meaning of section 56 of the *Health Care Consent Act, 1996* shall be deemed to be a substitute decision-maker of the individual in respect of the collection, use or disclosure of personal health information about the individual if the purpose of the collection, use or disclosure is necessary for, or ancillary to, a decision about a personal assistance service under Part IV of that Act.

6. (1) **Interpretation** — For the purposes of this Act, the providing of personal health information between a health information custodian and an agent of the custodian is a use by the custodian, and not a disclosure by the person providing the information or a collection by the person to whom the information is provided.

(2) **Provisions based on consent** — A provision of this Act that applies to the collection, use or disclosure of personal health information about an individual by a health information custodian with the consent of the individual, whatever the nature of the consent, does not affect the collection, use or disclosure that this Act permits or requires the health information custodian to make of the information without the consent of the individual.

(3) **Permissive disclosure** — A provision of this Act that permits a health information custodian to disclose personal health information about an individual without the consent of the individual,

(a) does not require the custodian to disclose it unless required to do so by law;

(b) does not relieve the custodian from a legal requirement to disclose the information; and

(c) does not prevent the custodian from obtaining the individual's consent for the disclosure.

Part III
Consent Concerning Personal Health Information

General

18. (1) **Elements of consent** — If this Act or any other Act requires the consent of an individual for the collection, use or disclosure of personal health information by a health information custodian, the consent,

(a) must be a consent of the individual;

(b) must be knowledgeable;

(c) must relate to the information; and

(d) must not be obtained through deception or coercion.

(2) **Implied consent** — Subject to subsection (3), a consent to the collection, use or disclosure of personal health information about an individual may be express or implied.

(3) **Exception** — A consent to the disclosure of personal health information about an individual must be express, and not implied, if,

(a) a health information custodian makes the disclosure to a person that is not a health information custodian; or

(b) a health information custodian makes the disclosure to another health information custodian and the disclosure is not for the purposes of providing health care or assisting in providing health care.

(4) **Same** — Subsection (3) does not apply to,

(a) a disclosure pursuant to an implied consent described in subsection 20 (4);

(b) a disclosure pursuant to clause 32 (1) (b); or

(c) a prescribed type of disclosure that does not include information about an individual's state of health.

(5) **Knowledgeable consent** — A consent to the collection, use or disclosure of personal health information about an individual is knowledgeable if it is reasonable in the circumstances to believe that the individual knows,

(a) the purposes of the collection, use or disclosure, as the case may be; and

(b) that the individual may give or withhold consent.

(6) **Notice of purposes** — Unless it is not reasonable in the circumstances, it is reasonable to believe that an individual knows the purposes of the collection, use or disclosure of personal health information about the individual by a health information custodian if the custodian posts or makes readily available a notice describing the purposes where it is likely to come to the individual's attention or provides the individual with such a notice.

(7) **Transition** – A consent that an individual gives, before the day that subsection (1) comes into force, to a collection, use or disclosure of information that is personal health information is a valid consent if it meets the requirements of this Act for consent.

19. (1) **Withdrawal of consent** — If an individual consents to have a health information custodian collect, use or disclose personal health information about the individual, the individual may withdraw the consent, whether the consent is express or implied, by providing notice to the health information custodian, but the withdrawal of the consent shall not have retroactive effect.

(2) **Conditional consent** — If an individual places a condition on his or her consent to have a health information custodian collect, use or disclose personal health information about the individual, the condition is not effective to the extent that it purports to prohibit or restrict any recording of personal health information by a health information custodian that is required by law or by established standards of professional practice or institutional practice.

20. (1) **Assumption of validity** — A health information custodian who has obtained an individual's consent to a collection, use or disclosure of personal health information about the individual or who has received a copy of a document purporting to record the individual's consent to the collection, use or disclosure is entitled to assume that the consent fulfils the requirements of this Act and the individual has not withdrawn it, unless it is not reasonable to assume so.

(2) **Implied consent —** A health information custodian described in paragraph 1, 2, 3 or 4 of the definition of "health information custodian" in subsection 3 (1), that receives personal health information about an individual from the individual, the individual's substitute decision-maker or another health information custodian for the purpose of providing health care or assisting in the provision of health care to the individual, is entitled to assume that it has the individual's implied consent to collect, use or disclose the information for the purposes of providing health care or assisting in providing health care to the individual, unless the custodian that receives the information is aware that the individual has expressly withheld or withdrawn the consent.

(3) **Limited consent —** If a health information custodian discloses, with the consent of an individual, personal health information about the individual to a health information custodian described in paragraph 1, 2, 3 or 4 of the definition of "health information custodian" in subsection 3 (1) for the purpose of the provision of health care to the individual and if the disclosing custodian does not have the consent of the individual to disclose all the personal health information about the individual that it considers reasonably necessary for that purpose, the disclosing custodian shall notify the custodian to whom it disclosed the information of that fact.

(4) **Implied consent, affiliation —** If an individual who is a resident or patient in a facility that is a health information custodian provides to the custodian information about his or her religious or other organizational affiliation, the facility may assume that it has the individual's implied consent to provide his or her name and location in the facility to a representative of the religious or other organization, where the custodian has offered the individual the opportunity to withhold or withdraw the consent and the individual has not done so.

Capacity and Substitute Decision-Making

21. (1) **Capacity to consent —** An individual is capable of consenting to the collection, use or disclosure of personal health information if the individual is able,

(a) to understand the information that is relevant to deciding whether to consent to the collection, use or disclosure, as the case may be; and

(b) to appreciate the reasonably foreseeable consequences of giving, not giving, withholding or withdrawing the consent.

(2) **Different information —** An individual may be capable of consenting to the collection, use or disclosure of some parts of personal health information, but incapable of consenting with respect to other parts.

(3) **Different times —** An individual may be capable of consenting to the collection, use or disclosure of personal health information at one time, but incapable of consenting at another time.

(4) **Presumption of capacity** — An individual is presumed to be capable of consenting to the collection, use or disclosure of personal health information.

(5) **Non-application** — A health information custodian may rely on the presumption described in subsection (4) unless the custodian has reasonable grounds to believe that the individual is incapable of consenting to the collection, use or disclosure of personal health information.

22. (1) **Determination of incapacity** — A health information custodian that determines the incapacity of an individual to consent to the collection, use or disclosure of personal health information under this Act shall do so in accordance with the requirements and restrictions, if any, that are prescribed.

(2) **Information about determination** — If it is reasonable in the circumstances, a health information custodian shall provide, to an individual determined incapable of consenting to the collection, use or disclosure of his or her personal health information by the custodian, information about the consequences of the determination of incapacity, including the information, if any, that is prescribed.

(3) **Review of determination** — An individual whom a health information custodian determines is incapable of consenting to the collection, use or disclosure of his or her personal health information by a health information custodian may apply to the Board for a review of the determination unless there is a person who is entitled to act as the substitute decision-maker of the individual under subsection 5 (2), (3) or (4).

(4) **Parties** — The parties to the application are:

1. The individual applying for the review of the determination.
2. The health information custodian that has custody or control of the personal health information.
3. All other persons whom the Board specifies.

(5) **Powers of Board** — The Board may confirm the determination of incapacity or may determine that the individual is capable of consenting to the collection, use or disclosure of personal health information.

(6) **Restriction on repeated applications** — If a determination that an individual is incapable with respect to consenting to the collection, use or disclosure of personal health information is confirmed on the final disposition of an application under this section, the individual shall not make a new application under this section for a determination with respect to the same or a similar issue within six months after the final disposition of the earlier application, unless the Board gives leave in advance.

(7) **Grounds for leave** — The Board may give leave for the new application to be made if it is satisfied that there has been a material change in circumstances that justifies reconsideration of the individual's capacity.

(8) **Procedure** — Sections 73 to 81 of the *Health Care Consent Act, 1996* apply with necessary modifications to an application under this section.

23. (1) **Persons who may consent —** If this Act or any other Act refers to a consent required of an individual to a collection, use or disclosure of personal health information about the individual, a person described in one of the following paragraphs may give, withhold or withdraw the consent:

1. If the individual is capable of consenting to the collection, use or disclosure of the information,
   i. the individual, or
   ii. if the individual is at least 16 years of age, any person who is capable of consenting, whom the individual has authorized in writing to act on his or her behalf and who, if a natural person, is at least 16 years of age.
2. If the individual is a child who is less than 16 years of age, a parent of the child or a children's aid society or other person who is lawfully entitled to give or refuse consent in the place of the parent unless the information relates to,
   i. treatment within the meaning of the *Health Care Consent Act, 1996*, about which the child has made a decision on his or her own in accordance with that Act, or
   ii. counselling in which the child has participated on his or her own under the *Child and Family Services Act*.
3. If the individual is incapable of consenting to the collection, use or disclosure of the information, a person who is authorized under subsection 5 (2), (3) or (4) or section 26 to consent on behalf of the individual.
4. If the individual is deceased, the deceased's estate trustee or the person who has assumed responsibility for the administration of the deceased's estate, if the estate does not have an estate trustee.
5. A person whom an Act of Ontario or Canada authorizes or requires to act on behalf of the individual.

(2) **Definition —** In subsection (1),

"parent" does not include a parent who has only a right of access to the child.

(3) **Conflict if child capable —** If the individual is a child who is less than 16 years of age and who is capable of consenting to the collection, use or disclosure of the information and if there is a person who is entitled to act as the substitute decision-maker of the child under paragraph 2 of subsection (1), a decision of the child to give, withhold or withdraw the consent or to provide the information prevails over a conflicting decision of that person.

24. (1) **Factors to consider for consent —** A person who consents under this Act or any other Act on behalf of or in the place of an individual to a collection, use or disclosure of personal health information by a health information custodian, who withholds or withdraws such a consent or who provides an express instruction under clause 37 (1) (a), 38 (1) (a) or 50 (1) (e) shall take into consideration,

(a) the wishes, values and beliefs that,

(i) if the individual is capable, the person knows the individual holds and believes the individual would want reflected in decisions made concerning the individual's personal health information, or

(ii) if the individual is incapable or deceased, the person knows the individual held when capable or alive and believes the individual would have wanted reflected in decisions made concerning the individual's personal health information;

(b) whether the benefits that the person expects from the collection, use or disclosure of the information outweigh the risk of negative consequences occurring as a result of the collection, use or disclosure;

(c) whether the purpose for which the collection, use or disclosure is sought can be accomplished without the collection, use or disclosure; and

(d) whether the collection, use or disclosure is necessary to satisfy any legal obligation.

(2) **Determination of compliance** — If a substitute decision-maker, on behalf of an incapable individual, gives, withholds or withdraws a consent to a collection, use or disclosure of personal health information about the individual by a health information custodian or provides an express instruction under clause 37 (1) (a), 38 (1) (a) or 50 (1) (e) and if the custodian is of the opinion that the substitute decision-maker has not complied with subsection (1), the custodian may apply to the Board for a determination as to whether the substitute decision-maker complied with that subsection.

(3) **Parties** — The parties to the application are:

1. The health information custodian.
2. The incapable individual.
3. The substitute decision-maker.
4. Any other person whom the Board specifies.

(4) **Power of Board** — In determining whether the substitute decision-maker complied with subsection (1), the Board may substitute its opinion for that of the substitute decision-maker.

(5) **Directions** — If the Board determines that the substitute decision-maker did not comply with subsection (1), it may give him or her directions and, in doing so, shall take into consideration the matters set out in clauses (1) (a) to (d).

(6) **Time for compliance** — The Board shall specify the time within which the substitute decision-maker must comply with its directions.

(7) **Deemed not authorized** — If the substitute decision-maker does not comply with the Board's directions within the time specified by the Board, he or she shall be deemed not to meet the requirements of subsection 26 (2).

(8) **Public Guardian and Trustee** — If the substitute decision-maker who is given directions is the Public Guardian and Trustee, he or she is required to comply with the directions and subsection (6) does not apply to him or her.

(9) **Procedure —** Sections 73 to 81 of the *Health Care Consent Act, 1996* apply with necessary modifications to an application under this section.

25. (1) **Authority of substitute decision-maker —** If this Act permits or requires an individual to make a request, give an instruction or take a step and a substitute decision-maker is authorized to consent on behalf of the individual to the collection, use or disclosure of personal health information about the individual, the substitute decision-maker may make the request, give the instruction or take the step on behalf of the individual.

(2) **Same —** If a substitute decision-maker makes a request, gives an instruction or takes a step under subsection (1) on behalf of an individual, references in this Act to the individual with respect to the request made, the instruction given or the step taken by the substitute decision-maker shall be read as references to the substitute decision-maker, and not to the individual.

26. (1) **Incapable individual: persons who may consent —** If an individual is determined to be incapable of consenting to the collection, use or disclosure of personal health information by a health information custodian, a person described in one of the following paragraphs may, on the individual's behalf and in the place of the individual, give, withhold or withdraw the consent:

1. The individual's guardian of the person or guardian of property, if the consent relates to the guardian's authority to make a decision on behalf of the individual.
2. The individual's attorney for personal care or attorney for property, if the consent relates to the attorney's authority to make a decision on behalf of the individual.
3. The individual's representative appointed by the Board under section 27, if the representative has authority to give the consent.
4. The individual's spouse or partner.
5. A child or parent of the individual, or a children's aid society or other person who is lawfully entitled to give or refuse consent in the place of the parent. This paragraph does not include a parent who has only a right of access to the individual. If a children's aid society or other person is lawfully entitled to consent in the place of the parent, this paragraph does not include the parent.
6. A parent of the individual with only a right of access to the individual.
7. A brother or sister of the individual.
8. Any other relative of the individual.

(2) **Requirements —** A person described in subsection (1) may consent only if the person,

(a) is capable of consenting to the collection, use or disclosure of personal health information by a health information custodian;

(b) in the case of an individual, is at least 16 years old or is the parent of the individual to whom the personal health information relates;

(c) is not prohibited by court order or separation agreement from having access to the individual to whom the personal health information relates or from giving or refusing consent on the individual's behalf;

(d) is available; and

(e) is willing to assume the responsibility of making a decision on whether or not to consent.

(3) **Meaning of "available"** — For the purpose of clause (2) (d), a person is available if it is possible, within a time that is reasonable in the circumstances, to communicate with the person and obtain a consent.

(4) **Ranking** — A person described in a paragraph of subsection (1) may consent only if no person described in an earlier paragraph meets the requirements of subsection (2).

(5) **Same** — Despite subsection (4), a person described in a paragraph of subsection (1) who is present or has otherwise been contacted may consent if the person believes that,

(a) no other person described in an earlier paragraph or the same paragraph exists; or

(b) although such other person exists, the other person is not a person described in paragraph 1 or 2 of subsection (1) and would not object to the person who is present or has otherwise been contacted making the decision.

(6) **Public Guardian and Trustee** — If no person described in subsection (1) meets the requirements of subsection (2), the Public Guardian and Trustee may make the decision to consent.

(7) **Conflict between persons in same paragraph** — If two or more persons who are described in the same paragraph of subsection (1) and who meet the requirements of subsection (2) disagree about whether to consent, and if their claims rank ahead of all others, the Public Guardian and Trustee may make the decision in their stead.

(8) **Transition, representative appointed by individual** — Where an individual, to whom personal health information relates, appointed a representative under section 36.1 of the *Mental Health Act* before the day this section comes into force, the representative shall be deemed to have the same authority as a person mentioned in paragraph 2 of subsection (1).

(9) **Limited authority** — The authority conferred on the representative by subsection (8) is limited to the purposes for which the representative was appointed.

(10) **Revocation** — An individual who is capable of consenting with respect to personal health information may revoke the appointment mentioned in subsection (8) in writing.

(11) **Ranking** — A person who is entitled to be the substitute decision-maker of the individual under this section may act as the substitute decision-maker only

in circumstances where there is no person who may act as the substitute decision-maker of the individual under subsection 5 (2), (3) or (4).

27. (1) **Appointment of representative —** An individual who is 16 years old or older and who is determined to be incapable of consenting to the collection, use or disclosure of personal health information may apply to the Board for appointment of a representative to consent on the individual's behalf to a collection, use or disclosure of the information by a health information custodian.

(2) **Application by proposed representative —** If an individual is incapable of consenting to the collection, use or disclosure of personal health information, another individual who is 16 years old or older may apply to the Board to be appointed as a representative to consent on behalf of the incapable individual to a collection, use or disclosure of the information.

(3) **Exception —** Subsections (1) and (2) do not apply if the individual to whom the personal health information relates has a guardian of the person, a guardian of property, an attorney for personal care, or an attorney for property, who has authority to give or refuse consent to the collection, use or disclosure.

(4) **Parties —** The parties to the application are:

1. The individual to whom the personal health information relates.
2. The proposed representative named in the application.
3. Every person who is described in paragraph 4, 5, 6 or 7 of subsection 26 (1).
4. All other persons whom the Board specifies.

(5) **Appointment —** In an appointment under this section, the Board may authorize the representative to consent, on behalf of the individual to whom the personal health information relates, to,

(a) a particular collection, use or disclosure at a particular time;

(b) a collection, use or disclosure of the type specified by the Board in circumstances specified by the Board, if the individual is determined to be incapable of consenting to the collection, use or disclosure of personal health information at the time the consent is sought; or

(c) any collection, use or disclosure at any time, if the individual is determined to be incapable of consenting to the collection, use or disclosure of personal health information at the time the consent is sought.

(6) **Criteria for appointment —** The Board may make an appointment under this section if it is satisfied that the following requirements are met:

1. The individual to whom the personal health information relates does not object to the appointment.
2. The representative consents to the appointment, is at least 16 years old and is capable of consenting to the collection, use or disclosure of personal health information.
3. The appointment is in the best interests of the individual to whom the personal health information relates.

(7) **Powers of Board** — Unless the individual to whom the personal health information relates objects, the Board may,

(a) appoint as representative a different individual than the one named in the application;

(b) limit the duration of the appointment;

(c) impose any other condition on the appointment; or

(d) on any person's application, remove, vary or suspend a condition imposed on the appointment or impose an additional condition on the appointment.

(8) **Termination** — The Board may, on any person's application, terminate an appointment made under this section if,

(a) the individual to whom the personal health information relates or the representative requests the termination;

(b) the representative is no longer capable of consenting to the collection, use or disclosure of personal health information;

(c) the appointment is no longer in the best interests of the individual to whom the personal health information relates; or

(d) the individual to whom the personal health information relates has a guardian of the person, a guardian of property, an attorney for personal care, or an attorney for property, who has authority to give or refuse consent to the types of collections, uses and disclosures for which the appointment was made and in the circumstances to which the appointment applies.

(9) **Procedure** — Sections 73 to 81 of the *Health Care Consent Act, 1996* apply with necessary modifications to an application under this section.

28. (1) **Transition, representative appointed by Board** — This Act applies to a representative whom the Board appointed under section 36.2 of the *Mental Health Act* or who was deemed to be appointed under that section before the day this section comes into force for an individual with respect to the individual's personal health information, as if the representative were the individual's representative appointed by the Board under section 27.

(2) **Limited authority** — The authority conferred on the representative by subsection (1) is limited to the purposes for which the representative was appointed.

Part IV

Collection, Use and Disclosure of Personal Health Information

Disclosure

38. (1) **Disclosures related to providing health care** — A health information custodian may disclose personal health information about an individual,

(a) to a person described in paragraph 1, 2, 3 or 4 of the definition of "health information custodian" in subsection 3 (1), if the disclosure is reasonably necessary for the provision of health care and it is not reasonably possible to obtain the individual's consent in a timely manner, but not if the individual has expressly instructed the custodian not to make the disclosure;

(b) in order for the Minister or another health information custodian to determine or provide funding or payment to the custodian for the provision of health care; or

(c) for the purpose of contacting a relative, friend or potential substitute decision-maker of the individual, if the individual is injured, incapacitated or ill and unable to give consent personally.

(2) **Notice of instruction** — If a health information custodian discloses personal health information about an individual under clause (1) (a) and if an instruction of the individual made under that clause prevents the custodian from disclosing all the personal health information that the custodian considers reasonably necessary to disclose for the provision of health care or assisting in the provision of health care to the individual, the custodian shall notify the person to whom it makes the disclosure of that fact.

(3) **Facility that provides health care** — A health information custodian that is a facility that provides health care may disclose to a person the following personal health information relating to an individual who is a patient or a resident in the facility if the custodian offers the individual the option, at the first reasonable opportunity after admission to the facility, to object to such disclosures and if the individual does not do so:

1. The fact that the individual is a patient or resident in the facility.
2. The individual's general health status described as critical, poor, fair, stable or satisfactory, or in similar terms.
3. The location of the individual in the facility.

(4) **Deceased individual** — A health information custodian may disclose personal health information about an individual who is deceased, or is reasonably suspected to be deceased,

(a) for the purpose of identifying the individual;

(b) for the purpose of informing any person whom it is reasonable to inform in the circumstances of,

  (i) the fact that the individual is deceased or reasonably suspected to be deceased, and

  (ii) the circumstances of death, where appropriate; or

(c) to the spouse, partner, sibling or child of the individual if the recipients of the information reasonably require the information to make decisions about their own health care or their children's health care.

39. (1) **Disclosures for health or other programs** — Subject to the requirements and restrictions, if any, that are prescribed, a health information custodian may disclose personal health information about an individual,

(a) for the purpose of determining or verifying the eligibility of the individual to receive health care or related goods, services or benefits provided under an Act of Ontario or Canada and funded in whole or in part by the Government of Ontario or Canada or by a municipality;

(b) to a person conducting an audit or reviewing an application for accreditation or reviewing an accreditation, if the audit or review relates to services provided by the custodian and the person does not remove any records of personal health information from the custodian's premises; or

(c) to a prescribed person who compiles or maintains a registry of personal health information for purposes of facilitating or improving the provision of health care or that relates to the storage or donation of body parts or bodily substances.

(2) **Same** — A health information custodian may disclose personal health information about an individual,

(a) to the Chief Medical Officer of Health or a medical officer of health within the meaning of the *Health Protection and Promotion Act* if the disclosure is made for a purpose of that Act; or

(b) to a public health authority that is similar to the persons described in clause (a) and that is established under the laws of Canada, another province or a territory of Canada or other jurisdiction, if the disclosure is made for a purpose that is substantially similar to a purpose of the *Health Protection and Promotion Act.*

(3) **Removal allowed** — Despite clause (1) (b), the person described in that clause may remove records of personal health information from the custodian's premises if,

(a) the removal is authorized by or under an Act of Ontario or Canada; or

(b) an agreement between the custodian and the person authorizes the removal and provides that the records will be held in a secure and confidential manner and will be returned when the audit or review is completed.

(4) **Authorization to collect** — A person who is not a health information custodian is authorized to collect the personal health information that a health information custodian may disclose to the person under clause (1) (c).

40. (1) **Disclosures related to risks** — A health information custodian may disclose personal health information about an individual if the custodian believes on reasonable grounds that the disclosure is necessary for the purpose of eliminating or reducing a significant risk of serious bodily harm to a person or group of persons.

(2) **Disclosures related to care or custody** — A health information custodian may disclose personal health information about an individual to the head of a

penal or other custodial institution in which the individual is being lawfully detained or to the officer in charge of a psychiatric facility within the meaning of the *Mental Health Act* in which the individual is being lawfully detained for the purposes described in subsection (3).

(3) **Same —** A health information custodian may disclose personal health information about an individual under subsection (2) to assist an institution or a facility in making a decision concerning,

(a) arrangements for the provision of health care to the individual; or

(b) the placement of the individual into custody, detention, release, conditional release, discharge or conditional discharge under Part IV of the *Child and Family Services Act*, the *Mental Health Act*, the *Ministry of Correctional Services Act*, the *Corrections and Conditional Release Act* (Canada), Part XX.1 of the *Criminal Code* (Canada), the *Prisons and Reformatories Act* (Canada) or the *Youth Criminal Justice Act* (Canada).

Part V
Access to Records of Personal Health Information and Correction

Access

51. (1) **Application of Part —** This Part does not apply to a record that contains,

(a) quality of care information;

(b) personal health information collected or created for the purpose of complying with the requirements of a quality assurance program within the meaning of the Health Professions Procedural Code that is Schedule 2 to the *Regulated Health Professions Act, 1991*;

(c) raw data from standardized psychological tests or assessments; or

(d) personal health information of the prescribed type in the custody or under the control of a prescribed class or classes of health information custodians.

(2) **Severable record —** Despite subsection (1), this Part applies to that part of a record of personal health information that can reasonably be severed from the part of the record that contains the information described in clauses (1) (a) to (d).

(3) **Agent of a non-custodian —** This Part does not apply to a record in the custody or under the control of a health information custodian acting as an agent of an institution within the meaning of the *Freedom of Information and Protection of Privacy Act* or the *Municipal Freedom of Information and Protection of Privacy Act* that is not a health information custodian if the individual has the right to request access to the record under one of those Acts.

52. (1) **Individual's right of access —** Subject to this Part, an individual has a right of access to a record of personal health information about the individual that is in the custody or under the control of a health information custodian unless,

(a) the record or the information in the record is subject to a legal privilege that restricts disclosure of the record or the information, as the case may be, to the individual;

(b) another Act, an Act of Canada or a court order prohibits disclosure to the individual of the record or the information in the record in the circumstances;

(c) the information in the record was collected or created primarily in anticipation of or use in a proceeding, and the proceeding, together with all appeals or processes resulting from it, have not been concluded;

(d) the following conditions are met:

(i) the information was collected or created in the course of an inspection, investigation or similar procedure authorized by law, or undertaken for the purpose of the detection, monitoring or prevention of a person's receiving or attempting to receive a service or benefit, to which the person is not entitled under an Act or a program operated by the Minister, or a payment for such a service or benefit, and

(ii) the inspection, investigation, or similar procedure, together with all proceedings, appeals or processes resulting from them, have not been concluded;

(e) granting the access could reasonably be expected to,

(i) result in a risk of serious harm to the treatment or recovery of the individual or a risk of serious bodily harm to the individual or another person,

(ii) lead to the identification of a person who was required by law to provide information in the record to the custodian, or

(iii) lead to the identification of a person who provided information in the record to the custodian explicitly or implicitly in confidence if the custodian considers it appropriate in the circumstances that the name of the person be kept confidential; or

(f) the following conditions are met:

(i) the custodian is an institution within the meaning of the *Freedom of Information and Protection of Privacy Act* or the *Municipal Freedom of Information and Protection of Privacy Act* or is acting as part of such an institution, and

(ii) the custodian would refuse to grant access to the part of the record,

(A) under clause 49 (a), (c) or (e) of the *Freedom of Information and Protection of Privacy Act*, if the request were made under that Act and that Act applied to the record, or

(B) under clause 38 (a) or (c) of the *Municipal Freedom of Information and Protection of Privacy Act*, if the request were made under that Act and that Act applied to the record.

(2) **Severable record** — Despite subsection (1), an individual has a right of access to that part of a record of personal health information about the individual that can reasonably be severed from the part of the record to which the individual does not have a right of access as a result of clauses (1) (a) to (f).

(3) **Same** — Despite subsection (1), if a record is not a record dedicated primarily to personal health information about the individual requesting access, the individual has a right of access only to the portion of personal health information about the individual in the record that can reasonably be severed from the record for the purpose of providing access.

(4) **Individual's plan of service** — Despite subsection (1), a health information custodian shall not refuse to grant the individual access to his or her plan of service within the meaning of the *Long-Term Care Act, 1994*.

(5) **Consultation regarding harm** — Before deciding to refuse to grant an individual access to a record of personal health information under subclause (1) (e) (i), a health information custodian may consult with a member of the College of Physicians and Surgeons of Ontario or a member of the College of Psychologists of Ontario.

(6) **Informal access** — Nothing in this Act prevents a health information custodian from,

(a) granting an individual access to a record of personal health information, to which the individual has a right of access, if the individual makes an oral request for access or does not make any request for access under section 53; or

(b) with respect to a record of personal health information to which an individual has a right of access, communicating with the individual or his or her substitute decision-maker who is authorized to consent on behalf of the individual to the collection, use or disclosure of personal health information about the individual.

(7) **Duty of health information custodian** — Nothing in this Part relieves a health information custodian from a legal duty to provide, in a manner that is not inconsistent with this Act, personal health information as expeditiously as is necessary for the provision of health care to the individual.

53. (1) **Request for access** — An individual may exercise a right of access to a record of personal health information by making a written request for access to the health information custodian that has custody or control of the information.

(2) **Detail in request** — The request must contain sufficient detail to enable the health information custodian to identify and locate the record with reasonable efforts.

(3) **Assistance** — If the request does not contain sufficient detail to enable the health information custodian to identify and locate the record with reasonable

efforts, the custodian shall offer assistance to the person requesting access in reformulating the request to comply with subsection (2).

54. (1) **Response of health information custodian** — A health information custodian that receives a request from an individual for access to a record of personal health information shall,

(a) make the record available to the individual for examination and, at the request of the individual, provide a copy of the record to the individual and if reasonably practical, an explanation of any term, code or abbreviation used in the record;

(b) give a written notice to the individual stating that, after a reasonable search, the custodian has concluded that the record does not exist or cannot be found, if that is the case;

(c) if the custodian is entitled to refuse the request, in whole or in part, under any provision of this Part other than clause 52 (1) (c), (d) or (e), give a written notice to the individual stating that the custodian is refusing the request, in whole or in part, providing a reason for the refusal and stating that the individual is entitled to make a complaint about the refusal to the Commissioner under Part VI; or

(d) if the custodian is entitled to refuse the request, in whole or in part, under clause 52 (1) (c), (d) or (e), give a written notice to the individual stating that the custodian is refusing to confirm or deny the existence of any record subject to any of those provisions and that the individual is entitled to make a complaint about the refusal to the Commissioner under Part VI.

(2) **Time for response** — Subject to subsection (3), the health information custodian shall give the response required by clause (1) (a), (b), (c) or (d) as soon as possible in the circumstances but no later than 30 days after receiving the request.

(3) **Extension of time for response** — Within 30 days after receiving the request for access, the health information custodian may extend the time limit set out in subsection (2) for a further period of time of not more than 30 days if,

(a) meeting the time limit would unreasonably interfere with the operations of the custodian because the information consists of numerous pieces of information or locating the information would necessitate a lengthy search; or

(b) the time required to undertake the consultations necessary to reply to the request within 30 days after receiving it would make it not reasonably practical to reply within that time.

(4) **Notice of extension** — Upon extending the time limit under subsection (3), the health information custodian shall give the individual written notice of the extension setting out the length of the extension and the reason for the extension.

(5) **Expedited access** — Despite subsection (2), the health information custodian shall give the response required by clause (1) (a), (b), (c) or (d) within the time period that the individual specifies if,

(a) the individual provides the custodian with evidence satisfactory to the custodian, acting on a reasonable basis, that the individual requires access to the requested record of personal health information on an urgent basis within that time period; and

(b) the custodian is reasonably able to give the required response within that time period.

(6) **Frivolous or vexatious requests** — A health information custodian that believes on reasonable grounds that a request for access to a record of personal health information is frivolous or vexatious or is made in bad faith may refuse to grant the individual access to the requested record.

(7) **Effect of non-compliance** — If the health information custodian does not respond to the request within the time limit or before the extension, if any, expires, the custodian shall be deemed to have refused the individual's request for access.

(8) **Right to complain** — If the health information custodian refuses or is deemed to have refused the request, in whole or in part,

(a) the individual is entitled to make a complaint about the refusal to the Commissioner under Part VI; and

(b) in the complaint, the burden of proof in respect of the refusal lies on the health information custodian.

(9) **Identity of individual** — A health information custodian shall not make a record of personal health information or a part of it available to an individual under this Part or provide a copy of it to an individual under clause (1) (a) without first taking reasonable steps to be satisfied as to the individual's identity.

(10) **Fee for access** — A health information custodian that makes a record of personal health information or a part of it available to an individual under this Part or provides a copy of it to an individual under clause (1) (a) may charge the individual a fee for that purpose if the custodian first gives the individual an estimate of the fee.

(11) **Amount of fee** — The amount of the fee shall not exceed the prescribed amount or the amount of reasonable cost recovery, if no amount is prescribed.

(12) **Waiver of fee** — A health information custodian mentioned in subsection (10) may waive the payment of all or any part of the fee that an individual is required to pay under that subsection if, in the custodian's opinion, it is fair and equitable to do so.

Correction

55. (1) **Correction** — If a health information custodian has granted an individual access to a record of his or her personal health information and if the individual believes that the record is inaccurate or incomplete for the purposes for which the custodian has collected or used the information, the individual may request in writing that the custodian correct the record.

(2) **Informal request** — If the individual makes an oral request that the health information custodian correct the record, nothing in this Part prevents the custodian from making the requested correction.

(3) **Reply** — As soon as possible in the circumstances but no later than 30 days after receiving a request for a correction under subsection (1), the health information custodian shall, by written notice to the individual, grant or refuse the individual's request or extend the deadline for replying for a period of not more than 30 days if,

(a) replying to the request within 30 days would unreasonably interfere with the activities of the custodian; or

(b) the time required to undertake the consultations necessary to reply to the request within 30 days would make it not reasonably practical to reply within that time.

(4) **Extension of time for reply** — A health information custodian that extends the time limit under subsection (3) shall,

(a) give the individual written notice of the extension setting out the length of the extension and the reason for the extension; and

(b) grant or refuse the individual's request as soon as possible in the circumstances but no later than the expiry of the time limit as extended.

(5) **Deemed refusal** — A health information custodian that does not grant a request for a correction under subsection (1) within the time required shall be deemed to have refused the request.

(6) **Frivolous or vexatious requests** — A health information custodian that believes on reasonable grounds that a request for a correction under subsection (1) is frivolous or vexatious or is made in bad faith may refuse to grant the request and, in that case, shall provide the individual with a notice that sets out the reasons for the refusal and that states that the individual is entitled to make a complaint about the refusal to the Commissioner under Part VI.

(7) **Right to complain** — The individual is entitled to make a complaint to the Commissioner under Part VI about a refusal made under subsection (6).

(8) **Duty to correct** — The health information custodian shall grant a request for a correction under subsection (1) if the individual demonstrates, to the satisfaction of the custodian, that the record is incomplete or inaccurate for the purposes for which the custodian uses the information and gives the custodian the information necessary to enable the custodian to correct the record.

(9) **Exceptions** — Despite subsection (8), a health information custodian is not required to correct a record of personal health information if,

(a) it consists of a record that was not originally created by the custodian and the custodian does not have sufficient knowledge, expertise and authority to correct the record; or

(b) it consists of a professional opinion or observation that a custodian has made in good faith about the individual.

(10) **Duties upon correction** — Upon granting a request for a correction under subsection (1), the health information custodian shall,

(a) make the requested correction by,

(i) recording the correct information in the record and,

(A) striking out the incorrect information in a manner that does not obliterate the record, or

(B) if that is not possible, labelling the information as incorrect, severing the incorrect information from the record, storing it separately from the record and maintaining a link in the record that enables a person to trace the incorrect information, or

(ii) if it is not possible to record the correct information in the record, ensuring that there is a practical system in place to inform a person who accesses the record that the information in the record is incorrect and to direct the person to the correct information;

(b) give notice to the individual of what it has done under clause (a);

(c) at the request of the individual, give written notice of the requested correction, to the extent reasonably possible, to the persons to whom the custodian has disclosed the information with respect to which the individual requested the correction of the record, except if the correction cannot reasonably be expected to have an effect on the ongoing provision of health care or other benefits to the individual.

(11) **Notice of refusal** — A notice of refusal under subsection (3) or (4) must give the reasons for the refusal and inform the individual that the individual is entitled to,

(a) prepare a concise statement of disagreement that sets out the correction that the health information custodian has refused to make;

(b) require that the health information custodian attach the statement of disagreement as part of the records that it holds of the individual's personal health information and disclose the statement of disagreement whenever the custodian discloses information to which the statement relates;

(c) require that the health information custodian make all reasonable efforts to disclose the statement of disagreement to any person who would have been notified under clause (10) (c) if the custodian had granted the requested correction; and

(d) make a complaint about the refusal to the Commissioner under Part VI.

(12) **Rights of individual** — If a health information custodian, under subsection (3) or (4), refuses a request for a correction under subsection (1), in whole or in part, or is deemed to have refused the request, the individual is entitled to take the actions described in any of clauses (11) (a), (b), (c) and (d).

(13) **Custodian's duty** — If the individual takes an action described in clause (11) (b) or (c), the health information custodian shall comply with the requirements described in the applicable clause.

Part VIII
Complementary Amendments

Mental Health Act

90. (1) The definition of "mentally competent" in subsection 1 (1) of the *Mental Health Act* is repealed.

(2) Subsection 1 (1) of the Act, as amended by the Statutes of Ontario, 1992, chapter 32, section 20, 1996, chapter 2, section 72 and 2000, chapter 9, section 1, is amended by adding the following definitions:

"personal health information" has the same meaning as in the *Personal Health Information Protection Act, 2004*;

"record of personal health information", in relation to a person, means a record of personal health information that is compiled in a psychiatric facility in respect of the person;

(3) The definition of "substitute decision-maker" in subsection 1 (1) of the Act, as enacted by the Statutes of Ontario, 1996, chapter 2, section 72, is repealed and the following substituted:

"substitute decision-maker", in relation to a patient, means the person who would be authorized under the *Health Care Consent Act, 1996* to give or refuse consent to a treatment on behalf of the patient, if the patient were incapable with respect to the treatment under that Act, unless the context requires otherwise;

(4) Section 29 of the Act, as amended by the Statutes of Ontario, 2000, chapter 9, section 11, is amended by adding the following subsection:

(1.1) **Transfer of records from one facility to another** — The officer in charge of the psychiatric facility from which the patient is transferred may transfer the patient's record of personal health information to the officer in charge of the psychiatric facility to which the patient is transferred.

(5) The Act is amended by adding the following section:

34.1 Conflict — Where there is a conflict between the *Personal Health Information Protection Act, 2004* and section 35 or 35.1 of this Act or any provision of this Act relating to the issuance or renewal of a community treatment order or the treatment, care or supervision of a person in accordance with a community treatment plan, the provisions of this Act apply.

(6) The following provisions of the Act are repealed:

1. **Subsection 35 (1), as amended by the Statutes of Ontario, 1996, chapter 2, section 72.**
2. **Subsection 35 (2), as amended by the Statutes of Ontario, 1992, chapter 32, section 20.**

3. **Subsection 35 (3), as amended by the Statutes of Ontario, 1992, chapter 32, section 20, 1996, chapter 2, section 72 and 2000, chapter 9, section 16.**
4. **Subsection 35 (4).**

(7) Section 35 of the Act, as amended by the Statutes of Ontario, 1992, chapter 32, section 20, 1996, chapter 2, section 72 and 2000, chapter 9, section 16, is amended by adding the following subsections:

(1) **Personal health information** — In this section,

"patient" includes former patient, out-patient, former out-patient and anyone who is or has been detained in a psychiatric facility.

(2) **Disclosure, etc., for purpose of detention or order** — The officer in charge of a psychiatric facility may collect, use and disclose personal health information about a patient, with or without the patient's consent, for the purposes of,

(a) examining, assessing, observing or detaining the patient in accordance with this Act; or

(b) complying with Part XX.1 (Mental Disorder) of the *Criminal Code* (Canada) or an order or disposition made pursuant to that Part.

(3) **Disclosure to Board** — In a proceeding before the Board under this or any other Act in respect of a patient, the officer in charge shall, at the request of any party to the proceeding, disclose to the Board the patient's record of personal health information.

(4) **Disclosure of record** — The officer in charge may disclose or transmit a person's record of personal health information to or permit the examination of the record by,

(a) a physician who is considering issuing or renewing, or who has issued or renewed, a community treatment order under section 33.1;

(b) a physician appointed under subsection 33.5 (2);

(c) another person named in the person's community treatment plan as being involved in the person's treatment or care and supervision upon the written request of the physician or other named person; or

(d) a prescribed person who is providing advocacy services to patients in the prescribed circumstances.

(8) The following provisions of the Act are amended by striking out "clinical record" wherever it appears and substituting in each case "record of personal health information":

1. **Subsection 35 (5).**
2. **Subsection 35 (6).**
3. **Subsection 35 (7).**

(9) Subsection 35 (8.1) of the Act, as enacted by Statutes of Ontario, 1992, chapter 32, section 20, is repealed.

(10) Subsection 35 (9) of the Act, as re-enacted by the Statutes of Ontario, 1992, chapter 32, section 20 and amended by 1996, chapter 2, section 72, is repealed and the following substituted:

(9) **Disclosure in proceeding —** No person shall disclose in a proceeding in any court or before any body any information in respect of a patient obtained in the course of assessing or treating the patient, or in the course of assisting in his or her assessment or treatment, or in the course of employment in the psychiatric facility, except,

(a) where the patient is mentally capable within the meaning of the *Personal Health Information Protection Act, 2004*, with the patient's consent;

(b) where the patient is not mentally capable, with the consent of the patient's substitute decision-maker within the meaning of the *Personal Health Information Protection Act, 2004*; or

(c) where the court or, in the case of a proceeding not before a court, the Divisional Court determines, after a hearing from which the public is excluded and that is held on notice to the patient or, if the patient is not mentally capable, the patient's substitute decision-maker referred to in clause (b), that the disclosure is essential in the interests of justice.

(11) Subsection 35 (12) of the Act, as enacted by Statutes of Ontario, 1996, chapter 2, section 72, is repealed.

(12) Section 36 of the Act, as amended by the Statutes of Ontario, 1992, chapter 32, section 20, 1996, chapter 2, section 72 and 2000, chapter 9, section 18, is repealed and the following substituted:

36. Despite subsection 90 (12) Patient access to clinical record — of Schedule A to the *Health Information Protection Act, 2004*, this section, as it read immediately before that subsection came into force, continues to apply to a request for access that a patient made under this section before that subsection came into force.

(13) Section 36.1 of the Act, as enacted by the Statutes of Ontario, 1992, chapter 32, section 20 and amended by 1996, chapter 2, section 72 and 2000, chapter 9, section 19, is repealed.

(14) Section 36.2 of the Act, as enacted by the Statutes of Ontario, 1992, chapter 32, section 20 and amended by 1996, chapter 2, section 72 and 2000, chapter 9, section 20, is repealed.

(15) Section 36.3 of the Act, as enacted by the Statutes of Ontario, 1996, chapter 2, section 72, is repealed.

(16) Subsections 38 (4) and (5) of the Act, as re-enacted by the Statutes of Ontario, 1992, chapter 32, section 20, are repealed.

(17) Subsection 38 (8) of the Act, as enacted by the Statutes of Ontario, 1992, chapter 32, section 20, is amended by striking out "(5)".

(18) Subsection 53 (1) of the Act is amended by striking out "clinical record" and substituting "record of personal health information".

(19) Subsection 54 (3) of the Act, as re-enacted by the Statutes of Ontario, 1992, chapter 32, section 20, is amended by striking out "clinical record" and substituting "record of personal health information".

(20) Subclause 81 (1) (b) (v) of the Act is repealed and the following substituted:

(v) prescribing the forms, records, books, returns and reports to be made and kept in that respect and the period for which the psychiatric facility involved shall retain each, and providing for returns, reports and information to be furnished to the Ministry;

(21) Section 81 of the Act, as amended by the Statutes of Ontario, 1996, chapter 2, section 72, 1997, chapter 15, section 11 and 2000, chapter 9, section 30, is amended by adding the following clauses:

(h.2) requiring that a physician who determines that a patient is incapable of consenting to the collection, use or disclosure of personal health information promptly,

(i) give the patient a written notice that sets out the advice that the regulation specifies with respect to the patient's rights, and

(ii) notify a rights adviser;

(h.3) requiring the rights adviser mentioned in clause (h.2) to give the patient the explanations that the regulation specifies and governing the content of the explanations;

(22) Clause 81 (1) (i) of the Act, as enacted by the Statutes of Ontario, 1996, chapter 2, section 72, is amended by adding at the end "or the regulations".

(23) Clause 81 (1) (j) of the Act, as enacted by the Statutes of Ontario, 1996, chapter 2, section 72, is amended by striking out "who are incapable, within the meaning of the *Health Care Consent Act, 1996*, with respect to treatment of a mental disorder" in the portion before subclause (i) and substituting "who are either incapable, within the meaning of the *Health Care Consent Act, 1996*, with respect to treatment of a mental disorder or are incapable, within the meaning of the *Personal Health Information Protection Act, 2004*, with respect to personal health information".

(24) Clause 81 (1) (k.2) of the Act, as enacted by the Statutes of Ontario, 1996, chapter 2, section 72, is repealed.

(25) Clause 81 (1) (k.3) of the Act, as re-enacted by the Statutes of Ontario, 2000, chapter 9, section 30, is amended by striking out "clinical record under clause 35 (3) (d.1), (e.3), (e.4) or (e.5)" at the end and substituting "record of personal health information under subsection 35 (4)".

(26) Subsection 81 (1) of the Act, as amended by the Statutes of Ontario, 1996, chapter 2, section 72, 1997, chapter 15, section 11 and 2000, chapter 9, section 30, is amended by adding the following clause:

(k.4) prescribing a person and circumstances for the purpose of clause 35 (4) (d);

GENERAL

(O. Reg. 329/04, s. 9)

9. Substitute decision maker — An application to the Board under subsection 24 (2), 27 (1) or (2) of the Act shall be deemed to include an application to the Board under subsection 22 (3) of the Act with respect to the individual's capacity to consent to the collection, use or disclosure of his or her personal health information unless the individual's capacity has been determined by the Board within the previous six months.

SUMMARY OF FORMS

FORM	DESCRIPTION
P-1	Application to the Board to Review a Finding of Incapacity to Consent to the Collection, Use or Disclosure of Personal Health Information under Subsection 22(3) of the Act
P-2	Application to the Board to Determine Compliance under Subsection 24(2) of the Act
P-3	Application to the Board to Appoint a Representative under Subsection 27(1) of the Act
P-4	Application to the Board to Appoint a Representative under Subsection 27(2) of the Act

FORMS

Consent and Capacity Board

Form P-1
Personal Health Information Protection Act

Application to the Board to Review a Finding of Incapacity to Consent to the Collection, Use or Disclosure of Personal Health Information under Subsection 22(3) of the Act

Full Name of Applicant *(please print)*

I apply to the Board for a hearing to determine whether or not I am capable, *(check appropriate box(es))*

☐ to consent to the collection of personal health information;

☐ to consent to the use of personal health information;

☐ to consent to the disclosure of personal health information.

Note: An application may only be made if a health information custodian has made a relevant determination of incapacity.

Provide the name, address, telephone and fax numbers of the person who made the determination of incapacity.

Name	Address
Telephone No. *(incl. area code)*	Fax No. *(incl. area code)*

Are you currently an in-patient or resident at a health or residential facility?

☐ No

☐ Yes (if "Yes", provide Name, Address and Telephone Number of facility)

Name of Facility	Address
Telephone No. *(incl. area code)*	

Your home address and telephone number or other way to contact you.

Home Address	Telephone No. *(incl. area code)*

Name, address, telephone and fax numbers of your lawyer or agent *(if any)*.

Name of Lawyer/Agent	Address
Telephone No. *(incl. area code)*	Fax No. *(incl. area code)*

(Disponible en version française)

4351-04 (2004/10) Form P-1 (Page 1 of 4) www.ccboard.on.ca

© Queen's Printer for Ontario, 2004

If someone helped you to fill out this application form, please provide his / her name, address, telephone and fax numbers.

Name	Address
Telephone No. *(incl. area code)*	Fax No. *(incl. area code)*

Have you applied to the Board during the past year for a review of a determination regarding your capacity to consent to the collection, use or disclosure of personal Health Information?

☐ No

☐ Yes (if "Yes", provide Place and Date of last hearing)

Location *(Place)*	Date *(yyyy/mm/dd)*

Signature of Applicant	Date *(yyyy/mm/dd)*

For your information

What will happen if I don't apply to the Board?

If you have been determined to be incapable of consenting to the collection, use or disclosure of personal health information, someone else will be asked to make the decision for you. This is usually a close family member. If you have a court-appointed guardian or an attorney for personal care with the authority to make the decision, that person will make it for you.

Who may apply to the Board?

Anyone who has been determined to be incapable of consenting to the collection, use or disclosure of personal health information may apply unless:

- they have substitute decision maker with authority to make the required decision under subsections 5(2), (3) or (4), of the Personal Health Information Protection Act;
- they have applied within six months of a final determination of a previous application except with Board permission.

When and Where will the hearing be?

The hearing will be held somewhere close to where you are. It will probably take place within a week after the Board receives your application.

How will the Board make its decision?

The Board will base its decision on whether or not it believes that you are:

- able to understand the information that is relevant to deciding whether to consent to the collection, use or disclosure of personal health information, and
- able to appreciate the reasonable foreseeable consequences of giving, not giving, withholding or withdrawing the consent.

Collection of this information is for the purpose of conducting a proceeding before this Board. It is collected/used for this purpose under the authority of subsection 22(3) of the *Personal Health Information Protection Act*. For information about collection practices, contact the Board or call toll free at 1 800 461–2036.

Fax completed form to the Board at 416-924-8873 or call toll free at 1 800 461–2036 for assistance.

4351-04F (04/10) formule P-1 (Page 2 of 4) www.ccboard.on.ca © Imprimeur de la Reine pour l'Ontario, 2004

Consent and Capacity Board

Form P-2
Personal Health Information Protection Act

Application to the Board to Determine Compliance under Subsection 24(2) of the Act

This application is made with respect to the incapable person noted below, a person whom a health information custodian has determined to be incapable,

Full Name of incapable person *(please print)*

(check appropriate box(es))

- ☐ to consent to the collection of personal health information;
- ☐ to consent to the use of personal health information;
- ☐ to consent to the disclosure of personal health information.

Note: You may only bring an application to determine compliance if you are the health information custodian or the agent authorized to make the application.

I am the health information custodian or the agent of the health information custodian authorized to make the application.

I apply to the Board for a determination as to whether or not the substitute decision-maker in this case has complied with the principles for substitute decision-making as they are set out in the Act.

Full Name of health information custodian / Agent	Address
Telephone No. *(incl. area code)*	Fax No. *(incl. area code)*

Name, address, telephone and fax numbers of Substitute Decision-Maker

Name of Substitute Decision-Maker	Address
Telephone No. *(incl. area code)*	Fax No. *(incl. area code)*

(Disponible en version française)

4352-04 (2004/10) Form P-2 (Page 1 of 4) www.ccboard.on.ca © Queen's Printer for Ontario, 2004

Is the person who has been determined to be incapable currently an in-patient or resident at a health or residential facility?

☐ No

☐ Yes (if "Yes", provide Name, Address and Telephone Number of facility)

Name of Facility	Address
Telephone No. *(incl. area code)*	

If "No", provide Home address and telephone number of incapable person

Home Address	Telephone No. *(incl. area code)*

Name, address, telephone and fax numbers of the lawyer or agent *(if any)* for the person who has been determined to be incapable with respect to this matter.

Name of Lawyer / Agent	Address
Telephone No. *(incl. area code)*	Fax No. *(incl. area code)*

Name, address, telephone and fax numbers of **your** lawyer or agent *(if any)*.

Name of Lawyer / Agent	Address
Telephone No. *(incl. area code)*	Fax No. *(incl. area code)*

Signature of Applicant	Date *(yyyy/mm/dd)*

For your information

Whenever an application of this type is received, the law provides that the patient is deemed to have applied for a review of his or her capacity to make the relevant decision. This does not apply if the Board has determined this issue of capacity within the last six (6) months.

Collection of this information is for the purpose of conducting a proceeding before this Board. It is collected/used for this purpose under the authority of subsection 24(2) of the *Personal Health Information Protection Act*. For information about collection practices, contact the Board or call toll free at 1 800 461–2036.

Fax completed form to the Board at 416-924-8873 or call toll free at 1 800 461–2036 for assistance.

PERSONAL HEALTH INFORMATION PROTECTION ACT, 2004

4352-04 (04/10) formule P-2 (Page 2 of 4) www.ccboard.on.ca

© Imprimeur de la Reine pour l'Ontario, 2004

Consent and Capacity Board

Form P-3
Personal Health Information Protection Act

Application to the Board to Appoint a Representative under Subsection 27(1) of the Act

Full Name of Applicant *(please print)*

I apply to the Board to have a representative appointed to give or refuse consent on my behalf.

A health information custodian has determined that I am not capable, *(check appropriate box(es))*

- ☐ to consent to the collection of personal health information;
- ☐ to consent to the use of personal health information;
- ☐ to consent to the disclosure of personal health information.

Note: An application may only be made if a health information custodian has made a relevant determination of incapacity.

Provide the name, address, telephone and fax numbers of the proposed representative.

Full Name of proposed representative *(please print)*	Address
Telephone No. *(incl. area code)*	Fax No. *(incl. area code)*

Provide the name, address, telephone and fax numbers of the person who made the determination of incapacity.

Full Name of person *(please print)*	Address
Telephone No. *(incl. area code)*	Fax No. *(incl. area code)*

Are you currently an in-patient or resident at a health or residential facility?

- ☐ No
- ☐ Yes (if "Yes", provide Name, Address and Telephone Number of facility)

Name of Facility	Address
Telephone No. *(incl. area code)*	

Your home address and telephone number or other way to contact you.

Home Address	Telephone No. *(incl. area code)*

(Disponible en version française)

4353-04 (2004/10) Form P-3 (Page 1 of 4) www.ccboard.on.ca

© Queen's Printer for Ontario, 2004

You must list your spouse, partner, parent, brother(s) and sister(s) and your children. If you are under eighteen (18) years old, you must also list any agency or person legally authorized to make treatment decisions on your behalf.

Name	Relationship	Address	Telephone No. *(incl. area code)*
1.			
2.			
3.			
4.			
5.			

(☐ Check here if you required additional space and attached another sheet.)

If you were unable to provide a complete and accurate list, please explain below:

Explanation

WARNING: All persons in the required categories together with correct and complete contact information must be listed unless you are unable to do so and have so indicated. Intentional omissions or misinformation may result in a cost award against you, dismissal of your application or other sanctions.

Name, address, telephone and fax numbers of **your** lawyer or agent *(if any)*.

Name of Lawyer / Agent	Address
Telephone No. *(incl. area code)*	Fax No. *(incl. area code)*

If someone helped you to fill out this application form, please provide his / her name, address, telephone and fax numbers.

Name	Address
Telephone No. *(incl. area code)*	Fax No. *(incl. area code)*

I confirm that the proposed representative and I both are at least sixteen (16) years of age.

Signature of Applicant	Date *(yyyy/mm/dd)*

For your information

Whenever an application of this type is received, the law provides that the patient is deemed to have applied for a review of his or her capacity to make the relevant decision. This does not apply if the Board has determined this issue of capacity within the last six (6) months.

Collection of this information is for the purpose of conducting a proceeding before this Board. It is collected/used for this purpose under the authority of subsection 27(1) of the *Personal Health Information Protection Act*. For information about collection practices, contact the Board or call toll free at 1 800 461-2036.

Fax completed form to the Board at 416-924-8873 or call toll free at 1 800 461–2036 for assistance.

4353-04 (04/10) formule P-3 (Page 2 of 4) www.ccboard.on.ca

© Imprimeur de la Reine pour l'Ontario, 2004

PERSONAL HEALTH INFORMATION PROTECTION ACT, 2004

Consent to Disclose Personal Health Information
Pursuant to the Personal Health Information Protection Act, 2004 (PHIPA)

I, ______________________, **authorize** ______________________
(Print your name) *(Print name of health information custodian)*

to disclose
☐ my personal health information consisting of:

____

____
(Describe the personal health information to be disclosed)

or
☐ the personal health information of ______________________
(Name of person for whom you are the substitute decision-maker)*

consisting of: ______________________

____
(Describe the personal health information to be disclosed)

to ______________________
(Print name and address of person requiring the information)

I understand the purpose for disclosing this personal health information to the person noted above. I understand that I can refuse to sign this consent form.

My Name: ______________ **Address:** ______________

Home Tel.: ______________ **Work Tel.:** ______________

Signature: ______________ **Date:** ______________

Witness Name: ______________ **Address:** ______________

Home Tel.: ______________ **Work Tel.:** ______________

Signature: ______________ **Date:** ______________

***Please note: A substitute decision-maker is a person authorized under PHIPA to consent, on behalf of an individual, to disclose personal health information about the individual.**

Consent and Capacity Board

Form P-4
Personal Health Information Protection Act

Application to the Board to Appoint a Representative under Subsection 27(2) of the Act

This application is made with respect to the incapable person noted below, a person whom a health information custodian has determined to be incapable,

Full Name of incapable person *(please print)*

(check appropriate box(es))

- ☐ to consent to the collection of personal health information;
- ☐ to consent to the use of personal health information;
- ☐ to consent to the disclosure of personal health information.

Note: An application may only be made if a health information custodian has made a relevant determination of incapacity.

I apply to the Board to be appointed a representative for the above named person with respect to this matter.

Full Name of proposed representative *(please print)*	Address
Telephone No. *(incl. area code)*	Fax No. *(incl. area code)*

Provide the name, address, telephone and fax numbers of the person who made the determination of incapacity.

Full Name of person *(please print)*	Address
Telephone No. *(incl. area code)*	Fax No. *(incl. area code)*

Is the person who has been determined to be incapable with respect to this matter currently an in-patient or resident at a health or residential facility?

- ☐ No
- ☐ Yes (if "Yes", provide Name, Address and Telephone Number of facility)

Name of Facility	Address
Telephone No. *(incl. area code)*	

Home address and telephone number of incapable person.

Home Address	Telephone No. *(incl. area code)*

(Disponible en version française)

4354-04 (2004/10) Form P-4 (Page 1 of 4) www.ccboard.on.ca © Queen's Printer for Ontario, 2004

PERSONAL HEALTH INFORMATION PROTECTION ACT, 2004

Name, address, telephone and fax numbers of the lawyer or agent *(if any)* for the person who has been determined to be incapable with respect to this matter.

Name of Lawyer / Agent	Address
Telephone No. *(incl. area code)*	Fax No. *(incl. area code)*

Name, address, telephone and fax numbers of **your** lawyer or agent *(if any)*.

Name of Lawyer / Agent	Address
Telephone No. *(incl. area code)*	Fax No. *(incl. area code)*

You must list the spouse, partner, parent, brother(s) and sister(s) and children of the incapable person. If the person is under eighteen (18) years old, you must also list any agency or person legally authorized to make treatment decisions on his or her behalf.

Name	Relationship	Address	Telephone No. *(incl. area code)*
1.			
2.			
3.			
4.			
5.			

(☐ Check here if you required additional space and attached another sheet.)

If you were unable to provide a complete and accurate list, please explain below:

Explanation

WARNING: **All persons in the required categories together with correct and complete contact information must be listed unless you are unable to do so and have so indicated. Intentional omissions or misinformation may result in a cost award against you, dismissal of your application or other sanctions.**

I confirm that I am at least sixteen (16) years of age.

Signature of Applicant	Date *(yyyy/mm/dd)*

For your information

Whenever an application of this type is received, the law provides that the patient is deemed to have applied for a review of his or her capacity to make the relevant decision. This does not apply if the Board has determined this issue of capacity within the last six (6) months.

Collection of this information is for the purpose of conducting a proceeding before this Board. It is collected/used for this purpose under the authority of subsection 27(2) of the *Personal Health Information Protection Act*. For information about collection practices, contact the Board or call toll free at 1 800 461–2036.

Fax completed form to the Board at 416-924-8873 or call toll free at 1 800 461–2036 for assistance.

4354-04 (04/10) formule P-4 (Page 2 of 4) www.ccboard.on.ca

© Imprimeur de la Reine pour l'Ontario, 2004

STATUTORY POWERS PROCEDURE ACT

COMMENTARY

Purpose and Application

The Statutory Powers Procedure Act ("SPPA") applies to Ontario tribunals created by statute, which are required to hold hearings. The Consent and Capacity Board is such a tribunal, since it is established under the *Health Care Consent Act, 1996*, and is required to hold hearings.

The SPPA grants certain powers to the tribunals to which it applies to permit them to operate in accordance with the rules of procedure also set out in this Act, and codifies the common law administrative principles of natural justice and fairness for parties appearing before these tribunals. The rules of conduct required by the SPPA constitute minimum procedural safeguards. The Consent and Capacity Board has chosen to enact its own Rules of Practice in accordance with the SPPA provision permitting this step, in order to clarify the specific application to this Board of some of the basic procedural safeguards set out under the SPPA. In practising before the Board, regard must be had to both the SPPA's basic provisions and the Rules of Practice of the Board, in determining whether the tribunal has acted in accordance with the natural justice and fundamental due process principles enunciated in the development of our common law jurisprudence in administrative law.

The SPPA governs all aspects of a tribunal proceeding from before the hearing (eg. notice provisions, disclosure, pre-hearing conferences, motions,) throughout the conduct of the hearing (general and specific rules of evidence for tribunals), and steps to be taken after the conclusion of the hearing (the requirement to render decisions and reasons for decisions as well as amending decisions of the tribunal and challenging these decisions.)

While the SPPA should be read in its entirety and we do not propose to canvass it exhaustively here, a short introduction to how some of the provisions in the SPPA are commonly used by and before the Consent and Capacity Board is offered below.

Waiver of Procedural Requirements

Section 4(1) of the SPPA allows any procedural requirement under the Act to be waived with the consent of the parties and the tribunal. This is useful in certain applications before the Board where there are many statutory parties to a proceeding. For example, statutory parties to Form B, C, D, E, F, and G applications under the *HCCA* potentially include a great many relatives of the incapable person. In the event that any of those statutory parties is uninterested in the proceeding, they may waive (with the parties' and the Board's consent) their right to further notice of the proceedings. This has the effect of simplifying and streamlining the scheduling of these hearings, which must be turned around within seven days of an application being received by the Board.

Notice of Hearing

Pursuant to section 6.(1) of the SPPA, parties to a proceeding must be given reasonable notice of the hearing by the tribunal. "Reasonable notice" is context-specific. Given the seven-day turn-around time in scheduling hearings before the Board, notices of hearings are often received the day before the hearing, something parties to the proceedings often find very frustrating. Further, the Board rarely knows even the day before the hearing where within a psychiatric facility a hearing will be held, which means that this Board does not comply with section 6(3)(a) requiring the place of the hearing to be specified, except in the most general sense of identifying the facility. In day to day practice, hearings actually commence late on many occasions as parties try to find the hearing room within a large hospital setting.

Where proceedings before the Board require notice to many parties to the hearing (such as the Form A-G applications under the HCCA referenced above), it is the Board's responsibility to get these notices into the hands of those parties; however, the process is seriously delayed if the application does not contain current and correct detailed contact information for all the statutory parties. Not only will the commencement of the hearing be delayed substantially past the seven days (although the hearing may convene, it would not be able to proceed without notice to all the necessary parties), but any decision the Board renders in a matter will be vulnerable to an appeal by any statutory party who did not receive the requisite notice under the SPPA.

Where Character, Conduct or Competence of a Party is In Issue

Section 8 of the SPPA requires notice of particulars of any allegation regarding the character, conduct or competence of a party to the tribunal proceedings. In the context of Consent and Capacity Board proceedings, this requires notice to physician parties whose conduct or competence is in issue, and to substitute decision makers (SDMs) who are statutory parties to certain applications under the HCCA whose character, conduct or competence may be brought into issue either by the incapable person or the health care practitioner proposing a treatment.

Orders Excluding the Public

Section 9(1) of the SPPA provides that oral hearings are open to the public, with certain limited exceptions. This provision comes into play when a party to the proceeding wishes to exclude the public, meaning that the Board is asked to make an Order excluding from the hearing anyone who is not a statutory party to the proceeding (ie. stipulated under the applicable legislation as a party) or a party appointed by the Board. Generally, a patient applicant before the Board may try to keep family members out of the hearing room or media who may be in attendance. On occasion, other patients in a psychiatric facility will come into a hearing room seeking to attend as members of the public. Also on occasion, staff members at the psychiatric facility will want to attend to observe, even though they have no immediate connection to the proceedings. Sometimes members of the Board will be in attendance training as observers, but not part of the Panel hearing the matter.

Section 9(1)(b) essentially provides that an Order excluding the public may be made by a tribunal where the desirability of avoiding public disclosure of intimate financial or personal matters outweighs the public interest in holding public hearings, which is the general principle.

Any hearing of the Consent and Capacity Board involves intimate personal information since an individual's mental health history and issues will be discussed. Given that hearings are generally intended to be public, there must be some particularly sensitive matter in issue which is expected to be addressed in the hearing for the Board to consider such an unusual order. An example of an appropriate case where a party may seek such an Order is a young child who is expected to testify as to sexual abuse by a parent; in such a case, counsel for the child may indicate that the child is not comfortable providing this testimony in front of the parent whose conduct is in issue, and that absent an Order excluding the public, that parent would otherwise be permitted to remain in the hearing room (if not before his or her testimony in the event there is an Order excluding witnesses) after they've completed their testimony, if any, and throughout the proceeding otherwise.

Orders Excluding Witnesses

Orders to exclude the public are different and apart from Orders sought to exclude witnesses. Consent and Capacity Board hearings routinely commence with a request from counsel for the patient applicant that the Board make an Order excluding witnesses. The Board has this power as part of its general power to control its own processes. The rationale for this type of Order is to maintain the integrity of the proceeding and to ensure that testimony of each witness providing evidence is not tainted or influenced by the testimony of witnesses before him or her. A witness is excluded from attending the proceedings only until after they have completed their testimony, after which time they are welcome to remain in attendance (absent an Order to exclude the public.) However, no party to the proceeding can be excluded for any part of the proceeding.

In practice, Orders to exclude witnesses are routinely granted, where Orders to exclude the public are rarely, if ever, granted by the Consent and Capacity Board. Where an Order to exclude witnesses is made by the Board and physicians or health care practitioners who are parties to the proceeding wish to call the evidence of a family member or nursing staff, they often choose to call the evidence of that family or staff member before providing their own testimony. This way, the other witness for the physician may remain in attendance while the physician is testifying. Another common occurrence once an Order to exclude witnesses is sought is that family members may apply to be made a party to the proceeding at the Board's discretion, to avoid being excluded from the hearing room while a physician or health practitioner is testifying.

Orders to Maintain Control of Proceedings

Parties to a hearing have a right to attend hearings and to remain in attendance throughout the hearing. However, if the conduct of a party to the hearing is so disruptive that order cannot be maintained in the proceeding, the Board can exclude a party from the hearing. The Consent and Capacity Board will make every effort to allow parties to remain in the hearing room throughout the proceeding. However, on occasion physicians will inform the Board that a patient applicant before the Board must remain in hospital gowns, in waist-wrist restraints or other physical restraints or must be maintained in a seclusion room due to aggressive behaviour at the time of the hearing. Counsel for the patient will argue that all of these things are prejudicial to his or her client and will request that the individual be permitted to attend in street clothes and without physical restraint, or, if the individual must be maintained outside of the hearing room, that the hearing be held in the seclusion room of the individual. All attempts to facilitate the participation of the individual in the hearing process as fully as possible will be made.

Proceedings Involving Similar Questions

Pursuant to section 9.1 of the SPPS, if two or more proceedings before a tribunal involve the same or similar questions of fact, law or policy, the tribunal may (a) combine the proceedings with the consent of the parties; (b) hear the proceedings at the same time, with the consent of the parties; (c) hear the proceedings one immediately after the other; or (d) stay one or more of the proceedings until after the determination of another one of them. In 2004 for example, the Consent and Capacity Board relied on this provision and stayed the constitutional challenges to the Community Treatment Order provisions of the *Mental Health Act* in a number of similar cases before it in, pending the determination of the issue in the first case of this nature to come before the Board.

Interim Orders

The SPPA has recently been amended to include a provision (s. 16.1) allowing tribunals to make interim decisions and orders including applicable conditions. While the Board had made interim orders staying the constitutional component of a number of hearings to review Community Treatment Orders (CTOs) in 2004 as indicated above, it refused to grant interim relief to the subject of a CTO who requested that her CTO be stayed pending the resolution of her constitutional challenge to the legislation.[1]

On a number of different occasions recently, a hearing panel of the Board has raised the question of whether as an interim measure it may order an applicant treated or transferred to a long term care facility pending the resolution of the matter before the Board on the issue of an applicant's capacity to make either treatment or long-term care placement decisions. Certainly, in the event the the person objects to the proposed treatment or admission, counsel for the applicant in these matters, if present, can be expected to oppose vigorously this type of

---

[1] In re KT TO 04-2855 October 15, 2004

contemplated order since the individual's application to review a finding of incapacity in relation to these issues would be essentially rendered moot by forcing upon the individual treatment or placement to which the person objects. In addition, even where the applicant is simply contesting the finding of incapacity without necessarily wishing to refuse the treatment or admission proposed, operation of the HCCA would appear to prohibit such interim orders permitting the administration of the treatment or the placement of the individiual in long term care, given that no treatment can be commenced and no admission may be authorized pending the final resolution of these issues.[2] In any event, an appeal to the Superior Court of Justice arguably lies from such contemplated interim orders pursuant to s. 80 of the HCCA, failing which an application for judicial review to Divisional Court may be well-founded. In either case, the interim order of the Board would be stayed pending final resolution of the issues before the Court.

2 HCCA, 1996, section 18 (treatment not to be commenced) and section 46 (admission not to be authorized).

STATUTORY POWERS PROCEDURE ACT

(R.S.O. 1990, CHAPTER S. 22)

Amended: 1993, c. 27, Sched.; 1994, c. 27, s. 56; 1997, c. 23, s. 13; 1999, c. 12, Sched. B., s. 16; 2002, c. 17, Sched. F, Table.

1. (1) **Interpretation —** In this Act,

"electronic hearing" means a hearing held by conference telephone or some other form of electronic technology allowing persons to hear one another;

"hearing" means a hearing in any proceeding;

"licence" includes any permit, certificate, approval, registration or similar form of permission required by law;

"municipality" has the same meaning as in the *Municipal Affairs Act*;

"oral hearing" means a hearing at which the parties or their counsel or agents attend before the tribunal in person;

"proceeding" means a proceeding to which this Act applies;

"statutory power of decision" means a power or right, conferred by or under a statute, to make a decision deciding or prescribing,

(a) the legal rights, powers, privileges, immunities, duties or liabilities of any person or party, or

(b) the eligibility of any person or party to receive, or to the continuation of, a benefit or licence, whether the person is legally entitled thereto or not;

"tribunal" means one or more persons, whether or not incorporated and however described, upon which a statutory power of decision is conferred by or under a statute;

"written hearing" means a hearing held by means of the exchange of documents, whether in written form or by electronic means.

[1994, c. 27, s. 56; 2002, c. 17, Sched. F, Table]

(2) **Meaning of "person" extended —** A municipality, an unincorporated association of employers, a trade union or council of trade unions who may be a party to a proceeding in the exercise of a statutory power of decision under the statute conferring the power shall be deemed to be a person for the purpose of any provision of this Act or of any rule made under this Act that applies to parties.

2. Liberal construction of Act and rules — This Act, and any rule made by a tribunal under section 25.1, shall be liberally construed to secure the just, most expeditious and cost-effective determination of every proceeding on its merits.

[1999, c. 12, Sched. B, s. 16]

3. (1) **Application of Act —** Subject to subsection (2), this Act applies to a proceeding by a tribunal in the exercise of a statutory power of decision conferred by or under an Act of the Legislature, where the tribunal is required by or under such Act or otherwise by law to hold or to afford to the parties to the proceeding an opportunity for a hearing before making a decision.

(2) **Where Act does not apply —** This Act does not apply to a proceeding,

(a) before the Assembly or any committee of the Assembly;

(b) in or before,

(i) the Court of Appeal,

(ii) the Ontario Court (General Division),

(iii) the Ontario Court (Provincial Division),

(iv) the Unified Family Court,

(v) the Small Claims Court, or

(vi) a justice of the peace;

(c) to which the Rules of Civil Procedure apply;

(d) before an arbitrator to which the *Arbitrations Act* or the *Labour Relations Act* applies;

(e) at a coroner's inquest;

(f) of a commission appointed under the *Public Inquiries Act*;

(g) of one or more persons required to make an investigation and to make a report, with or without recommendations, where the report is for the information or advice of the person to whom it is made and does not in any way legally bind or limit that person in any decision he or she may have power to make; or

(h) of a tribunal empowered to make regulations, rules or by-laws in so far as its power to make regulations, rules or by-laws is concerned.

[1994, c. 27, s. 56 (6).

4. (1) **Waiver of procedural requirement —** Any procedural requirement of this Act, or of another Act or a regulation that applies to a proceeding, may be waived with the consent of the parties and the tribunal.

(2) **Same, rules —** Any provision of a tribunal's rules made under section 25.1 may be waived in accordance with the rules.

[1994, c. 27, s. 56; 1997, c. 23, s. 13]

4.1 Disposition without hearing — If the parties consent, a proceeding may be disposed of by a decision of the tribunal given without a hearing, unless another Act or a regulation that applies to the proceeding provides otherwise.

[1997, c. 23, s. 13]

4.2 (1) **Panels, certain matters —** A procedural or interlocutory matter in a proceeding may be heard and determined by a panel consisting of one or more members of the tribunal, as assigned by the chair of the tribunal.

(2) **Assignments** — In assigning members of the tribunal to a panel, the chair shall take into consideration any requirement imposed by another Act or a regulation that applies to the proceeding that the tribunal be representative of specific interests.

(3) **Decision of panel** — The decision of a majority of the members of a panel, or their unanimous decision in the case of a two-member panel, is the tribunal's decision.

[1994, c. 27, s. 56; 1997, c. 23, s. 13]

4.2.1 (1) **Panel of one** — The chair of a tribunal may decide that a proceeding be heard by a panel of one person and assign the person to hear the proceeding unless there is a statutory requirement in another Act that the proceeding be heard by a panel of more than one person.

(2) **Reduction in number of panel members** — Where there is a statutory requirement in another Act that a proceeding be heard by a panel of a specified number of persons, the chair of the tribunal may assign to the panel one person or any lesser number of persons than the number specified in the other Act if all parties to the proceeding consent.

[1999, c. 12, Sched. B, s. 16]

4.3 Expiry of term — If the term of office of a member of a tribunal who has participated in a hearing expires before a decision is given, the term shall be deemed to continue, but only for the purpose of participating in the decision and for no other purpose.

[1997, c. 23, s. 13]

4.4 (1) **Incapacity of member** — If a member of a tribunal who has participated in a hearing becomes unable, for any reason, to complete the hearing or to participate in the decision, the remaining member or members may complete the hearing and give a decision.

(2) **Other Acts and regulations** — Subsection (1) does not apply if another Act or a regulation specifically deals with the issue of what takes place in the circumstances described in subsection (1).

[1994, c. 27, s. 56; 1997, c. 23, s. 13]

4.5 (1) **Decision not to process commencement of proceeding** — Subject to subsection (3), upon receiving documents relating to the commencement of a proceeding, a tribunal or its administrative staff may decide not to process the documents relating to the commencement of the proceeding if,

(a) the documents are incomplete;

(b) the documents are received after the time required for commencing the proceeding has elapsed;

(c) the fee required for commencing the proceeding is not paid; or

(d) there is some other technical defect in the commencement of the proceeding.

(2) **Notice** — A tribunal or its administrative staff shall give the party who commences a proceeding notice of its decision under subsection (1) and shall set

out in the notice the reasons for the decision and the requirements for resuming the processing of the documents.

(3) **Rules under s. 25.1** — A tribunal or its administrative staff shall not make a decision under subsection (1) unless the tribunal has made rules under section 25.1 respecting the making of such decisions and those rules shall set out,

(a) any of the grounds referred to in subsection (1) upon which the tribunal or its administrative staff may decide not to process the documents relating to the commencement of a proceeding; and

(b) the requirements for the processing of the documents to be resumed.

(4) **Continuance of provisions in other statutes** — Despite section 32, nothing in this section shall prevent a tribunal or its administrative staff from deciding not to process documents relating to the commencement of a proceeding on grounds that differ from those referred to in subsection (1) or without complying with subsection (2) or (3) if the tribunal or its staff does so in accordance with the provisions of an Act that are in force on the day this section comes into force.

[1999, c. 12, Sched. B, s. 16]

4.6 (1) **Dismissal of proceeding without hearing** — Subject to subsections (5) and (6), a tribunal may dismiss a proceeding without a hearing if,

(a) the proceeding is frivolous, vexatious or is commenced in bad faith;

(b) the proceeding relates to matters that are outside the jurisdiction of the tribunal; or

(c) some aspect of the statutory requirements for bringing the proceeding has not been met.

(2) **Notice** — Before dismissing a proceeding under this section, a tribunal shall give notice of its intention to dismiss the proceeding to,

(a) all parties to the proceeding if the proceeding is being dismissed for reasons referred to in clause (1) (b); or

(b) the party who commences the proceeding if the proceeding is being dismissed for any other reason.

(3) **Same** — The notice of intention to dismiss a proceeding shall set out the reasons for the dismissal and inform the parties of their right to make written submissions to the tribunal with respect to the dismissal within the time specified in the notice.

(4) **Right to make submissions** — A party who receives a notice under subsection (2) may make written submissions to the tribunal with respect to the dismissal within the time specified in the notice.

(5) **Dismissal** — A tribunal shall not dismiss a proceeding under this section until it has given notice under subsection (2) and considered any submissions made under subsection (4).

(6) **Rules —** A tribunal shall not dismiss a proceeding under this section unless it has made rules under section 25.1 respecting the early dismissal of proceedings and those rules shall include,

(a) any of the grounds referred to in subsection (1) upon which a proceeding may be dismissed;

(b) the right of the parties who are entitled to receive notice under subsection (2) to make submissions with respect to the dismissal; and

(c) the time within which the submissions must be made.

(7) **Continuance of provisions in other statutes —** Despite section 32, nothing in this section shall prevent a tribunal from dismissing a proceeding on grounds other than those referred to in subsection (1) or without complying with subsections (2) to (6) if the tribunal dismisses the proceeding in accordance with the provisions of an Act that are in force on the day this section comes into force.

[1999, c. 12, Sched. B, s. 16]

4.7 Classifying proceedings — A tribunal may make rules under section 25.1 classifying the types of proceedings that come before it and setting guidelines as to the procedural steps or processes (such as preliminary motions, pre-hearing conferences, alternative dispute resolution mechanisms, expedited hearings) that apply to each type of proceeding and the circumstances in which other procedures may apply.

[1999, c. 12, Sched. B, s. 16]

4.8 (1) **Alternative dispute resolution —** A tribunal may direct the parties to a proceeding to participate in an alternative dispute resolution mechanism for the purposes of resolving the proceeding or an issue arising in the proceeding if,

(a) it has made rules under section 25.1 respecting the use of alternative dispute resolution mechanisms; and

(b) all parties consent to participating in the alternative dispute resolution mechanism.

(2) **Definition —** In this section,

"alternative dispute resolution mechanism" includes mediation, conciliation, negotiation or any other means of facilitating the resolution of issues in dispute.

(3) **Rules —** A rule under section 25.1 respecting the use of alternative dispute resolution mechanisms shall include procedural guidelines to deal with the following:

1. The circumstances in which a settlement achieved by means of an alternative dispute resolution mechanism must be reviewed and approved by the tribunal.

2. Any requirement, statutory or otherwise, that there be an order by the tribunal.

(4) **Mandatory alternative dispute resolution —** A rule under subsection (3) may provide that participation in an alternative dispute resolution mechanism is mandatory or that it is mandatory in certain specified circumstances.

(5) **Person appointed to mediate, etc —**.A rule under subsection (3) may provide that a person appointed to mediate, conciliate, negotiate or help resolve a matter by means of an alternative dispute resolution mechanism be a member of the tribunal or a person independent of the tribunal. However, a member of the tribunal who is so appointed with respect to a matter in a proceeding shall not subsequently hear the matter if it comes before the tribunal unless the parties consent.

(6) **Continuance of provisions in other statutes —** Despite section 32, nothing in this section shall prevent a tribunal from directing parties to a proceeding to participate in an alternative dispute resolution mechanism even though the requirements of subsections (1) to (5) have not been met if the tribunal does so in accordance with the provisions of an Act that are in force on the day this section comes into force.

[1999, c. 12, Sched. B, s. 16]

4.9 Mediators, etc., not compellable — (1) No person employed as a mediator, conciliator or negotiator or otherwise appointed to facilitate the resolution of a matter before a tribunal by means of an alternative dispute resolution mechanism shall be compelled to give testimony or produce documents in a proceeding before the tribunal or in a civil proceeding with respect to matters that come to his or her knowledge in the course of exercising his or her duties under this or any other Act.

(2) **Evidence in civil proceedings —** No notes or records kept by a mediator, conciliator or negotiator or by any other person appointed to facilitate the resolution of a matter before a tribunal by means of an alternative dispute resolution mechanism under this or any other Act are admissible in a civil proceeding.

[1999, c. 12, Sched. B, s. 16]

5. Parties — The parties to a proceeding shall be the persons specified as parties by or under the statute under which the proceeding arises or, if not so specified, persons entitled by law to be parties to the proceeding.

5.1 (1) **Written hearings —** A tribunal whose rules made under section 25.1 deal with written hearings may hold a written hearing in a proceeding.

(2) **Exception —** The tribunal shall not hold a written hearing if a party satisfies the tribunal that there is good reason for not doing so.

(2.1) **Same —** Subsection (2) does not apply if the only purpose of the hearing is to deal with procedural matters.

(3) **Documents —** In a written hearing, all the parties are entitled to receive every document that the tribunal receives in the proceeding.

[1994, c. 27, s. 56; 1997, c. 23, s. 13; 1999, c. 12, Sched. B, s. 16]

5.2 (1) **Electronic hearings —** A tribunal whose rules made under section 25.1 deal with electronic hearings may hold an electronic hearing in a proceeding.

(2) **Exception —** The tribunal shall not hold an electronic hearing if a party satisfies the tribunal that holding an electronic rather than an oral hearing is likely to cause the party significant prejudice.

(3) **Same —** Subsection (2) does not apply if the only purpose of the hearing is to deal with procedural matters.

(4) **Participants to be able to hear one another —** In an electronic hearing, all the parties and the members of the tribunal participating in the hearing must be able to hear one another and any witnesses throughout the hearing.

[1994, c. 27, s. 56; 1997, c. 23, s. 13]

5.2.1 Different kinds of hearings in one proceeding — A tribunal may, in a proceeding, hold any combination of written, electronic and oral hearings.

[1997, c. 23, s. 13]

5.3 Pre-hearing conferences — (1) If the tribunal's rules made under section 25.1 deal with pre-hearing conferences, the tribunal may direct the parties to participate in a pre-hearing conference to consider,

(a) the settlement of any or all of the issues;

(b) the simplification of the issues;

(c) facts or evidence that may be agreed upon;

(d) the dates by which any steps in the proceeding are to be taken or begun;

(e) the estimated duration of the hearing; and

(f) any other matter that may assist in the just and most expeditious disposition of the proceeding.

(1.1) **Other Acts and regulations —** The tribunal's power to direct the parties to participate in a pre-hearing conference is subject to any other Act or regulation that applies to the proceeding.

(2) **Who presides —** The chair of the tribunal may designate a member of the tribunal or any other person to preside at the pre-hearing conference.

(3) **Orders —** A member who presides at a pre-hearing conference may make such orders as he or she considers necessary or advisable with respect to the conduct of the proceeding, including adding parties.

(4) **Disqualification —** A member who presides at a pre-hearing conference at which the parties attempt to settle issues shall not preside at the hearing of the proceeding unless the parties consent.

(5) **Application of s. 5.2 —** Section 5.2 applies to a pre-hearing conference, with necessary modifications.

[1994, c. 27, s. 56; 1997, c. 23, s. 13]

5.4 Disclosure — (1) If the tribunal's rules made under section 25.1 deal with disclosure, the tribunal may, at any stage of the proceeding before all hearings are complete, make orders for,

(a) the exchange of documents;

(b) the oral or written examination of a party;

(c) the exchange of witness statements and reports of expert witnesses;

(d) the provision of particulars;

(e) any other form of disclosure.

(1.1) **Other Acts and regulations** — The tribunal's power to make orders for disclosure is subject to any other Act or regulation that applies to the proceeding.

(2) **Exception, privileged information** — Subsection (1) does not authorize the making of an order requiring disclosure of privileged information.

[1994, c. 27, s. 56; 1997, c. 23, s. 13]

6. (1) **Notice of hearing** — The parties to a proceeding shall be given reasonable notice of the hearing by the tribunal.

(2) **Statutory authority** — A notice of a hearing shall include a reference to the statutory authority under which the hearing will be held.

(3) **Oral hearing** — A notice of an oral hearing shall include,

(a) a statement of the time, place and purpose of the hearing; and

(b) a statement that if the party notified does not attend at the hearing, the tribunal may proceed in the party's absence and the party will not be entitled to any further notice in the proceeding.

(4) **Written hearing** — A notice of a written hearing shall include,

(a) a statement of the date and purpose of the hearing, and details about the manner in which the hearing will be held;

(b) a statement that the hearing shall not be held as a written hearing if the party satisfies the tribunal that there is good reason for not holding a written hearing (in which case the tribunal is required to hold it as an electronic or oral hearing) and an indication of the procedure to be followed for that purpose;

(c) a statement that if the party notified neither acts under clause (b) nor participates in the hearing in accordance with the notice, the tribunal may proceed without the party's participation and the party will not be entitled to any further notice in the proceeding.

(5) **Electronic hearing** — A notice of an electronic hearing shall include,

(a) a statement of the time and purpose of the hearing, and details about the manner in which the hearing will be held;

(b) a statement that the only purpose of the hearing is to deal with procedural matters, if that is the case;

(c) if clause (b) does not apply, a statement that the party notified may, by satisfying the tribunal that holding the hearing as an electronic hearing is likely to cause the party significant prejudice, require the tribunal to hold the hearing as an oral hearing, and an indication of the procedure to be followed for that purpose; and

(d) a statement that if the party notified neither acts under clause (c), if applicable, nor participates in the hearing in accordance with the notice, the tribunal may proceed without the party's participation and the party will not be entitled to any further notice in the proceeding.

[1994, c. 27, s. 56; 1997, c. 23, s. 13; 1999, c. 12, Sched. B, s. 16]

7. (1) **Effect of non-attendance at hearing after due notice** — Where notice of an oral hearing has been given to a party to a proceeding in accordance with this Act and the party does not attend at the hearing, the tribunal may proceed in the absence of the party and the party is not entitled to any further notice in the proceeding. R.S.O. 1990, c. S.22, s. 7; 1994, c. 27, s. 56 (14).

(2) **Same, written hearings** — Where notice of a written hearing has been given to a party to a proceeding in accordance with this Act and the party neither acts under clause 6 (4) (b) nor participates in the hearing in accordance with the notice, the tribunal may proceed without the party's participation and the party is not entitled to any further notice in the proceeding.

(3) **Same, electronic hearings** — Where notice of an electronic hearing has been given to a party to a proceeding in accordance with this Act and the party neither acts under clause 6 (5) (c), if applicable, nor participates in the hearing in accordance with the notice, the tribunal may proceed without the party's participation and the party is not entitled to any further notice in the proceeding.

[1994, c. 27, s. 56]

8. Where character, etc., of a party is in issue — Where the good character, propriety of conduct or competence of a party is an issue in a proceeding, the party is entitled to be furnished prior to the hearing with reasonable information of any allegations with respect thereto.

9. (1) **Hearings to be public, exceptions** — An oral hearing shall be open to the public except where the tribunal is of the opinion that,

(a) matters involving public security may be disclosed; or

(b) intimate financial or personal matters or other matters may be disclosed at the hearing of such a nature, having regard to the circumstances, that the desirability of avoiding disclosure thereof in the interests of any person affected or in the public interest outweighs the desirability of adhering to the principle that hearings be open to the public,

in which case the tribunal may hold the hearing in the absence of the public.

(1.1) **Written hearings** — In a written hearing, members of the public are entitled to reasonable access to the documents submitted, unless the tribunal is of the opinion that clause (1) (a) or (b) applies.

(1.2) **Electronic hearings** — An electronic hearing shall be open to the public unless the tribunal is of the opinion that,

(a) it is not practical to hold the hearing in a manner that is open to the public; or

(b) clause (1) (a) or (b) applies.

(2) **Maintenance of order at hearings** — A tribunal may make such orders or give such directions at an oral or electronic hearing as it considers necessary for the maintenance of order at the hearing, and, if any person disobeys or fails to comply with any such order or direction, the tribunal or a member thereof may call for the assistance of any peace officer to enforce the order or direction, and every peace officer so called upon shall take such action as is necessary to enforce

the order or direction and may use such force as is reasonably required for that purpose.

[1994, c. 27, s. 56; 1997, c. 23, s. 13]

9.1 (1) **Proceedings involving similar questions** — If two or more proceedings before a tribunal involve the same or similar questions of fact, law or policy, the tribunal may,

(a) combine the proceedings or any part of them, with the consent of the parties;

(b) hear the proceedings at the same time, with the consent of the parties;

(c) hear the proceedings one immediately after the other; or

(d) stay one or more of the proceedings until after the determination of another one of them.

(2) **Exception** — Subsection (1) does not apply to proceedings to which the *Consolidated Hearings Act* applies.

(3) **Same** — Clauses (1) (a) and (b) do not apply to a proceeding if,

(a) any other Act or regulation that applies to the proceeding requires that it be heard in private;

(b) the tribunal is of the opinion that clause 9 (1) (a) or (b) applies to the proceeding.

(4) **Conflict, consent requirements** — The consent requirements of clauses (1) (a) and (b) do not apply if another Act or a regulation that applies to the proceedings allows the tribunal to combine them or hear them at the same time without the consent of the parties.

(5) **Use of same evidence** — If the parties to the second-named proceeding consent, the tribunal may treat evidence that is admitted in a proceeding as if it were also admitted in another proceeding that is heard at the same time under clause (1) (b).

[1994, c. 27, s. 56; 1997, c. 23, s. 13]

10. Right to counsel — A party to a proceeding may be represented by counsel or an agent.

[1994, c. 27, s. 56]

10.1 Examination of witnesses — A party to a proceeding may, at an oral or electronic hearing,

(a) call and examine witnesses and present evidence and submissions; and

(b) conduct cross-examinations of witnesses at the hearing reasonably required for a full and fair disclosure of all matters relevant to the issues in the proceeding.

[1994, c. 27, s. 56]

11. (1) **Rights of witnesses to counsel** — A witness at an oral or electronic hearing is entitled to be advised by counsel or an agent as to his or her rights but such counsel or agent may take no other part in the hearing without leave of the tribunal.

(2) **Idem** — Where an oral hearing is closed to the public, the counsel or agent for a witness is not entitled to be present except when that witness is giving evidence.

[1994, c. 27, s. 56]

12. (1) **Summonses** — A tribunal may require any person, including a party, by summons,

(a) to give evidence on oath or affirmation at an oral or electronic hearing; and

(b) to produce in evidence at an oral or electronic hearing documents and things specified by the tribunal,

relevant to the subject-matter of the proceeding and admissible at a hearing.

(2) **Form and service of summons** — A summons issued under subsection (1) shall be in the prescribed form (in English or French) and,

(a) where the tribunal consists of one person, shall be signed by him or her;

(b) where the tribunal consists of more than one person, shall be signed by the chair of the tribunal or in such other manner as documents on behalf of the tribunal may be signed under the statute constituting the tribunal.

(3) **Same** — The summons shall be served personally on the person summoned.

(3.1) **Fees and allowances** — The person summoned is entitled to receive the same fees or allowances for attending at or otherwise participating in the hearing as are paid to a person summoned to attend before the Ontario Court (General Division).

(4) **Bench warrant** — A judge of the Ontario Court (General Division) may issue a warrant against a person if the judge is satisfied that,

(a) a summons was served on the person under this section;

(b) the person has failed to attend or to remain in attendance at the hearing (in the case of an oral hearing) or has failed otherwise to participate in the hearing (in the case of an electronic hearing) in accordance with the summons; and

(c) the person's attendance or participation is material to the ends of justice.

(4.1) **Same** — The warrant shall be in the prescribed form (in English or French), directed to any police officer, and shall require the person to be apprehended anywhere within Ontario, brought before the tribunal forthwith and,

(a) detained in custody as the judge may order until the person's presence as a witness is no longer required; or

(b) in the judge's discretion, released on a recognizance, with or without sureties, conditioned for attendance or participation to give evidence.

(5) **Proof of service** — Service of a summons may be proved by affidavit in an application to have a warrant issued under subsection (4).

(6) **Certificate of facts** — Where an application to have a warrant issued is made on behalf of a tribunal, the person constituting the tribunal or, if the tribunal

consists of more than one person, the chair of the tribunal may certify to the judge the facts relied on to establish that the attendance or other participation of the person summoned is material to the ends of justice, and the judge may accept the certificate as proof of the facts.

(7) **Same** — Where the application is made by a party to the proceeding, the facts relied on to establish that the attendance or other participation of the person is material to the ends of justice may be proved by the party's affidavit.

[1994, c. 27, s. 56]

13. (1) **Contempt proceedings** — Where any person without lawful excuse,

(a) on being duly summoned under section 12 as a witness at a hearing makes default in attending at the hearing; or

(b) being in attendance as a witness at an oral hearing or otherwise participating as a witness at an electronic hearing, refuses to take an oath or to make an affirmation legally required by the tribunal to be taken or made, or to produce any document or thing in his or her power or control legally required by the tribunal to be produced by him or her or to answer any question to which the tribunal may legally require an answer; or

(c) does any other thing that would, if the tribunal had been a court of law having power to commit for contempt, have been contempt of that court,

the tribunal may, of its own motion or on the motion of a party to the proceeding, state a case to the Divisional Court setting out the facts and that court may inquire into the matter and, after hearing any witnesses who may be produced against or on behalf of that person and after hearing any statement that may be offered in defence, punish or take steps for the punishment of that person in like manner as if he or she had been guilty of contempt of the court.

(2) **Same** — Subsection (1) also applies to a person who,

(a) having objected under clause 6 (4) (b) to a hearing being held as a written hearing, fails without lawful excuse to participate in the oral or electronic hearing of the matter; or

(b) being a party, fails without lawful excuse to attend a pre-hearing conference when so directed by the tribunal.

[1994, c. 27, s. 56; 1997, c. 23, s. 13]

14. (1) **Protection for witnesses** — A witness at an oral or electronic hearing shall be deemed to have objected to answer any question asked him or her upon the ground that the answer may tend to criminate him or her or may tend to establish his or her liability to civil proceedings at the instance of the Crown, or of any person, and no answer given by a witness at a hearing shall be used or be receivable in evidence against the witness in any trial or other proceeding against him or her thereafter taking place, other than a prosecution for perjury in giving such evidence.

(2) [Repealed, 1994, c. 27, s. 56]

[1994, c. 27, s. 56]

15. (1) **What is admissible in evidence at a hearing** — Subject to subsections (2) and (3), a tribunal may admit as evidence at a hearing, whether or not given or proven under oath or affirmation or admissible as evidence in a court,

(a) any oral testimony; and

(b) any document or other thing,

relevant to the subject-matter of the proceeding and may act on such evidence, but the tribunal may exclude anything unduly repetitious.

(2) **What is inadmissible in evidence at a hearing** — Nothing is admissible in evidence at a hearing,

(a) that would be inadmissible in a court by reason of any privilege under the law of evidence; or

(b) that is inadmissible by the statute under which the proceeding arises or any other statute.

(3) **Conflicts** — Nothing in subsection (1) overrides the provisions of any Act expressly limiting the extent to or purposes for which any oral testimony, documents or things may be admitted or used in evidence in any proceeding.

(4) **Copies** — Where a tribunal is satisfied as to its authenticity, a copy of a document or other thing may be admitted as evidence at a hearing.

(5) **Photocopies** — Where a document has been filed in evidence at a hearing, the tribunal may, or the person producing it or entitled to it may with the leave of the tribunal, cause the document to be photocopied and the tribunal may authorize the photocopy to be filed in evidence in the place of the document filed and release the document filed, or may furnish to the person producing it or the person entitled to it a photocopy of the document filed certified by a member of the tribunal.

(6) **Certified copy admissible in evidence** — A document purporting to be a copy of a document filed in evidence at a hearing, certified to be a copy thereof by a member of the tribunal, is admissible in evidence in proceedings in which the document is admissible as evidence of the document.

15.1 (1) **Use of previously admitted evidence** — The tribunal may treat previously admitted evidence as if it had been admitted in a proceeding before the tribunal, if the parties to the proceeding consent.

(2) **Definition** — In subsection (1),

"previously admitted evidence" means evidence that was admitted, before the hearing of the proceeding referred to in that subsection, in any other proceeding before a court or tribunal, whether in or outside Ontario.

(3) **Additional power** — This power conferred by this section is in addition to the tribunal's power to admit evidence under section 15.

[1994, c. 27, s. 56; 1997, c. 23, s. 13]

15.2 Witness panels — A tribunal may receive evidence from panels of witnesses composed of two or more persons, if the parties have first had an opportunity to make submissions in that regard.

[1994, c. 27, s. 56]

16. Notice of facts and opinions — A tribunal may, in making its decision in any proceeding,

(a) take notice of facts that may be judicially noticed; and

(b) take notice of any generally recognized scientific or technical facts, information or opinions within its scientific or specialized knowledge.

16.1 (1) **Interim decisions and orders** — A tribunal may make interim decisions and orders.

(2) **Conditions** — A tribunal may impose conditions on an interim decision or order.

(3) **Reasons** — An interim decision or order need not be accompanied by reasons.

[1994, c. 27, s. 56]

16.2 Time frames — A tribunal shall establish guidelines setting out the usual time frame for completing proceedings that come before the tribunal and for completing the procedural steps within those proceedings.

[1999, c. 12, Sched. B, s. 16]

17. (1) **Decision** — A tribunal shall give its final decision and order, if any, in any proceeding in writing and shall give reasons in writing therefor if requested by a party.

(2) **Interest** — A tribunal that makes an order for the payment of money shall set out in the order the principal sum, and if interest is payable, the rate of interest and the date from which it is to be calculated.

[1993, c. 27, Sched; 1994, c. 27, s. 56]

17.1 Costs — (1) Subject to subsection (2), a tribunal may, in the circumstances set out in a rule made under section 25.1, order a party to pay all or part of another party's costs in a proceeding.

(2) **Exception** — A tribunal shall not make an order to pay costs under this section unless,

(a) the conduct or course of conduct of a party has been unreasonable, frivolous or vexatious or a party has acted in bad faith; and

(b) the tribunal has made rules under section 25.1 with respect to the ordering of costs which include the circumstances in which costs may be ordered and the amount of the costs or the manner in which the amount of the costs is to be determined.

(3) **Amount of costs** — The amount of the costs ordered under this section shall be determined in accordance with the rules made under section 25.1.

(4) **Continuance of provisions in other statutes** — Despite section 32, nothing in this section shall prevent a tribunal from ordering a party to pay all or

part of another party's costs in a proceeding in circumstances other than those set out in, and without complying with, subsections (1) to (3) if the tribunal makes the order in accordance with the provisions of an Act that are in force on the day this section comes into force.

[1999, c. 12, Sched. B, s. 16]

18. (1) **Notice of decision** — The tribunal shall send each party who participated in the proceeding, or the party's counsel or agent, a copy of its final decision or order, including the reasons if any have been given,

(a) by regular lettermail;

(b) by electronic transmission;

(c) by telephone transmission of a facsimile; or

(d) by some other method that allows proof of receipt, if the tribunal's rules made under section 25.1 deal with the matter.

(2) **Use of mail** — If the copy is sent by regular lettermail, it shall be sent to the most recent addresses known to the tribunal and shall be deemed to be received by the party on the fifth day after the day it is mailed.

(3) **Use of electronic or telephone transmission** — If the copy is sent by electronic transmission or by telephone transmission of a facsimile, it shall be deemed to be received on the day after it was sent, unless that day is a holiday, in which case the copy shall be deemed to be received on the next day that is not a holiday.

(4) **Use of other method** — If the copy is sent by a method referred to in clause (1) (d), the tribunal's rules made under section 25.1 govern its deemed day of receipt.

(5) **Failure to receive copy** — If a party that acts in good faith does not, through absence, accident, illness or other cause beyond the party's control, receive the copy until a later date than the deemed day of receipt, subsection (2), (3) or (4), as the case may be, does not apply.

[1994, c. 27, s. 56; 1997, c. 23, s. 13]

19. (1) **Enforcement of orders** — A certified copy of a tribunal's decision or order in a proceeding may be filed in the Ontario Court (General Division) by the tribunal or by a party and on filing shall be deemed to be an order of that court and is enforceable as such.

(2) **Notice of filing** — A party who files an order under subsection (1) shall notify the tribunal within 10 days after the filing.

(3) **Order for payment of money** — On receiving a certified copy of a tribunal's order for the payment of money, the sheriff shall enforce the order as if it were an execution issued by the Ontario Court (General Division).

[1994, c. 27, s. 56]

20. **Record of proceeding** — A tribunal shall compile a record of any proceeding in which a hearing has been held which shall include,

(a) any application, complaint, reference or other document, if any, by which the proceeding was commenced;

(b) the notice of any hearing;

(c) any interlocutory orders made by the tribunal;

(d) all documentary evidence filed with the tribunal, subject to any limitation expressly imposed by any other Act on the extent to or the purposes for which any such documents may be used in evidence in any proceeding;

(e) the transcript, if any, of the oral evidence given at the hearing; and

(f) the decision of the tribunal and the reasons therefor, where reasons have been given.

21. Adjournments — A hearing may be adjourned from time to time by a tribunal of its own motion or where it is shown to the satisfaction of the tribunal that the adjournment is required to permit an adequate hearing to be held.

21.1 Correction of errors — A tribunal may at any time correct a typographical error, error of calculation or similar error made in its decision or order.

[1994, c. 27, s. 56]

21.2 (1) **Power to review** — A tribunal may, if it considers it advisable and if its rules made under section 25.1 deal with the matter, review all or part of its own decision or order, and may confirm, vary, suspend or cancel the decision or order. 1997, c. 23, s. 13 (20).

(2) **Time for review** — The review shall take place within a reasonable time after the decision or order is made.

(3) **Conflict** — In the event of a conflict between this section and any other Act, the other Act prevails.

[1994, c. 27, s. 56; 1997, c. 23, s. 13]

22. Administration of oaths — A member of a tribunal has power to administer oaths and affirmations for the purpose of any of its proceedings and the tribunal may require evidence before it to be given under oath or affirmation.

23. (1) **Abuse of processes** — A tribunal may make such orders or give such directions in proceedings before it as it considers proper to prevent abuse of its processes.

(2) **Limitation on examination** — A tribunal may reasonably limit further examination or cross-examination of a witness where it is satisfied that the examination or cross-examination has been sufficient to disclose fully and fairly all matters relevant to the issues in the proceeding.

(3) **Exclusion of agents** — A tribunal may exclude from a hearing anyone, other than a barrister and solicitor qualified to practise in Ontario, appearing as an agent on behalf of a party or as an adviser to a witness if it finds that such person is not competent properly to represent or to advise the party or witness or does not understand and comply at the hearing with the duties and responsibilities of an advocate or adviser.

[1994, c. 27, s. 56]

24. (1) **Notice, etc —**.Where a tribunal is of the opinion that because the parties to any proceeding before it are so numerous or for any other reason, it is impracticable,

(a) to give notice of the hearing; or

(b) to send its decision and the material mentioned in section 18,

to all or any of the parties individually, the tribunal may, instead of doing so, cause reasonable notice of the hearing or of its decision to be given to such parties by public advertisement or otherwise as the tribunal may direct.

(2) **Contents of notice** — A notice of a decision given by a tribunal under clause (1) (b) shall inform the parties of the place where copies of the decision and the reasons therefor, if reasons were given, may be obtained.

25. (1) **Appeal operates as stay, exception** — An appeal from a decision of a tribunal to a court or other appellate body operates as a stay in the matter unless,

(a) another Act or a regulation that applies to the proceeding expressly provides to the contrary; or

(b) the tribunal or the court or other appellate body orders otherwise.

(2) **Idem** — An application for judicial review under the *Judicial Review Procedure Act*, or the bringing of proceedings specified in subsection 2 (1) of that Act is not an appeal within the meaning of subsection (1).

[1997, c. 23, s. 13]

25.0.1 Control of process — A tribunal has the power to determine its own procedures and practices and may for that purpose,

(a) make orders with respect to the procedures and practices that apply in any particular proceeding; and

(b) establish rules under section 25.1.

[1999, c. 12, Sched. B, s. 16]

25.1 Rules — (1) A tribunal may make rules governing the practice and procedure before it.

(2) **Application** — The rules may be of general or particular application.

(3) **Consistency with Acts** — The rules shall be consistent with this Act and with the other Acts to which they relate.

(4) **Public access** — The tribunal shall make the rules available to the public in English and in French.

(5) ***Regulations Act*** — Rules adopted under this section are not regulations as defined in the *Regulations Act*.

(6) **Additional power** — The power conferred by this section is in addition to any power to adopt rules that the tribunal may have under another Act.

[1994, c. 27, s. 56]

26. **Regulations** — The Lieutenant Governor in Council may make regulations prescribing forms for the purpose of section 12.

[1994, c. 27, s. 56]

27. Rules, etc., available to public — A tribunal shall make any rules or guidelines established under this or any other Act available for examination by the public.

[1999, c. 12, Sched. B, s. 16]

28. Substantial compliance — Substantial compliance with requirements respecting the content of forms, notices or documents under this Act or any rule made under this or any other Act is sufficient.

[1999, c. 12, Sched. B, s. 16]

29-31. [Repealed, 1994, c. 27, s. 56]

32. Conflict — Unless it is expressly provided in any other Act that its provisions and regulations, rules or by-laws made under it apply despite anything in this Act, the provisions of this Act prevail over the provisions of such other Act and over regulations, rules or by-laws made under such other Act which conflict therewith.

[1994, c. 27, s. 56]

33, 34. [Repealed, 1994, c. 27, s. 56]

Forms 1, 2 [Repealed, 1994, c. 27, s. 56]

THE CONSENT AND CAPACITY BOARD

Introduction

The Consent and Capacity Board is established under the *Health Care Consent Act, 1996* (HCCA).[1] It is the administrative tribunal which adjudicates issues of involuntary commital and community treatment orders under the *Mental Health Act* (MHA), consent and capacity issues in relation to treatment, admission to care facilities and personal assistance services under the HCCA, and management of property under both the *Substitute Decisions Act, 1992* (SDA) and the MHA. Other legislation under which the Board adjudicates are the *Long-Term Care Act, 1994, and effective November 1, 2004, the Personal Health Information Protection Act, 2004*. The Board is an expert tribunal.

Members of the Board Hearing Applications

The members of the Board are appointed by the Lieutenant Governor in Council[2] for a term of three years or less at a time, subject to reappointment.[3] Currently sitting members and the terms of their appointments are identified on the website of the office of the Public Appointments Secretariat for Ontario (www.pas.gov.on.ca)

Some applications that come before the Board such as matters of capacity under any of the Acts may be heard by a "senior lawyer member" of the Board sitting alone. Others, such as certain applications under the MHA, must be heard by panels of three or five members. The Chair of the Board assigns the members of the Board to sit alone or in panels of three or five members to deal with particular applications.[4] A member is not permitted to sit alone unless he or she has been assigned by the Chair to do so. The Chair must be of the opinion that the member has the necessary experience to adjudicate in relation to matters of capacity and fulfills all other qualifications required by the Chair. The member must also be a lawyer in Ontario for ten or more years and a member of the Board for two or more years immediately preceding the assignment.[5]

Only panels of three or five members may hear applications to review an individual's involuntary status[6] or community treatment order[7] and matters related to the detention of children as informal minors.[8]

---

1 *Health Care Consent Act,* 1996, c. 2, Sched. A s. 70 (1) and s. 70-80 generally.

2 *Ibid*, s. 70 (2).

3 s. 70 (3).

4 s. 73 (1).

5 s. 73(2).

6 s. 39(5.1) MHA.

7 s. 39.1(10) MHA.

The sections establishing the Board and its procedures under the HCCA are generally imported into the MHA for purposes of these reviews[9]

In panel hearings, one member is assigned to preside over the matter and decisions are binding when made by the majority of the panel.[10] Although there is no statutory requirement to assign a lawyer member to preside over hearings, this is the practice of the Board. The composition and quorum of panels of the Board are set out in the MHA under each section which requires a panel hearing. A three-member panel shall consist of a psychiatrist, a lawyer and a third person who is neither a psychiatrist nor a lawyer. All three members are required for a quorum. A five-member panel shall include one or two psychiatrists and one or two lawyers. The other member or members shall be persons who are neither psychiatrists nor lawyers. A majority of the members of the panel constitutes a quorum. A psychiatrist, a lawyer and a member who is neither a psychiatrist nor a lawyer are required to make up the quorum.[11]

A member of the Board shall not take part in the hearing of a matter that concerns a person who is or was the member's patient or client or a patient of a facility of which the member is an officer or employee or in which the member has a financial interest.[12]

No member of the Board shall participate in a decision unless he or she was present throughout the hearing and heard the parties' evidence and argument.[13]

The member or members of the Board conducting a hearing shall not communicate about the subject-matter of the hearing directly or indirectly with any party, counsel, agent or other person, unless all the parties and their counsel or agents receive notice and have an opportunity to participate. However, the member or members of the Board conducting the hearing may seek advice from an adviser independent of the parties, and in that case the nature of the advice shall be communicated to all the parties and their counsel or agents so that they may make submissions as to the law.[14]

Scheduling Hearings, Rendering Decisions and Reasons

When the Board receives an application, it must promptly fix a time and place for a hearing which must begin within seven days after the day the Board receives the application, unless the parties agree to a postponement. The Board must render its decision within one day after the day the hearing ends and written reasons must be provided within two business days after the day they are

---

8 s. 13(6) MHA.

9 HCCA, Clause 73 (3) (a), subs. 73 (4) and ss. 74 to 80 apply to an application under these sections, with necessary modifications., *e.g.* s. 39 (7) MHA.

10 s. 73(3).

11 s. 39(6) MHA.

12 s. 74 (1), (2).

13 s. 78.

14 s. 77(1), (2).

requested. The parties have the right to be informed that they may make a request for written reasons within 30 days after the day the hearing ends.[15]

Right of Access to Documents Prior to Hearing

Before the hearing, the parties shall be given an opportunity to examine and copy any documentary evidence that will be produced and any report whose contents will be given in evidence. The applicant before the Board and his or her counsel or agent are entitled to examine and to copy, at their own expense, any medical or other health record prepared in respect of the party, subject to limited exceptions.[16]

Legal Representation for Incapable Persons

If a person who is or may be incapable with respect to a treatment, admission to a care facility or a personal assistance service is a party to a proceeding before the Board and does not have legal representation, the Board may direct the Public Guardian and Trustee or the Children's Lawyer to arrange for legal representation to be provided for the person. The person is deemed to have capacity to retain and instruct counsel.[17]

Information About the Board

The Board's website[18] provides a great deal of useful information about the Board. It describes the applications which may be brought before the Board and provides information sheets (which are also available by calling the Board) for parties to the proceedings. The website provides links to the applicable legislation and forms, as well as to a free website[19] which catalogues some pre-selected decisions of the Board.

---

[15] s. 75(1) – (5).

[16] s. 76(1), (2).

[17] s. 81(1). The PGT is not responsible for payment of counsel's fees; the individual's estate is responsible for the fees or the person may make application for legal aid for assistance, if eligible. In the event that the individual for whom counsel has been arranged through the OPGT refuses to instruct or accept the services of counsel so assigned, the Court of Appeal for Ontario has left the door open for the "conversion" of counsel arranged through the OPGT into Amicus Counsel to the individual or the Board in Consent and Capacity Board proceedings, see *Pietrangelo v. Balachandra et al*, Court of Appeal for Ontario Docket: C37729 released August 12, 2004, which referred to In re AM TO-04-1921, July 26, 2004, where the board made such an appointment of Amicus counsel under similar circumstances.

[18] www.ccboard.on.ca; Tel No: 1-800-461-2036.

[19] www.canlii.org. Cases are pre-selected by the Board for relevance and date back only to October, 2000.

The Board's New Rules of Practice

The Rules of Practice have been adopted by the Board pursuant to section 25.1 of the *Statutory Powers Procedure Act*. The Rules apply to all proceedings before the Board. The Rules took effect on March 31, 2004. We do not propose to give an exhaustive review of the Rules in this introduction as they should be read in their entirety. Process issues such as computing times and rules for service, while important, we recommend to the reader without making comment on them.

However, there are a few provisions we think may be of particular interest to parties and counsel appearing before the Board. We focus on those aspects of the Rules which impact substantive issues before the Board. We also highlight changes in practice before the Board which result from the enactment of the Rules.

Purpose of the Rules

The stated purpose of these Rules is to provide "a just, fair, accessible and understandable process for parties to proceedings before the Board. The Rules attempt to facilitate access to the Board; to promote respectful hearings; to promote consistency of process; to make proceedings less adversarial, where appropriate; to make proceedings as cost effective as possible for all those involved in Board proceedings and for the Board by ensuring the efficiency and timeliness of proceedings; to avoid unnecessary length and delay of proceedings; and to assist the Board in fulfilling its statutory mandate of delivering a just and fair determination of the matters which come before it".[20]

Parties

Rule 5 provides guidance regarding the Board's interpretation of its discretionary power to grant party status to an applicant who is not a statutory party to proceedings. In deciding whether to specify a person as a party to an application, the Board may consider: (a) the nature of the case; (b) the issues; (c) whether the person has a genuine interest in the issues; (d) whether the person's interests may be directly and substantially affected by the hearing or its result; (e) whether the person is likely to make a useful and distinct contribution to the Board's understanding of the issues in the hearing; and (f) any other relevant factor.[21] The Board may require persons with similar interests to designate a spokesperson.[22]

Motions

Rule 13 establishes guidelines for the hearing of "motions." A motion is defined as a request for the Board's ruling or decision on a particular issue at any

---

[20] Rule 1.1.

[21] Rule 5.1.

[22] Rule 5.2.

stage within a proceeding or intended proceeding. A motion may be made by a party to the proceeding or by a person with an interest in the proceeding. At the earliest possible date before the hearing, and in any event no later than 4 p.m. on the day before the hearing, the party or person who wishes to bring a motion shall give notice of the motion to all other parties and to the Board. If necessary, leave to bring a motion may be sought at the commencement of the hearing.

Notice of a motion does not need to be in any particular form. In appropriate circumstances, notice may be given by telephone call. Notice of a motion must adequately set out the grounds for the motion and the relief requested. The Board may direct the procedure to be followed for dealing with a motion and set applicable time limits. The Board may direct that the motion will be dealt with in writing or by any other means.

Pre-hearing Conferences

Rule 14 establishes pre-hearing conferences which may be ordered by the Board even over the objection of a party. The Board may, at the request of a party or on its own initiative, direct the representatives for the parties, either with or without the parties, and any party not represented by counsel to appear before a member of the Board for a pre-hearing conference for the purpose of considering any or all of the following:

(a) the identification, simplification and/or resolution of some or all of the issues;

(b) identifying facts or evidence that may be agreed upon by the parties;

(c) identifying all parties to the hearing;

(d) the estimated duration of the hearing;

(e) identifying the witnesses;

(f) any other matter that may assist the just and most expeditious disposition of the proceeding.[23]

The Board may direct the parties to serve documents or submissions prior to the pre-hearing conference.[24] However, a pre-hearing conference will not be held unless the party who is the subject of the application has legal representation.[25] This provision opens up the possibility that the Board may order the PGT to arrange for legal representation of an individual at the pre-hearing conference stage, even where no hearing before the Board has commenced.[26] No communication shall be made to the panel presiding at the hearing of the proceeding with respect to any statement made at pre-hearing conference, except as disclosed in a memorandum signed by the parties or an order made at the pre-

[23] Rule 14.1.

[24] Rule 14.2.

[25] Rule 14.3.

[26] Rule 5.4 and 5.5.

hearing under Rule 14.7.[27] The member of the Board who presides over a pre-hearing conference shall not participate in the hearing unless all parties consent.[28]

Mediation

Rule 15 allows for mediation for the purpose of attempting to reach a settlement but only on consent of all parties. The subject of the application must have legal representation at the mediation. If a member of the Board presides over a mediation, that member shall not participate in the hearing unless all parties consent. If all parties to mediation wish to resolve all or some of the issues in dispute by way of an order of the Board, a request in writing shall be made by the parties to the mediator. The request shall record the agreements and undertakings made during mediation. The request shall be submitted forthwith to the Board by the mediator.

Amending a Decision

In addition to correcting errors of a typographical nature, the Board may at any time, if it considers it advisable, review all or part of its own decision or order, and may confirm, vary, suspend or cancel the decision or order.[29] This is a new provision, which may prove to be very helpful to parties. Since appeals from the Board's decisions must be filed within seven days and may have adverse consequences for the parties pending appeal,[30] an otherwise meritorious appeal is often simply not practicable to launch. The option of requesting the Board to reconsider a decision which the parties may even agree is clearly wrong in law provides a useful alternative.

Appeals

The Board's decisions are appealable as of right to the Superior Court of Justice on a question of law or fact or both.[31] The time for service and filing of the notice of appeal is seven days after receipt of the Board's decision.[32] The Board must be provided a copy of the notice of appeal.[33] On receipt of the copy of the notice of appeal, the Board promptly prepare the transcript and record of the proceeding, serve the parties and file the materials with the court.[34] The appellant and respondent each have 14 days only to serve and file their materials with the court.

---

[27] Rule 14.8.

[28] Rule 14.10.

[29] Rule 31.

[30] Appeal provisions under the MHA operate to continue an involuntary admission, and appeal provisions under the HCCA operate to stay treatment.

[31] s. 80(1) HCCA and s. 48 MHA.

[32] s. 80(2).

[33] s. 80(3).

[34] s. 80(4).

The appellant's clock runs from the date of receipt of the record of the matter and the respondent has 14 days from receipt of the appellant's factum.[35]

The court should be expediting these appeals as it must "fix for the hearing of the appeal the earliest date that is compatible with its just disposition".[36] The court shall hear the appeal on the record, including the transcript, but may receive new or additional evidence as it considers just.[37] On appeals from determinations of capacity by the Board, it is not appropriate to receive fresh evidence relating to the condition of the individual since the date of hearing, notwithstanding the broad language of the discretion to receive new evidence.[38] On the appeal, the court may: (a) exercise all the powers of the Board; (b) substitute its opinion for that of a health practitioner, an evaluator, a substitute decision-maker or the Board; or (c) refer the matter back to the Board, with directions, for rehearing in whole or in part.[39]

The Board has been recognized by the courts as an expert tribunal. The Board's decisions are entitled to curial deference in relation to factual determinations and certain questions of mixed fact and law within its specialized expertise. On appeal the Board's decisions are reviewed on a reasonableness simpliciter standard.[40] On pure questions of law or statutory interpretation, however, there is no deference owed to the Board. Its legal determinations are reviewed on a correctness standard.[41]

Practical Considerations

Generally

The law sets out the way in which applications before the Board should proceed. There are special issues, however, which arise in practice as a result of the unique nature of litigation before this Board. We take this opportunity to highlight some of these issues and offer some guidance for the reader's consideration.

The Board hears applications relating to individuals who may be seriously incapacitated in some way and who are often unhappy or angry with their particular situation. Family and health care professionals are very concerned about the individual; there are complex relationships among the parties and witnesses before such proceedings which do not end when the hearing is over or the decision is rendered. For this reason alone, it is always advisable that the professionals involved with the matter (be they counsel to the applicant or patient or health practitioners or others) co-operate as much as possible in reducing

[35] s. 80(5) (6).

[36] s. 80(8).

[37] s. 80(9).

[38] *Starson v. Swayze* (2003), 225 D.L.R. (4th) 385 (S.C.C.).

[39] s. 80(10).

[40] *T.(I.) v. L. (L.)* (1999), 46 O.R. (3d) 284 (C.A.).

[41] *Daugherty v. Stall* [2002] O.J. No. 4715 (S.C.J.) and *Starson*.

additional stressors which may unnecessarily heighten the emotion inherent in these proceedings.

(a) Where a hearing may be held

Although in practice the Board has always attempted to accommodate the individual who is the subject of the application before the Board, it has now specifically incorporated this principle under Rule 12.1 which stipulates that the hearing will be held as close as possible to the place where the person is located at the time of the hearing. The Board is a travelling tribunal and most of its hearings are held in the hospital, psychiatric facility or nursing home where the applicant is located. However, there are a number of applications which concern individuals residing in the community (for example, CTOs, financial capacity hearings under the SDA). While applicants may not want to return to a hospital where they have been held against their will in order to attend a hearing, there are competing considerations of physicians' schedules and the logistics of producing an original clinical record of a patient or former patient outside of the facility which controls and owns those records. The Board does have access to hearing rooms at its Toronto head office and will make hearing rooms available elsewhere across the province where necessary. Sometimes a neutral setting is itself helpful to facilitate the conduct of the proceedings.

(b) The 7-day Time Line for Hearings

The tight timelines for proceedings before the Board sometimes tax the patience of physicians and other parties to the hearing because scheduling the commencement of the hearing can be difficult, particularly where there are many parties to the proceeding. This is really the beginning point where co-operation between counsel for the applicant and physicians or other parties becomes useful. In practice, it may be that counsel is retained by an applicant to a proceeding only two or three days before the hearing. However, where an individual's involuntary detention is at stake or treatment cannot commence before the Board disposes of the matter, there are often compelling reasons to proceed with the hearing promptly.

Facilities where hearings are often held should establish a process for allowing patients' counsel to prepare for the hearing. It facilitates matters to provide unobstructed access to the health records of the applicant, copies where requested and a private area for counsel to meet with his or her client. Counsel for any party before the Board must be familiar with the applicable legislation and jurisprudence and ready to proceed when the hearing commences. This is not an area of practice where adjournments *sine die* or adjournments even for short periods of time serve anyone's interest. Counsel should decline the retainer unless he or she expects to be prepared to proceed. Similarly, physicians should make every effort to be available for the hearing. If the parties exchange documentation before the hearing, and issues which may be raised are brought to everyone's attention, the likelihood of requests for adjournment is reduced.

(c) At the hearing

It's always a good idea for the health practitioner or evaluator/assessor seeking to have a finding of incapacity or an involuntary admission confirmed to have a written summary of the case prepared in advance of the hearing, and preferably shared with the other parties before the hearing.

Proceedings of the Board are informal and not meant to be overly adversarial. For example, the Board's duty is to "inquire" whether the criteria for an involuntary admission continue to be met[42] on the date of hearing. In practice, however, the process is somewhat adversarial, or can be, due to the adjudicative nature of the Board even while it inquires into matters before it. It is a party-driven process and the parties choose the way in which they present evidence, or whether they choose to present evidence or testimony of witnesses to the Board.

The subject of the application before the Board (the detained patient or the incapable person) is not required to attend but may choose to do so for part or all of the proceeding; he or she may choose to provide testimony at the hearing but is not a compellable witness. The onus is entirely on the party seeking to have his or her opinion upheld by the Board (the attending physician under the MHA's involuntary status reviews, the issuing physician under the CTO provisions, and the health practitioner/evaluator/assessor under the HCCA or SDA.) The burden has sometimes been referred to as an "enhanced" balance of probability, although in capacity matters the Board has interpreted the *Starson* decision in the SCC (*Starson v. Swayze* [2003] S.C.J. No. 33) to lower that burden to a civil balance of probability[43]

Based on the *Starson* judgment in SCJ, affirmed at the SCC, however, there must be clear, cogent and compelling evidence before the Board to satisfy this burden. While hearsay evidence is admissible before the Board, uncorroborated hearsay which is contradicted by direct testimony should not be relied upon on key points in issue. Hearsay is to be assigned only the weight appropriate to it under all the circumstances and in light of the serious consequences for the subject of the application.

(d) Therapeutic Relationship

Hearings of the Board, notwithstanding the differing position of the parties before the Board, do not have to be countertherapeutic events in the clinical context. In fact, where there is mutual respect between the professionals involved with the proceeding, and shared respect for the subject of the application (client or patient), there can be very therapeutic effects of the hearing process. The individual hears the concerns about his or her situation in its entirety and is given an opportunity to address them, with the assistance of counsel. Often a resolution between the parties ensues after the hearing, regardless of outcome, which would not have been possible without the process.

---

42 s. 39.1 MHA.

43 *Re: D.M.* TO-03-0690/691/692, June 23, 2003.

CONSENT AND CAPACITY BOARD RULES OF PRACTICE

TABLE OF CONTENTS

March 1, 2004

PURPOSE OF THE RULES

1.1 The purpose of these Rules is to provide a just, fair, accessible and understandable process for parties to proceedings before the Board. The Rules attempt to facilitate access to the Board; to promote respectful hearings; to promote consistency of process; to make proceedings less adversarial, where appropriate; to make proceedings as cost effective as possible for all those involved in Board proceedings and for the Board by ensuring the efficiency and timeliness of proceedings; to avoid unnecessary length and delay of proceedings; and to assist the Board in fulfilling its statutory mandate of delivering a just and fair determination of the matters which come before it.

APPLICATION OF RULES

2.1 These Rules apply to all proceedings of the Board.

2.2 Where any of these Rules conflicts with any statute or regulation or where the application of these Rules is statutorily excluded, the provisions of the statute or regulation shall prevail.

2.3 Where something is not provided for in these Rules, the practice may be decided by referring to a similar provision in these Rules.

BOARD POWERS

3.1 The Board may exercise any of its powers under these Rules on its own initiative or at the request of any party. Unless otherwise provided, members of the Board, sitting alone or in a panel of three or five members to deal with particular applications, may exercise the powers provided to the Board in these Rules.

3.2 During any proceeding, the Board may do whatever is necessary and permitted by law to enable it to effectively and completely adjudicate on the matter before it. The Board may decide the procedure to be followed for any proceeding and may make procedural directions or orders at any time. The Board may impose such conditions as are appropriate and fair.

3.3 The Board may waive or vary any of these Rules at any time in order to ensure the fair and just determination of the proceedings before it.

COMPUTING TIMES

4.1 In computing time periods under these Rules or in an order or decision, except as provided by statute or where a contrary intention appears:

(a) where there is a reference to a number of days between two events, they shall be counted by excluding the day on which the first event happens and including the day on which the second event happens;

(b) where the time for doing an act under these Rules expires on a non-business day, the act may be done on the next day that is a business day;
(c) where, under these Rules, a document would be deemed to be received or service would be deemed to be effective on a day that is a non-business day, it shall be deemed to be received or effective on the next day which is a business day; and
(d) if a document is received after 4 p.m. on a business day, it shall be deemed to have been received on the next business day.

4.2 "Business day" means any day other than a Saturday, Sunday or a holiday. A "holiday" includes New Year's Day, Good Friday, Easter Monday, Christmas Day, Boxing Day, Civic and Provincial Holidays (including the first Monday in August), the birthday or the day fixed by proclamation of the Governor General for the celebration of the birthday of the reigning Sovereign, Victoria Day, Canada Day, Labour Day, Remembrance Day and any day appointed by proclamation of the Governor General or Lieutenant Governor as a public holiday or for a general fast or thanksgiving, and when any holiday, except Remembrance Day, falls on a Sunday, the day next following is in lieu thereof a holiday.

PARTIES

5.1 The following persons are parties to an application for the purpose of these Rules:

(a) persons specified as parties by the statute under which the application arises; and
(b) any other person the Board specifies.

5.2 In deciding whether to specify a person as a party to an application, the Board may consider:

(a) the nature of the case;
(b) the issues;
(c) whether the person has a genuine interest in the issues;
(d) whether the person's interests may be directly and substantially affected by the hearing or its result;
(e) whether the person is likely to make a useful and distinct contribution to the Board's understanding of the issues in the hearing; and
(f) any other relevant factor.

5.3 The Board may require persons who have similar interests to designate one person to act as their spokesperson, or to co-ordinate their submissions.

5.4 If it appears to the Board, prior to the commencement of or at any time during the hearing, that the subject of the application will not have legal representation at the hearing, the Board may exercise its powers under section 81 of the *Health Care Consent Act, 1996* to arrange legal representation for that person.

5.5 In order to exercise its powers under section 81 of the *Health Care Consent Act, 1996*, the Board or its administrative staff may make inquiries for the sole purpose of determining whether the subject of the application is or may be incapable with respect to treatment, admission to a care facility or a personal assistance service and/or whether he or she wishes to be represented by counsel at the hearing.

FILING APPLICATIONS AND OTHER DOCUMENTS WITH THE BOARD

6.1 In these Rules, "filing" of any document means the delivery in person or by fax of that document to the Board's Deputy Registrar and its receipt by the Board.

6.2 An application, notice or any other document shall be filed with the Board, unless otherwise directed by the Board.

6.3 Subject to Rule 4, documents are deemed to be filed as of the date and time they are received by the Board.

SERVICE OF DOCUMENTS

7.1 Service may be effected by:

(a) personal delivery of a document to a person or to the person's lawyer or agent in the proceeding;
(b) faxing the document to the last known fax number of the person or to the person's lawyer or agent in the proceeding;
(c) delivery of the document by courier or Priority Post, to the last known address of the person or to the person's lawyer or agent in the proceeding; or
(d) any other means authorized or permitted by the Board for delivery of the document or for communicating the information contained in the document.

7.2 If the Board is aware that the subject of an application is a young person under the age of 16, a document shall be served on the young person or the young person's lawyer in the proceeding, if any. If the young person does not have a lawyer, a document may be served on both the young person and the Children's Lawyer.

7.3 Unless advised to the contrary by a person's lawyer or agent, the Board shall assume that the lawyer or agent in the proceeding knows the whereabouts of the person and is able to contact that person.

7.4 Service is deemed to be effective, when delivered by:

(a) personal delivery, before 4 p.m. on the day of delivery, and after that time, on the next day;
(b) fax, before 4 p.m. on the date it was sent, and after that time, on the next day;
(c) courier, on the day after the courier picks it up for delivery; or
(d) any means authorized or permitted by the Board, on the date specified by the Board in its direction.

7.5 After an application is filed with the Board, a party may waive service by the Board or by any other party, of a notice of hearing or any other document.

7.6 Parties serving documents shall clearly show their name, address, and telephone and fax numbers on a covering document.

INCOMPLETE OR TECHNICALLY DEFECTIVE APPLICATIONS

8.1 In this section, "Board" includes the Board's administrative staff.

8.2 Upon receiving an application that appears incomplete, the Board will contact the person submitting the application to obtain the missing information. If information required to establish the nature of the application, the parties thereto or other facts material to the ability to hold a hearing cannot be obtained following reasonable inquiry, the Board may decide not to process the application.

8.3 Upon receiving an application that appears to be materially defective, the Board will notify the person submitting the application of the defect. If the defect is not remedied, the Board may decide not to process the application.

8.4 The Board shall give the applicant and such other persons as the Board deems appropriate notice of its decision not to process the application and set out the reasons for the decision and the requirements for commencement processing of the application.

8.5 The application will be deemed to have been received by the Board if and when these requirements have been met to the satisfaction of the Board.

DISMISSAL OF APPLICATION WITHOUT HEARING

9.1 The Board may dismiss an application without a hearing if:

(a) the application is frivolous, vexatious or is commenced in bad faith;
(b) the application relates to matters that are outside of the jurisdiction of the Board; or
(c) the statutory requirements for bringing the application have not been met.

9.2 Before dismissing an application under this section, the Board shall give notice of its intention to dismiss the application to:

(a) all parties to the application, if the application is being dismissed for reasons referred to in Rule 9.1(b); or
(b) the party who commenced the application, if the application is being dismissed for any other reason.

9.3 The notice of intention to dismiss an application shall set out the reasons for the intended dismissal and inform the parties of their right to make written submissions to the Board with respect to the dismissal within five days of service of the notice.

NOTICE OF WITHDRAWAL OF APPLICATION

10.1 An applicant who does not want to continue with all or part of an application may withdraw all or part of the application by faxing a notice of withdrawal to the Board.

10.2 A party in the proceedings before the Board who, before the time of the hearing, takes an action that makes a hearing unnecessary shall notify the Board about such action immediately by fax.

10.3 An application cannot be withdrawn until the Board receives a written notice of withdrawal or until the Board is reasonably satisfied that appropriate documentation has been completed. If, for any reason, the Board is not satisfied that an application has been properly withdrawn or that a hearing has become unnecessary, the Board may proceed with the hearing.

NOTICE OF HEARING

11.1 Notice of a hearing shall be served by the Board on the parties and other persons as permitted by statute.

11.2 In addition to providing the information required by statute, the Board may include in a notice of hearing any other information or directions it considers necessary for the proper conduct of the hearing.

11.3 The Board may serve notice of a hearing by way of telephone call, only if the Board considers this form of notice appropriate and necessary in the circumstances.

11.4 If, at the commencement of a hearing, the Board is not satisfied that all parties have received notice of the hearing, the Board may adjourn the hearing until all parties have received proper notice.

PLACE OF HEARING

12.1 Unless the Board decides otherwise, the hearing will be held as close as possible to the place where the person who is the subject of the application is physically located at the time of the hearing.

MOTIONS

13.1 "Motion" means a request for the Board's ruling or decision on a particular issue at any stage within a proceeding or intended proceeding.

13.2 A motion may be made by a party to the proceeding or by a person with an interest in the proceeding.

13.3 A person who has an interest in the proceeding and makes a motion will be dealt with by the Board as if he or she were a party for the purposes of the motion only.

13.4 At the earliest possible date before the hearing, and in any event no later than 4 p.m. on the day before the hearing, the party or person who wishes to bring a motion shall give notice of the motion to all other parties and to the Board. If necessary, leave to bring a motion may be sought at the commencement of the hearing.

13.5 Except as otherwise permitted by the Board, all motions shall be heard at the commencement of the hearing.

13.6 Notice of a motion does not need to be in any particular form. In appropriate circumstances, notice may be given by telephone call. Notice of a motion must adequately set out the grounds for the motion and the relief requested.

13.7 The Board may direct the procedure to be followed for dealing with a motion and set applicable time limits. The Board may direct that the motion will be dealt with in writing or by any other means.

PRE-HEARING CONFERENCES

14.1 The Board may, at the request of a party or on its own initiative, direct the representatives for the parties, either with or without the parties, and any party not represented by counsel to appear before a member of the Board for a pre-hearing conference for the purpose of considering any or all of the following:

(a) the identification, simplification and/or resolution of some or all of the issues;
(b) identifying facts or evidence that may be agreed upon by the parties;
(c) identifying all parties to the hearing;
(d) the estimated duration of the hearing;
(e) identifying the witnesses;
(f) any other matter that may assist the just and most expeditious disposition of the proceeding.

14.2 The Board may direct the parties to serve documents or submissions prior to the pre-hearing conference.

14.3 A pre-hearing conference will not be held unless the party who is the subject of the application has legal representation.

14.4 A pre-hearing conference shall be conducted by a Board member.

14.5 A pre-hearing conference may be held in person, in writing or electronically. A pre-hearing conference shall not be open to the public.

14.6 All documents intended to be used at the hearing that may be of assistance in achieving the purposes of a pre-hearing conference shall be made available to the member presiding at the prehearing conference.

14.7 (1) At the conclusion of the pre-hearing conference,

(a) counsel or any party not represented may sign a memorandum setting out the results of the conference; and/or
(b) the member of the Board who presides at a pre-hearing conference may make such orders as he or she considers necessary or advisable with respect to the conduct of the proceeding, including an order adding parties, and the memorandum or order binds the parties unless the member presiding at the hearing orders otherwise to prevent injustice.

(2) A copy of a memorandum or an order made under subrule (1) shall be placed in the hearing file and made accessible to the hearing panel.

14.8 No communication shall be made to the panel presiding at the hearing of the proceeding with respect to any statement made at pre-hearing conference, except as disclosed in the memorandum or order under Rule 14.7.

14.9 Upon conclusion of the pre-hearing conference, all original documents shall be returned to the party who provided them.

14.10 The member of the Board who presides over a pre-hearing conference shall not participate in the hearing unless all parties consent.

MEDIATION

15.1 Mediation, which is part of the proceeding but not a part of the hearing, may be held for the purpose of attempting to reach a settlement of any or all of the issues, or at least their simplification.

15.2 The Board may arrange for mediation only if all the parties consent to participate in the process. Any party can, at any time during the mediation, request an end to the mediation process. If such a request is made, mediation ends and a hearing will take place, if appropriate.

15.3 Mediation will not be held unless the party who is the subject of the application has legal representation.

15.4 Mediation shall be conducted by a person designated by the chair to sit as a mediator.

15.5 If a member of the Board presides over a mediation, that member shall not participate in the hearing unless all parties consent.

15.6 Mediation shall not be open to the public.

15.7 After mediation, all documents shall be returned to the party who provided them. Documents created or statements made for the sole purpose of mediation are not part of the record and are not admissible in a hearing unless all parties consent. Discussions held at mediation are privileged and may not be disclosed in further proceedings.

15.8 If all parties to mediation wish to resolve all or some of the issues in dispute by way of an order of the Board, a request in writing shall be made by the parties to the mediator. The request shall record the agreements and undertakings made during mediation. The request shall be submitted forthwith to the Board by the mediator.

WRITTEN AND ELECTRONIC HEARINGS

16.1 In appropriate cases and where permitted by law, the Board may decide in its discretion to conduct all or any part of the proceedings in person or by way of written or electronic hearing.

16.2 In deciding whether to hold a written or electronic proceeding, the Board may consider any relevant factors, including but not limited to:

(a) the suitability of a written or electronic hearing format considering the subject matter of the hearing;
(b) whether the nature of the evidence is appropriate for a written or electronic hearing, including whether credibility is in issue and the extent to which facts are in dispute;
(c) the extent to which the matters in dispute are questions of law;
(d) avoidance of unnecessary length or delay of the hearing;
(e) the convenience of the parties;
(f) the ability of the parties to participate in a written or electronic hearing;
(g) the cost, efficiency and timeliness of proceedings; and
(h) whether the hearing deals with procedural or substantive matters.

16.3 If possible, a party who objects to a written or electronic proceeding shall file a written objection with the Board before the hearing. An objection to an electronic hearing shall set out how an electronic hearing would cause that party significant prejudice. An objection to a written hearing shall set out the reasons why a written hearing is not appropriate.

HEARINGS IN ENGLISH AND FRENCH

17.1 Subject to the provisions of the *French Language Services Act*, the Board may conduct its proceedings in English or French, or partly in English and partly in French.

17.2 Parties are required to notify the Board if they or their witnesses wish to receive any or all services in the French language. This notification shall occur at the time the application is made or at the earliest possible opportunity thereafter.

INTERPRETERS

18.1 If a party or a party's witness requires an interpreter in a language other than the language of the hearing, the party shall notify the Board. This notification shall occur at the time the application is made or at the earliest possible opportunity thereafter.

18.2 If a health practitioner, legal counsel, helping professional or rights adviser is of the opinion that a party or a party's witness requires an interpreter at the hearing, that person shall notify the Board office at the earliest possible opportunity.

18.3 The Board, at its expense, will arrange for an interpreter as it deems necessary for the proper conduct of the hearing.

18.4 Where a written submission or written evidence is provided in a language other than the language of the hearing, the Board may order any person presenting the submission or evidence to provide it in the language of the hearing if the Board considers it necessary for the fair disposition of the matter.

SPECIAL NEEDS

19.1 Parties, lawyers and agents, and witnesses should notify the Board of their request for accommodation of any special needs during the hearing process. This notification shall occur at the time the application is made or at the earliest opportunity thereafter. The Board will determine, in its discretion, whether those special needs can be met.

19.2 If a health practitioner, a helping professional or a rights adviser is of the opinion that a party has special needs that should be met during the hearing process, that person shall notify the Board office at the earliest possible opportunity.

PROCEDURE AT A HEARING

20.1 The Board controls its own process and will determine its own practices and procedures during the hearing according to the legislation and principles of common law.

20.2 Unless directed otherwise by the chair of the Board, only members of the Board who are also members of the Law Society of Upper Canada shall preside over hearings.

PUBLIC ACCESS TO HEARINGS

21.1 All Board hearings shall be open to the public except where, in accordance with the criteria provided in section 9(1) of the *Statutory Powers Procedure Act*, the Board is of the opinion that a matter should be heard in the absence of the public. At any time after the commencement of the hearing, the Board may close the hearing on its own initiative or at the request of a party.

ADJOURNMENTS

22.1 Once commenced, a hearing may be adjourned at the discretion of the Board. The Board may adjourn the hearing on its own initiative or at the request of a party. In granting an adjournment, the Board may impose such conditions as it considers appropriate.

22.2 At the request of the parties or on its own initiative, the Board may recess or adjourn the hearing to allow parties to attempt to resolve the issues in dispute.

EVIDENCE

23.1 At a hearing, the Board may admit any evidence relevant to the subject matter of the proceeding. The Board may receive any facts agreed upon by the parties without proof or evidence.

The Board may direct the form in which evidence shall be received.

ORDER OF PRESENTATION OF EVIDENCE

24.1 Evidence at a hearing shall be presented by the parties in the order directed by the Board. Questioning of witnesses will follow in the same order as the parties adduced evidence.

FILING DOCUMENTS AT A HEARING

25.1 Any person tendering a document as evidence in a hearing shall provide one copy for each member of the Board at the hearing and one copy for each party. Except as otherwise permitted by the Board, documents shall be tendered and exchanged among the parties prior to the commencement of the hearing and any objections to those documents raised at the commencement of the hearing.

OATH OR AFFIRMATION

26.1 The Board may require that evidence be given under oath or affirmation.

WITNESSES

27.1 The Board may issue a summons to a party or any other person or witness, on its own initiative or upon the request of a party, to give evidence and produce documents relevant to the proceedings. A party shall inform the Board as soon as possible concerning the need to summon a witness. The party is responsible for providing the Board with all the information necessary to prepare the summons.

RECORDING OF PROCEEDINGS

28.1 The Board will arrange for the recording of the proceeding by:

(a) verbatim reporter; or
(b) a visual or audio recorder, or both.

28.2 Subject to Rule 28.1, recording devices of any sort are not permitted at a hearing. Provided the Board is notified of the request in advance of the hearing, the Board, in its discretion, may allow:

(a) a credentialed, professional journalist acting in the course of his or her duties to unobtrusively make an audio recording at a hearing for the sole purpose of supplementing or replacing that person's notes; and/or
(b) a person requiring an assistive device, who may use that device to enable them to participate in a hearing.

No other use shall be made of these recordings.

28.3 Any journalist permitted by Rule 28.2 to make an audio recording at a hearing shall give an undertaking in a form satisfactory to the Board that the recording will not be used for broadcast or any other purpose other than that permitted by Rule 28.2.

28.4 Except as provided in Rules 28.1 and 28.2, the panel of the Board conducting a hearing has no discretion to permit any other audio or visual recording of a hearing.

ARGUMENT AND SUBMISSIONS

29.1 After all of the parties have had an opportunity to present evidence, the Board shall give all parties an opportunity to make a final argument in support of the decision or order they want the Board to make. No new evidence may be presented during final argument.

29.2 The Board may order the parties to submit written arguments on any issue and shall direct the order and timing of submission of written arguments.

DECISIONS, ORDERS AND REASONS FOR DECISIONS

30.1 In addition to regular letter mail or fax, the Board may serve or deliver a decision and reasons for decision by any method it deems appropriate in the circumstances and which allows for proof of receipt, including but not limited to personal delivery.

AMENDING A DECISION

31.1 The Board may at any time correct a typographical error, error of calculation, clerical error, or other similar error made in its decision or reasons.

31.2 The Board may at any time, if considers it advisable, review all or part of its own decision or order, and may confirm, vary, suspend or cancel the decision or order.

REQUESTING LEAVE TO MAKE A NEW APPLICATION

32.1 A party to an application under section 32, section 34, section 50 or section 65 of the *Health Care Consent Act, 1996* which has been finally disposed of by the Board may request leave to make a new application within six months after the final disposition of the earlier application.

32.2 A request for leave to bring a new application shall be made in writing and signed by the person making the request.

32.3 The request must include:

(a) details of the material change in circumstances which justifies reconsideration of, depending on the application, the decision to admit to a place of treatment or the person's capacity; and

(b) any evidence which supports the request.

32.4 The Board shall issue a notice of the request to the parties to the application. The notice will include the information provided by the requester under Rule 32.3 (a) and will inform the parties of their right to deliver a written response and supporting evidence to the Board within seven days.

32.5 In exceptional circumstances, the Chair of the Board or a member designated by the Chair may order a hearing, which may be held in person or electronically, to hear the request for leave. The chair of the Board or a member designated by the chair may make any other procedural order to deal with the request for leave to bring a new application as he or she considers appropriate.

32.6 The Board shall issue a written decision to grant or refuse leave after the seven-day period referred to under Rule 32.4 has expired.

32.7 Until leave to bring a new application is granted, any application made under section 32, section 34, section 50 or section 65 of the *Health Care Consent Act, 1996* brought within six months after the final disposition of an earlier application shall be deemed not received by the Board.

Consent
and Capacity
Board

Notice of Withdrawal

My name is ______________________________
(full name of applicant)

I withdraw my application(s) to the Consent and Capacity Board dated ______________
(date)

regarding *(please check)*:

- ☐ involuntary status (Form 16)
- ☐ finding of incapacity with respect to treatment (Form A)
- ☐ finding of incapacity with respect to admission to a care facility (Form A)
- ☐ finding of incapacity with respect to a personal assistance service (Form A)
- ☐ finding of incapacity to manage my property (Form 18)
- ☐ being appointed as a patient's representative with respect to his or her treatment, admission to a care facility, or personal assistance service (Form C)
- ☐ whether the substitute decision-maker complied with the principles for giving or refusing consent under the *Health Care Consent Act* (Form G)
- ☐ other *(please specify)* ______________________________

____

______________________________ *(signature of applicant's lawyer/agent or applicant [if unrepresented])**

______________________________ *(date of signature)*

______________________________ *(print full name)*

(   ) ______________________________ *(telephone no.)*

* If the applicant is a **patient** in a **psychiatric facility** and does ***not*** **have legal representation**, this section **must** be completed:

My name is ______________________________ and *(select one)*:
(print full name)

- ☐ I have witnessed the patient's signature.
- ☐ the patient will not sign the Notice of Withdrawal, but has authorized me to make all necessary arrangements to withdraw the application.

______________________________ *(signature of witness)*

______________________________ *(date of signature)*

______________________________ *(title or relationship to the patient)*

(   ) ______________________________ *(telephone no.)*

For your information:

Application forms are treated independently: You must check every applicable box if you intend to withdraw more than one application.

Withdrawal of Forms B, C, D, E, F, or G: If one of these applications is withdrawn, the law will no longer provide that the patient is deemed to have applied for a review of his or her capacity to make the relevant decision. If the subject of the application still wants the Board to review a finding of incapacity, he or she must bring an application under a Form A.

4323-04(04/07) www.ccboard.on.ca *(Disponible en version française)*

CONSENT AND CAPACITY BOARD

INDEX

[Note: References not preceded by one of the following abbreviations are to page number; otherwise references are to section numbers]

The following abbreviations have been used in this index:

Substitute Decisions Act	SDA
Substitute Decisions Act Regulations – General	SDAR-G
Substitute Decisions Act Regulations – Register	SDAR-R
Substitute Decisions Act Regulations – Accounts and Records of Attorneys and Guardians	SDAR-AR
Substitute Decisions Act Regulations – Capacity Assessment	SDAR-CA
Substitute Decisions Act Forms	SDA Form
Powers of Attorney Act	PAA
Health Care Consent Act, 1996	HCCA
Health Care Consent Act Regulations – Evaluators	HCCA-E
Health Care Consent Act Forms	HCCA Form
Mental Health Act	MHA
Mental Health Act Regulations – General	MHAR-G
Mental Health Act Regulations – Grants	MHAR-Gr
Mental Health Act Forms	MHA Form
Personal Health Information Protection Act, 2004	PHIPA
Personal Health Information Protection Regulations - General	PHIPA-G
Personal Health Information Protection Forms	PHIPA Form
Statutory Powers Procedure Act	SPPA
Consent and Capacity Board Rules of Practice	CCBRP

A

I

Q

R

S

T